Shojo Beat

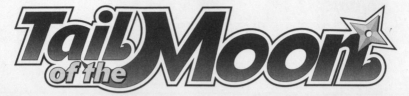

Tail of the Moon

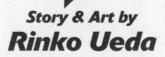

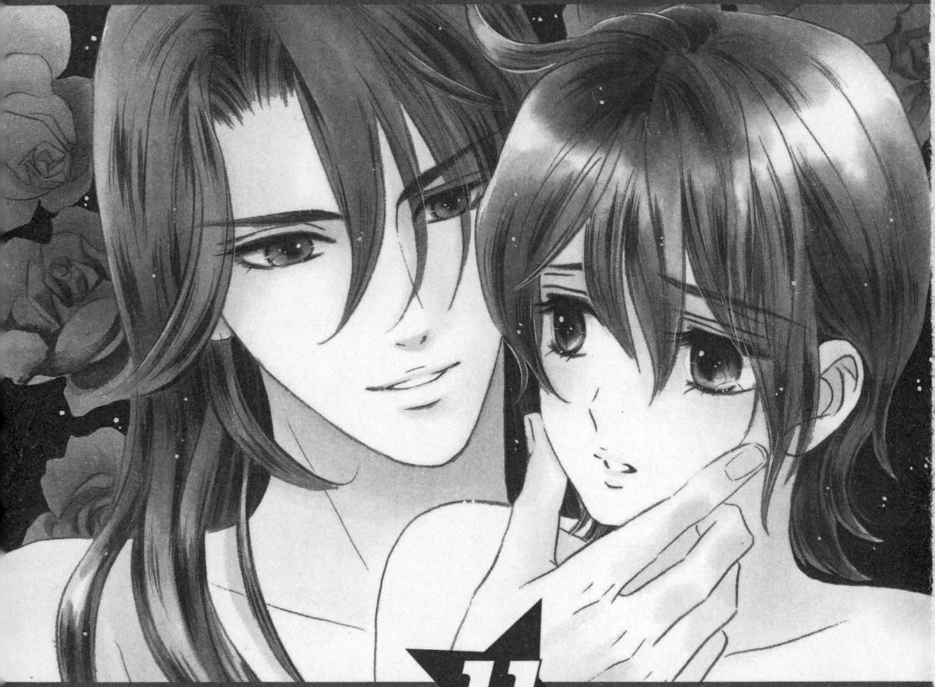

11

Story & Art by
Rinko Ueda

Volume 11

CONTENTS

Story Thus Far...

It is the Era of the Warring States. Usagi is a failure as a ninja, but she is a skilled herbalist. She is working hard to qualify as a ninja so she can be the bride of Hattori Hanzo (aka "Shimo no Hanzo")!

Usagi and her friend Kame are captured and locked inside a cell by Ranmaru, who is hunting down the Iga ninja. In order to escape, Kame suggests that Usagi seduce Ranmaru. Though Usagi doesn't think she's up to it, she succeeds in seducing him, and they are able to escape by stealing the key to the cell.

Usagi is reunited with Hanzo, and they head back to the capital to look for Mamezo. Along the way, they are caught in the rain and decide to seek shelter inside a cave. They take off their soaked clothes and warm themselves by the fire. Hanzo is no longer able to hold back his feelings, so he suddenly holds Usagi tightly in his arms and...?!

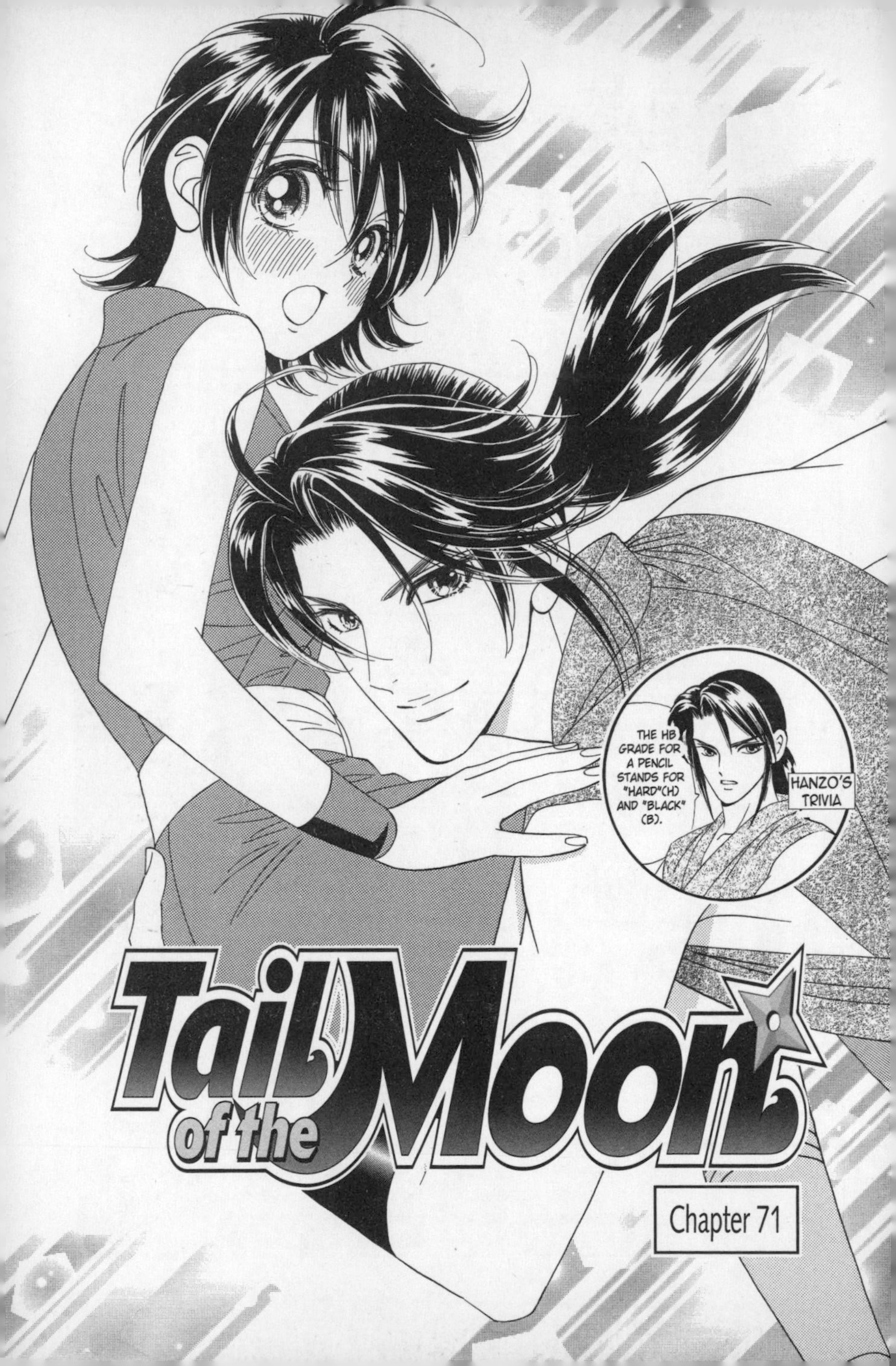
THE HB GRADE FOR A PENCIL STANDS FOR "HARD"(H) AND "BLACK" (B).
HANZO'S TRIVIA
Tail of the Moon
Chapter 71

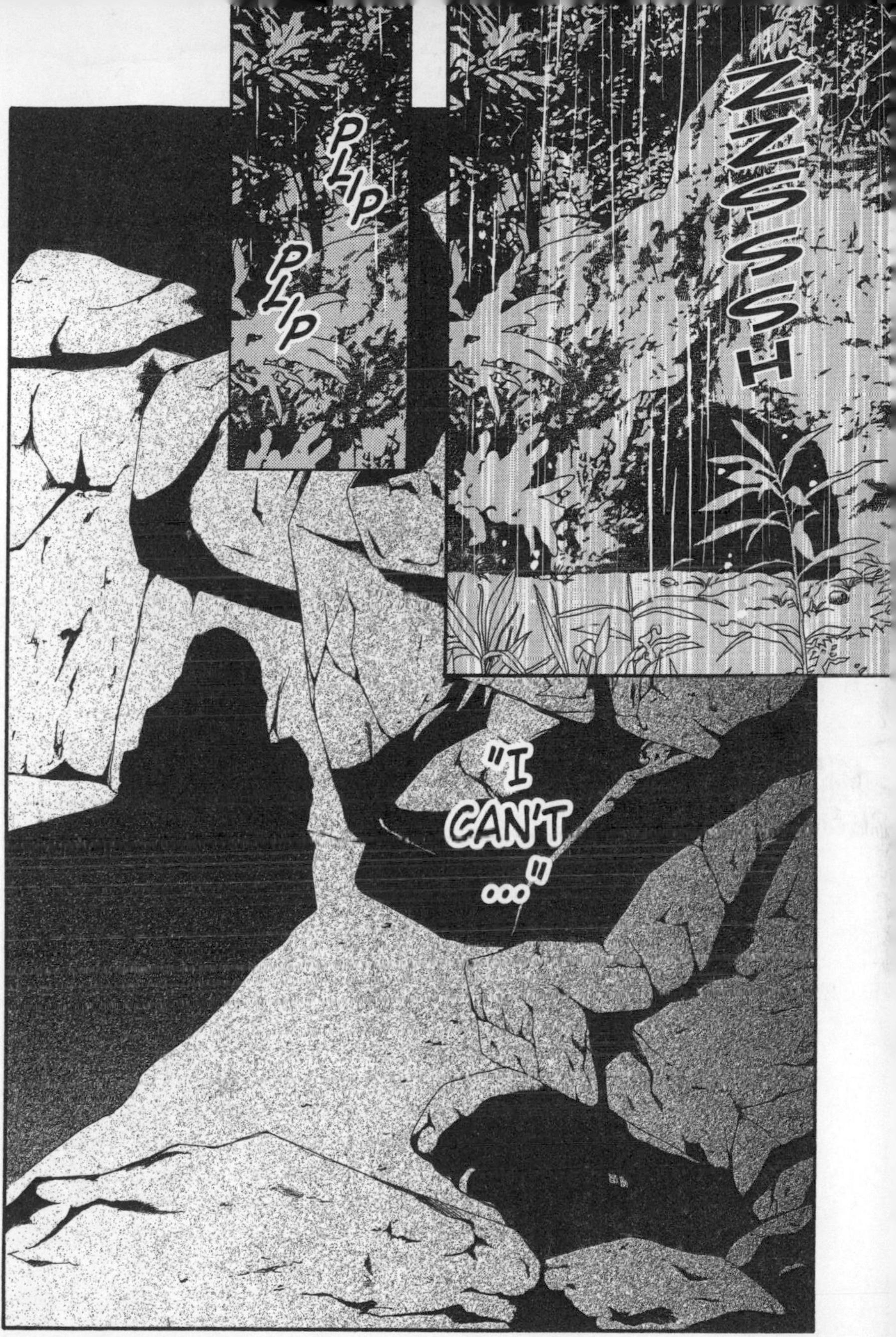
ZZSSSH
PLIP PLIP
"I CAN'T..."

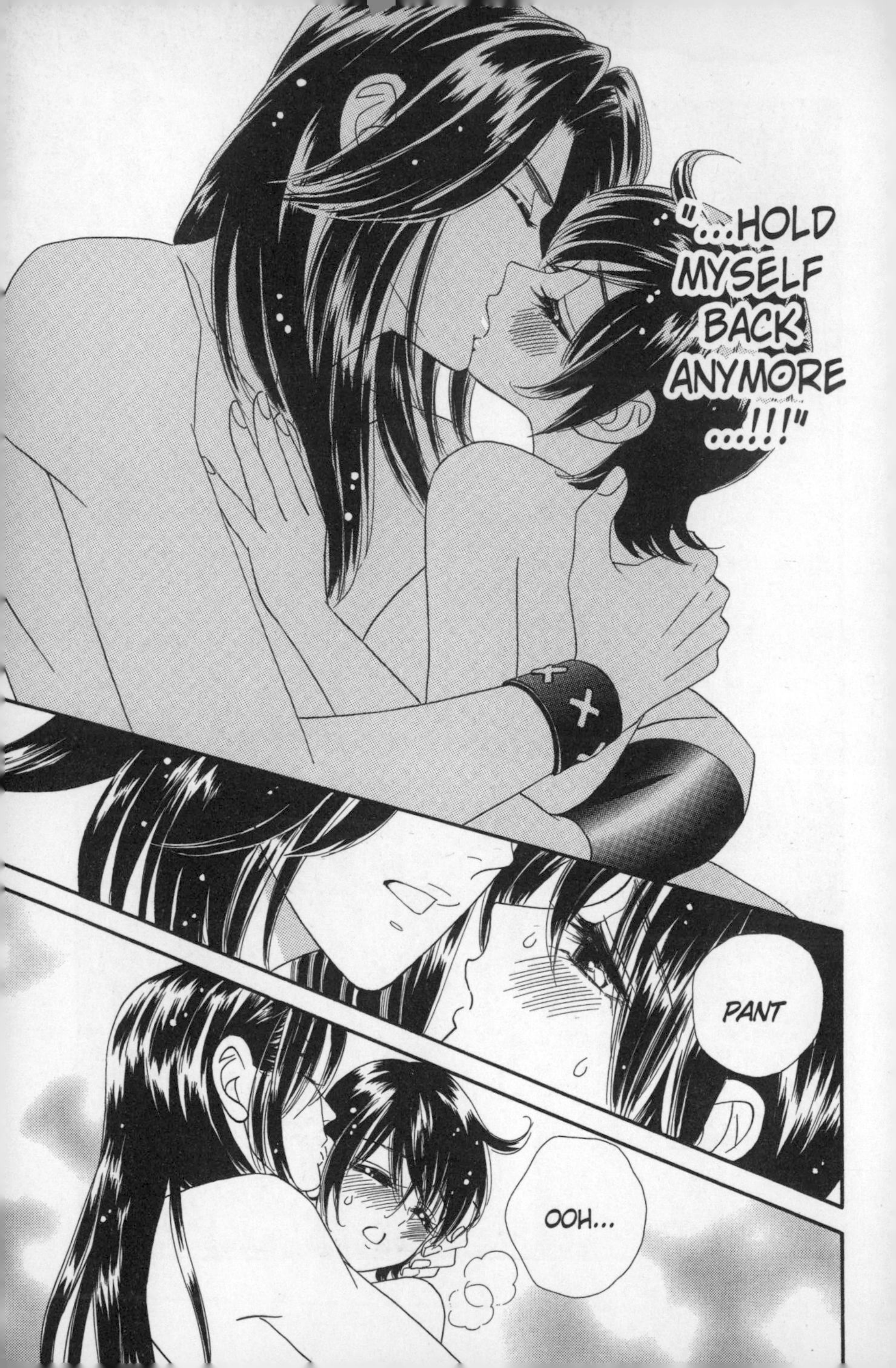
"...HOLD MYSELF BACK ANYMORE ...!!!"
PANT
OOH...

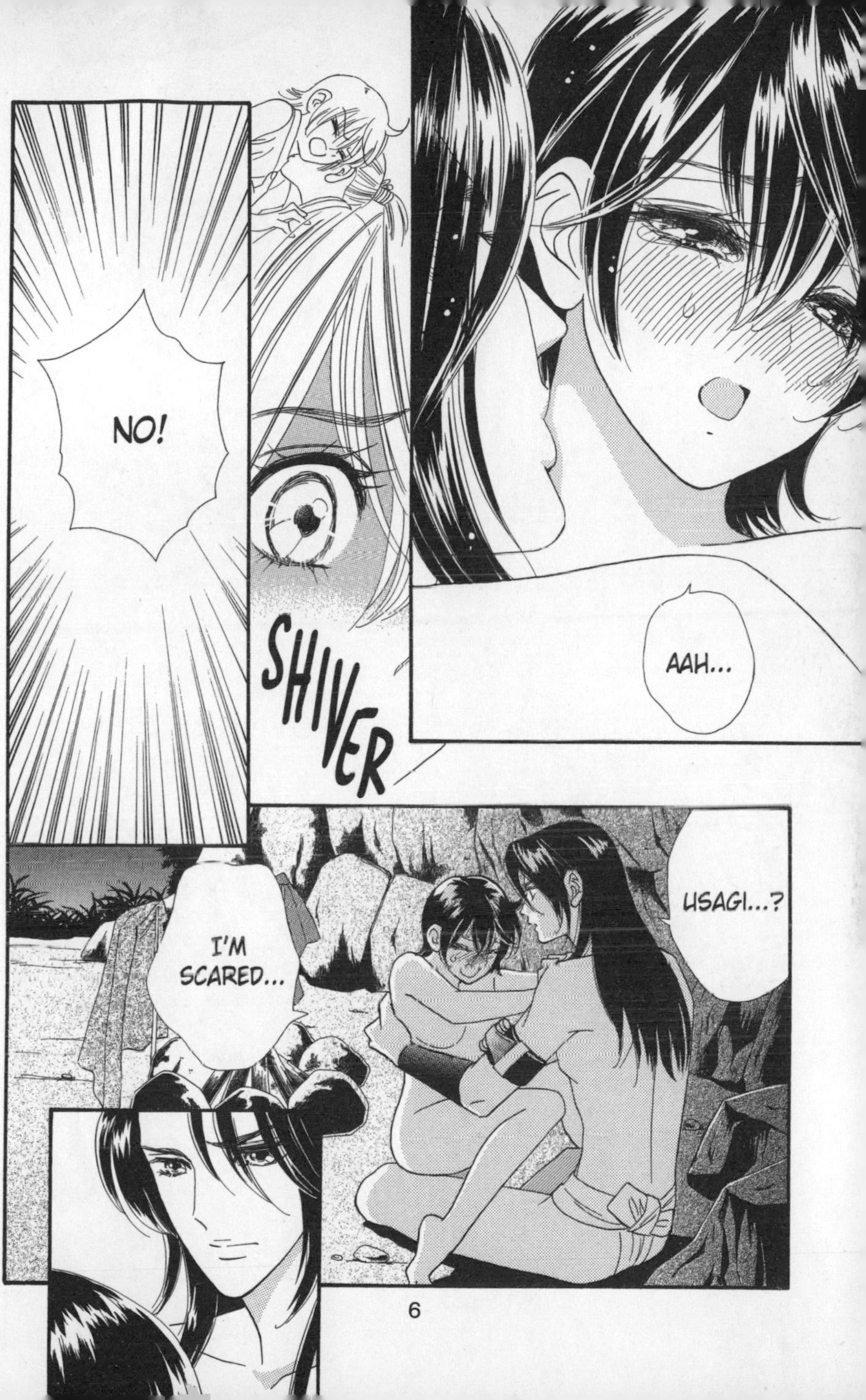
AAH...
SHIVER
NO!
USAGI...?
I'M SCARED...

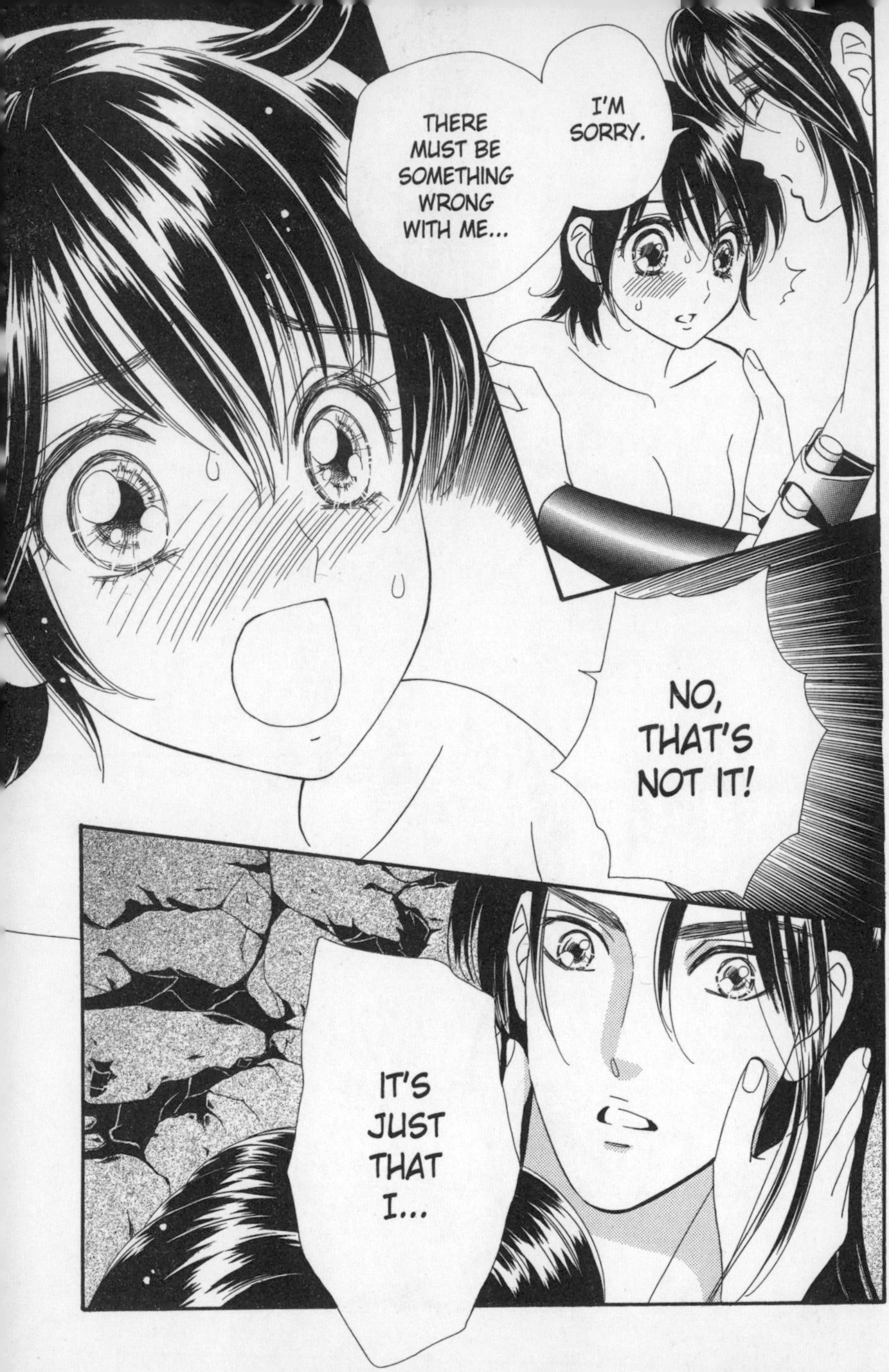
I'M SORRY.
THERE MUST BE SOMETHING WRONG WITH ME...
NO, THAT'S NOT IT!
IT'S JUST THAT I...

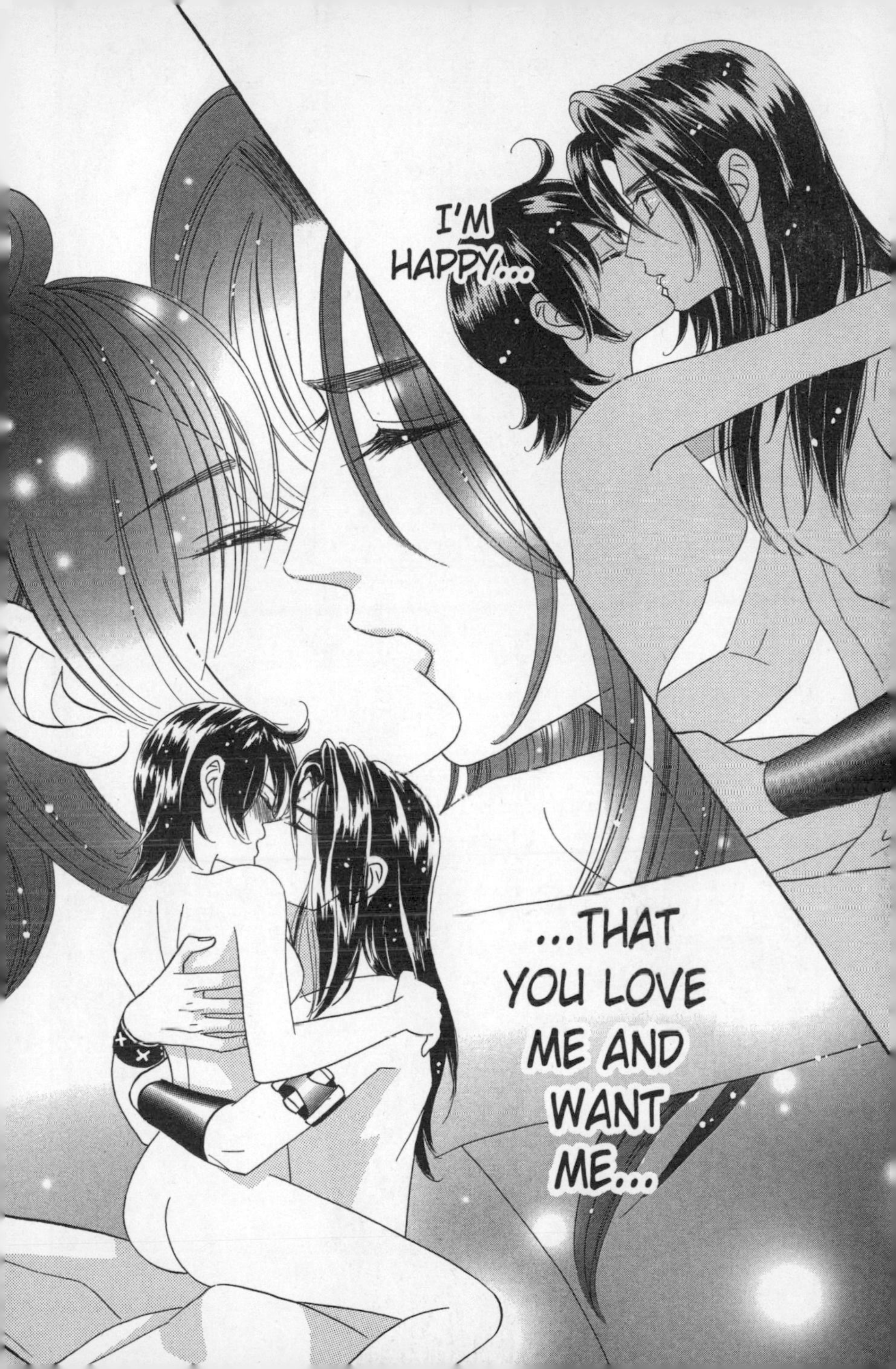
I'M HAPPY...
...THAT YOU LOVE ME AND WANT ME...

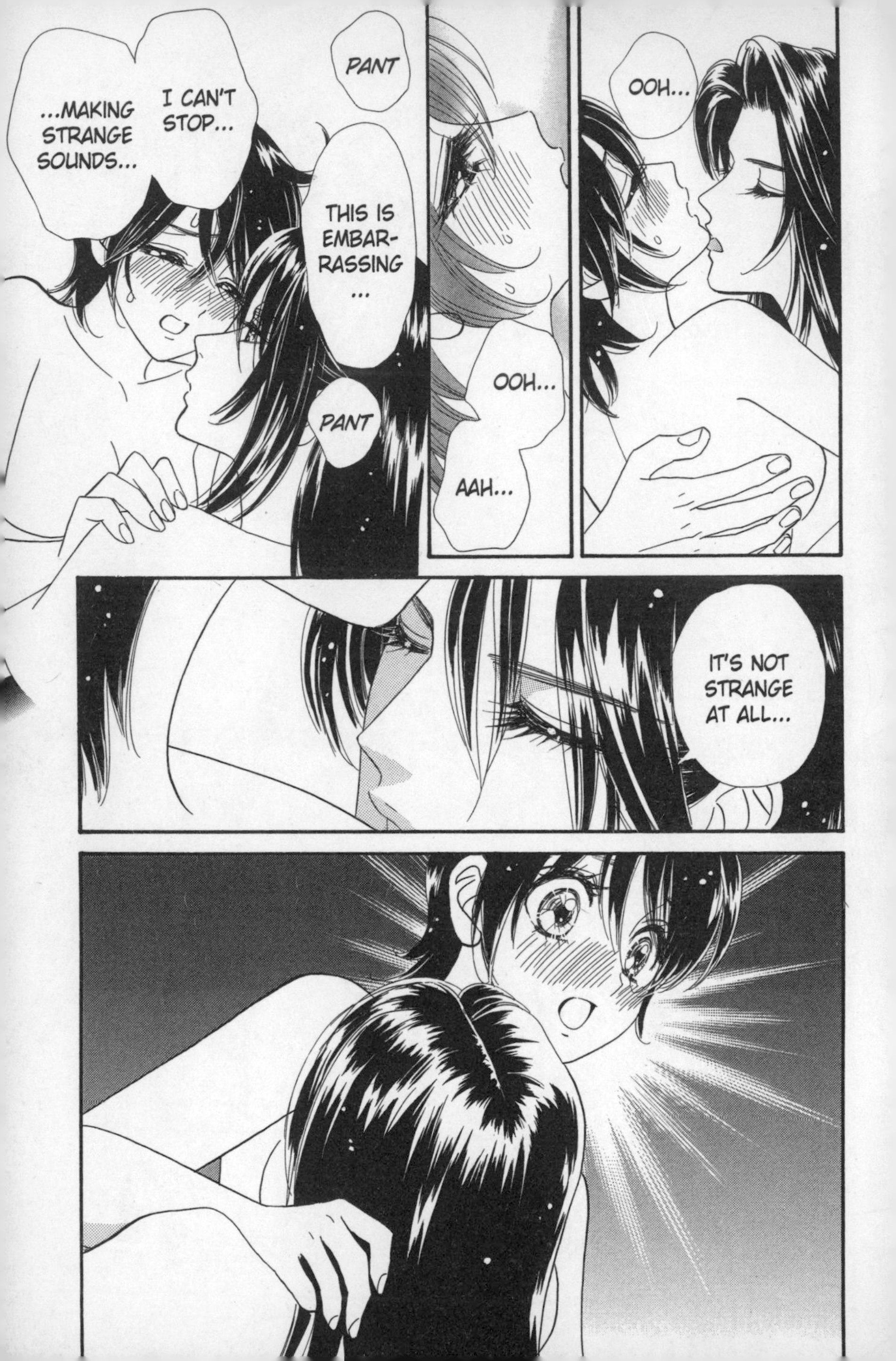
OOH...
OOH...
AAH...
PANT
I CAN'T STOP...
...MAKING STRANGE SOUNDS...
THIS IS EMBARRASSING...
PANT
IT'S NOT STRANGE AT ALL...

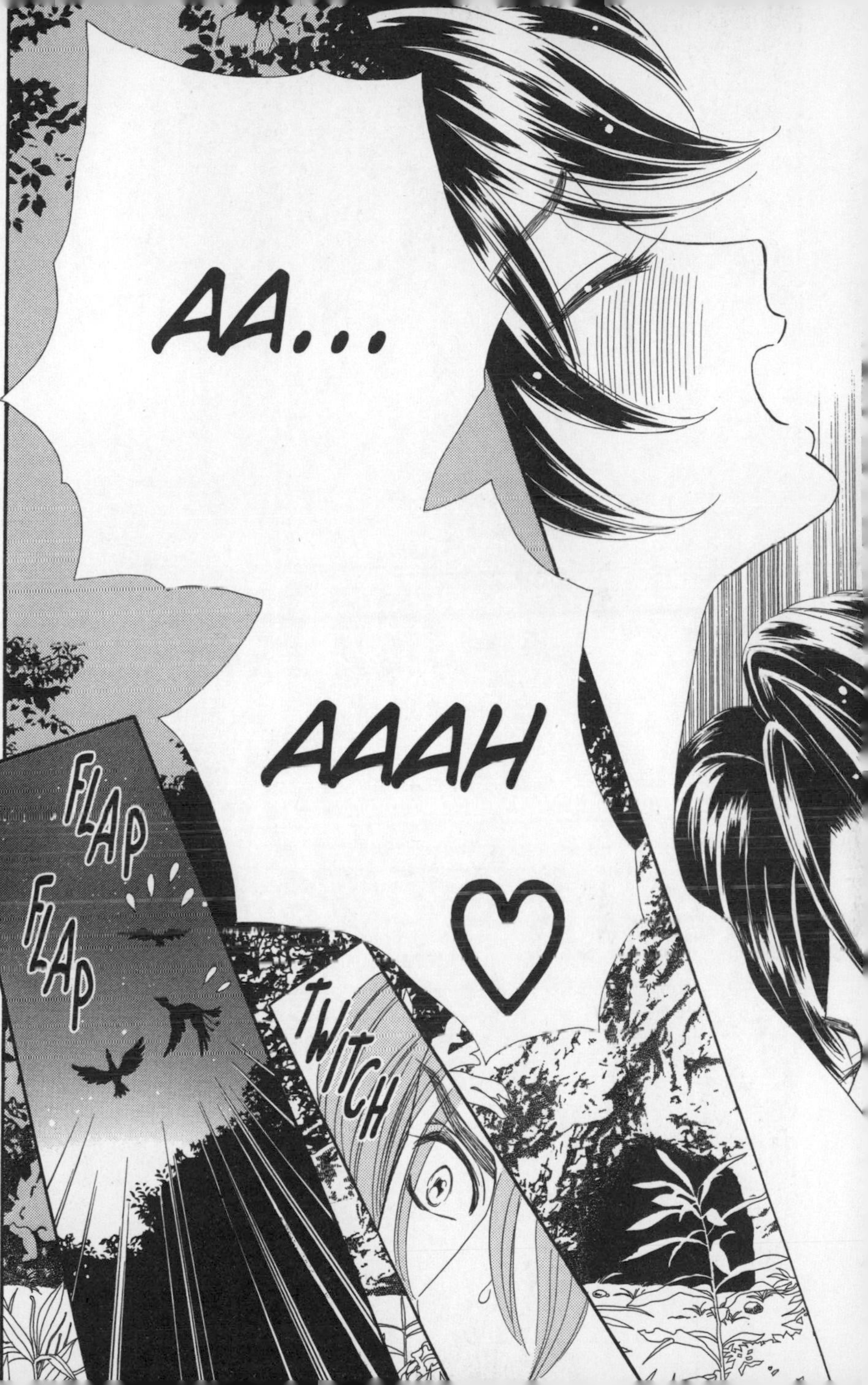
AA...
AAAH ♥
TWITCH
FLAP FLAP

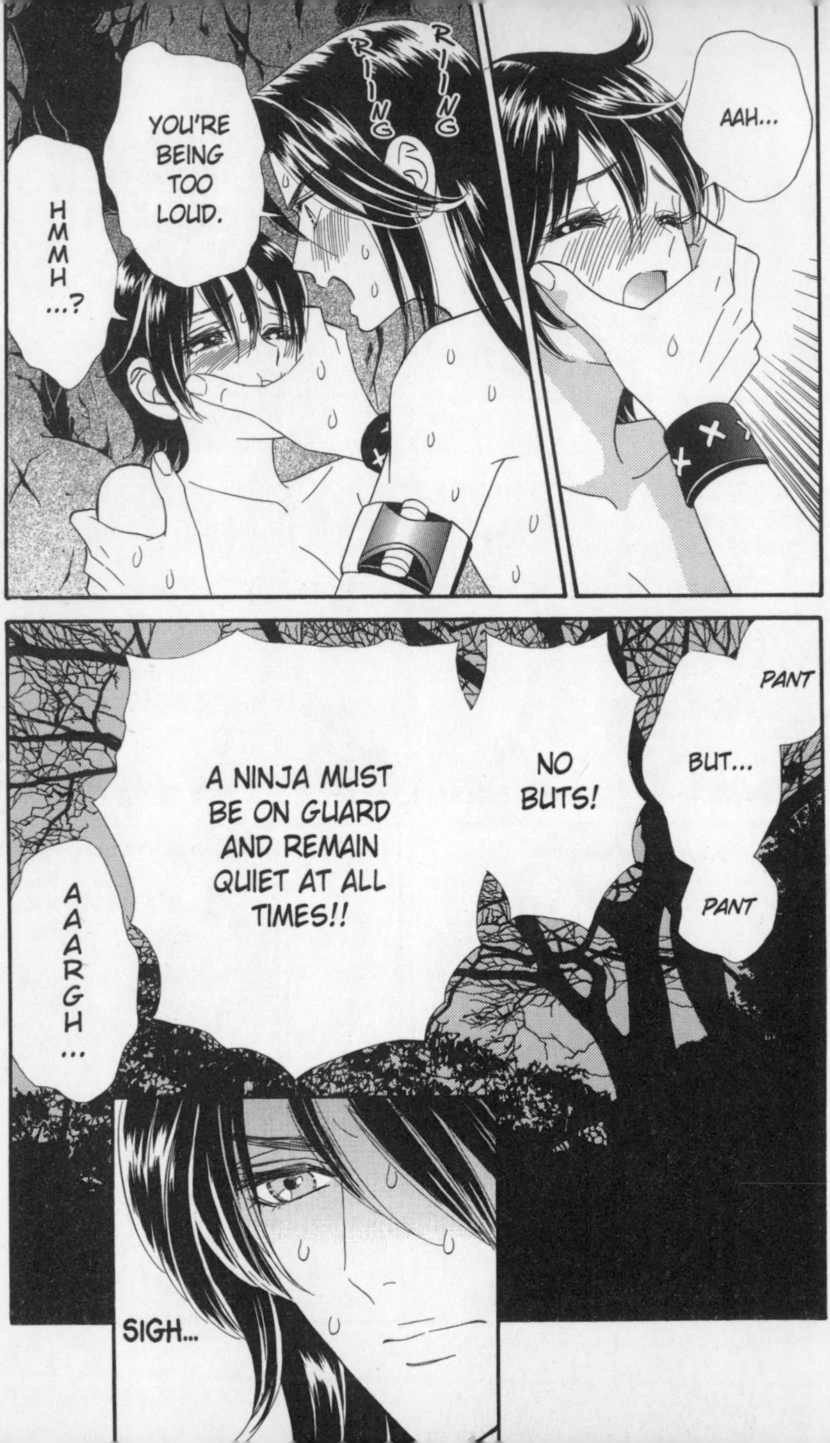
AAH...
RIIING RIIING
YOU'RE BEING TOO LOUD.
HMMH...?
PANT
BUT...
PANT
NO BUTS!
A NINJA MUST BE ON GUARD AND REMAIN QUIET AT ALL TIMES!!
AAARGH...
SIGH...

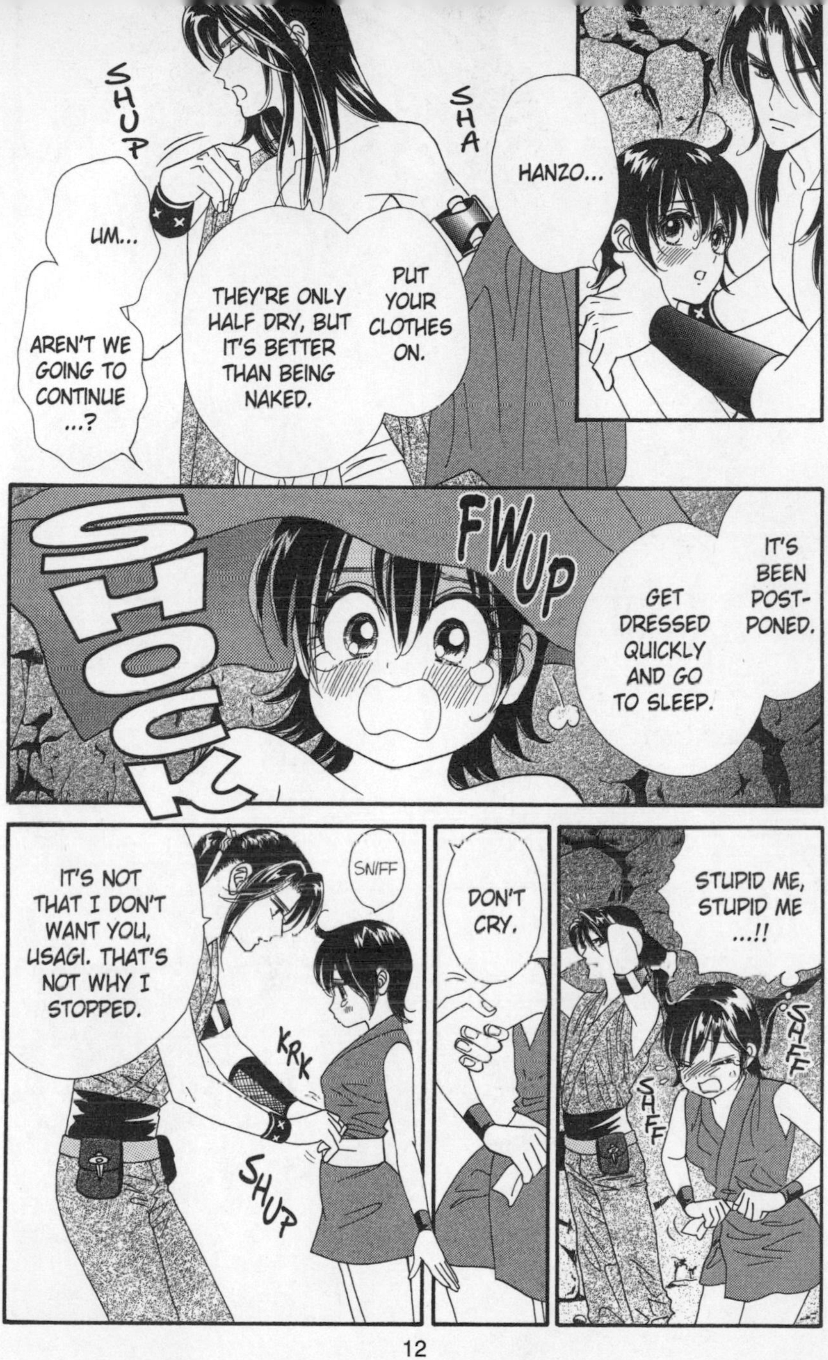
HANZO...
SHA
PUT YOUR CLOTHES ON.
THEY'RE ONLY HALF DRY, BUT IT'S BETTER THAN BEING NAKED.
SHUP
UM...
AREN'T WE GOING TO CONTINUE ...?
IT'S BEEN POST-PONED.
GET DRESSED QUICKLY AND GO TO SLEEP.
FWUP
SHOCK
STUPID ME, STUPID ME ...!!
SHFF
SHFF
DON'T CRY.
SNIFF
IT'S NOT THAT I DON'T WANT YOU, USAGI. THAT'S NOT WHY I STOPPED.
KRK
SHUP

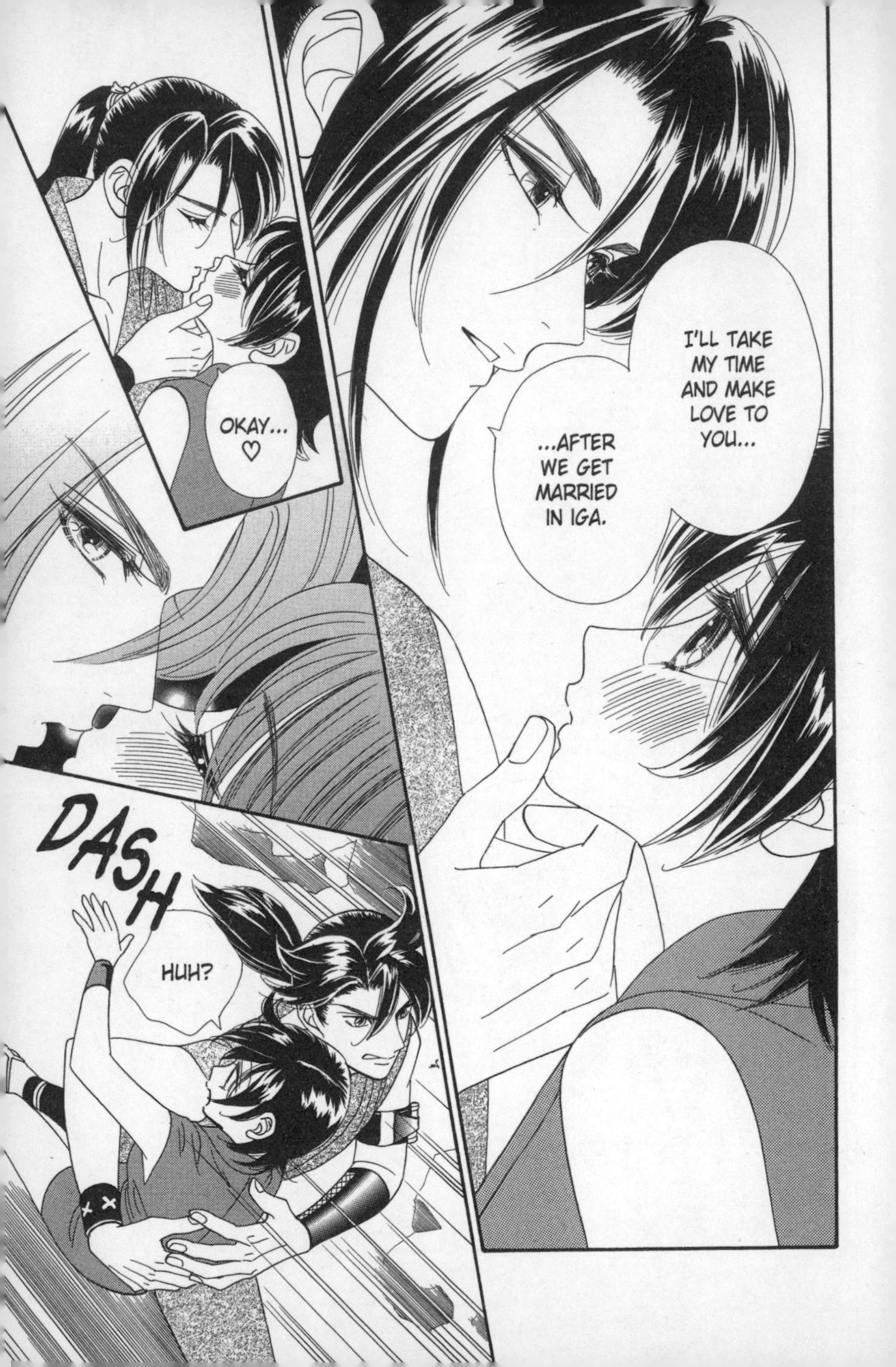
I'LL TAKE MY TIME AND MAKE LOVE TO YOU...
...AFTER WE GET MARRIED IN IGA.
OKAY... ♡
DASH
HUH?

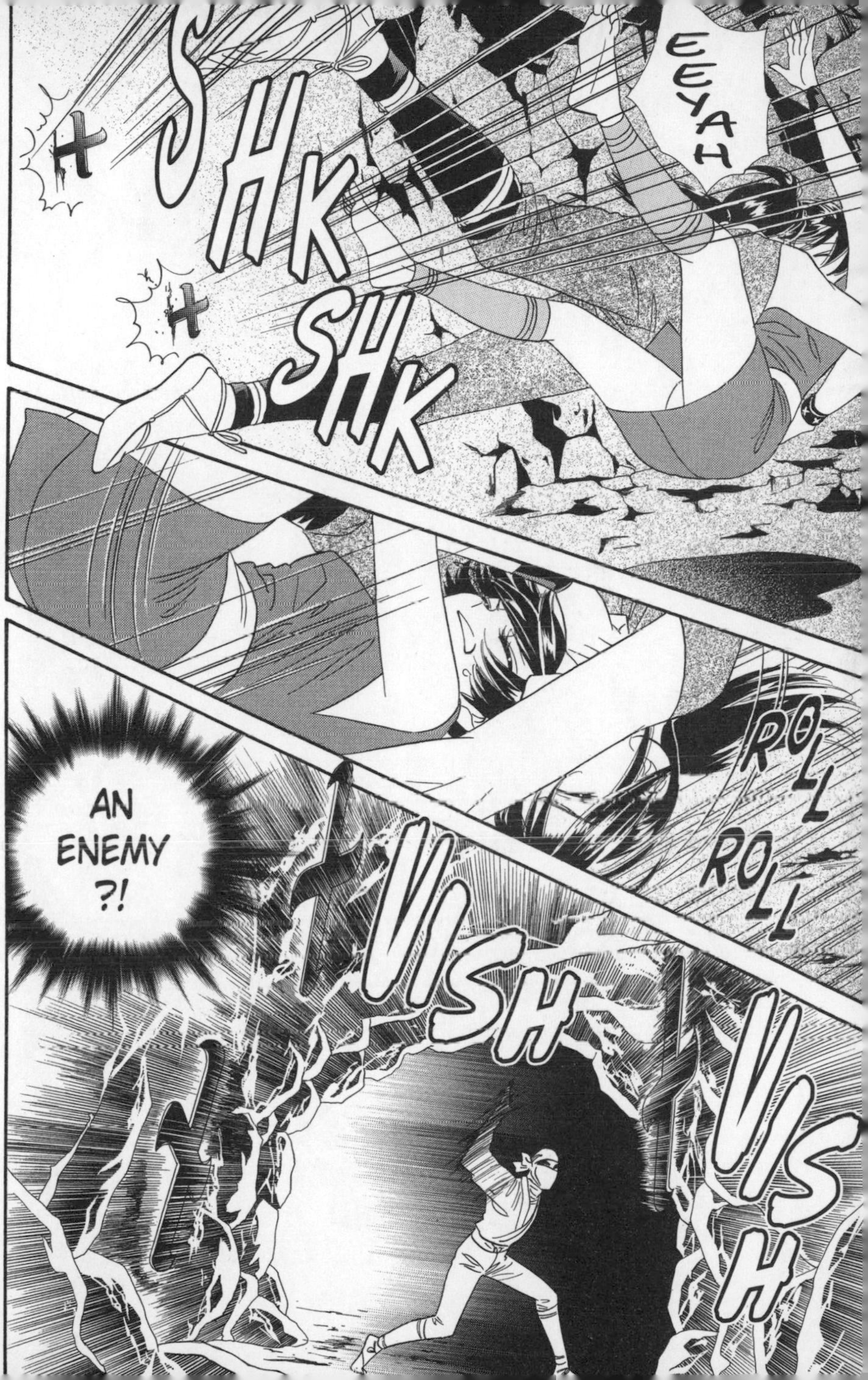
EEYAH
SHK
SHK
ROLL
ROLL
AN ENEMY ?!
VISH
VISH

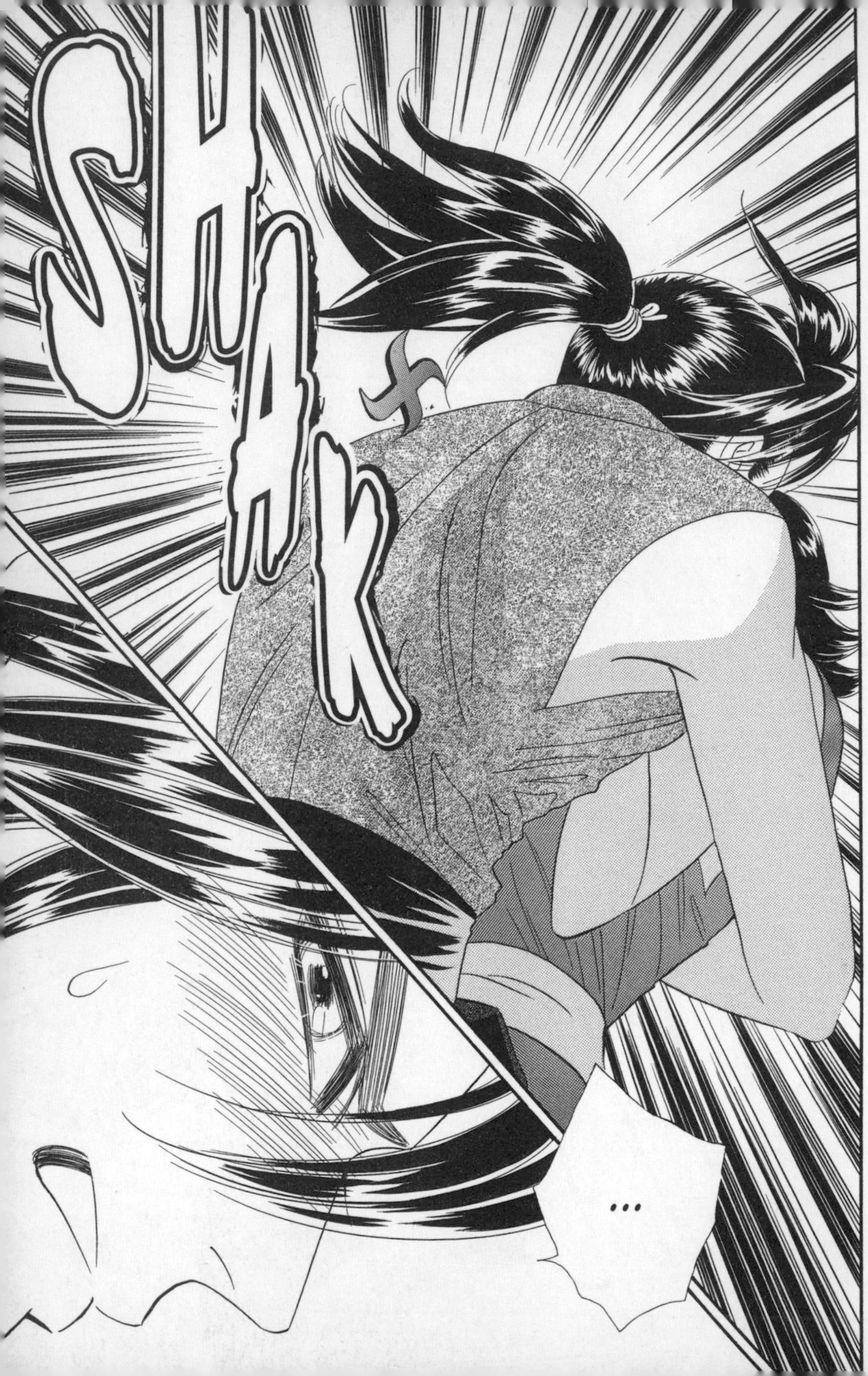
SHAK
...

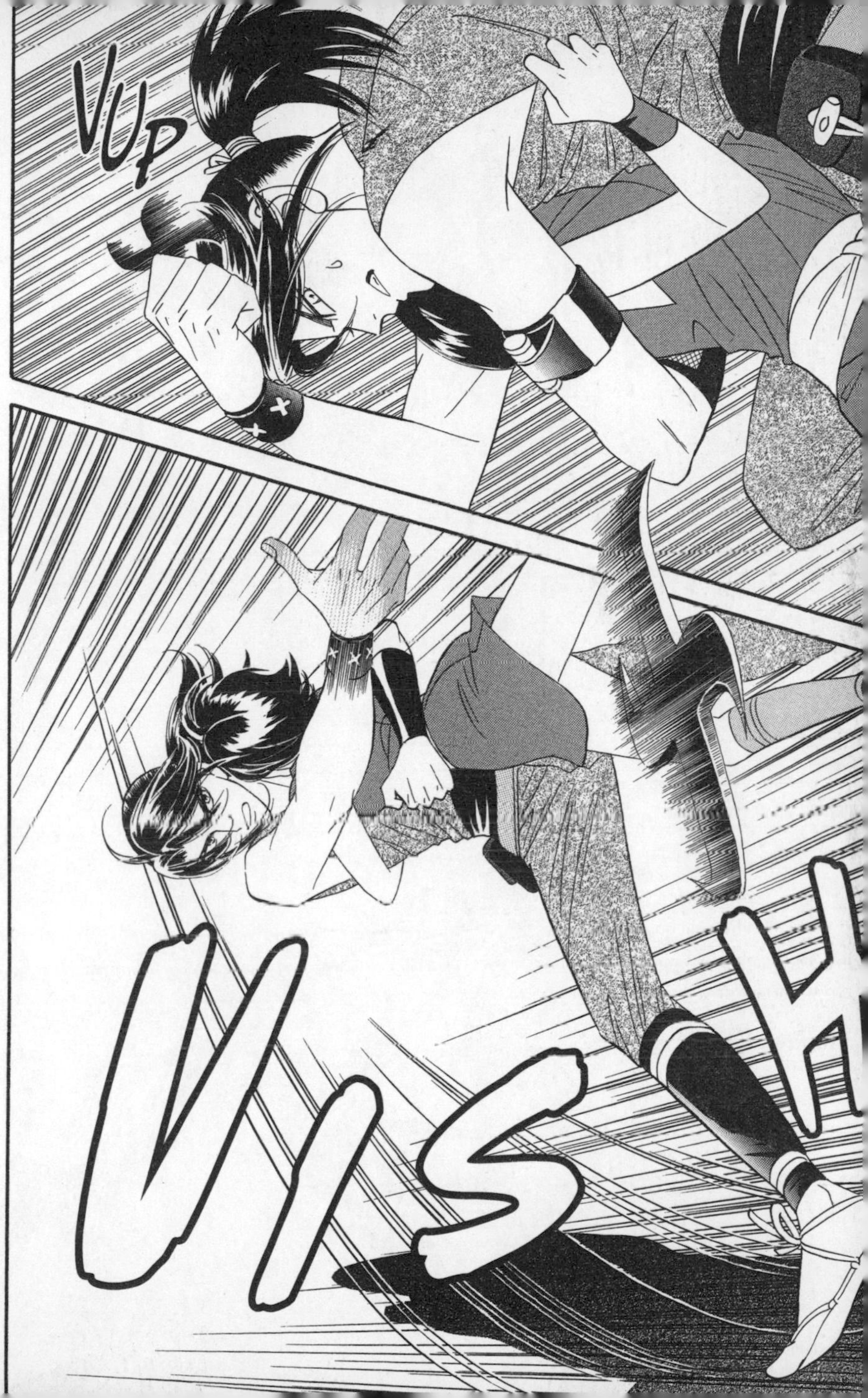
VUP
VISH

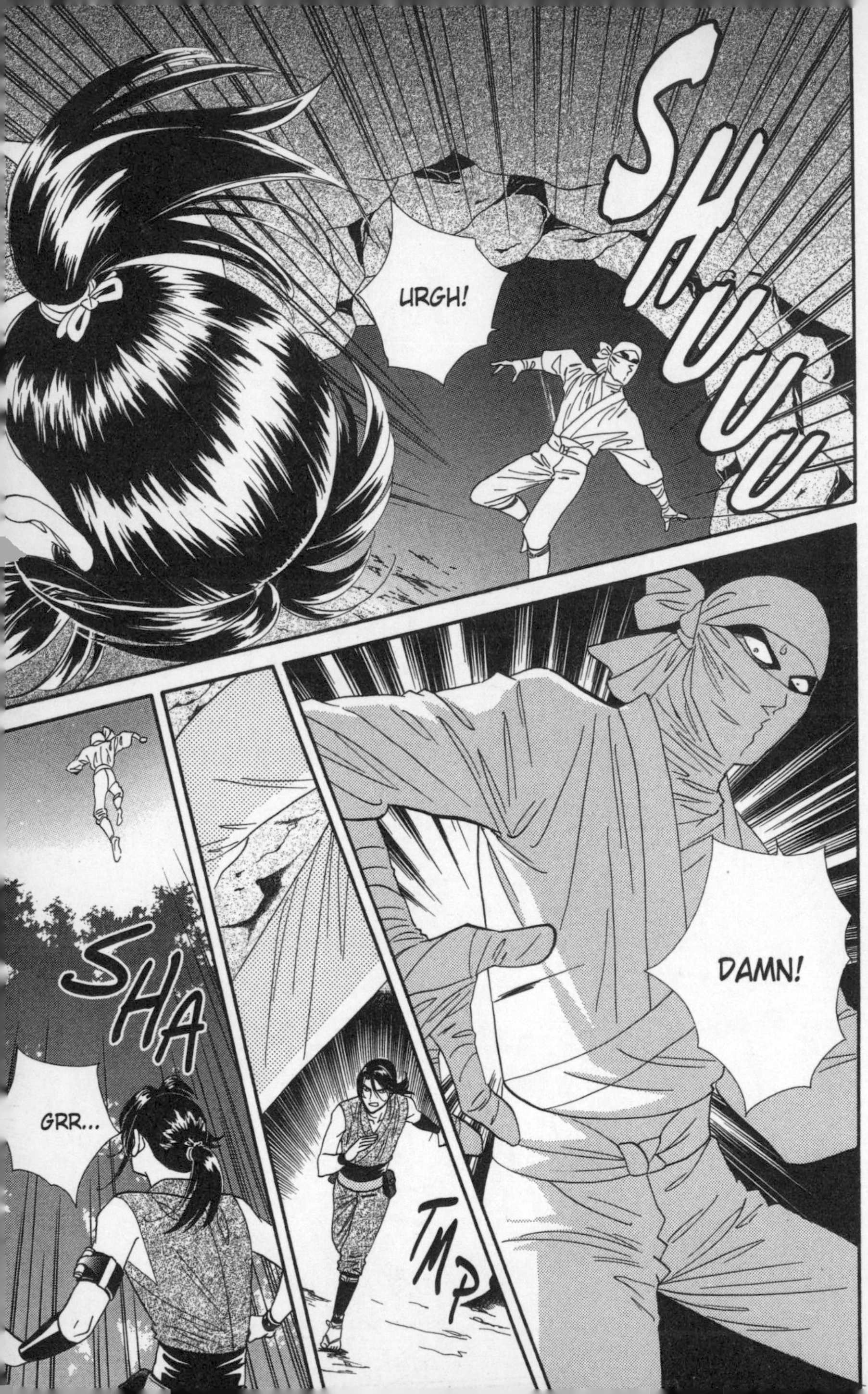
SHUUUU
URGH!
DAMN!
TMP
SHA
GRR...

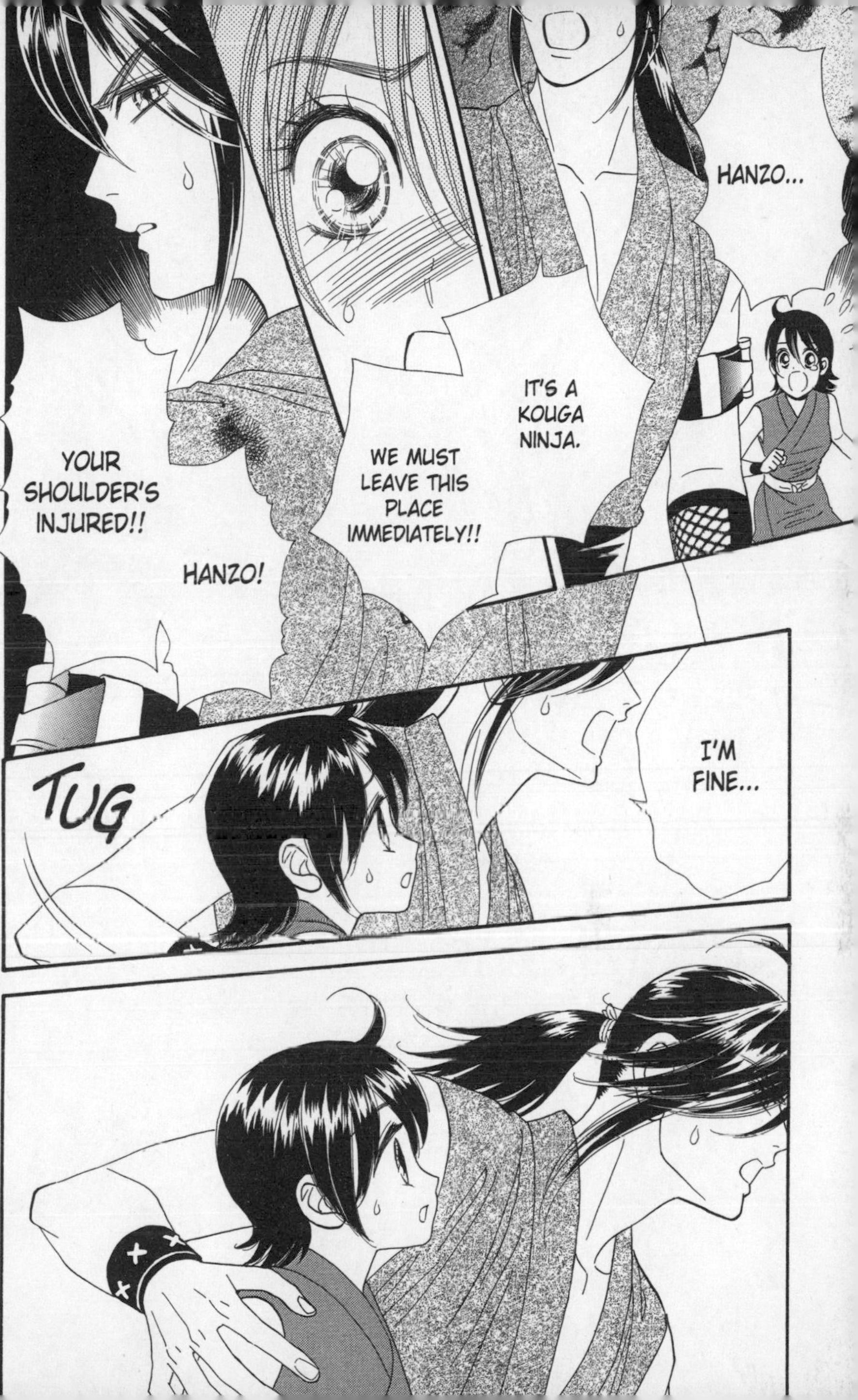
HANZO...
IT'S A KOUGA NINJA.
WE MUST LEAVE THIS PLACE IMMEDIATELY!!
HANZO!
YOUR SHOULDER'S INJURED!!
I'M FINE...
TUG

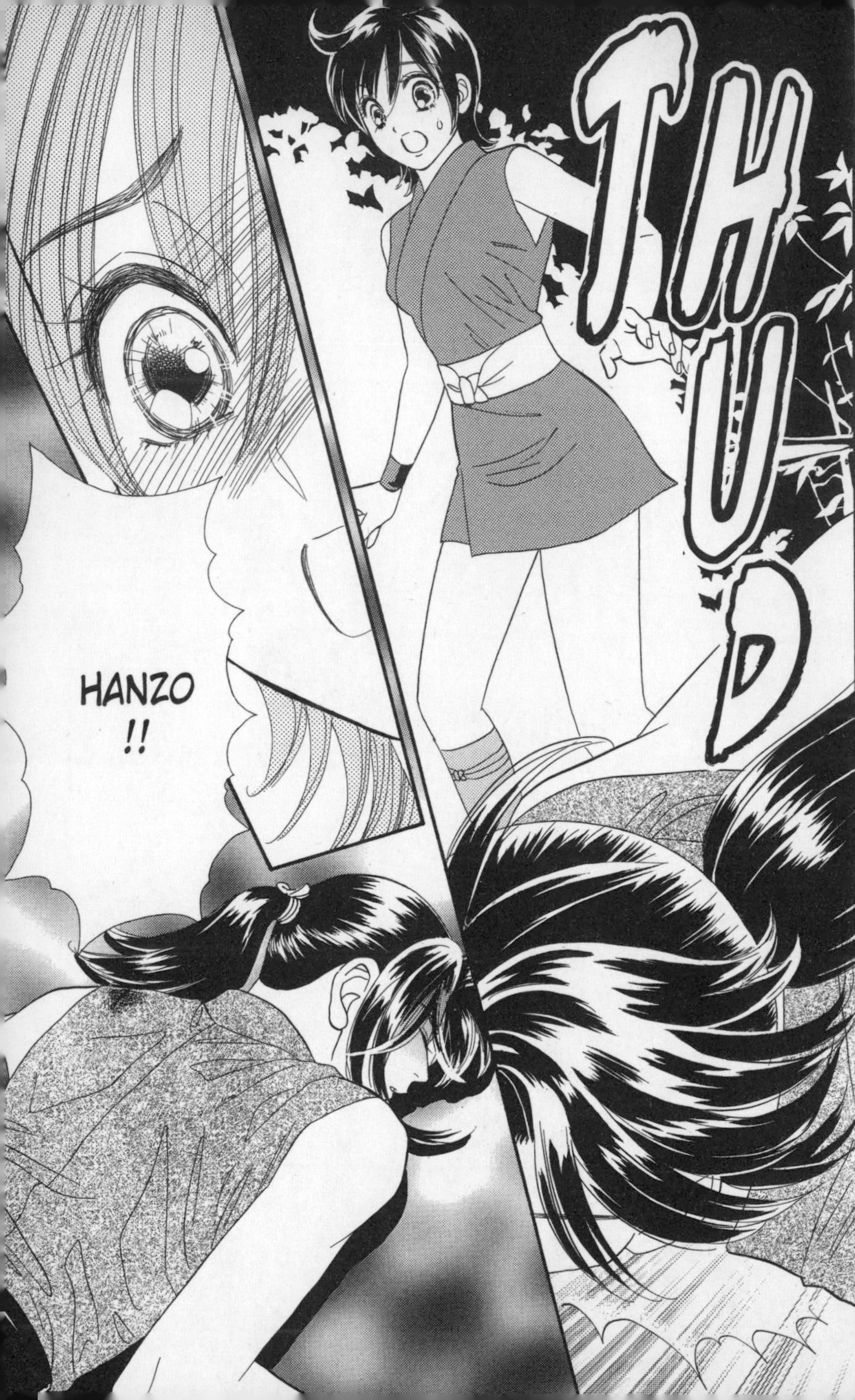
THUD
HANZO !!

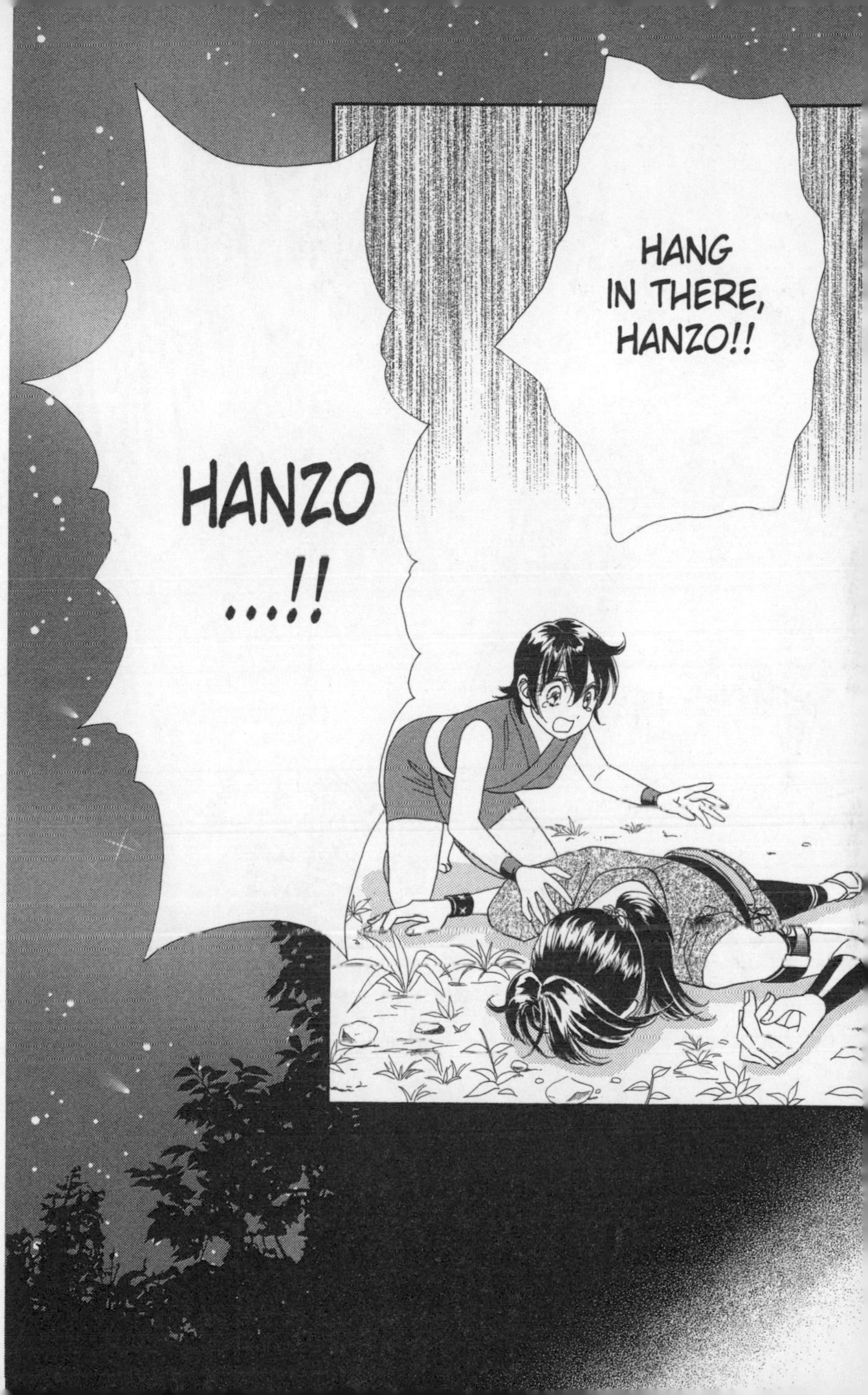
HANG IN THERE, HANZO!!
HANZO ...!!

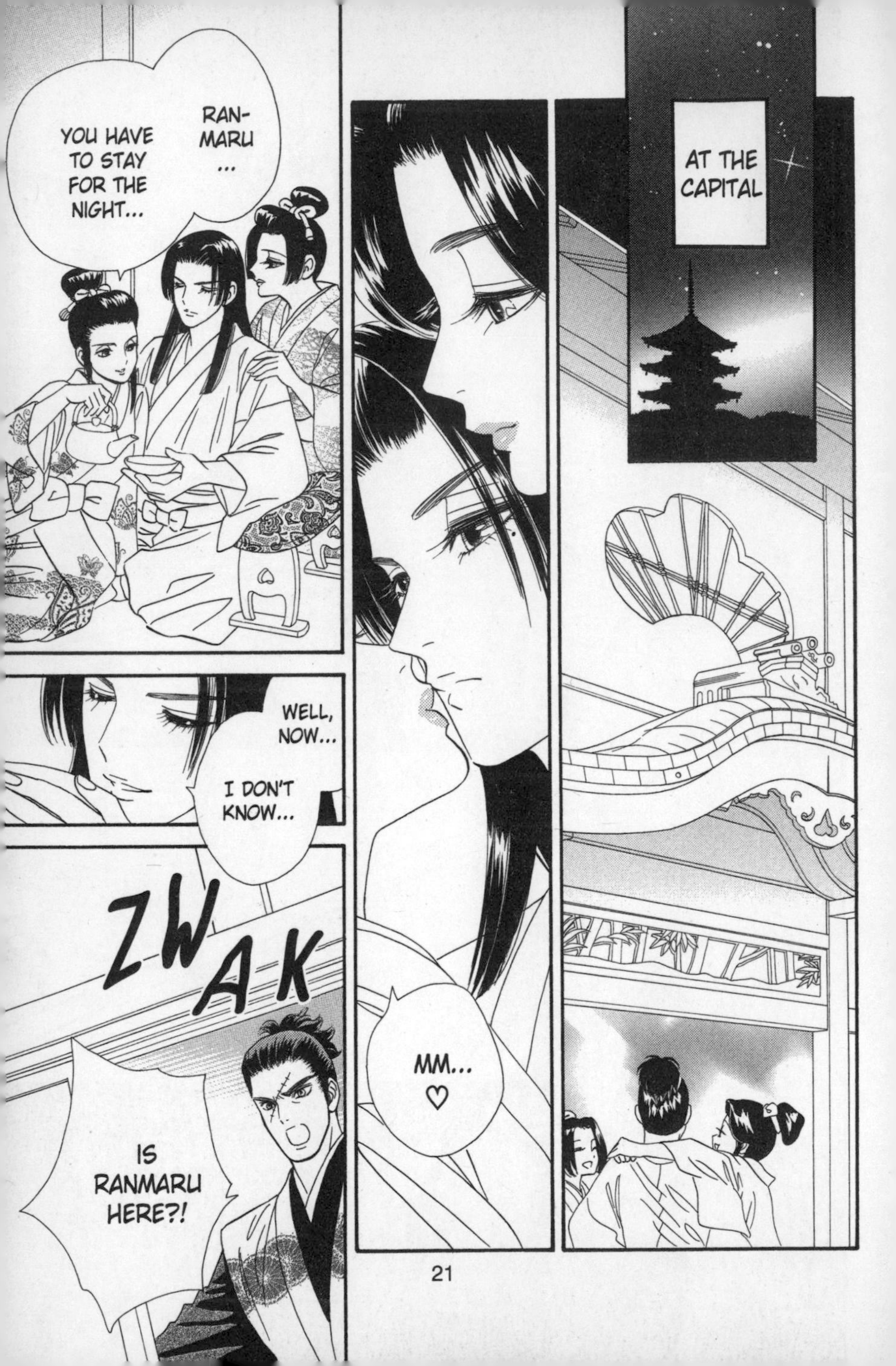
AT THE CAPITAL
MM... ♡
RAN-MARU...
YOU HAVE TO STAY FOR THE NIGHT...
WELL, NOW...
I DON'T KNOW...
ZWAK
IS RANMARU HERE?!

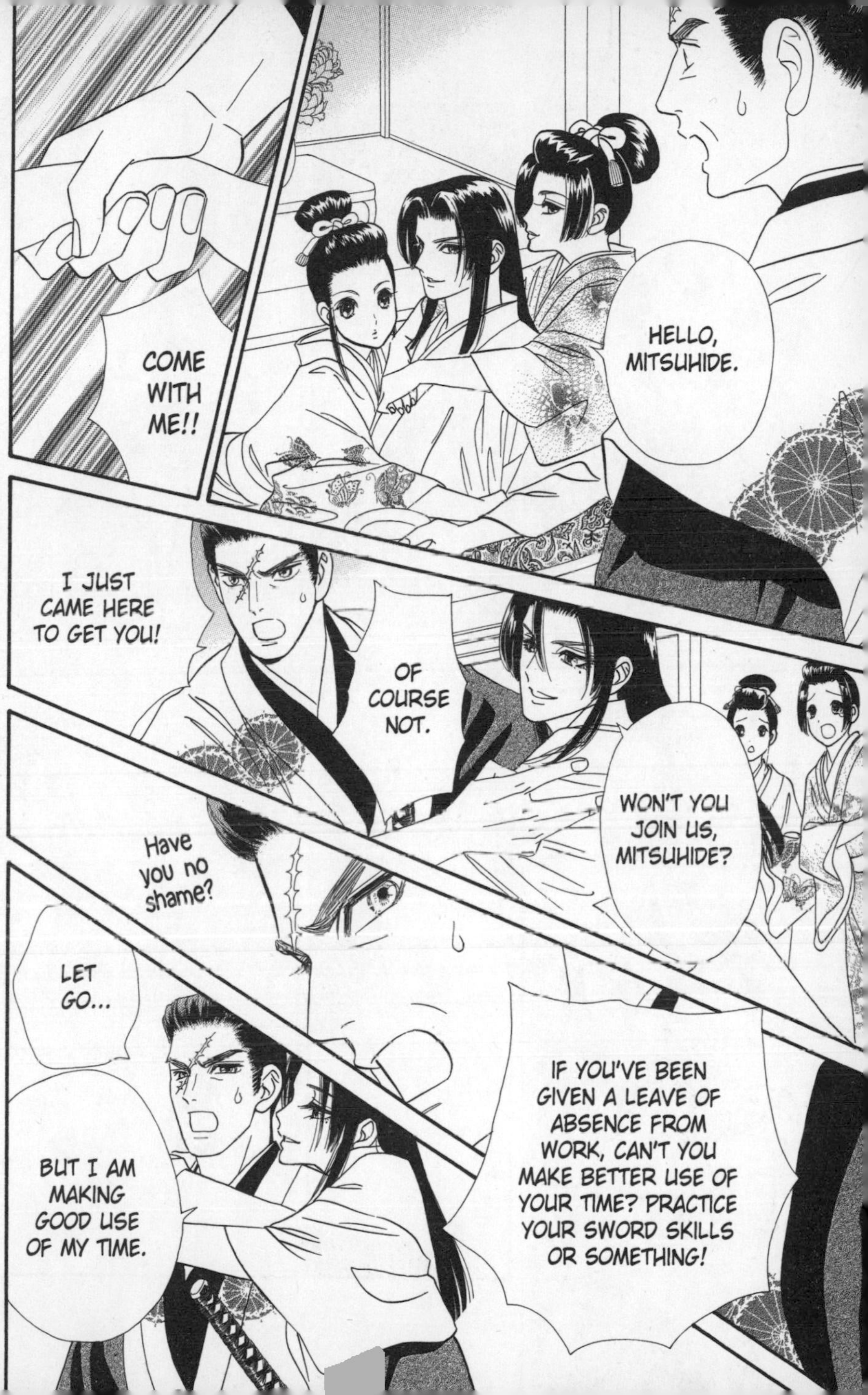
HELLO, MITSUHIDE.
COME WITH ME!!
WON'T YOU JOIN US, MITSUHIDE?
OF COURSE NOT.
I JUST CAME HERE TO GET YOU!
Have you no shame?
IF YOU'VE BEEN GIVEN A LEAVE OF ABSENCE FROM WORK, CAN'T YOU MAKE BETTER USE OF YOUR TIME? PRACTICE YOUR SWORD SKILLS OR SOMETHING!
LET GO...
BUT I AM MAKING GOOD USE OF MY TIME.

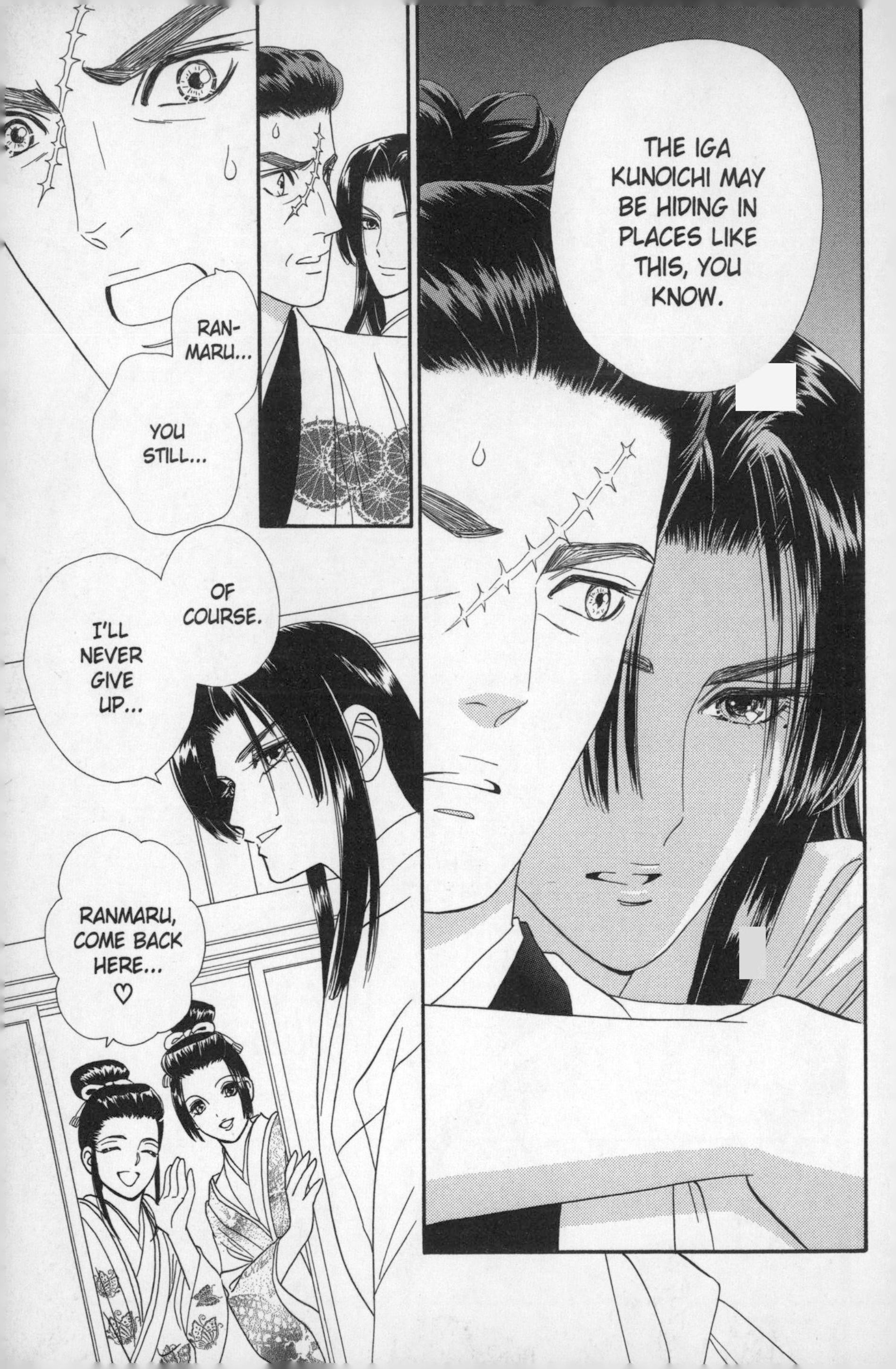
THE IGA KUNOICHI MAY BE HIDING IN PLACES LIKE THIS, YOU KNOW.
RAN-MARU...
YOU STILL...
OF COURSE.
I'LL NEVER GIVE UP...
RANMARU, COME BACK HERE... ♡

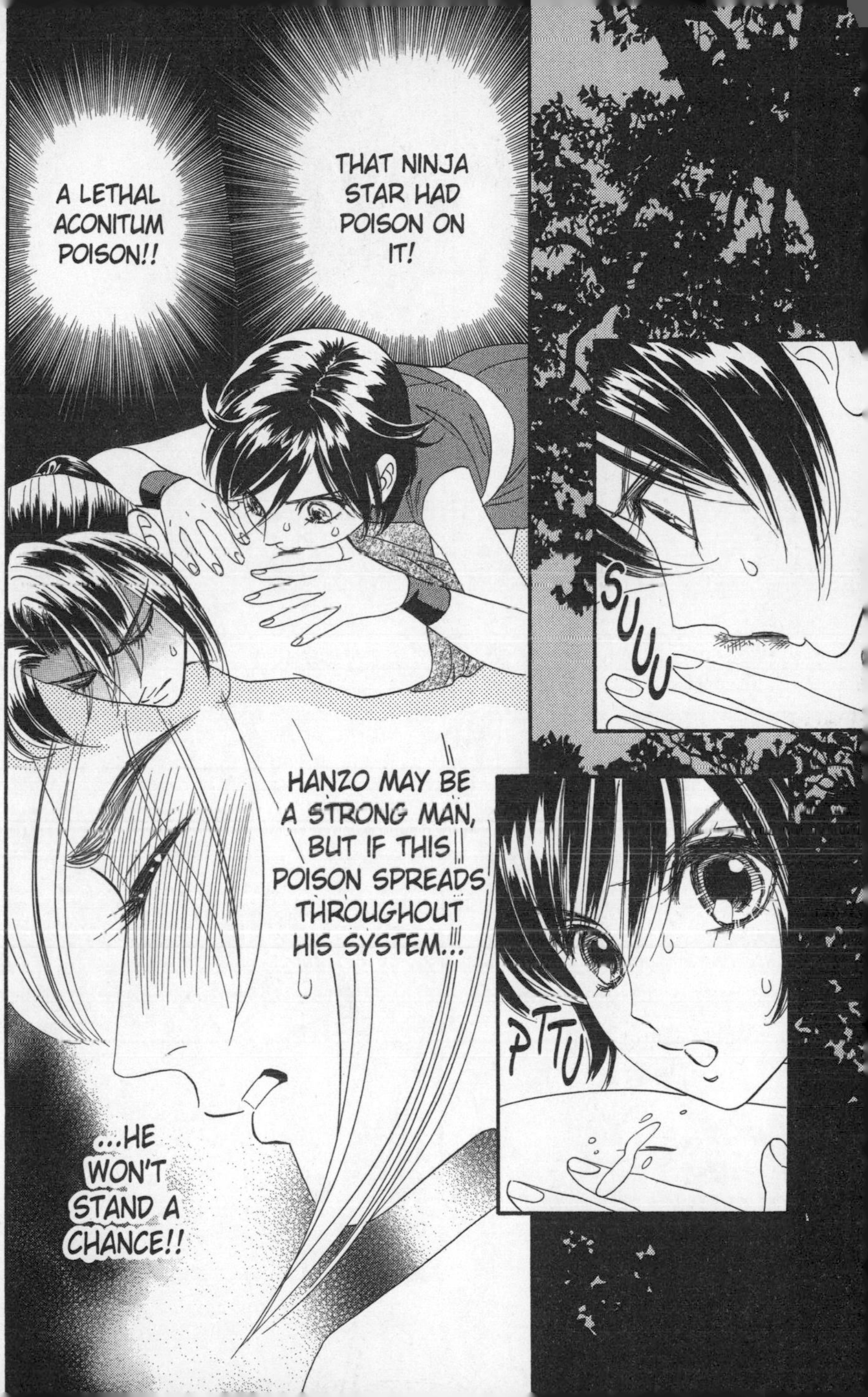
SUUUU
PTTU
THAT NINJA STAR HAD POISON ON IT!
A LETHAL ACONITUM POISON!!
HANZO MAY BE A STRONG MAN, BUT IF THIS POISON SPREADS THROUGHOUT HIS SYSTEM...!!
...HE WON'T STAND A CHANCE!!

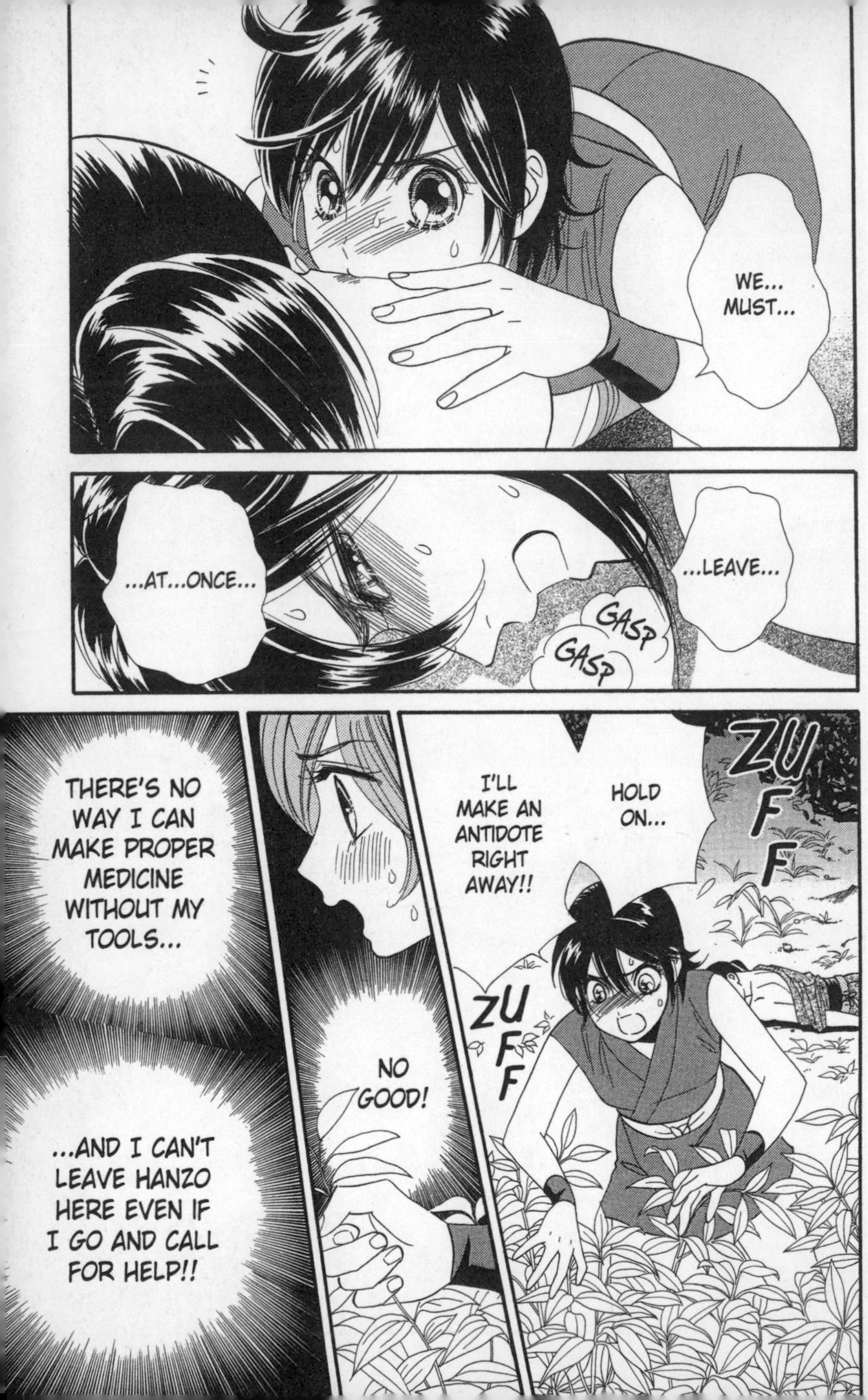
WE... MUST...
...LEAVE...
GASP
GASP
...AT...ONCE...
ZU F F
HOLD ON...
I'LL MAKE AN ANTIDOTE RIGHT AWAY!!
ZU F F
NO GOOD!
THERE'S NO WAY I CAN MAKE PROPER MEDICINE WITHOUT MY TOOLS...
...AND I CAN'T LEAVE HANZO HERE EVEN IF I GO AND CALL FOR HELP!!

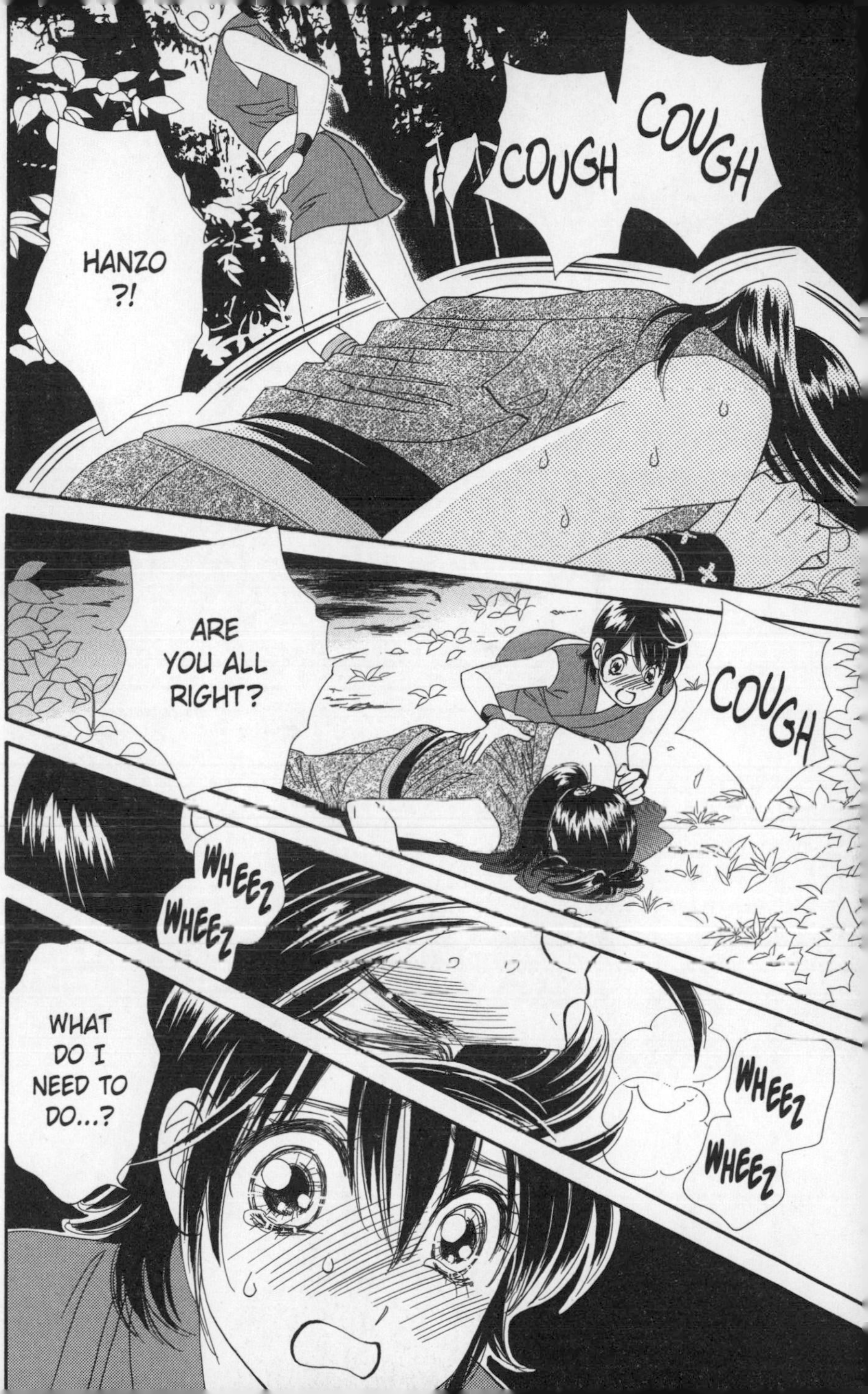
COUGH
COUGH
HANZO ?!
COUGH
ARE YOU ALL RIGHT?
WHEEZ
WHEEZ
WHEEZ
WHEEZ
WHAT DO I NEED TO DO...?

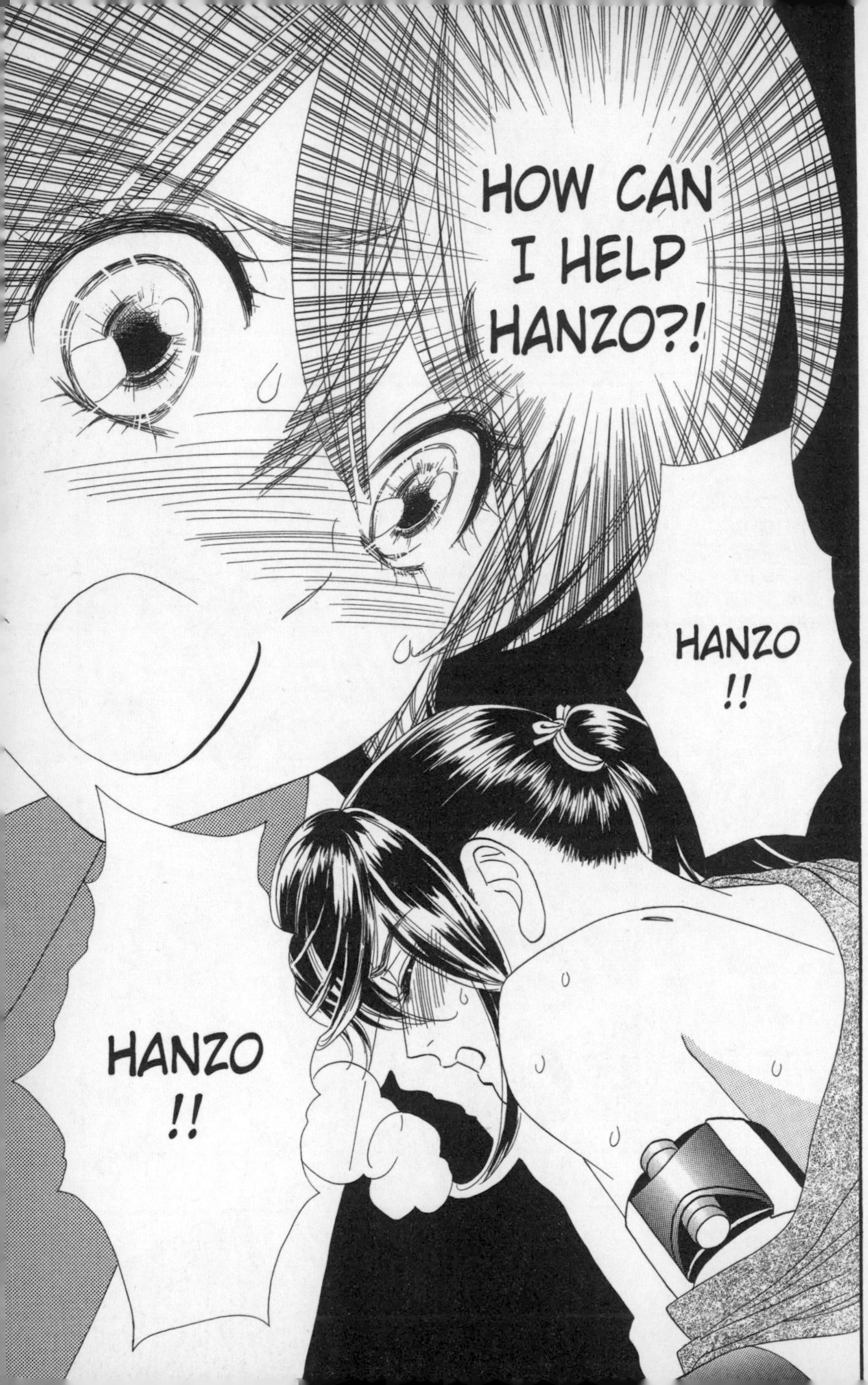
HOW CAN I HELP HANZO?!
HANZO !!
HANZO !!

TAIL OF THE MOON EXTRA: TODAY'S MISSION

"I WANT TO SEE HANZO MAKING MOCHI!"

-MARI, YAMAGUCHI PREFECTURE

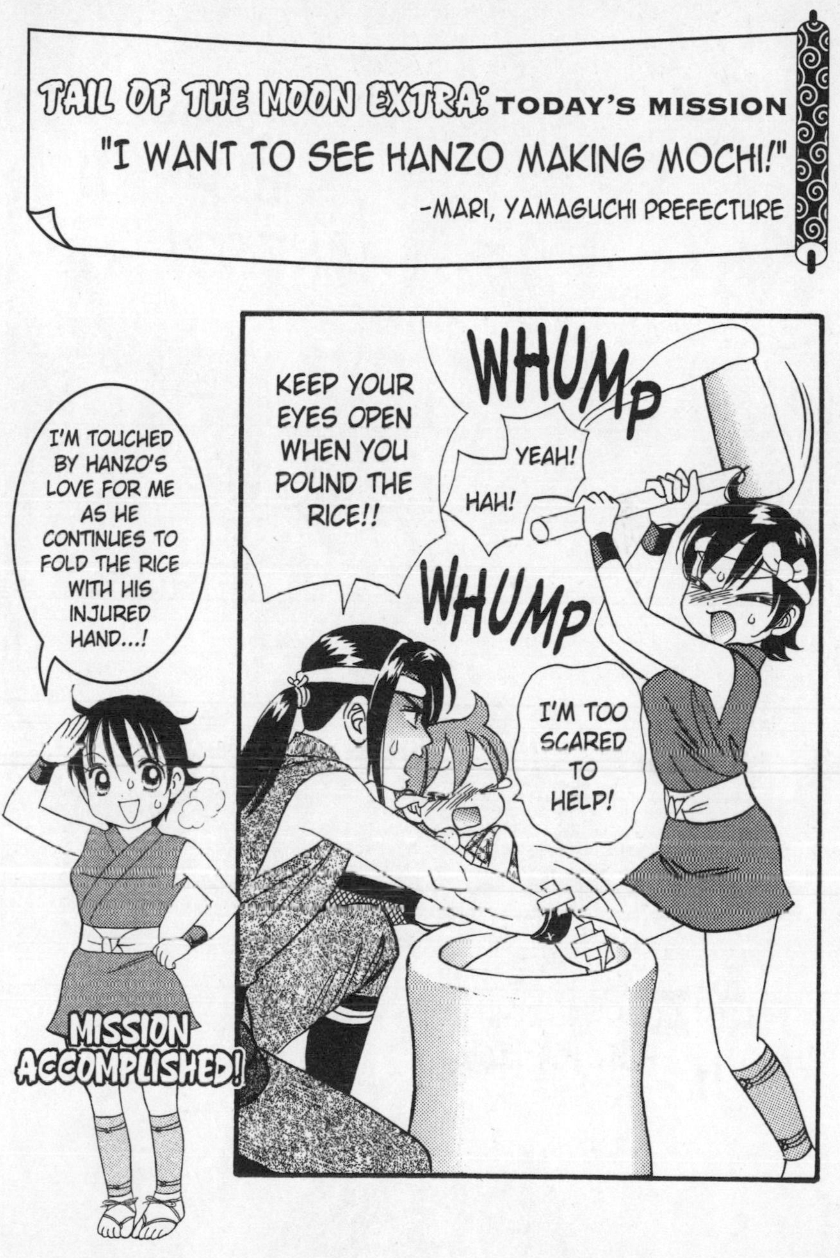
WHUMP
KEEP YOUR EYES OPEN WHEN YOU POUND THE RICE!!
YEAH!
HAH!
WHUMP
I'M TOO SCARED TO HELP!
I'M TOUCHED BY HANZO'S LOVE FOR ME AS HE CONTINUES TO FOLD THE RICE WITH HIS INJURED HAND...!
MISSION ACCOMPLISHED!

"I'LL LOVE YOU IN MY OWN WAY, USAGI."
I HAVE TO WORK HARD AND BECOME A FINE KUNOICHI FOR HANZO.

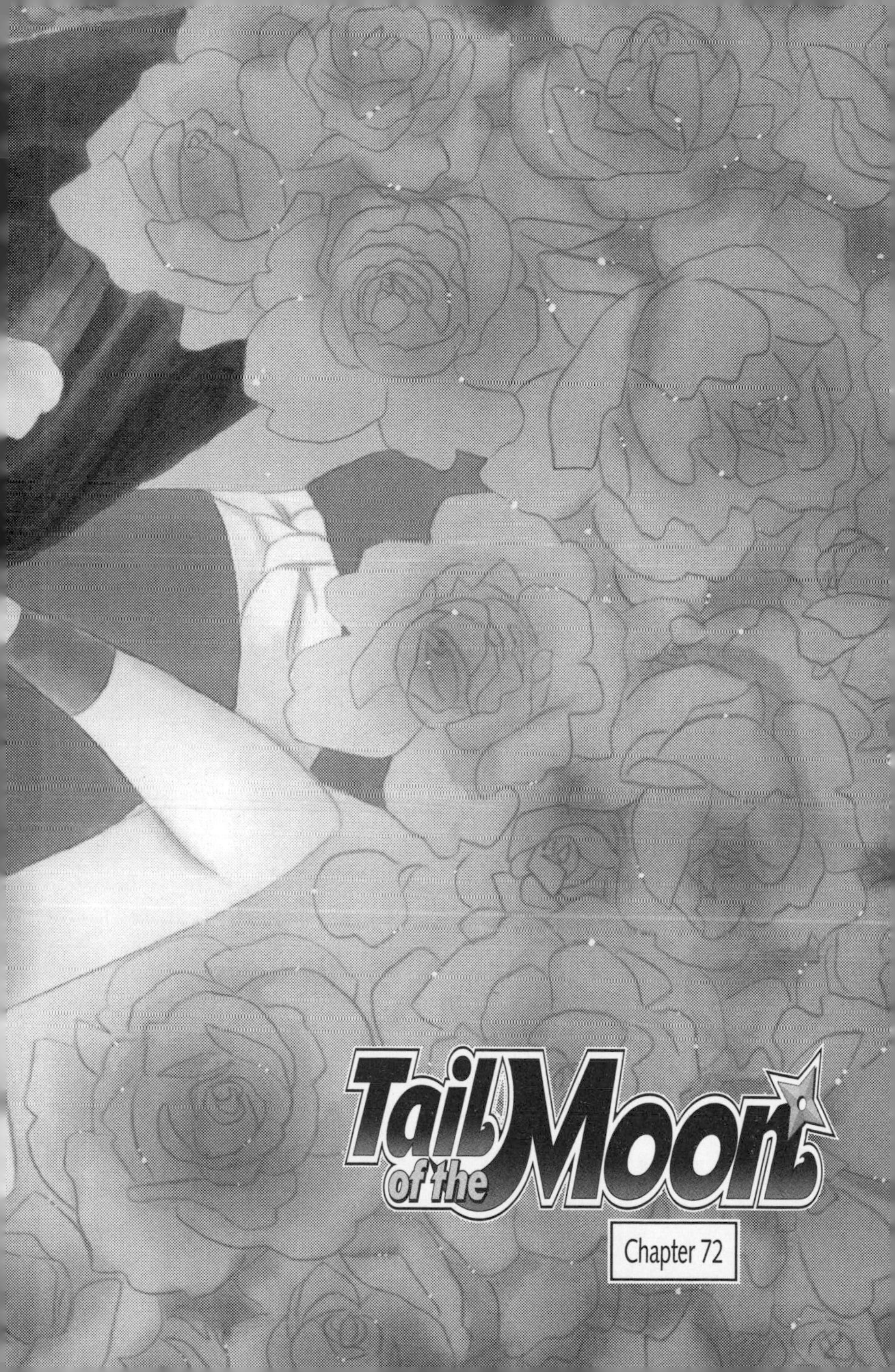

Tail of the Moon
Chapter 72

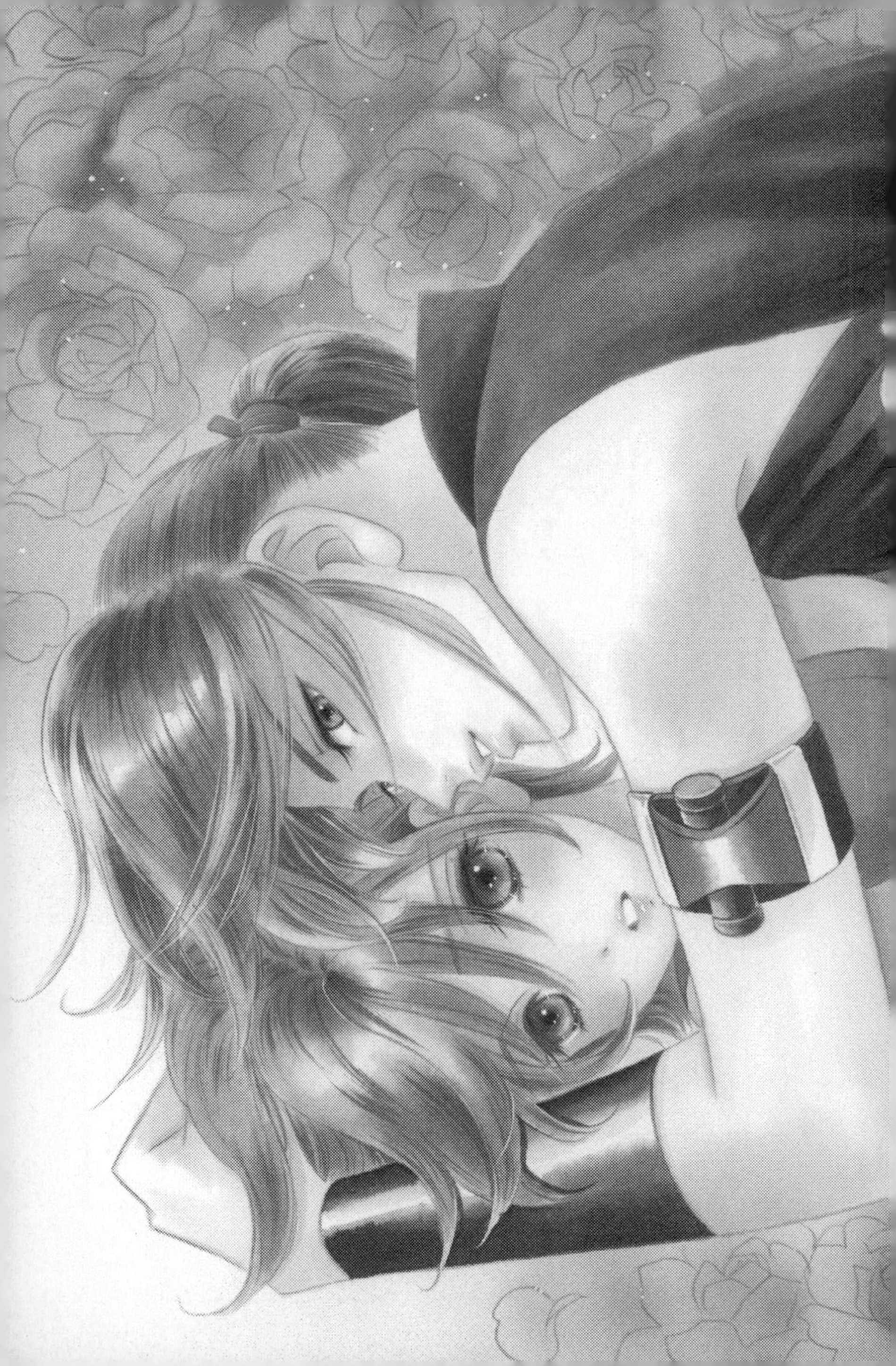

TAIL OF THE MOON EXTRA: TODAY'S MISSION

"I WANT TO SEE HANZO SKIING!"

-OCCHI, KANAGAWA PREFECTURE

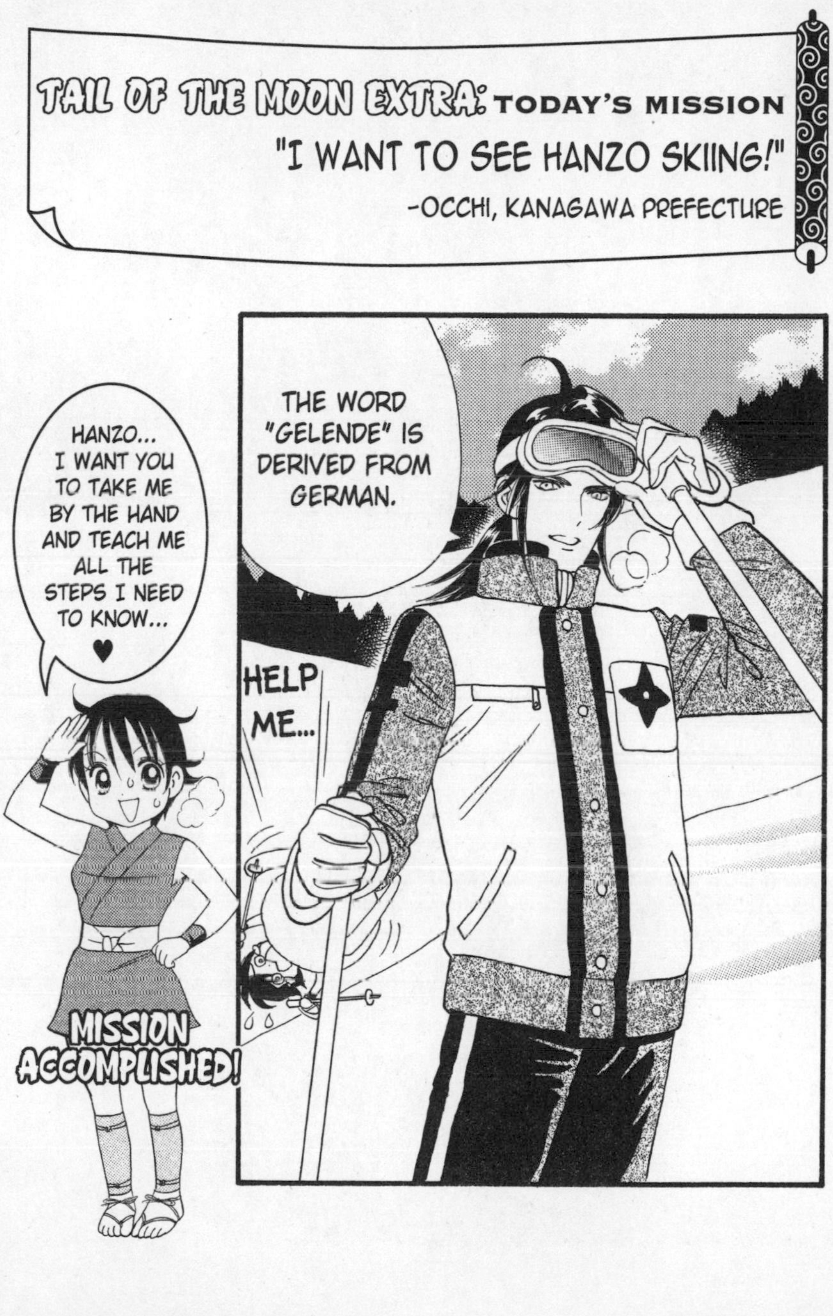
THE WORD "GELENDE" IS DERIVED FROM GERMAN.
HELP ME...
HANZO... I WANT YOU TO TAKE ME BY THE HAND AND TEACH ME ALL THE STEPS I NEED TO KNOW... ♥
MISSION ACCOMPLISHED!

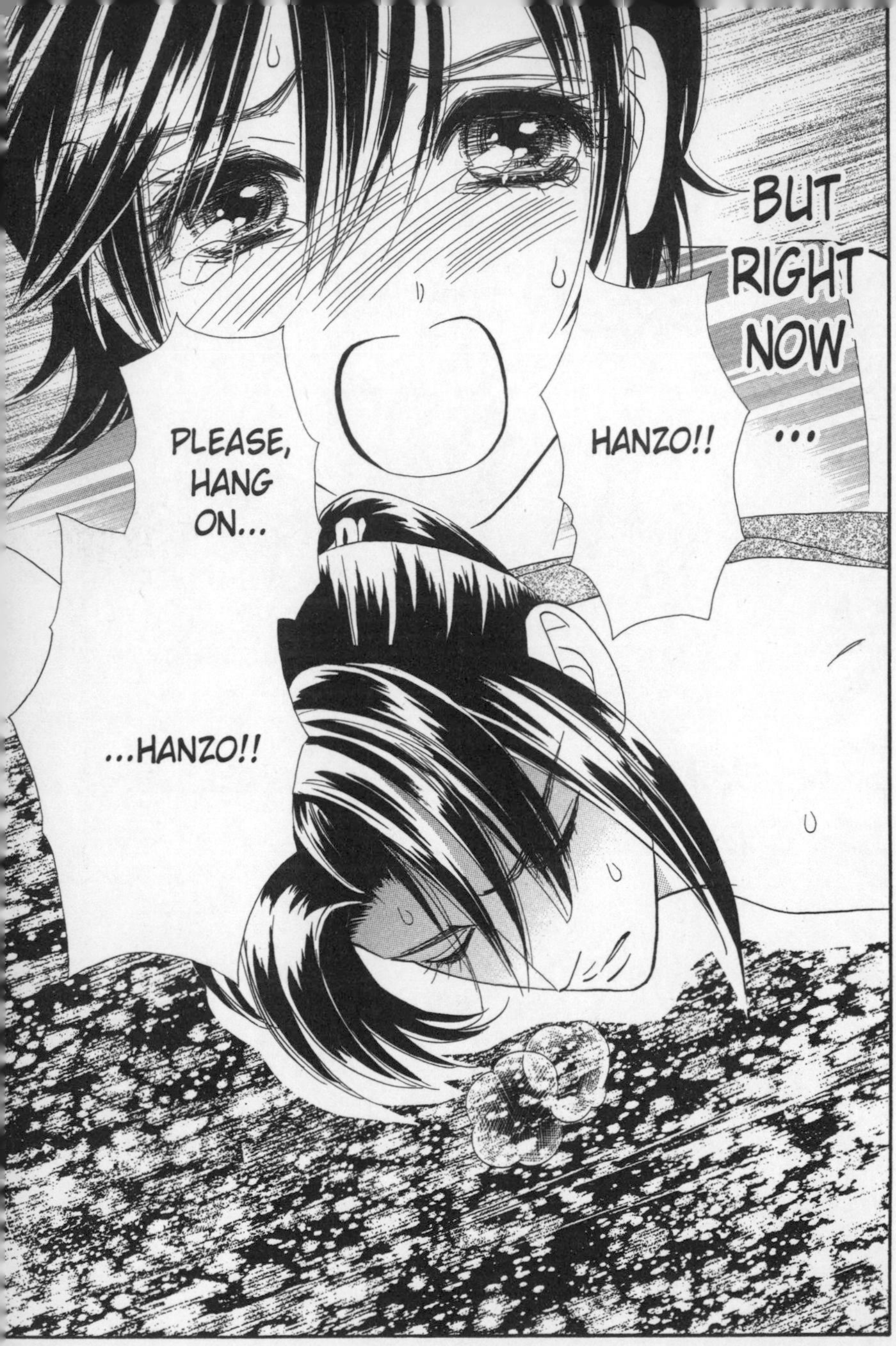
BUT RIGHT NOW...
HANZO!!
PLEASE, HANG ON...
...HANZO!!

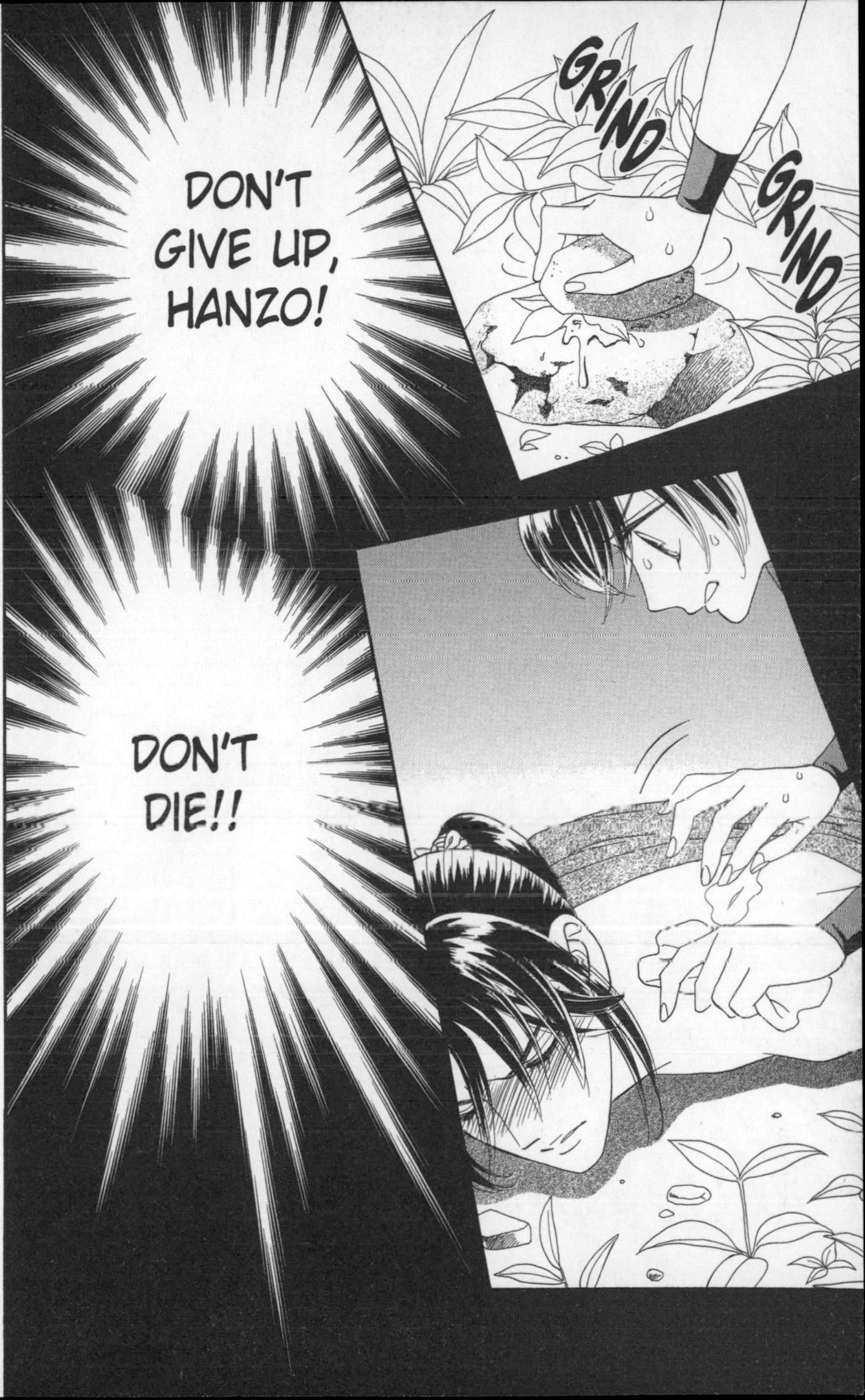
GRIND GRIND
DON'T GIVE UP, HANZO!
DON'T DIE!!

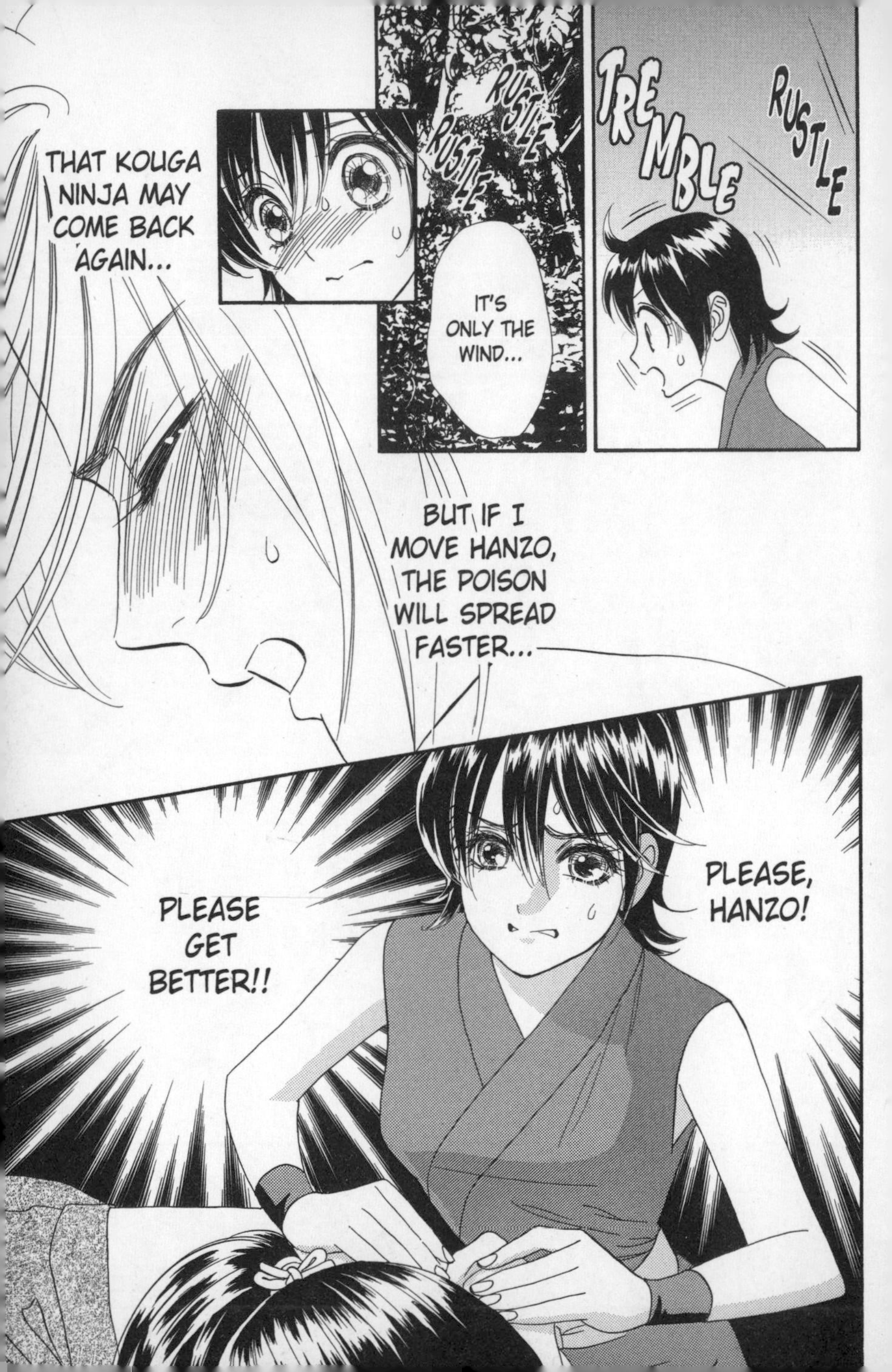
RUSTLE
TREMBLE
RUSTLE
RUSTLE
IT'S ONLY THE WIND...
THAT KOUGA NINJA MAY COME BACK AGAIN...
BUT IF I MOVE HANZO, THE POISON WILL SPREAD FASTER...
PLEASE, HANZO!
PLEASE GET BETTER!!

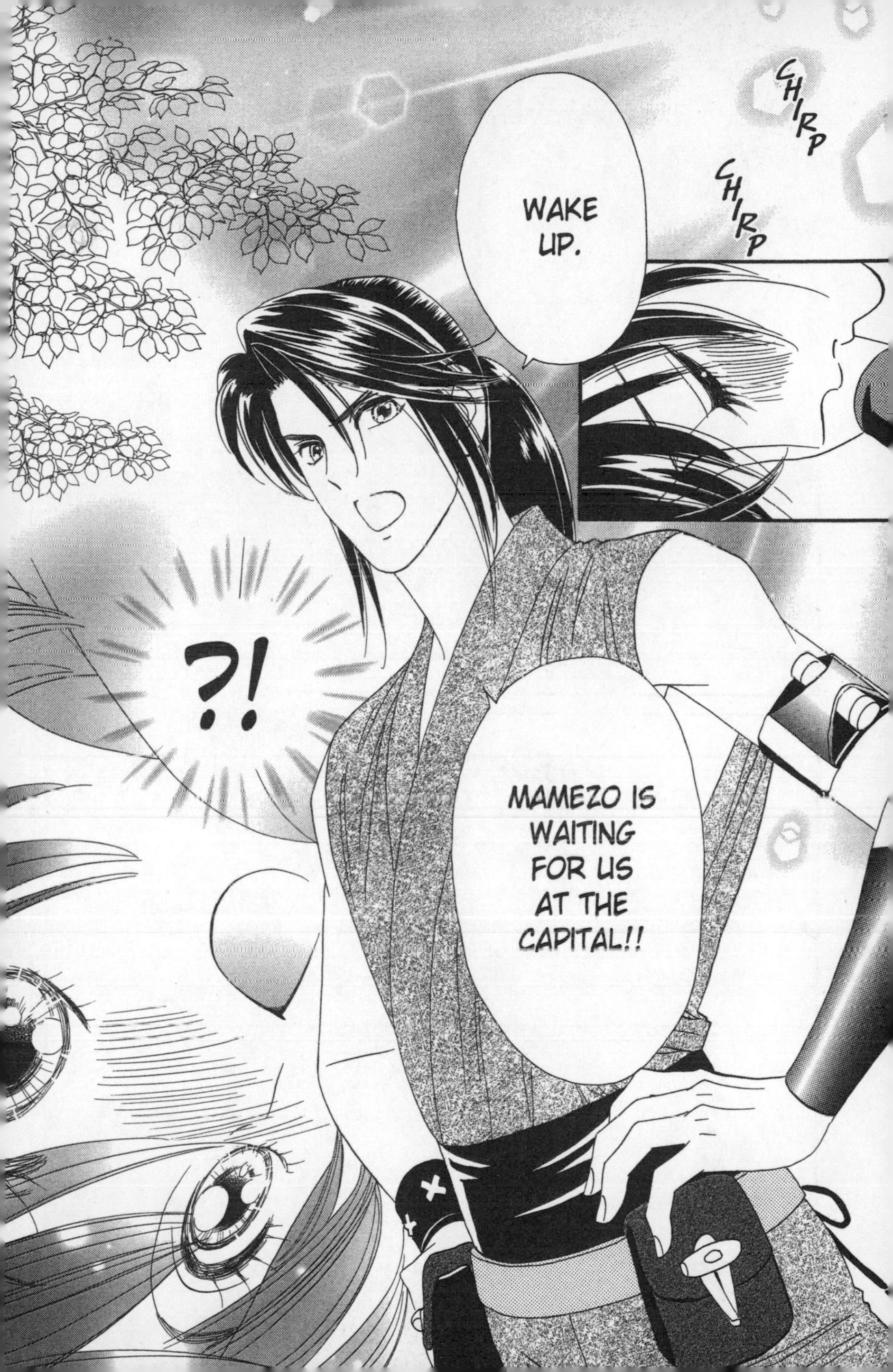
CHIRP
CHIRP
WAKE UP.
MAMEZO IS WAITING FOR US AT THE CAPITAL!!
?!

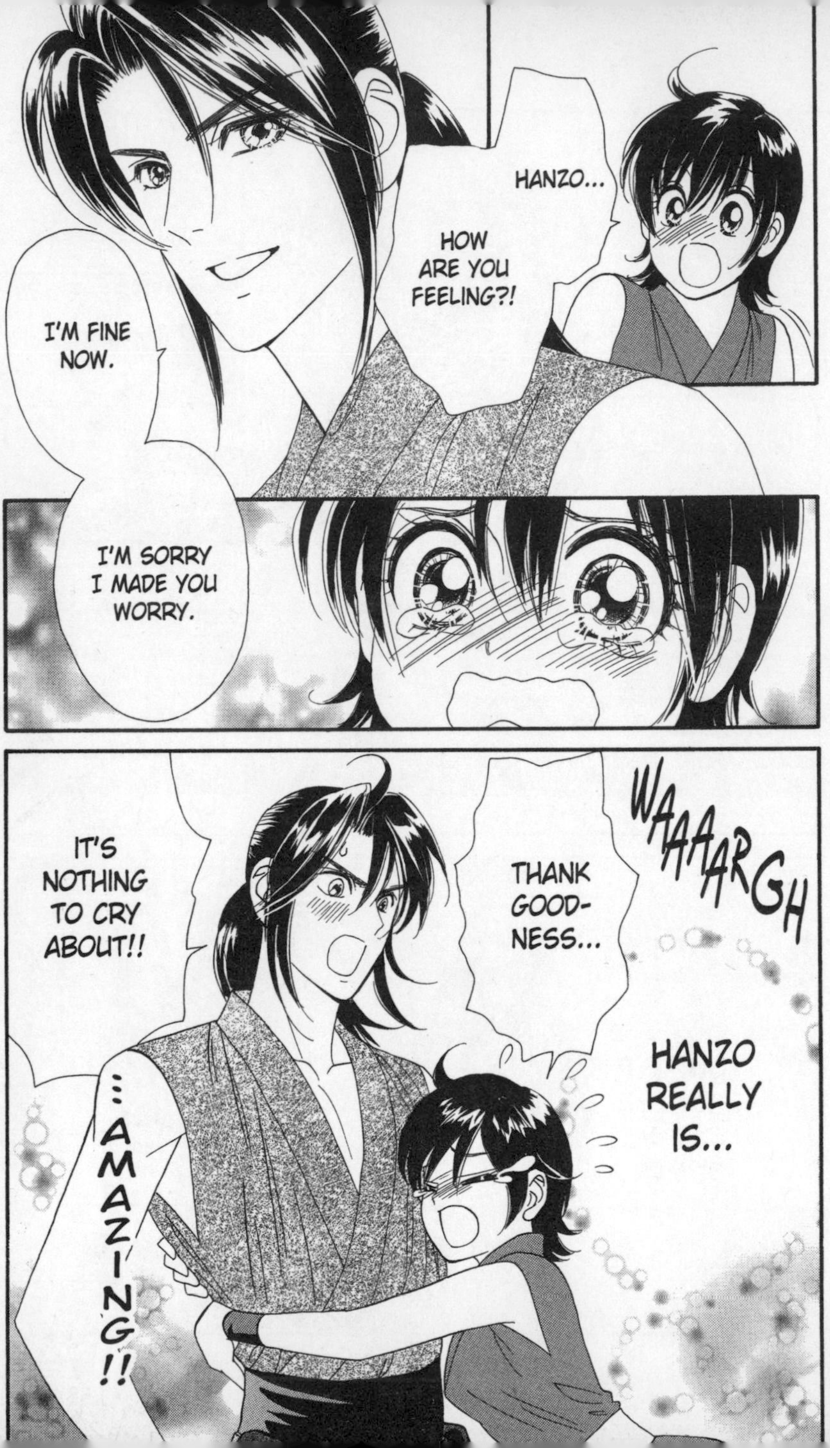
HANZO...
HOW ARE YOU FEELING?!
I'M FINE NOW.
I'M SORRY I MADE YOU WORRY.
WAAAAARGH
THANK GOOD-NESS...
IT'S NOTHING TO CRY ABOUT!!
HANZO REALLY IS...
...AMAZING!!

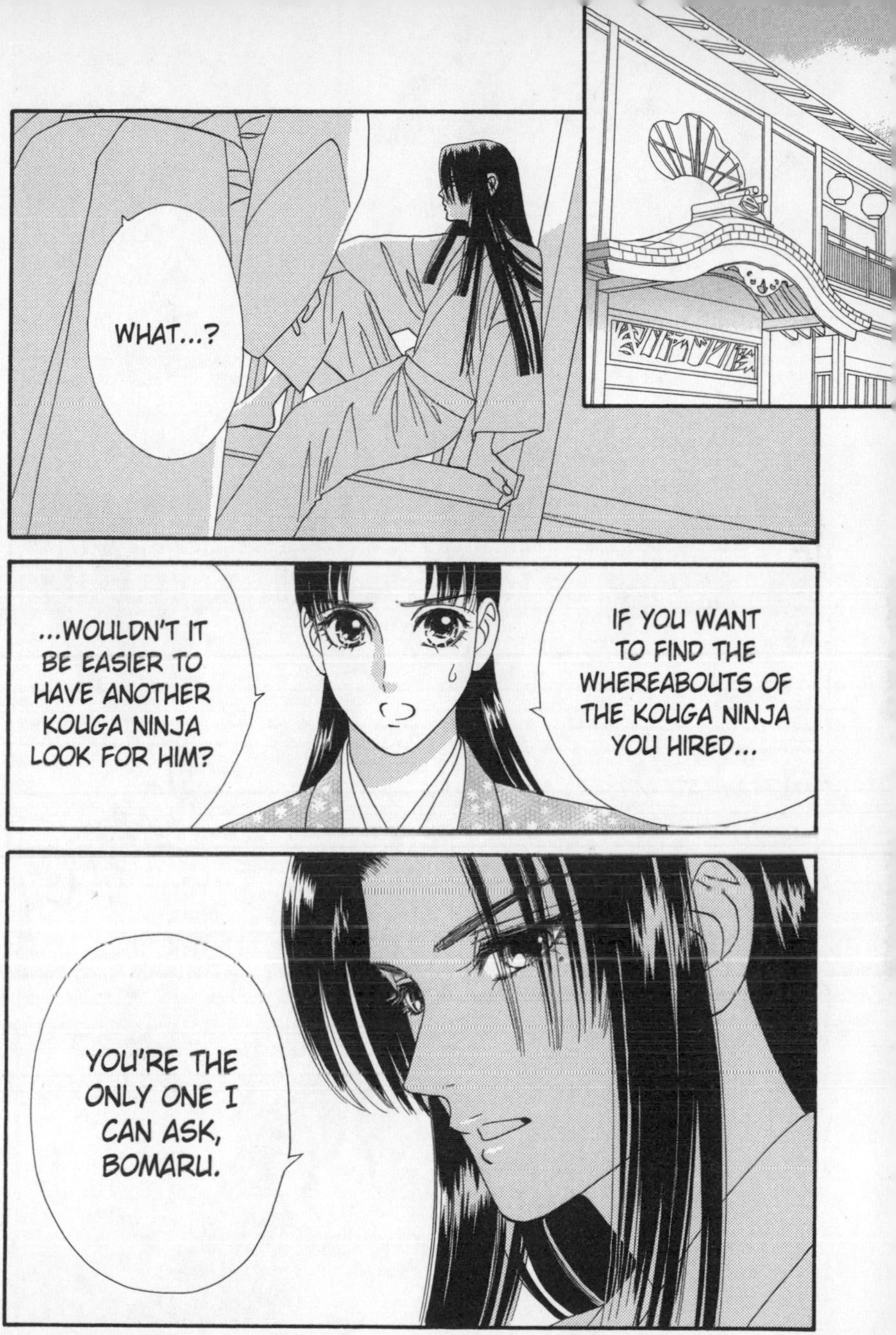
WHAT...?
IF YOU WANT TO FIND THE WHEREABOUTS OF THE KOUGA NINJA YOU HIRED...
...WOULDN'T IT BE EASIER TO HAVE ANOTHER KOUGA NINJA LOOK FOR HIM?
YOU'RE THE ONLY ONE I CAN ASK, BOMARU.

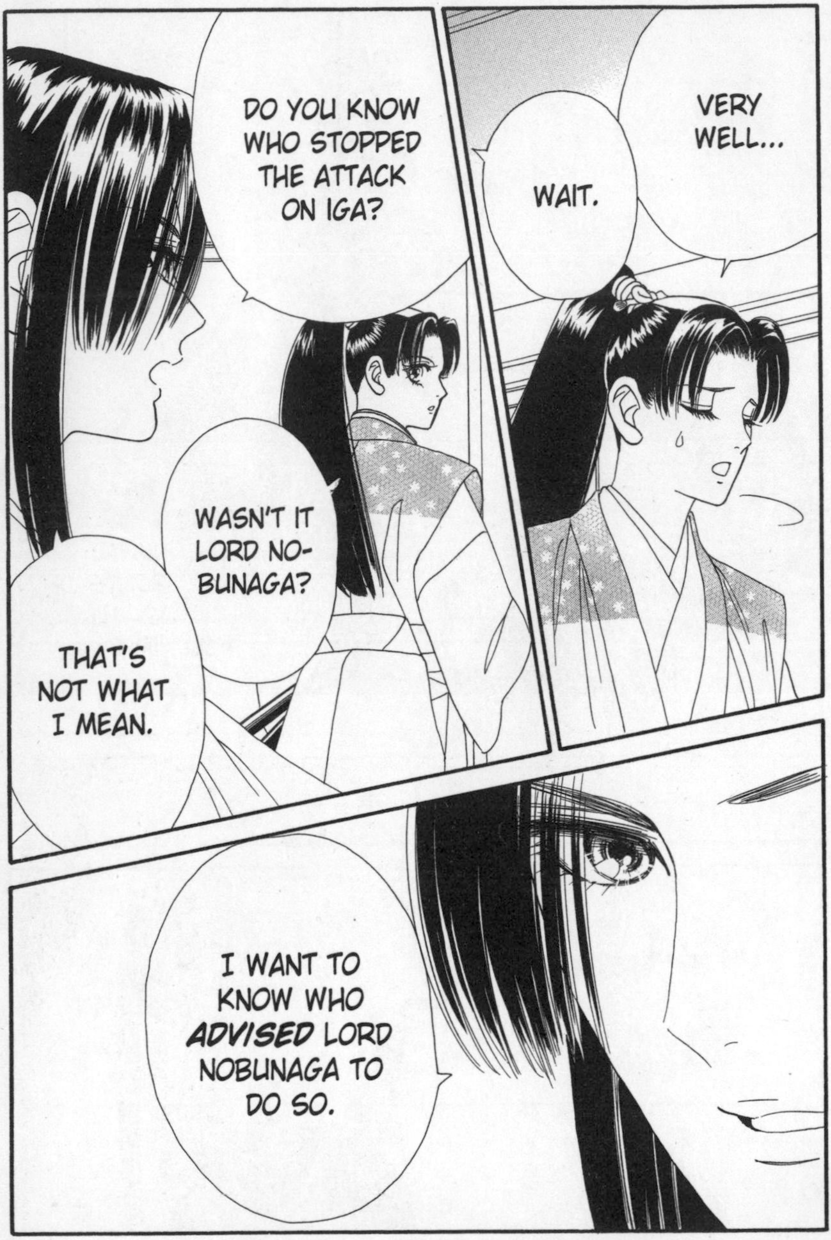
VERY WELL...
WAIT.
DO YOU KNOW WHO STOPPED THE ATTACK ON IGA?
WASN'T IT LORD NO-BUNAGA?
THAT'S NOT WHAT I MEAN.
I WANT TO KNOW WHO *ADVISED* LORD NOBUNAGA TO DO SO.

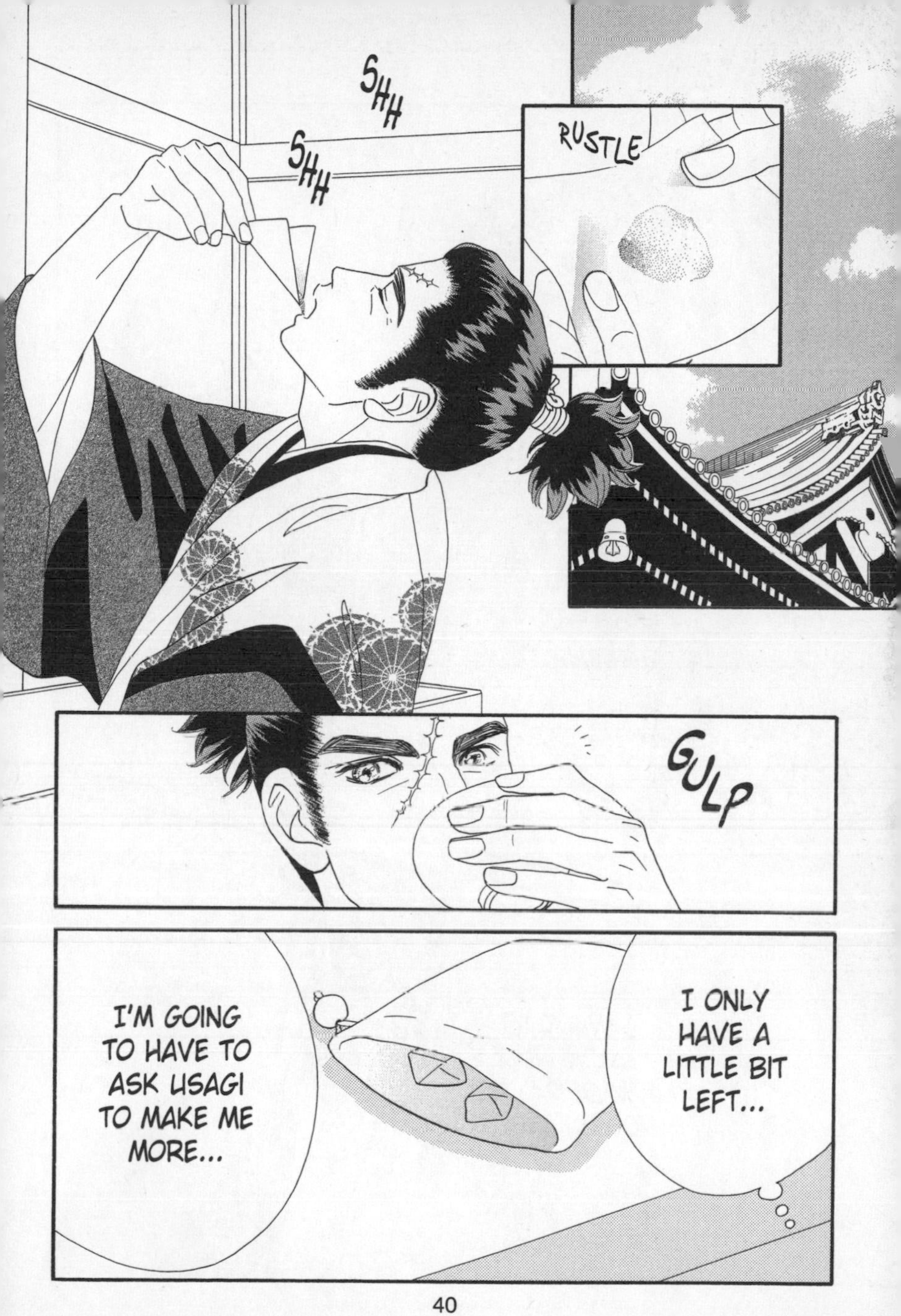
RUSTLE
SHH
SHH
GULP
I ONLY HAVE A LITTLE BIT LEFT...
I'M GOING TO HAVE TO ASK USAGI TO MAKE ME MORE...

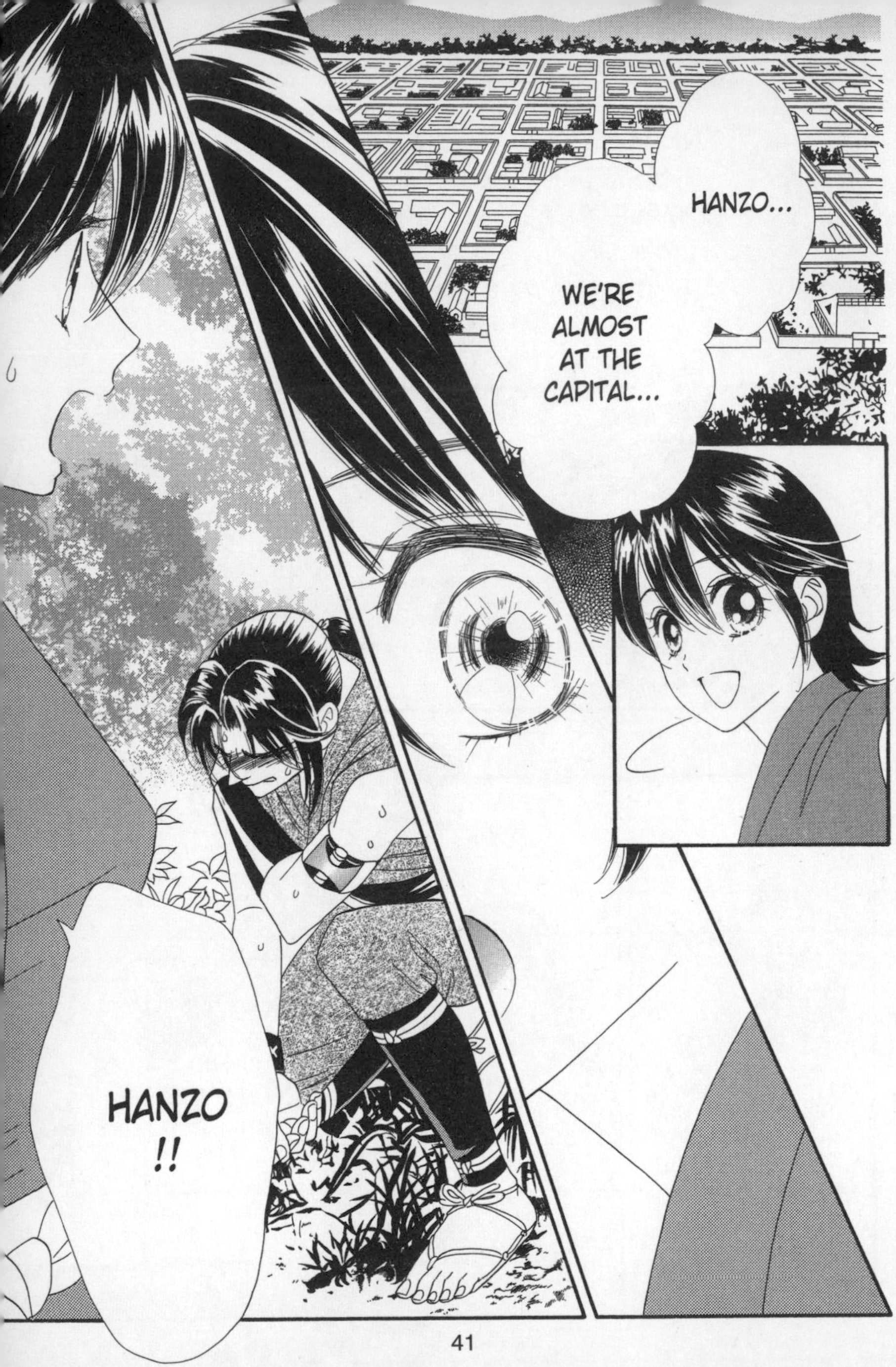
HANZO...
WE'RE ALMOST AT THE CAPITAL...
HANZO !!

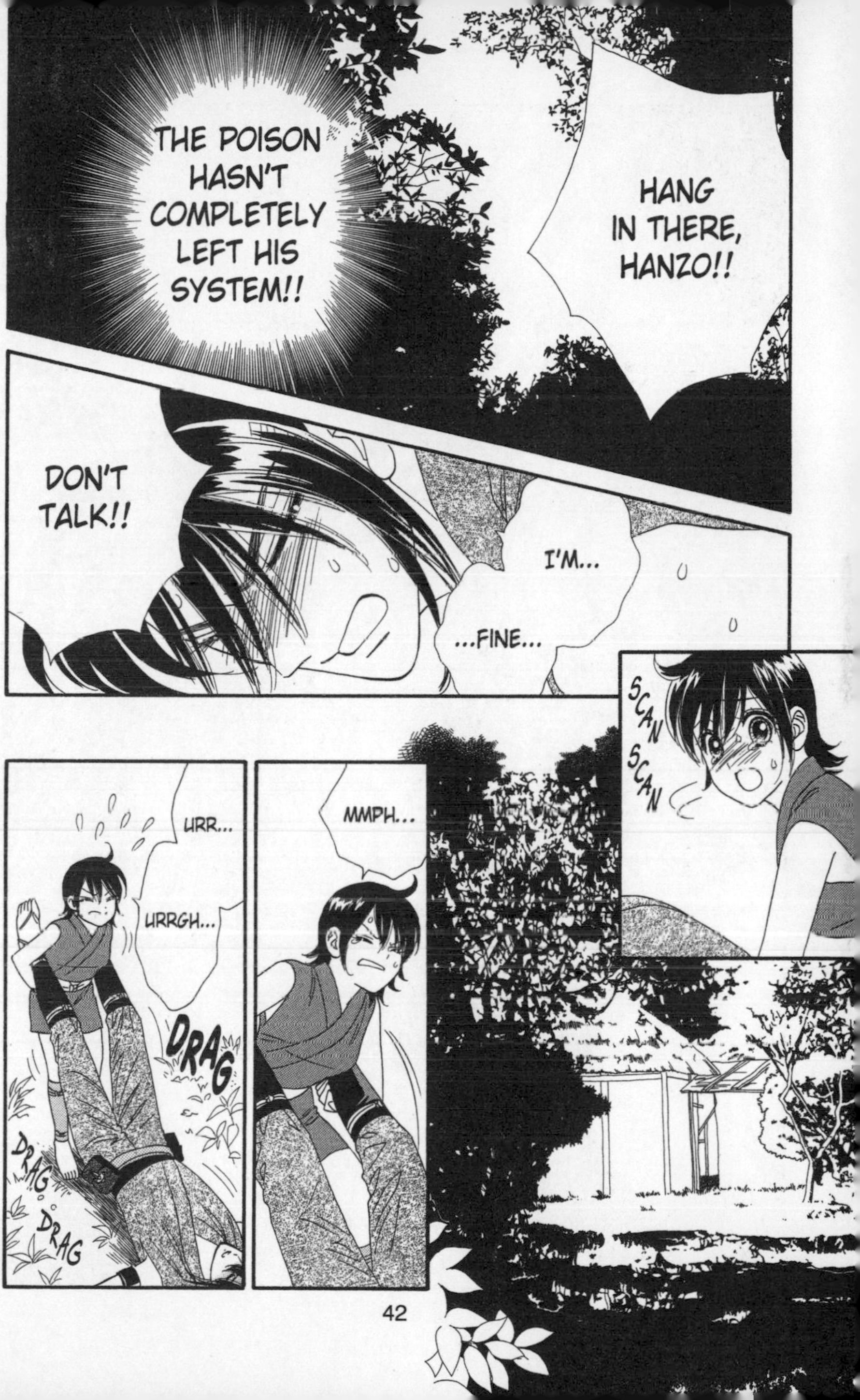
HANG IN THERE, HANZO!!
THE POISON HASN'T COMPLETELY LEFT HIS SYSTEM!!
I'M...
...FINE...
DON'T TALK!!
SCAN SCAN
MMPH...
URR...
URRGH...
DRAG
DRAG DRAG DRAG

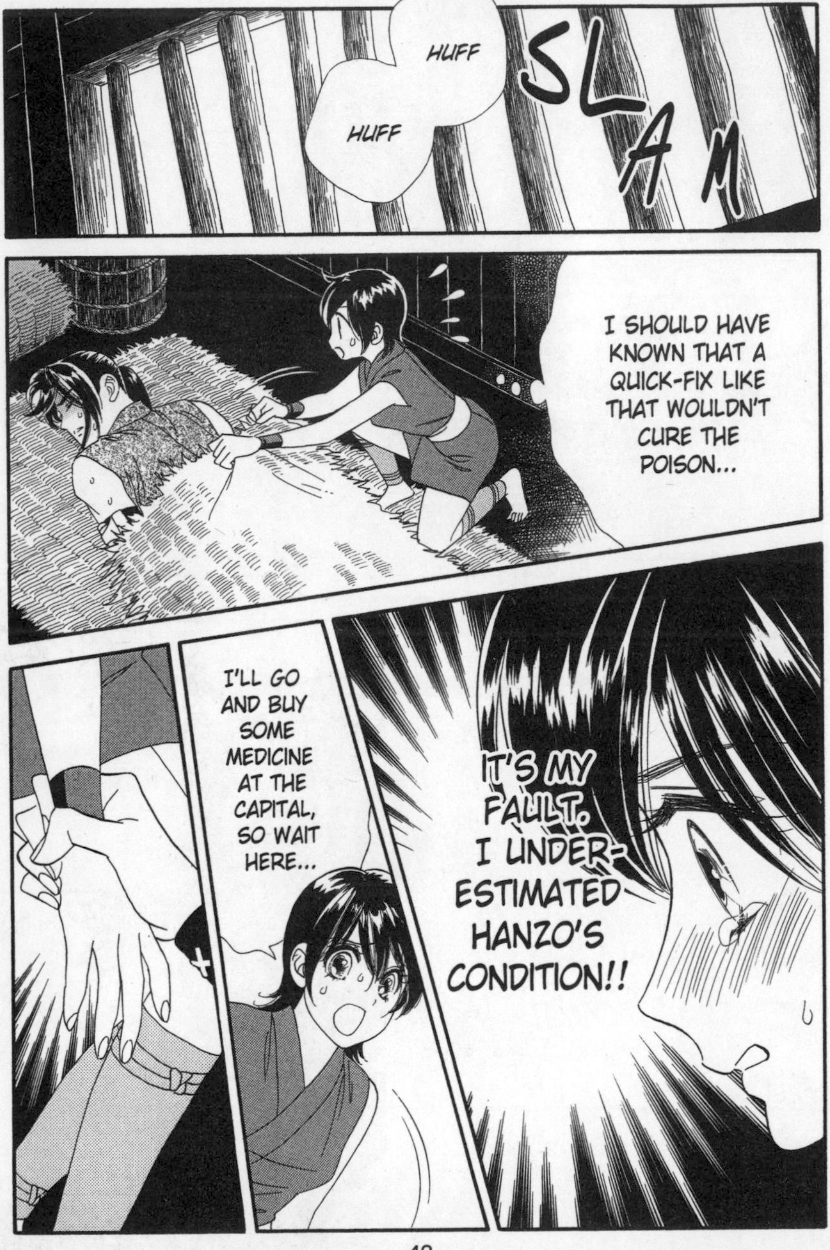
SLAM
HUFF
HUFF
I SHOULD HAVE KNOWN THAT A QUICK-FIX LIKE THAT WOULDN'T CURE THE POISON...
IT'S MY FAULT. I UNDER-ESTIMATED HANZO'S CONDITION!!
I'LL GO AND BUY SOME MEDICINE AT THE CAPITAL, SO WAIT HERE...

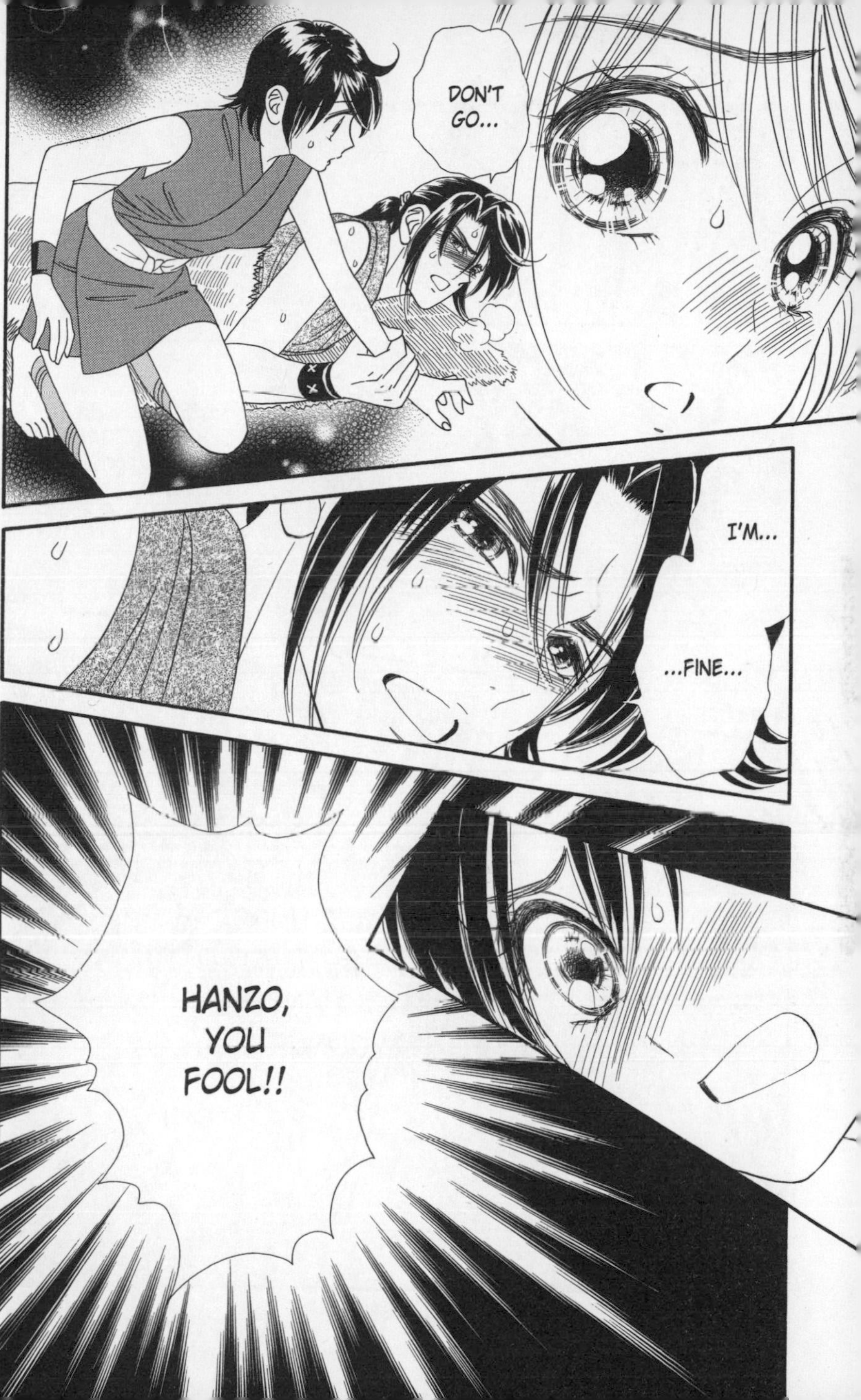
DON'T GO...
I'M...
...FINE...
HANZO, YOU FOOL!!

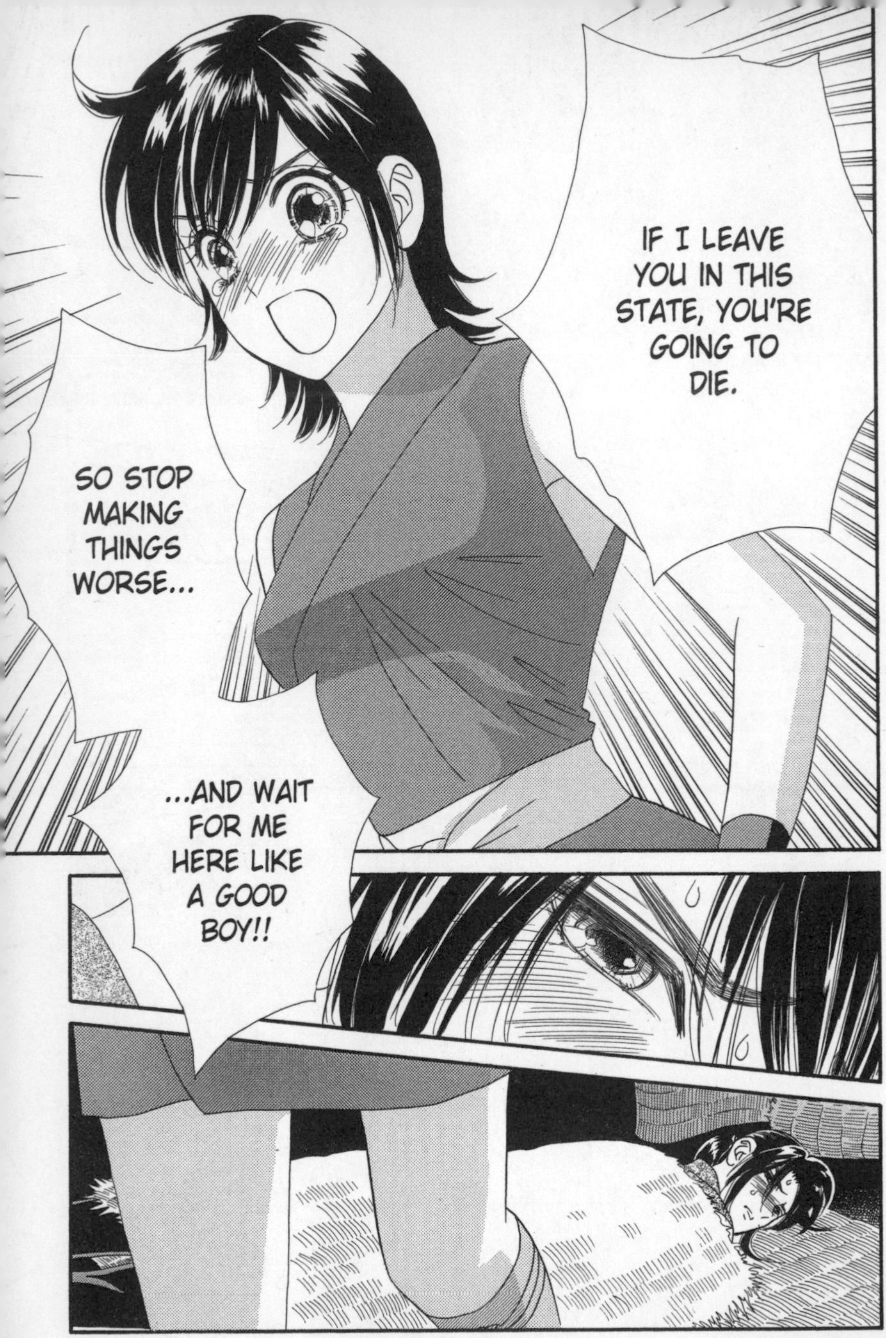
IF I LEAVE YOU IN THIS STATE, YOU'RE GOING TO DIE.
SO STOP MAKING THINGS WORSE...
...AND WAIT FOR ME HERE LIKE A GOOD BOY!!

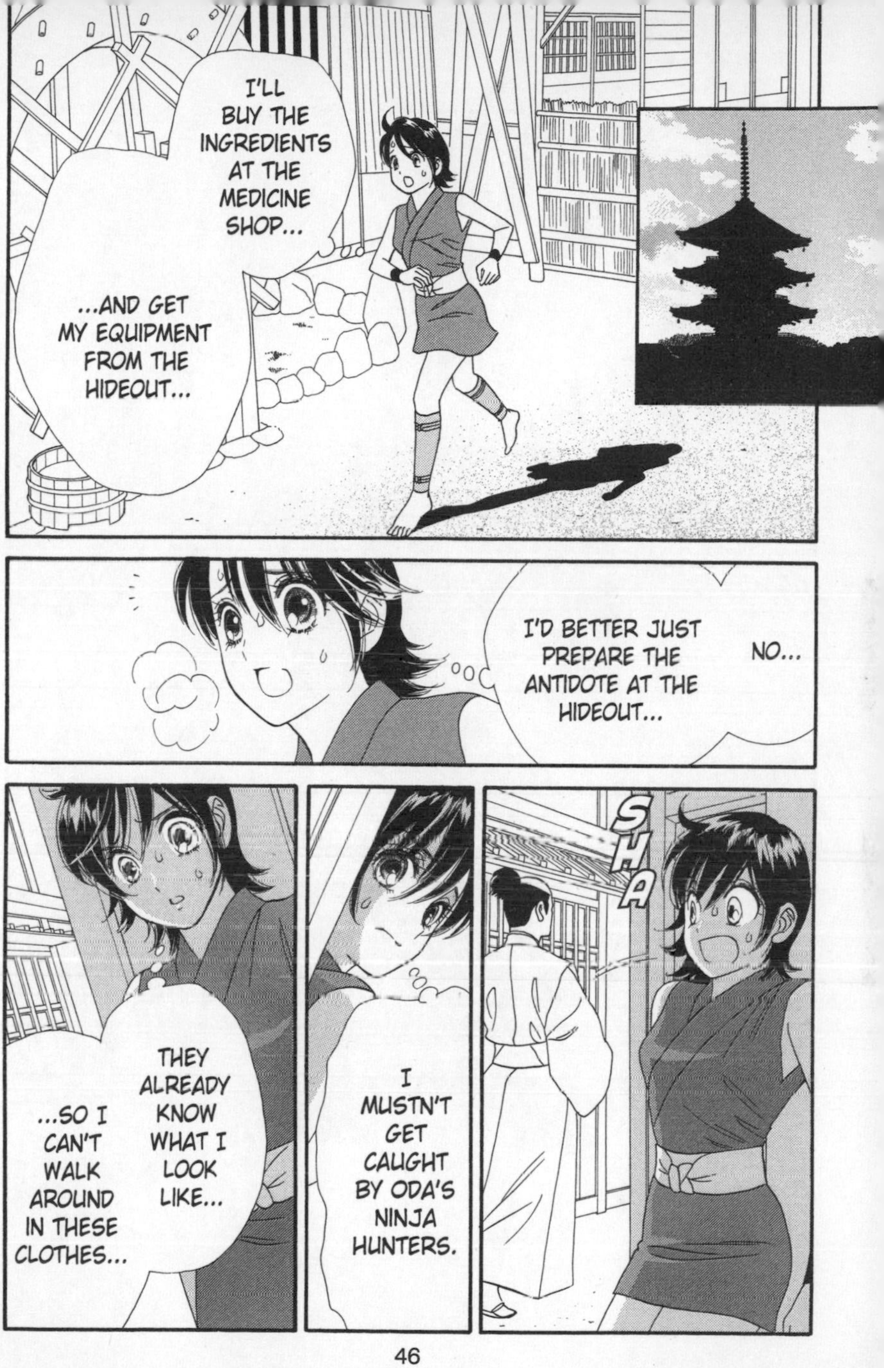
I'LL BUY THE INGREDIENTS AT THE MEDICINE SHOP...
...AND GET MY EQUIPMENT FROM THE HIDEOUT...
NO...
I'D BETTER JUST PREPARE THE ANTIDOTE AT THE HIDEOUT...
SHA
I MUSTN'T GET CAUGHT BY ODA'S NINJA HUNTERS.
THEY ALREADY KNOW WHAT I LOOK LIKE...
...SO I CAN'T WALK AROUND IN THESE CLOTHES...

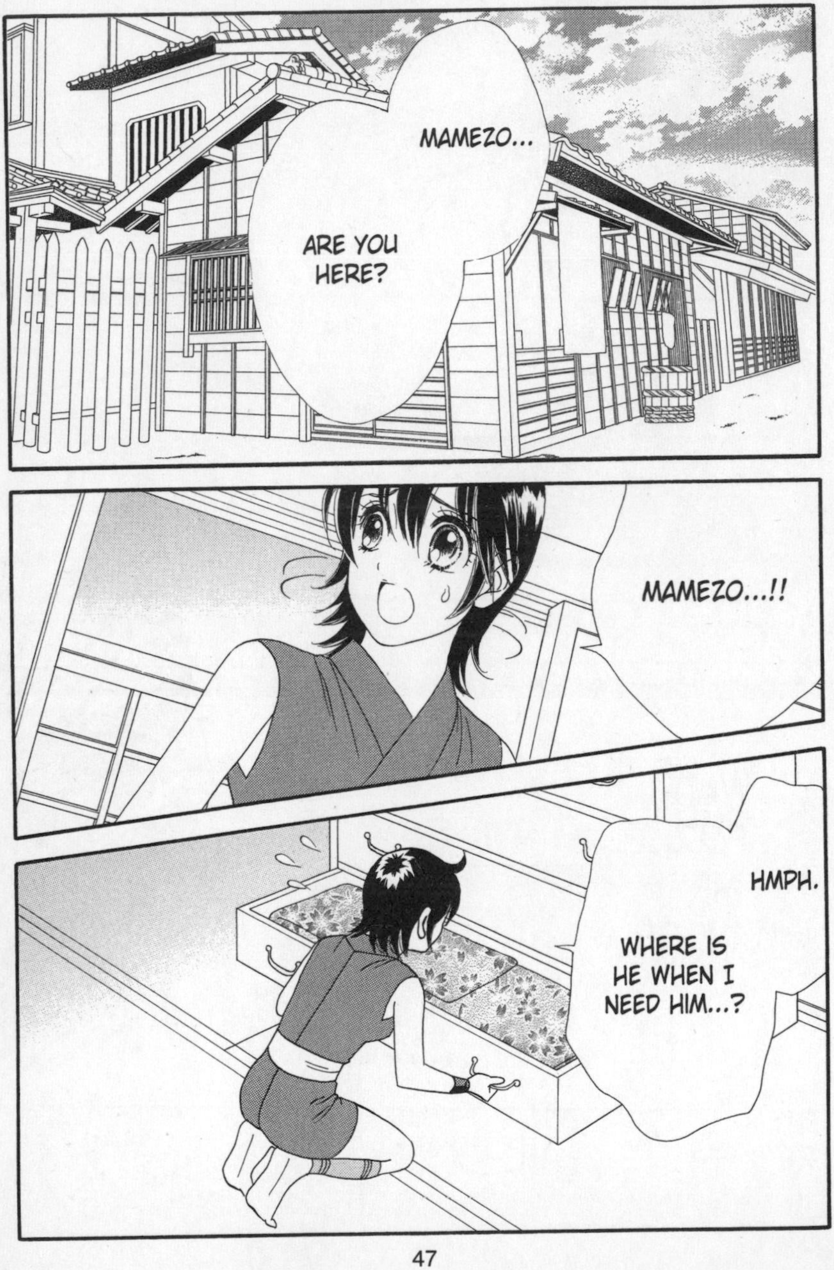
MAMEZO...
ARE YOU HERE?
MAMEZO...!!
HMPH.
WHERE IS HE WHEN I NEED HIM...?

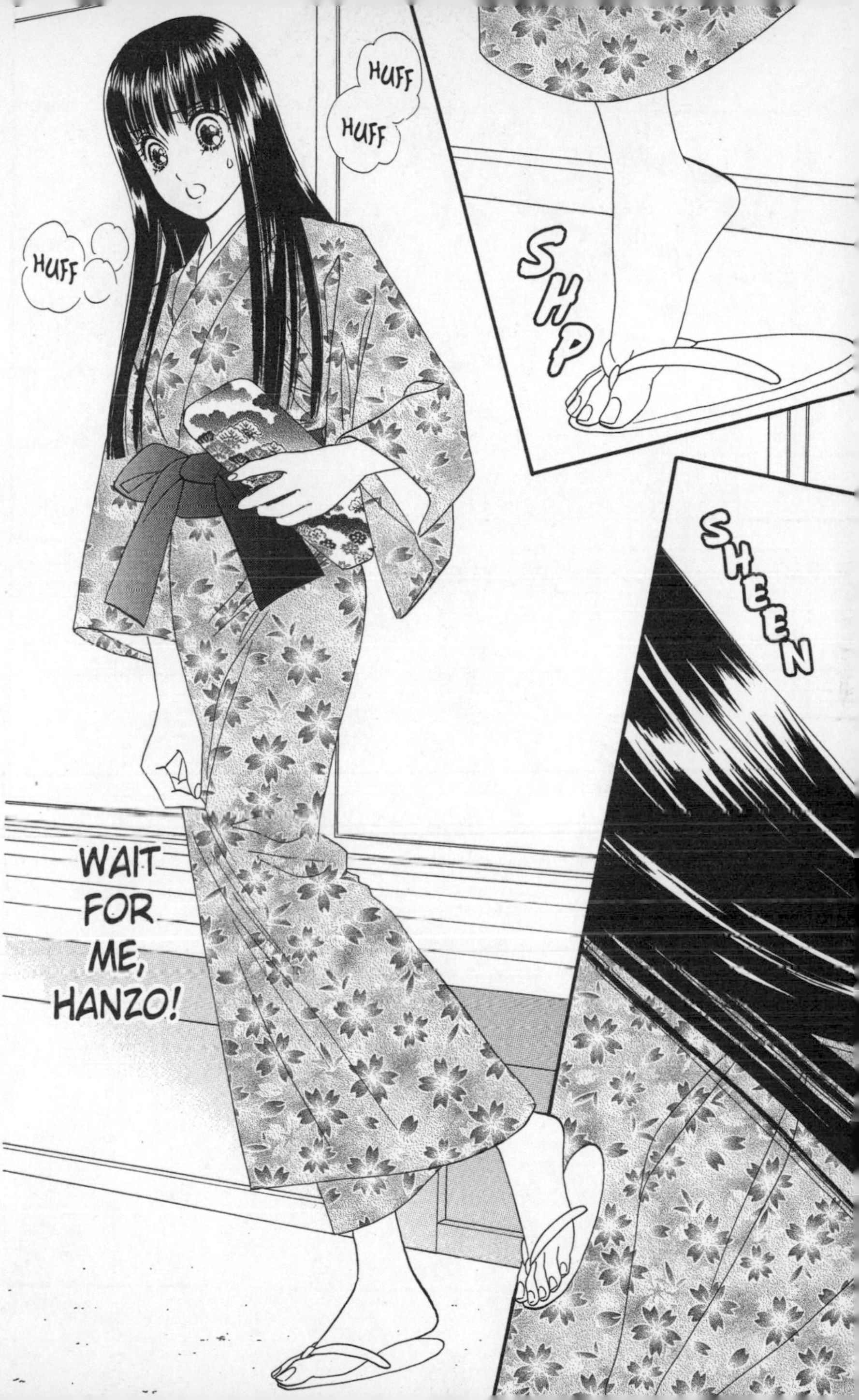
SHP
SHEEN
HUFF
HUFF
HUFF
WAIT FOR ME, HANZO!

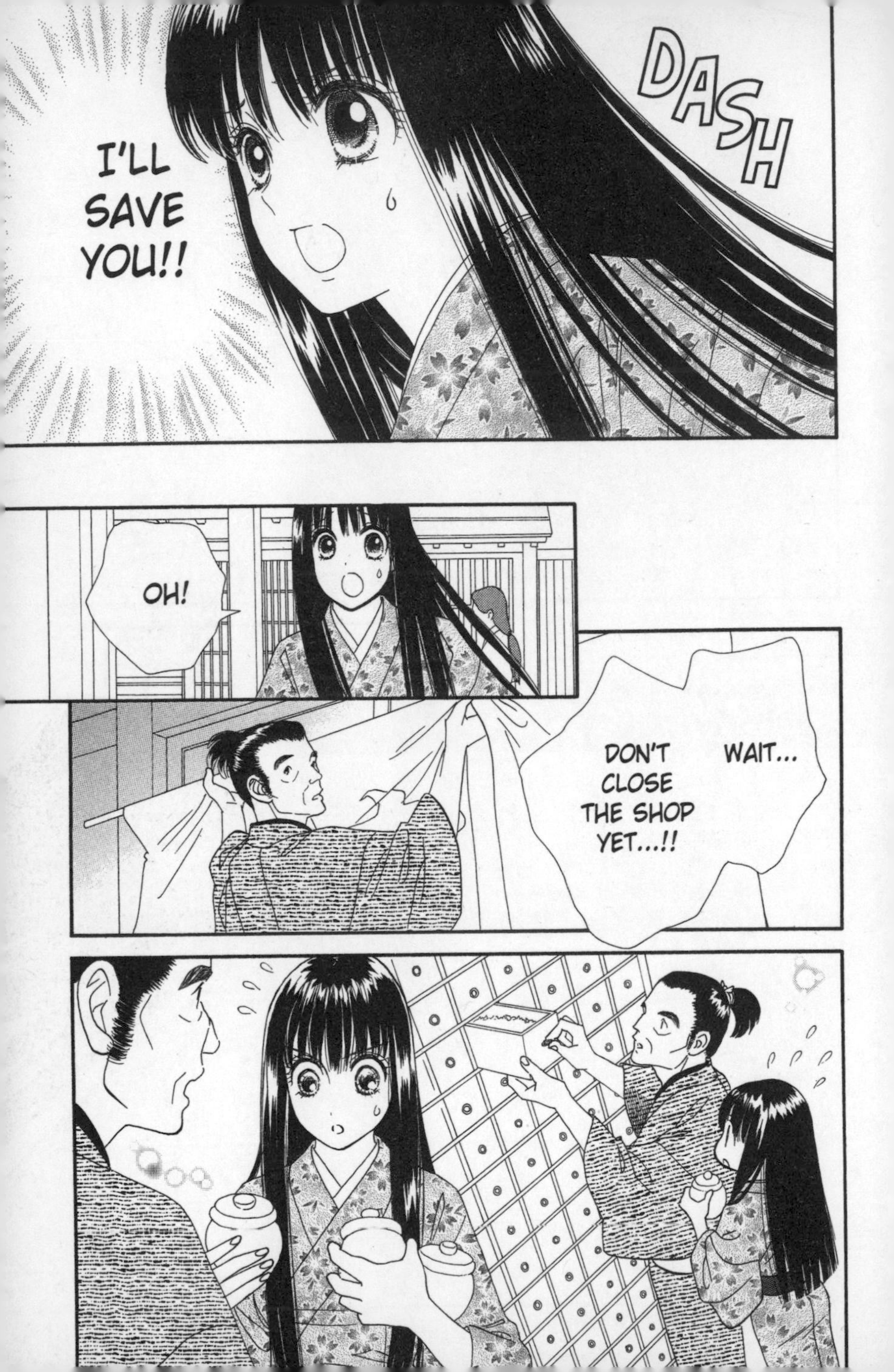
DASH
I'LL SAVE YOU!!
OH!
WAIT...
DON'T CLOSE THE SHOP YET...!!

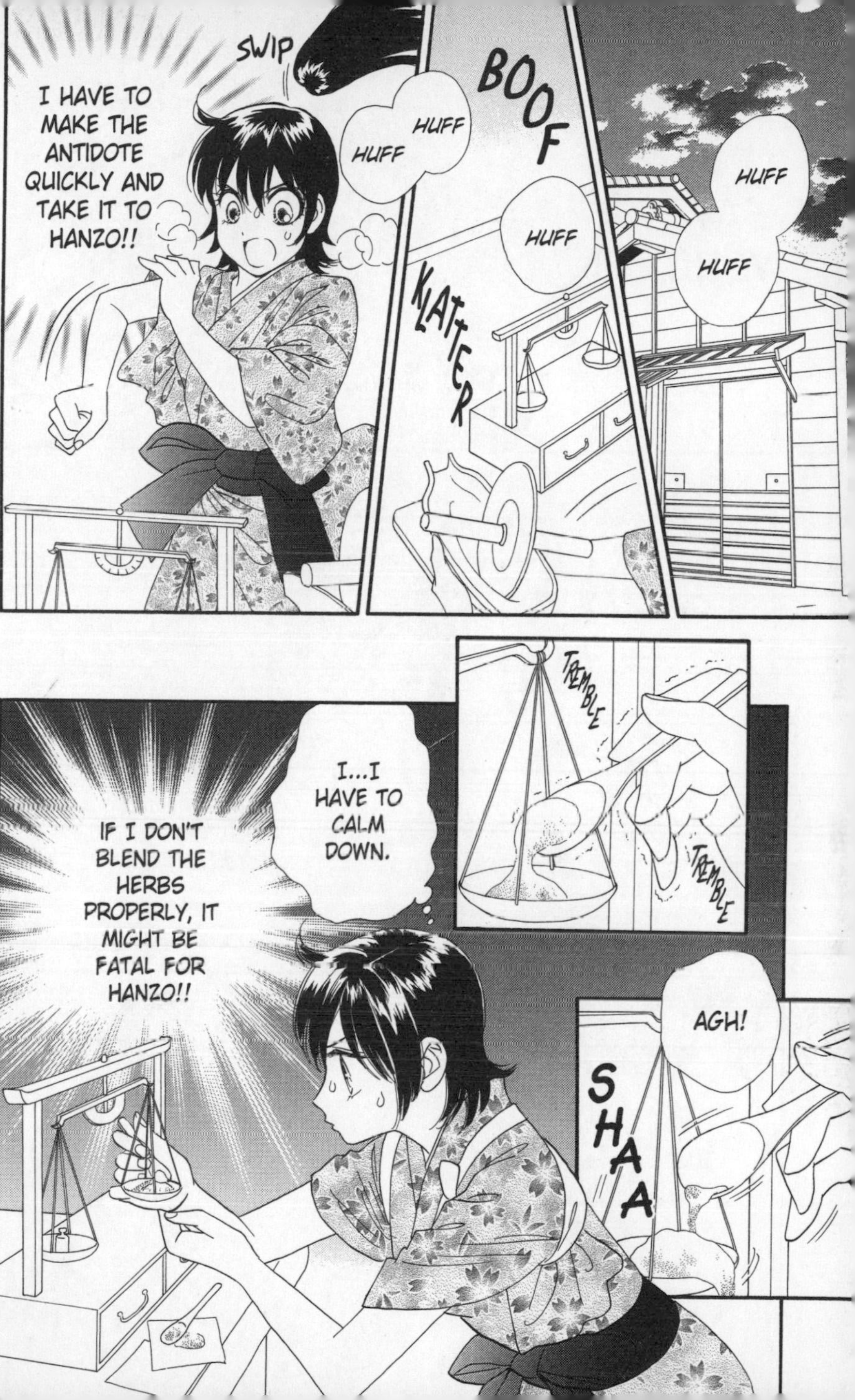
HUFF
HUFF
BOOF
HUFF
KLATTER
HUFF
HUFF
SWIP
I HAVE TO MAKE THE ANTIDOTE QUICKLY AND TAKE IT TO HANZO!!
TREMBLE
TREMBLE
AGH!
SHAA
I...I HAVE TO CALM DOWN.
IF I DON'T BLEND THE HERBS PROPERLY, IT MIGHT BE FATAL FOR HANZO!!

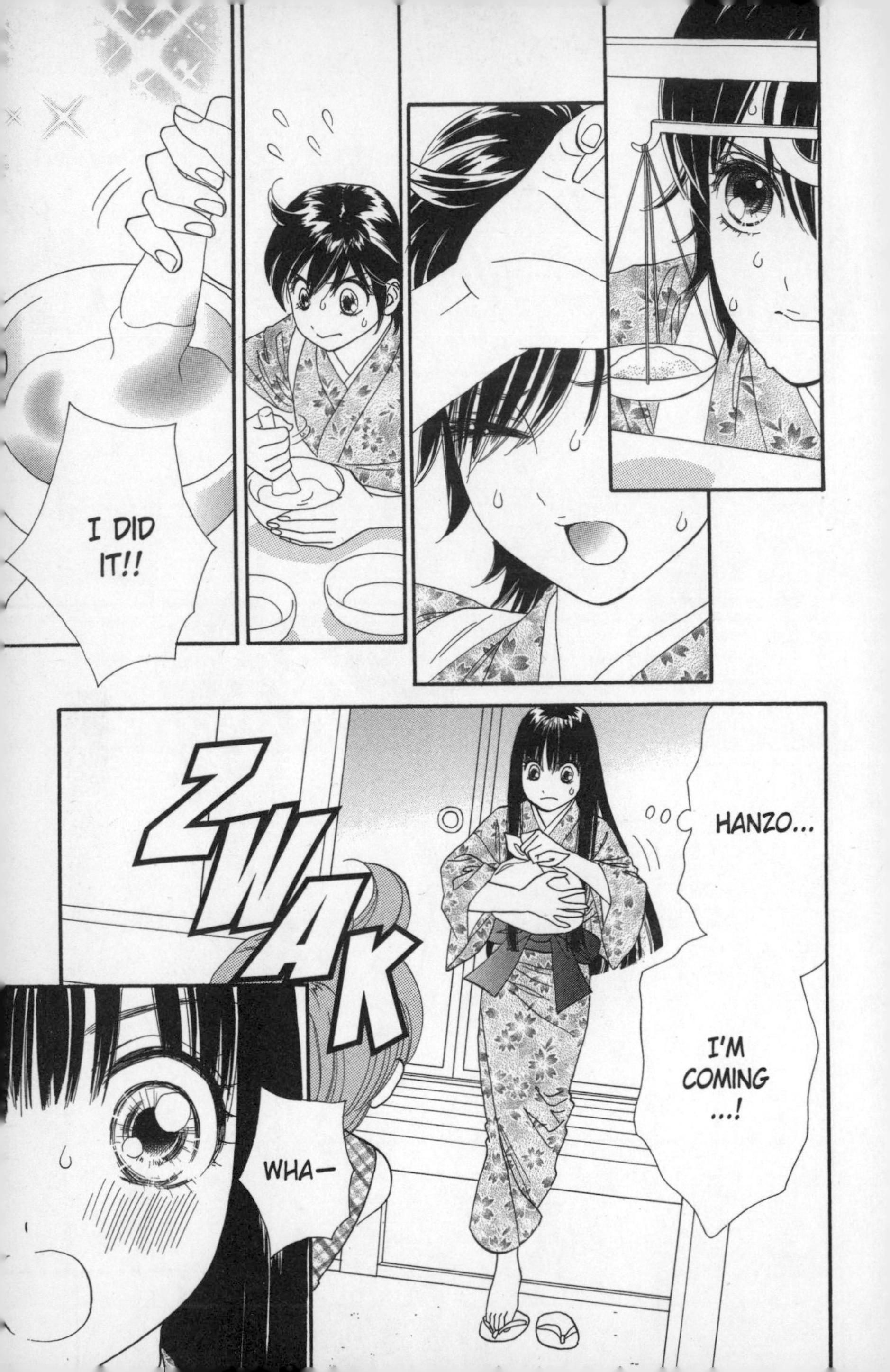
I DID IT!!
HANZO...
I'M COMING ...!
ZWAK
WHA—

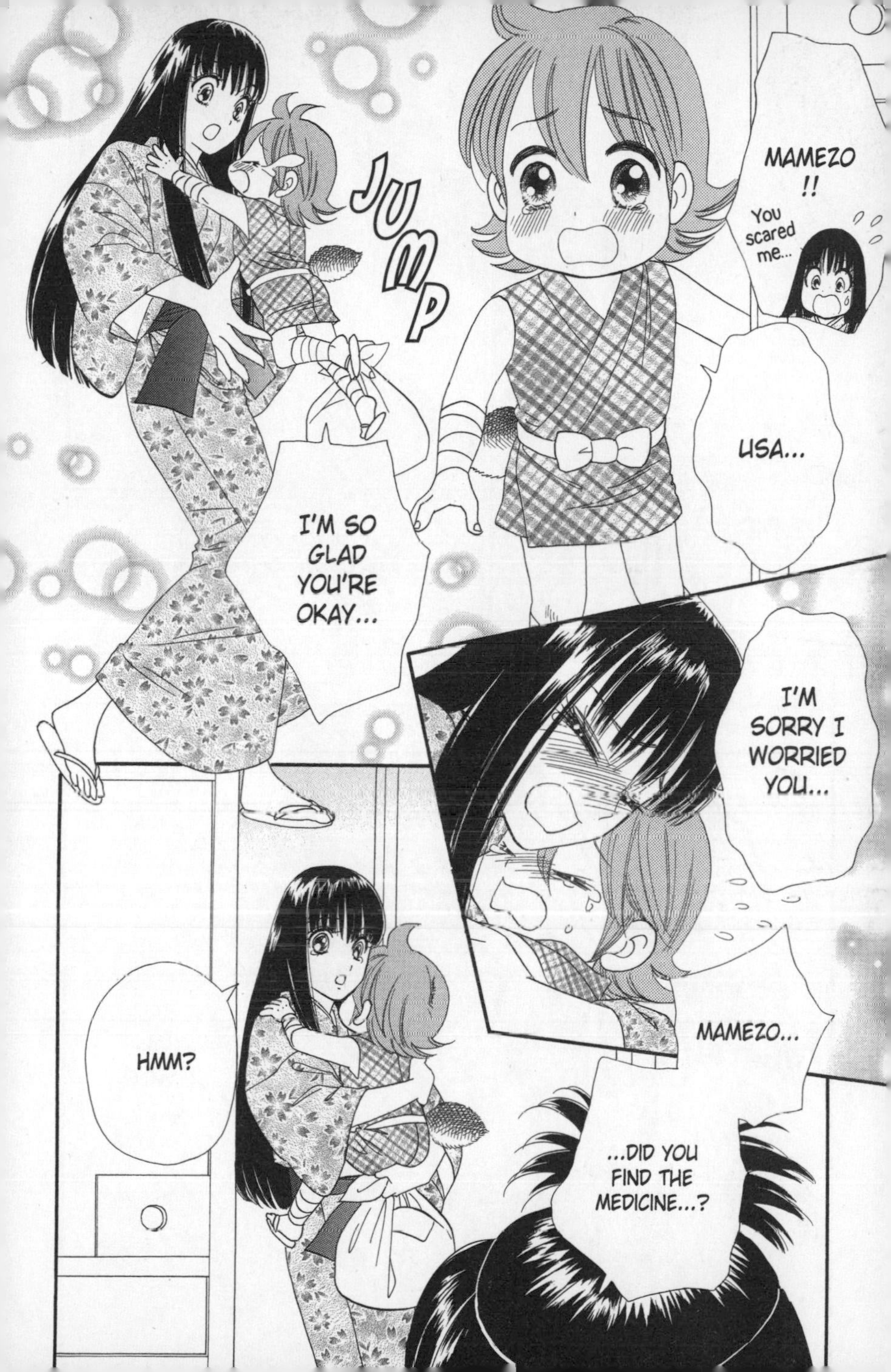

MAMEZO !!
You scared me...
USA...
JUMP
I'M SO GLAD YOU'RE OKAY...
I'M SORRY I WORRIED YOU...
MAMEZO...
...DID YOU FIND THE MEDICINE...?
HMM?

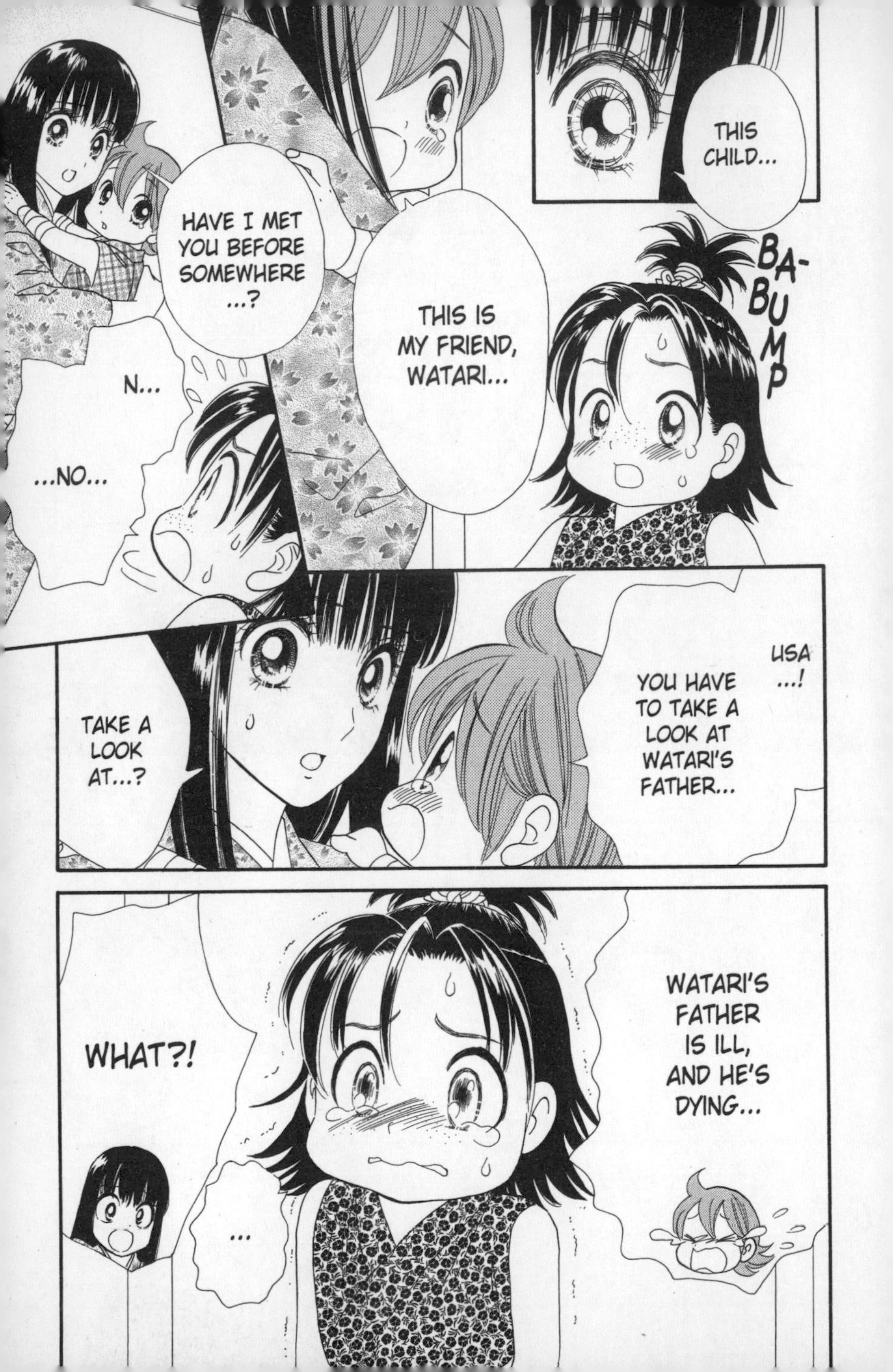
THIS CHILD...
BA-BUMP
THIS IS MY FRIEND, WATARI...
HAVE I MET YOU BEFORE SOMEWHERE ...?
N...
...NO...
USA ...!
YOU HAVE TO TAKE A LOOK AT WATARI'S FATHER...
TAKE A LOOK AT...?
WATARI'S FATHER IS ILL, AND HE'S DYING...
WHAT?!
...

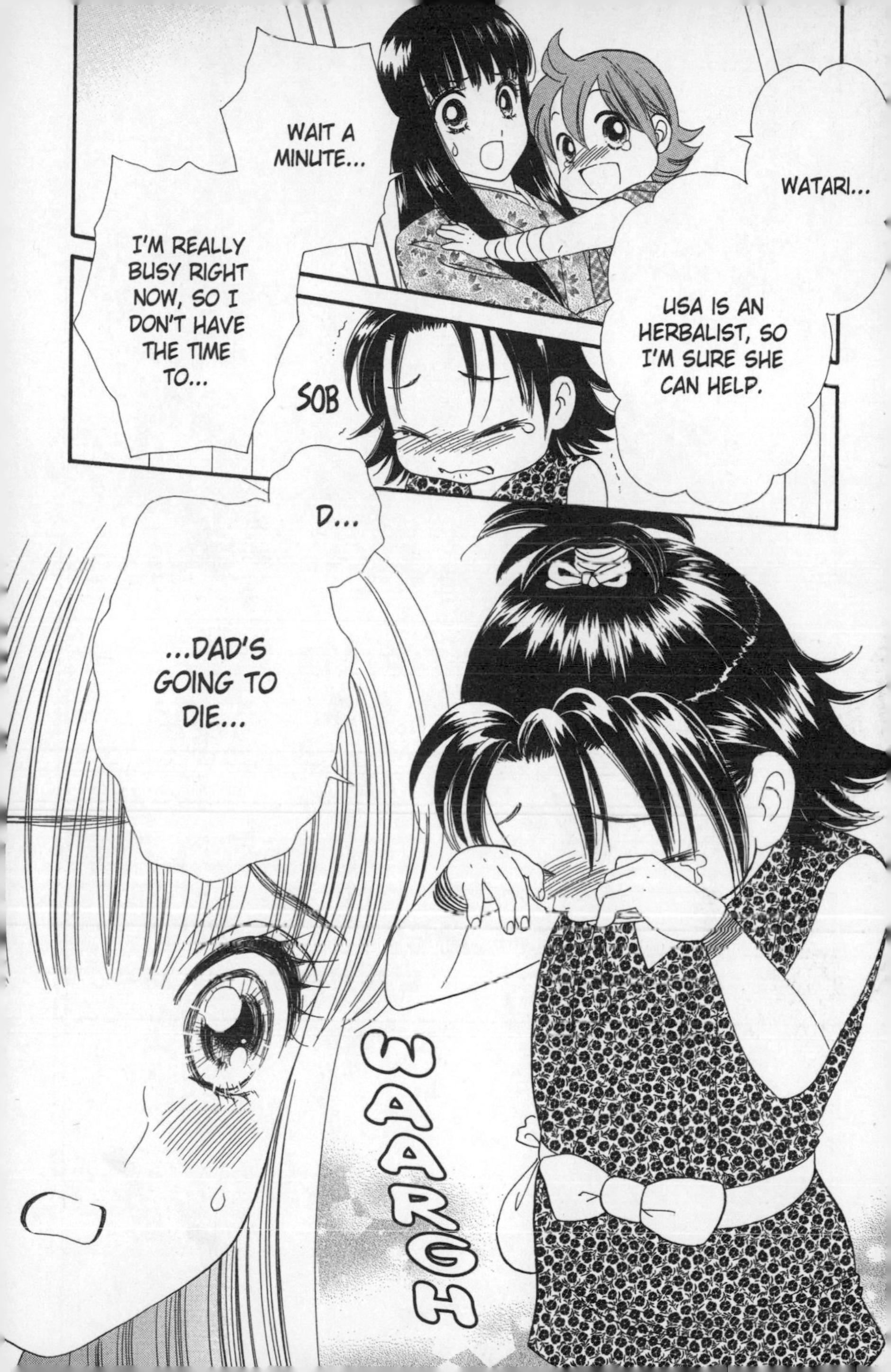
WATARI...
USA IS AN HERBALIST, SO I'M SURE SHE CAN HELP.
WAIT A MINUTE...
I'M REALLY BUSY RIGHT NOW, SO I DON'T HAVE THE TIME TO...
SOB
D...
...DAD'S GOING TO DIE...
WAARGH

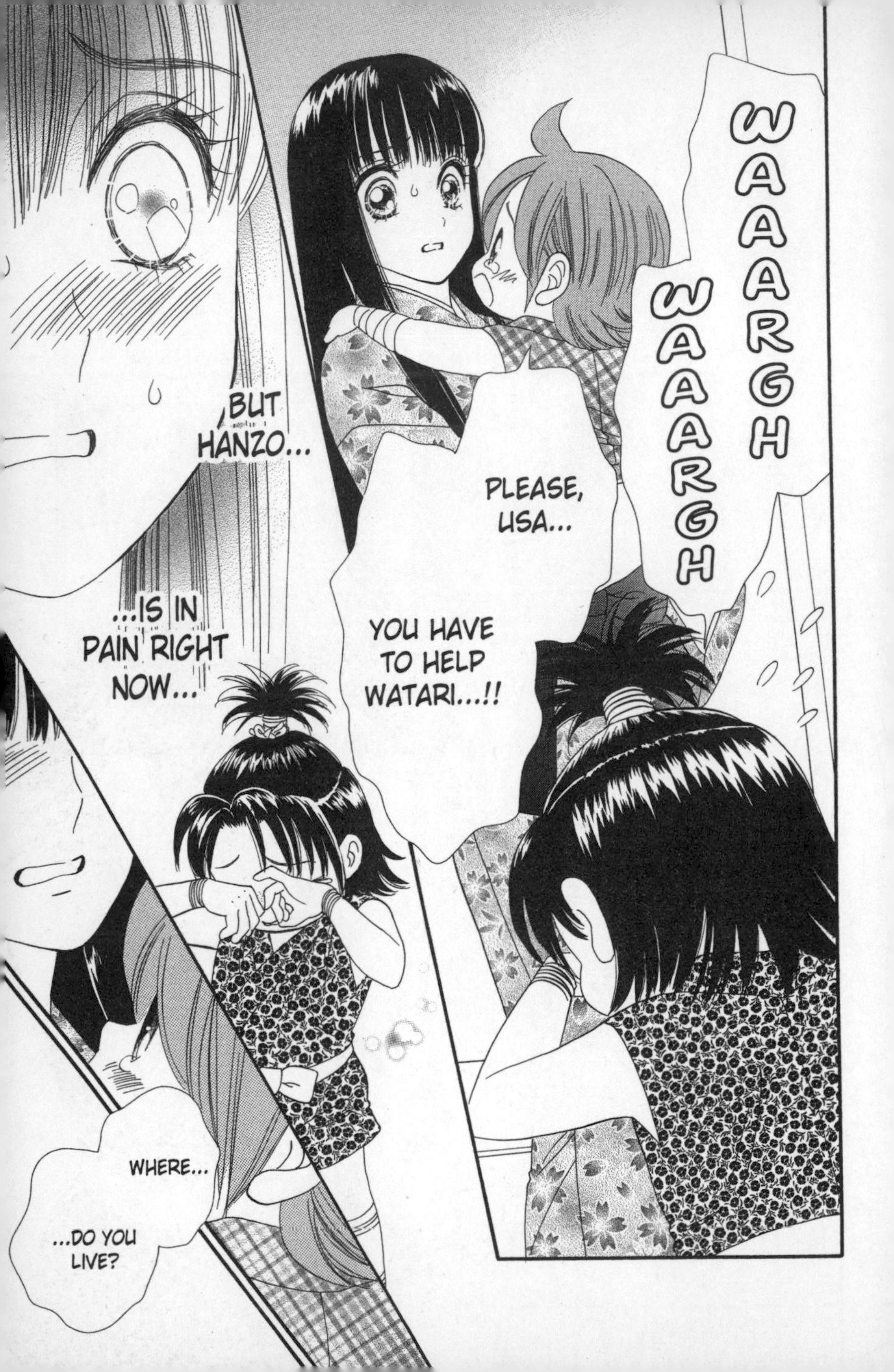
WAAARGH
WAAARGH
PLEASE, USA...
YOU HAVE TO HELP WATARI...!!
BUT HANZO...
...IS IN PAIN RIGHT NOW...
WHERE...
...DO YOU LIVE?

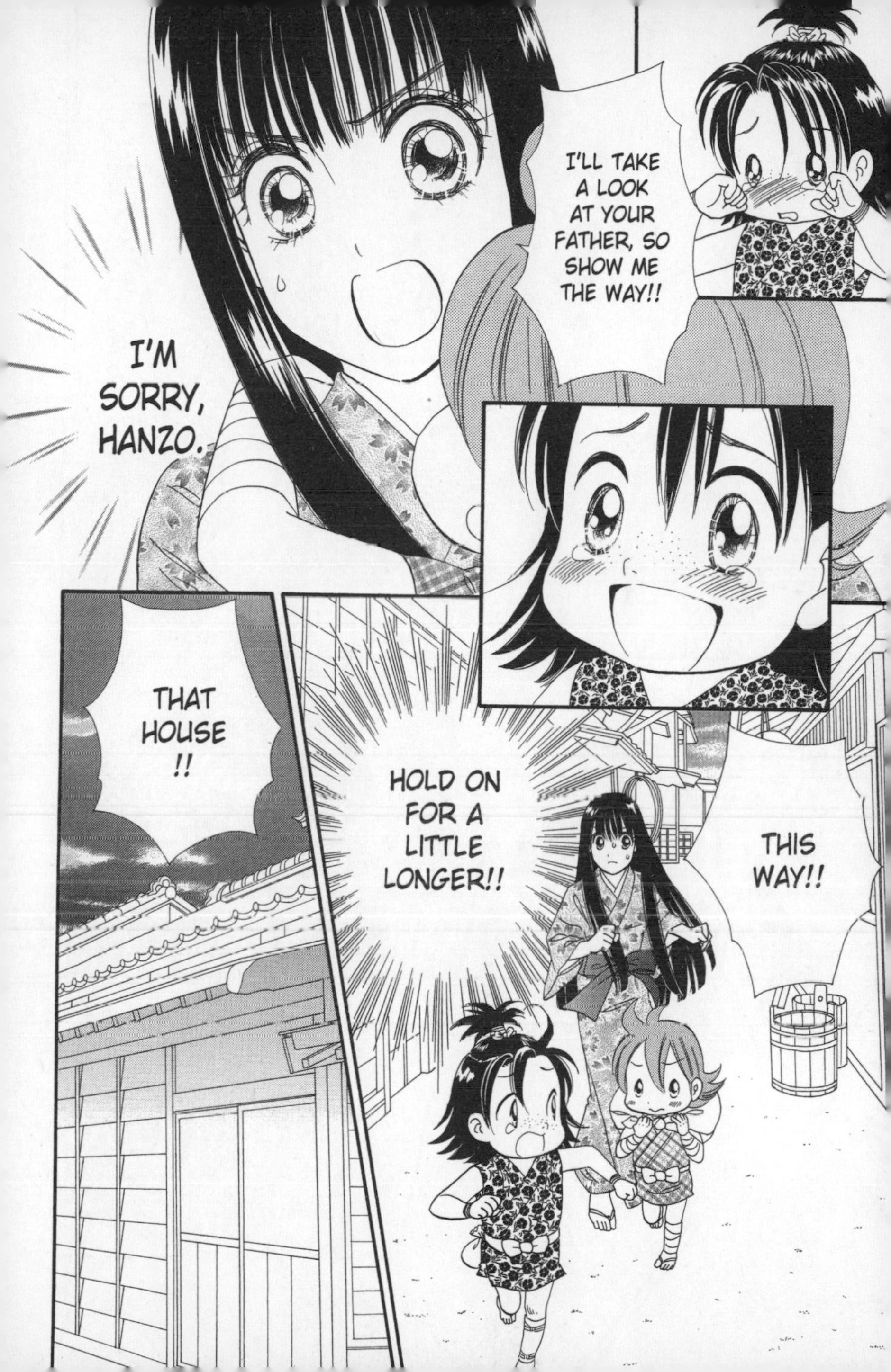
I'LL TAKE A LOOK AT YOUR FATHER, SO SHOW ME THE WAY!!
I'M SORRY, HANZO.
THIS WAY!!
HOLD ON FOR A LITTLE LONGER!!
THAT HOUSE !!

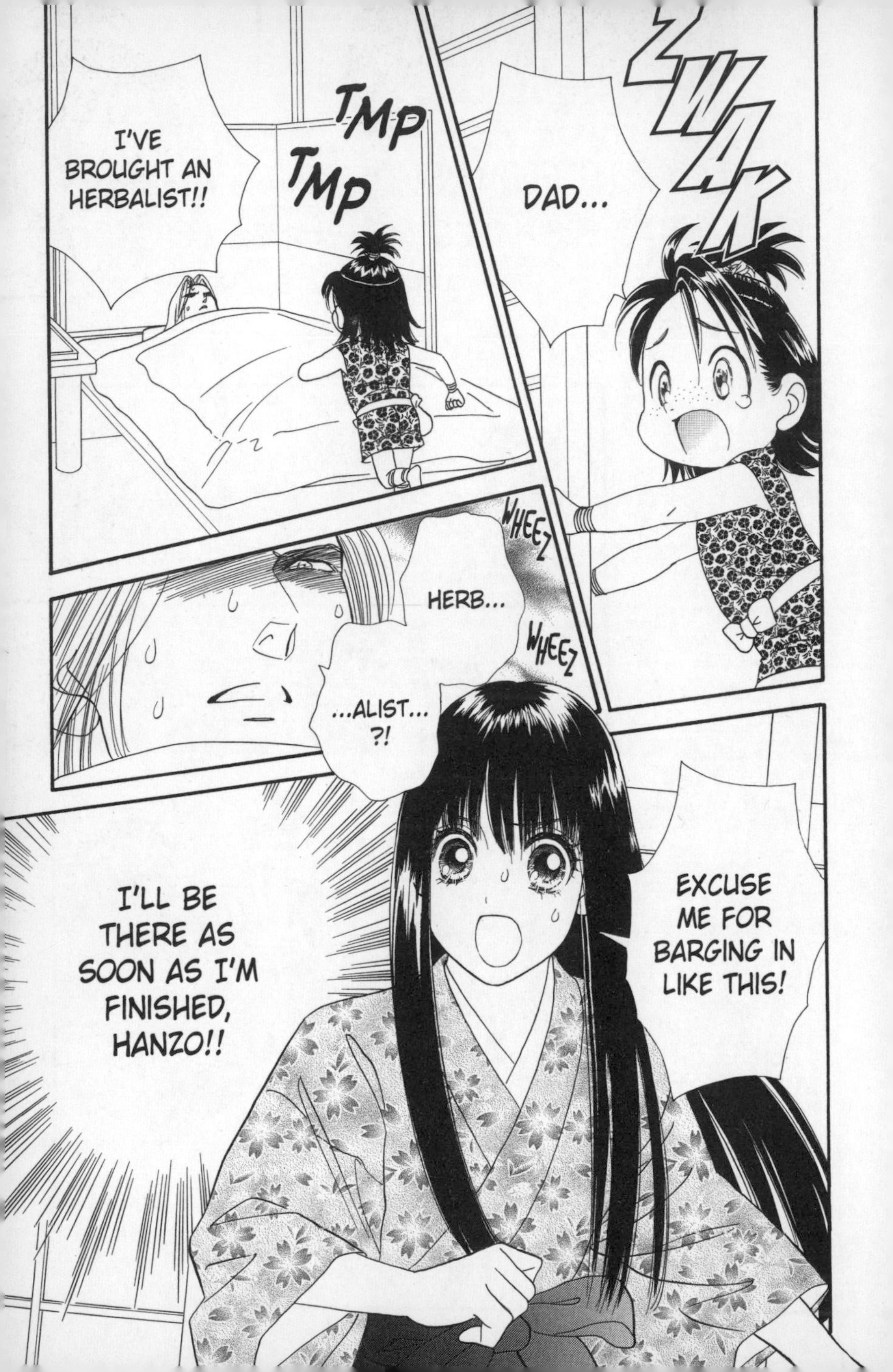
ZWAK
DAD...
I'VE BROUGHT AN HERBALIST!!
TMP TMP
WHEEZ
HERB...
WHEEZ
...ALIST...?!
EXCUSE ME FOR BARGING IN LIKE THIS!
I'LL BE THERE AS SOON AS I'M FINISHED, HANZO!!

TAIL OF THE MOON EXTRA: TODAY'S MISSION

"I WANT TO SEE HANZO AS A MANGA ARTIST!"

-KOZUE OYAMA, OITA PREFECTURE

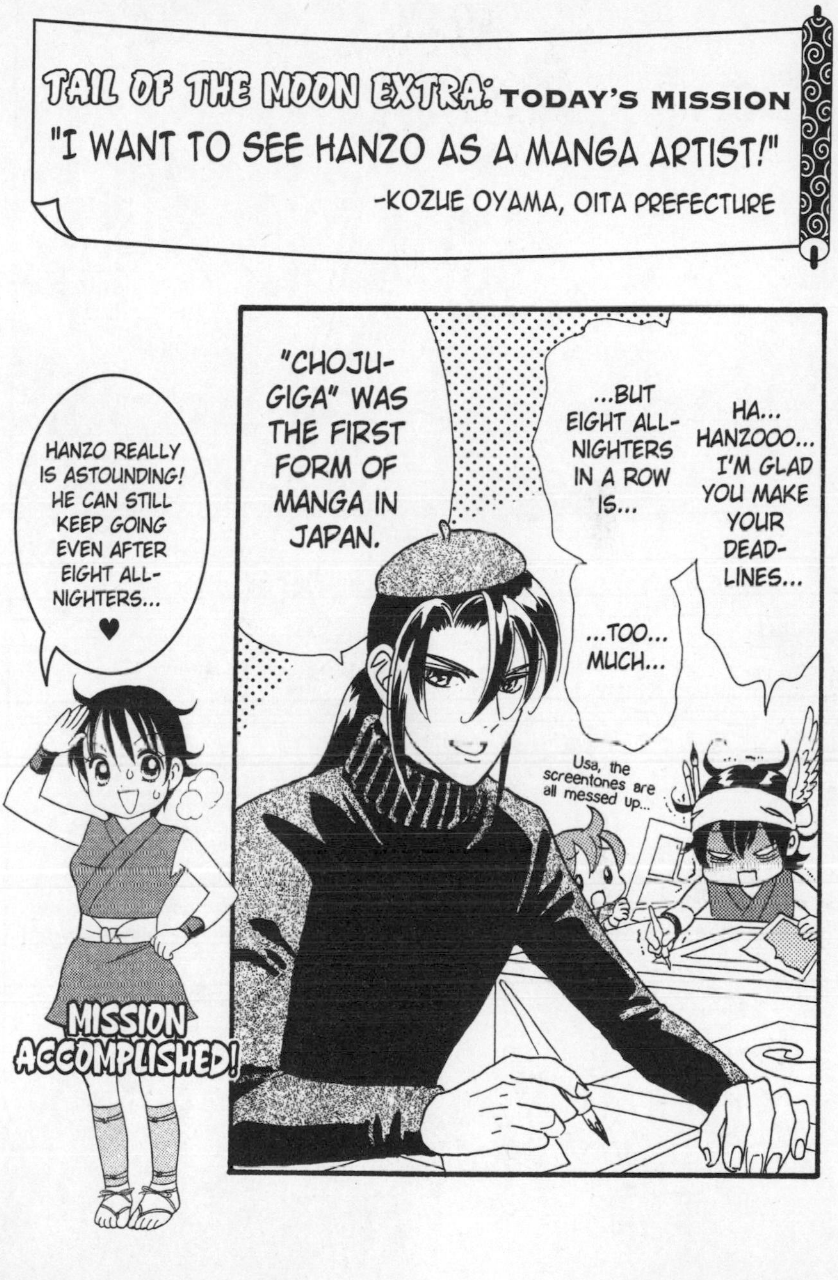
HA... HANZOOO... I'M GLAD YOU MAKE YOUR DEAD-LINES...
...BUT EIGHT ALL-NIGHTERS IN A ROW IS...
...TOO... MUCH...
Usa, the screentones are all messed up...
"CHOJU-GIGA" WAS THE FIRST FORM OF MANGA IN JAPAN.
HANZO REALLY IS ASTOUNDING! HE CAN STILL KEEP GOING EVEN AFTER EIGHT ALL-NIGHTERS... ♥
MISSION ACCOMPLISHED!

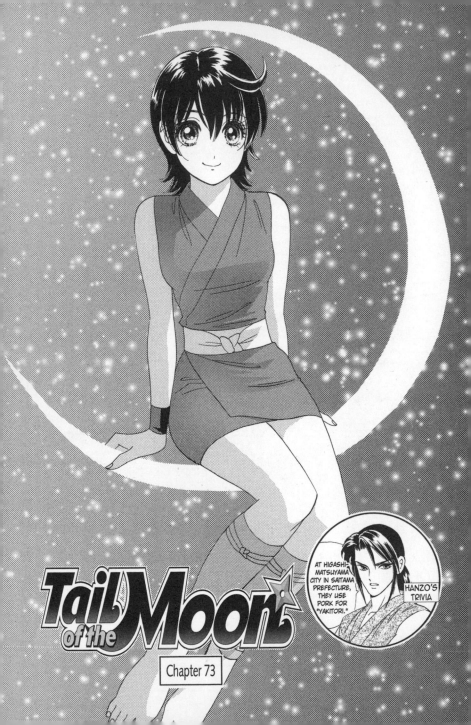

Tail of the Moon

Chapter 73

HANZO'S TRIVIA

AT HIGASHI-MATSUYAMA CITY IN SAITAMA PREFECTURE, THEY USE PORK FOR "YAKITORI."

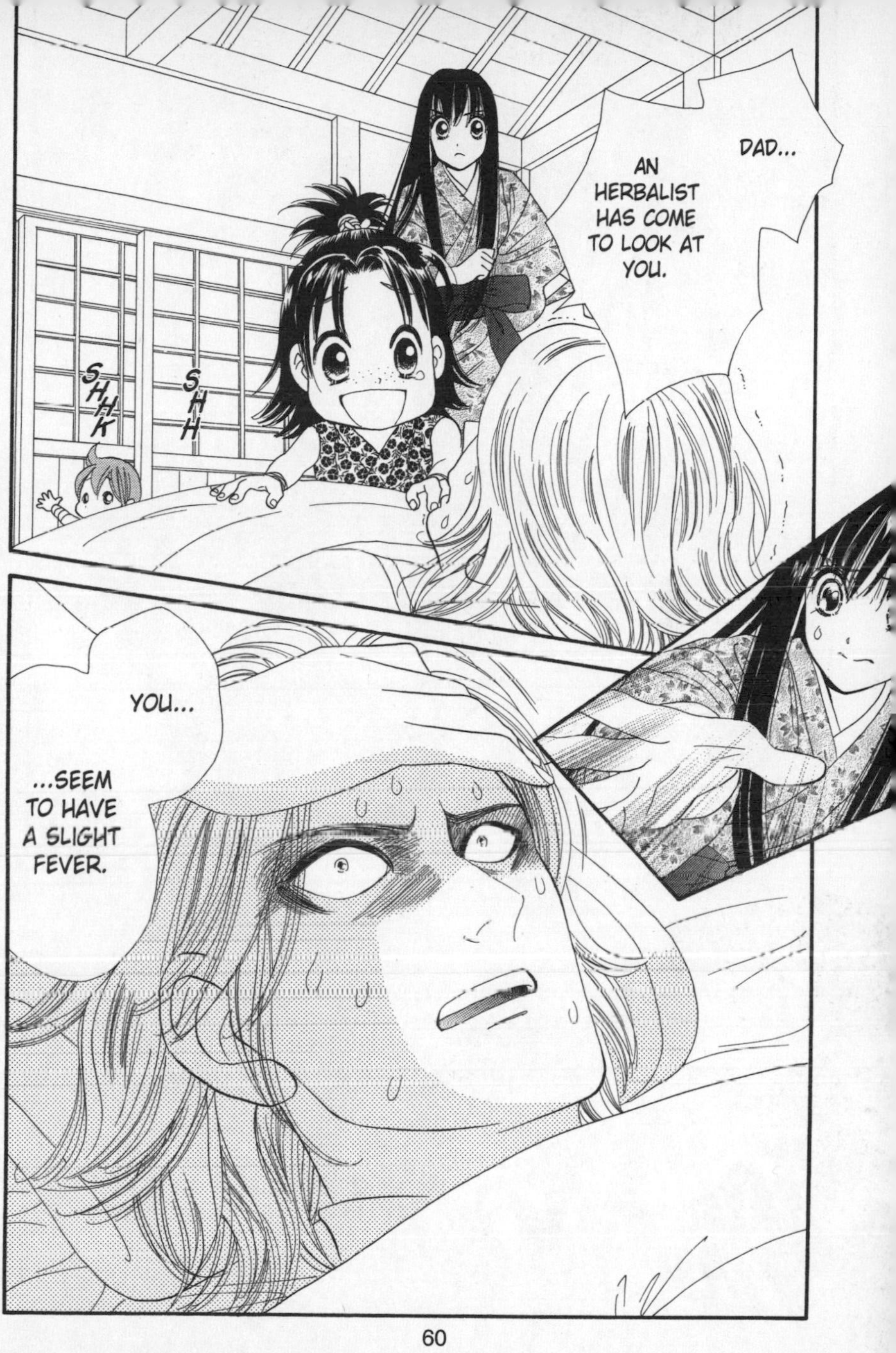
DAD...
AN HERBALIST HAS COME TO LOOK AT YOU.
SHH
SHHK
YOU...
...SEEM TO HAVE A SLIGHT FEVER.

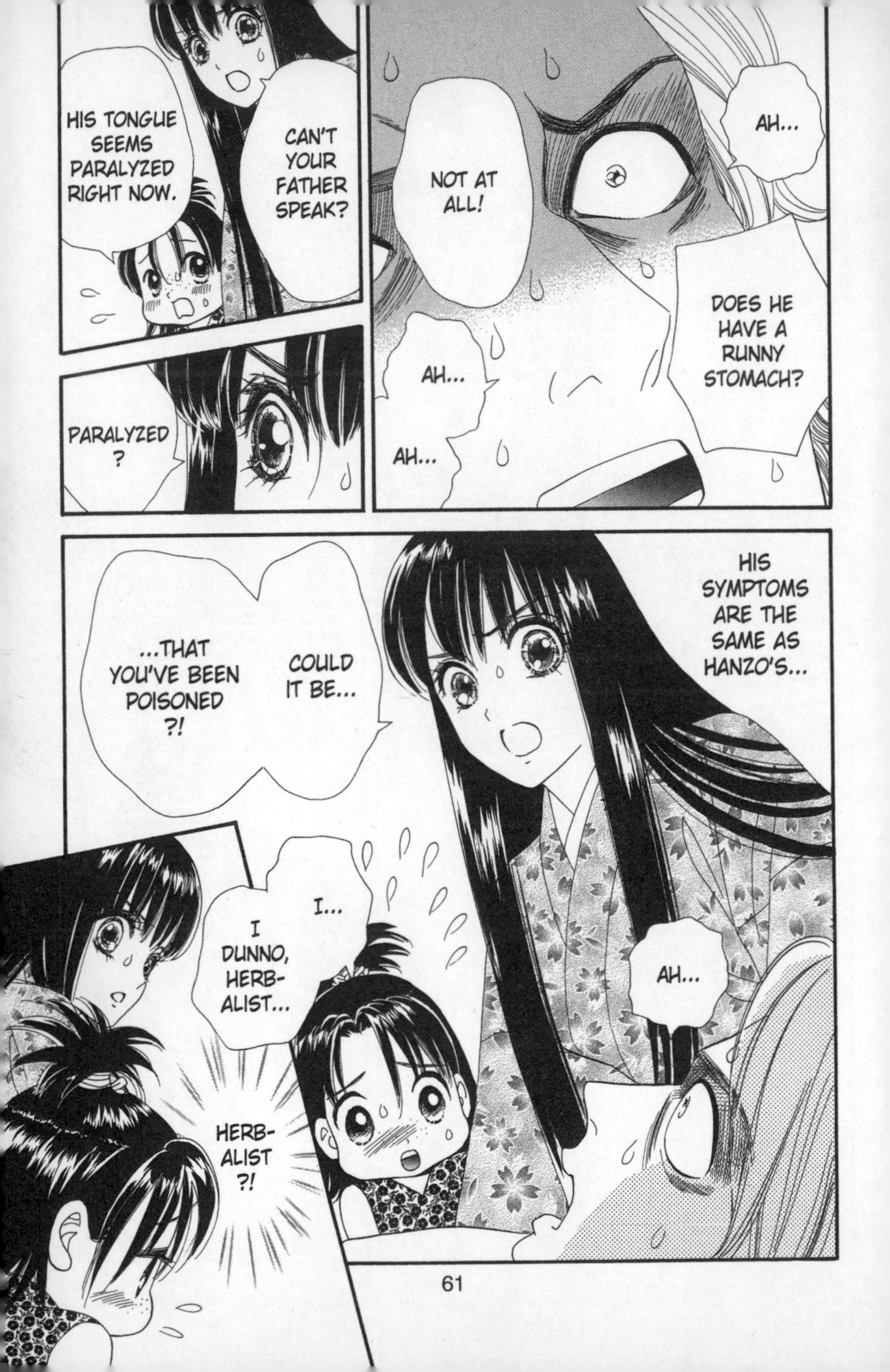
AH...
NOT AT ALL!
DOES HE HAVE A RUNNY STOMACH?
AH...
AH...
CAN'T YOUR FATHER SPEAK?
HIS TONGUE SEEMS PARALYZED RIGHT NOW.
PARALYZED?
HIS SYMPTOMS ARE THE SAME AS HANZO'S...
COULD IT BE...
...THAT YOU'VE BEEN POISONED?!
AH...
I...
I DUNNO, HERB-ALIST...
HERB-ALIST?!

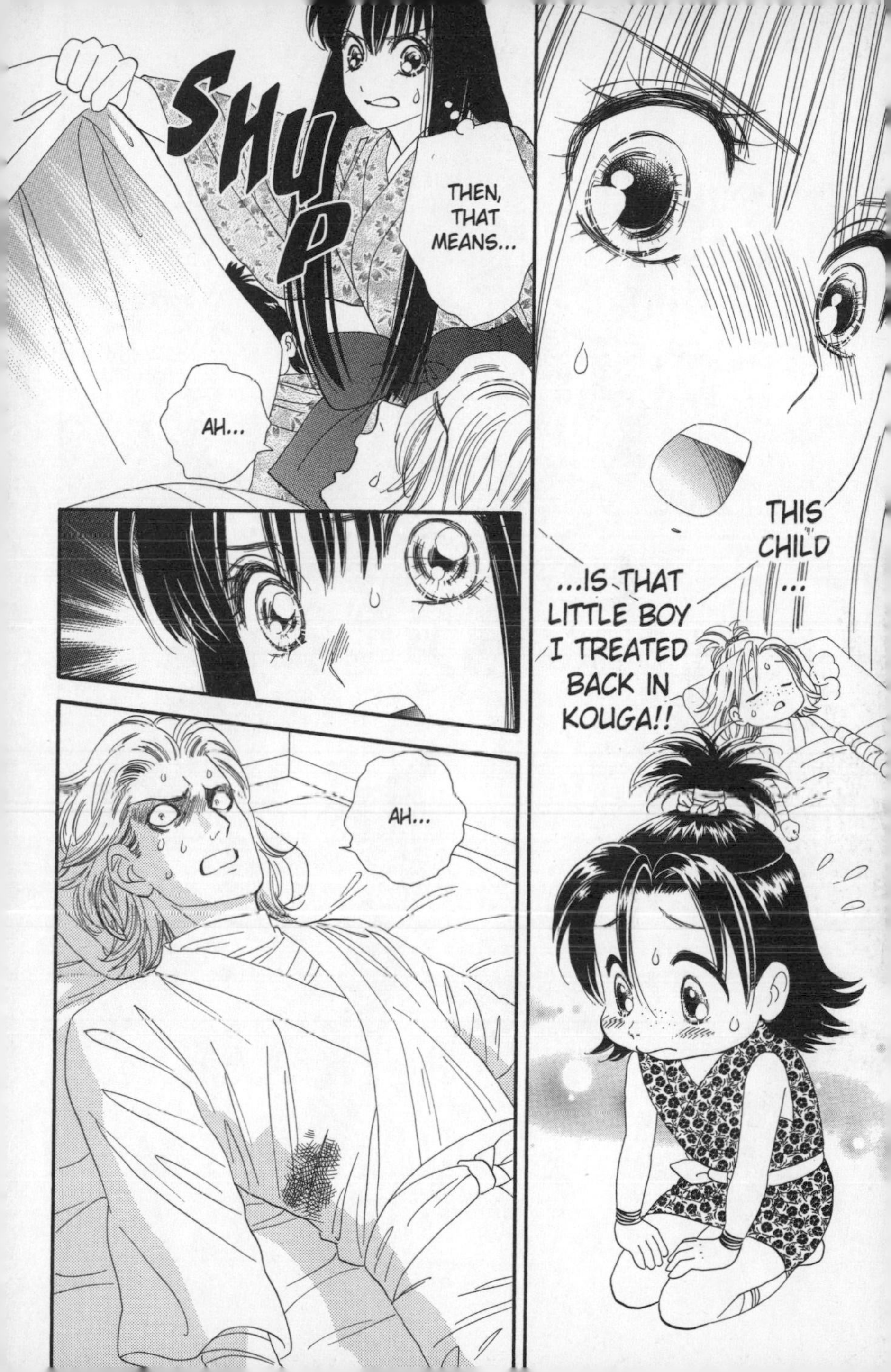
THIS CHILD ...
...IS THAT LITTLE BOY I TREATED BACK IN KOUGA!!
SHUP
THEN, THAT MEANS...
AH...
AH...

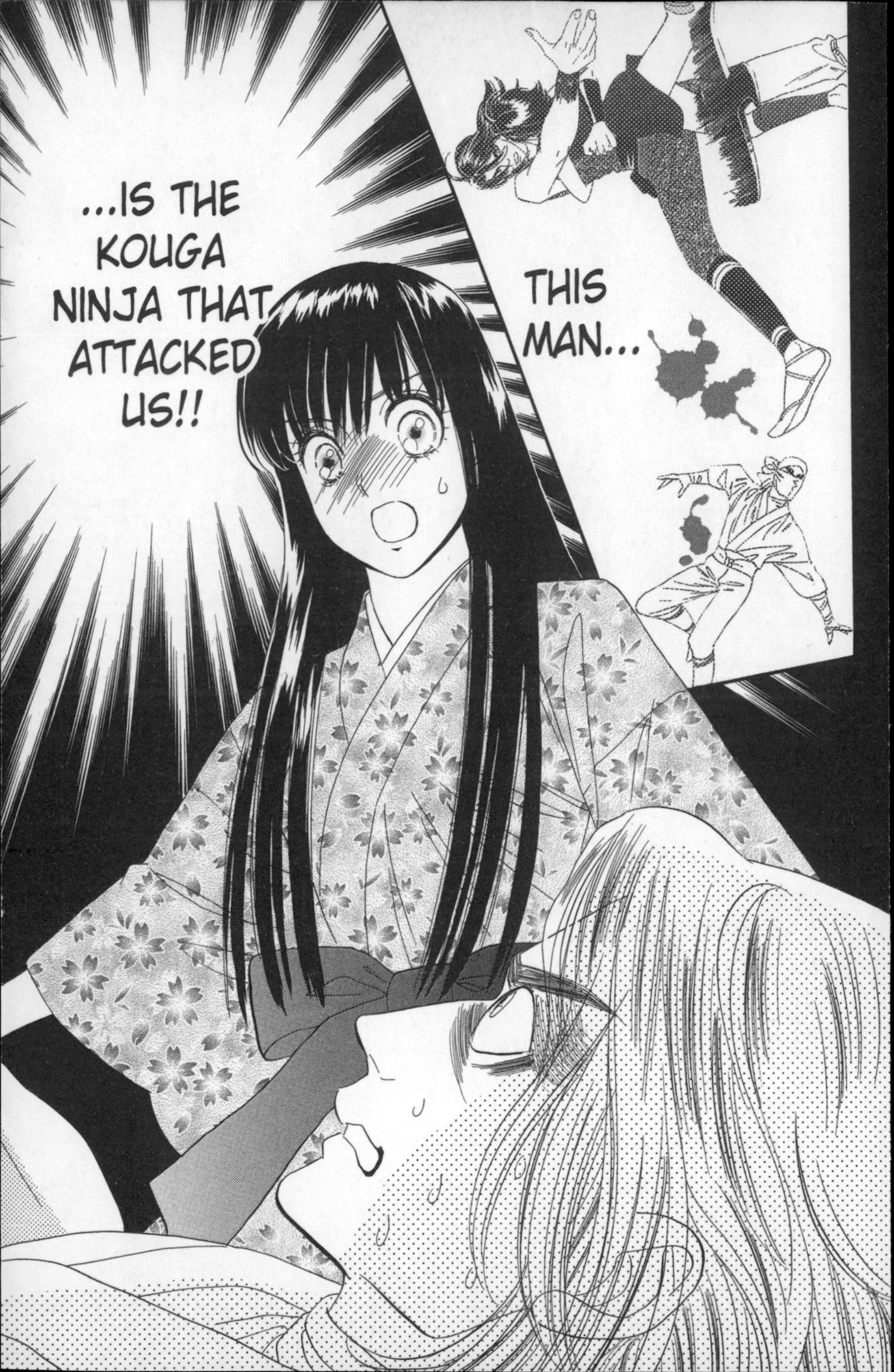
THIS MAN...
...IS THE KOUGA NINJA THAT ATTACKED US!!

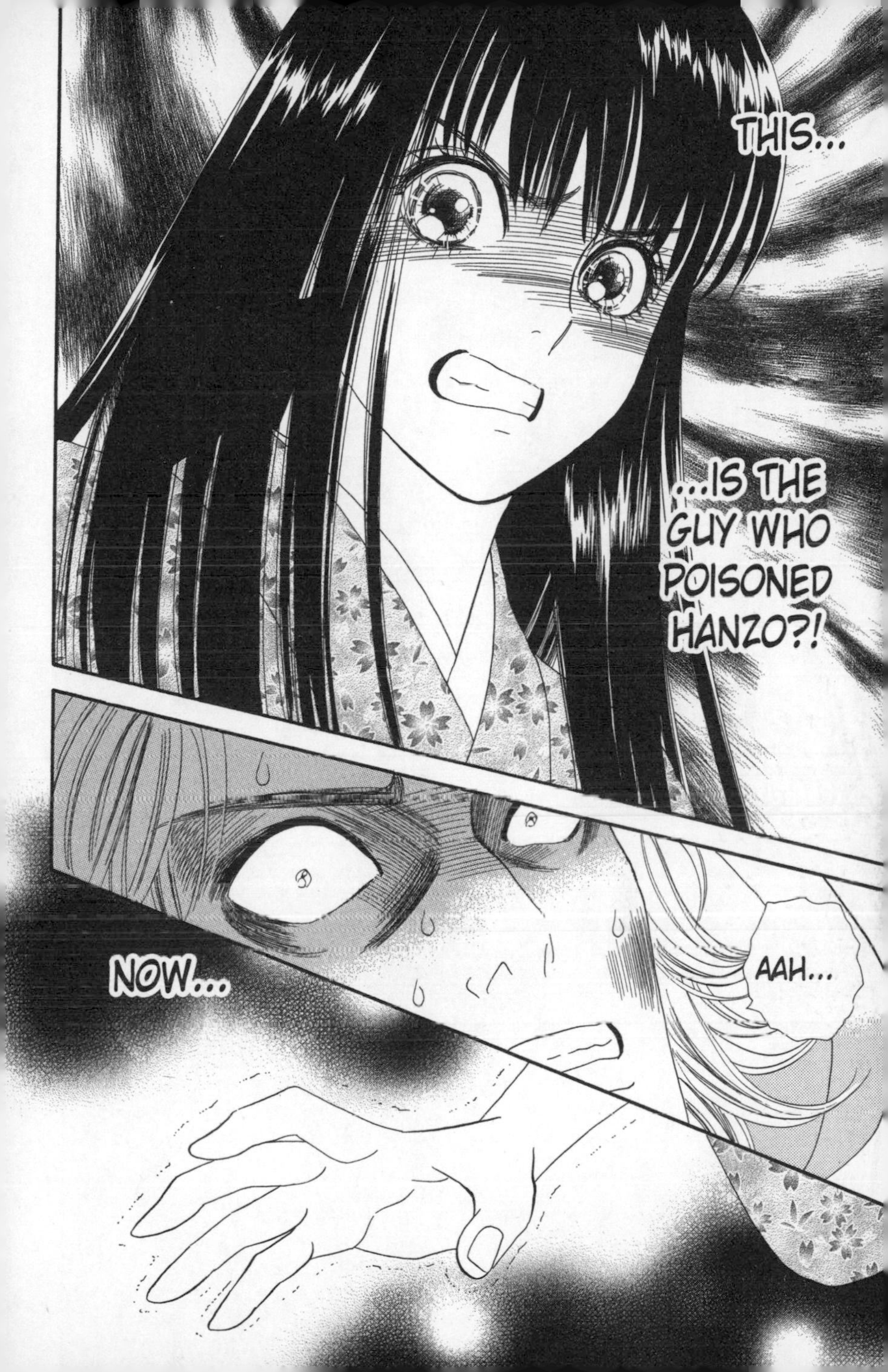
THIS...
...IS THE GUY WHO POISONED HANZO?!
AAH...
NOW...

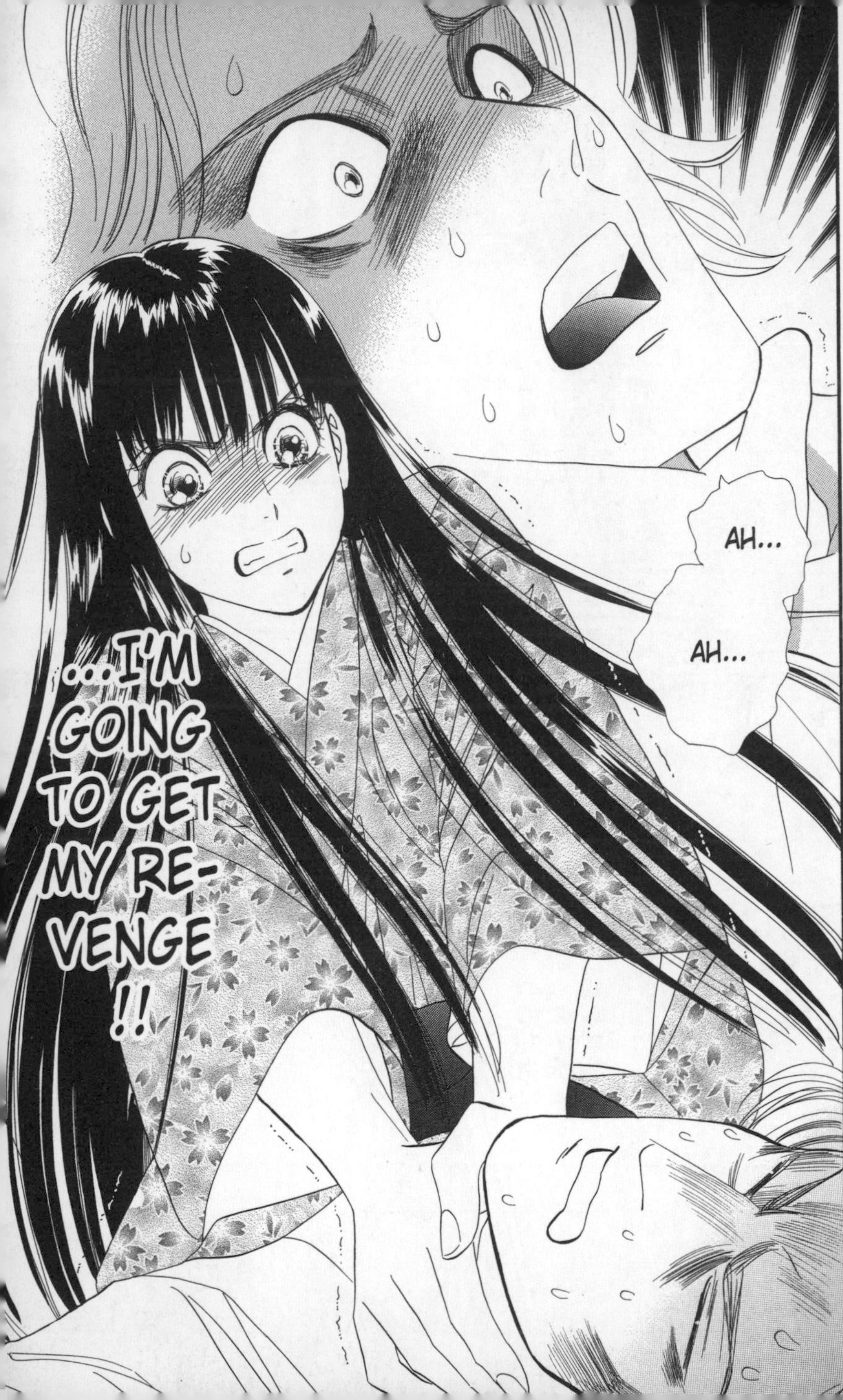
AH...
AH...
...I'M GOING TO GET MY RE-VENGE !!

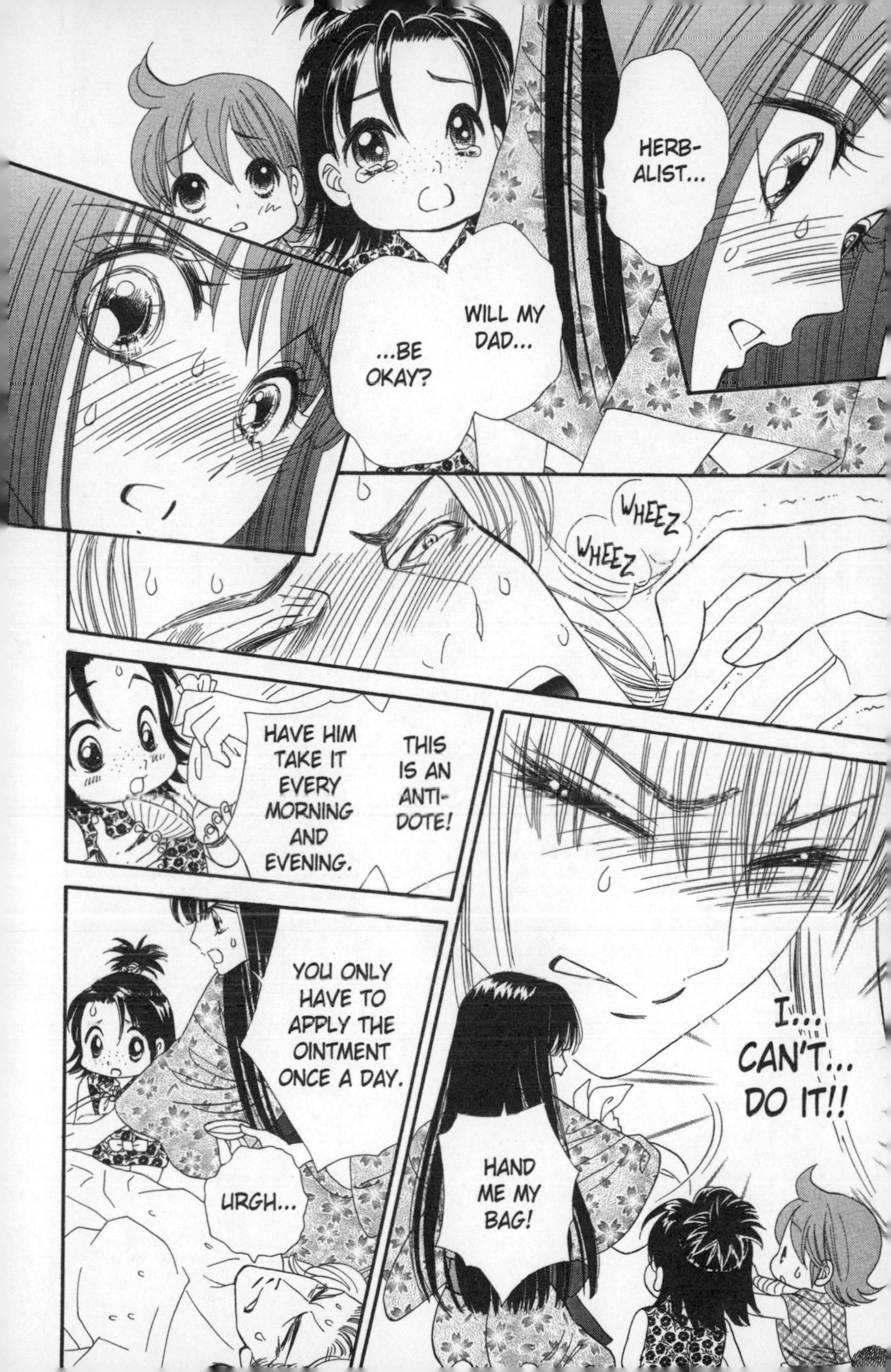
HERB-ALIST...
WILL MY DAD...
...BE OKAY?
WHEEZ WHEEZ
I... CAN'T... DO IT!!
HAND ME MY BAG!
THIS IS AN ANTI-DOTE!
HAVE HIM TAKE IT EVERY MORNING AND EVENING.
YOU ONLY HAVE TO APPLY THE OINTMENT ONCE A DAY.
URGH...

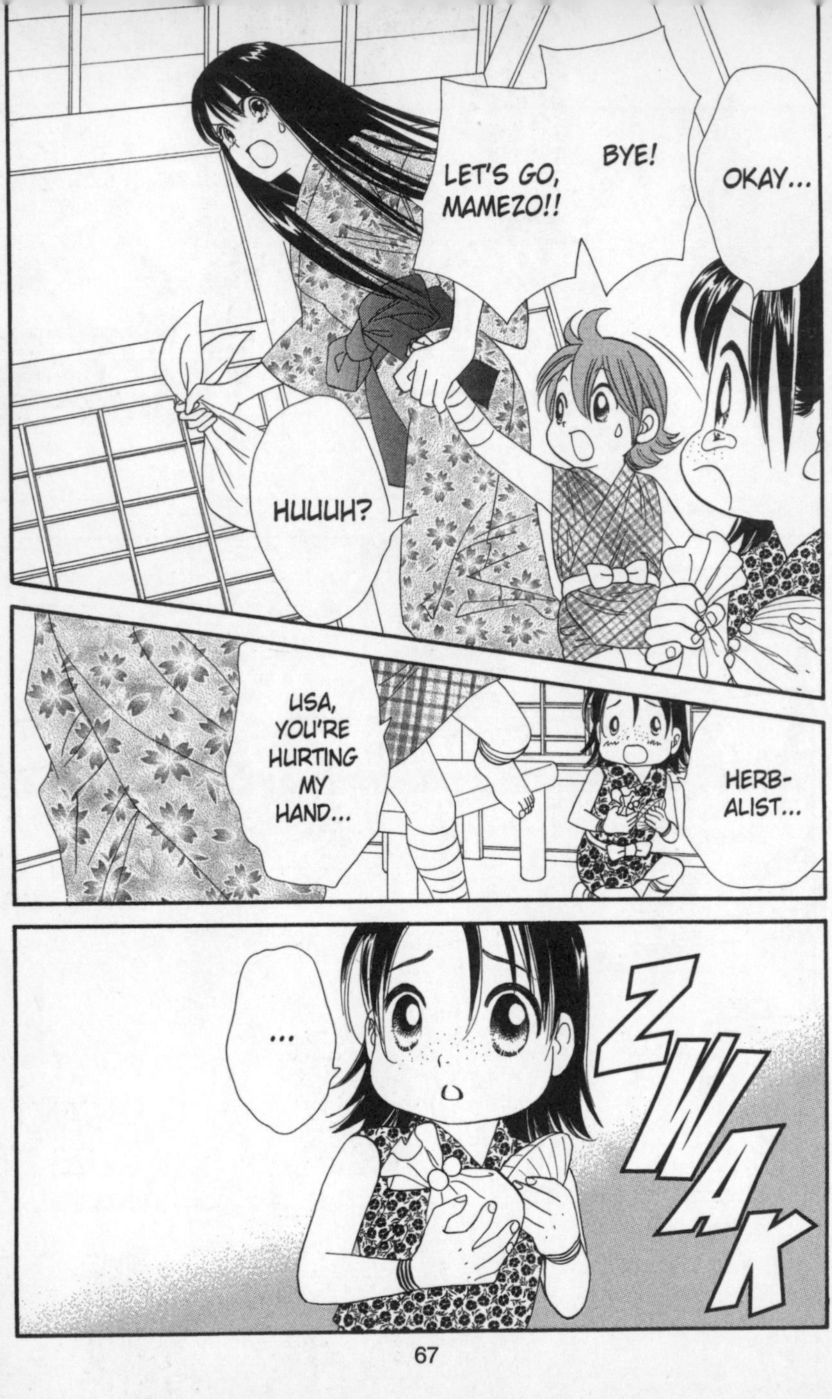
OKAY...
BYE!
LET'S GO, MAMEZO!!
HUUUH?
HERB-ALIST...
USA, YOU'RE HURTING MY HAND...
ZWAK
...

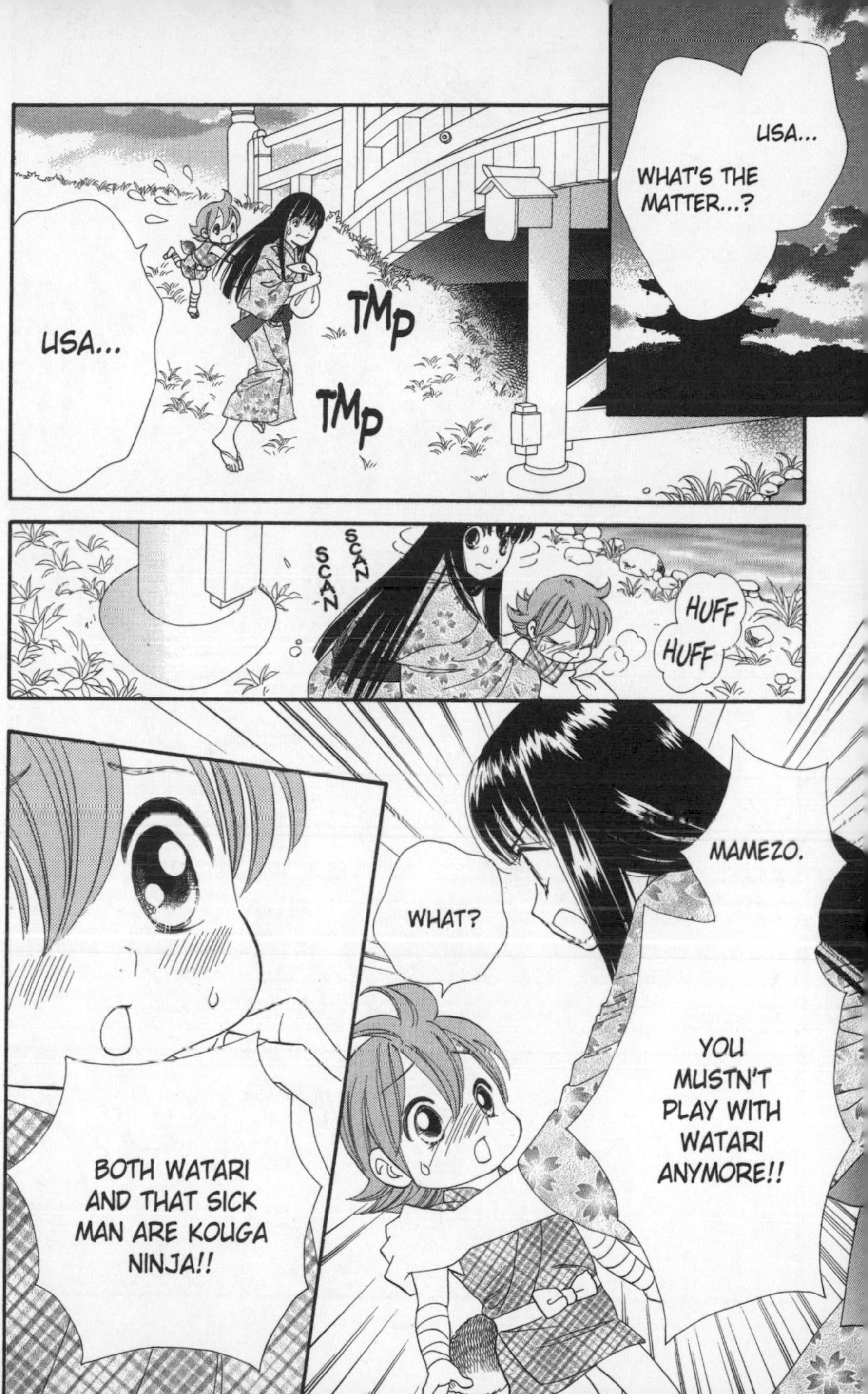
USA...
WHAT'S THE MATTER...?
USA...
TMP
TMP
HUFF HUFF
SCAN SCAN
MAMEZO.
WHAT?
YOU MUSTN'T PLAY WITH WATARI ANYMORE!!
BOTH WATARI AND THAT SICK MAN ARE KOUGA NINJA!!

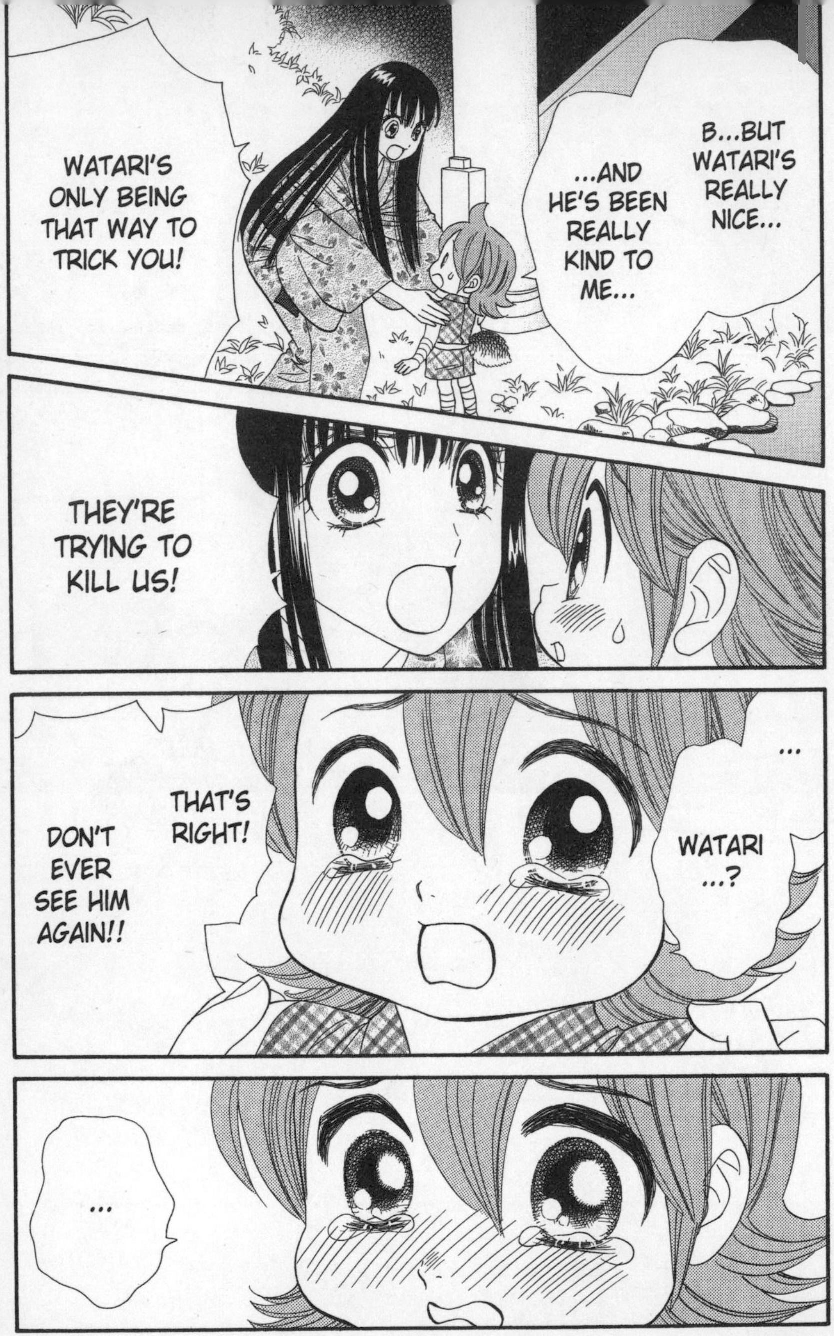
B...BUT WATARI'S REALLY NICE...
...AND HE'S BEEN REALLY KIND TO ME...
WATARI'S ONLY BEING THAT WAY TO TRICK YOU!
THEY'RE TRYING TO KILL US!
...
WATARI ...?
THAT'S RIGHT!
DON'T EVER SEE HIM AGAIN!!
...

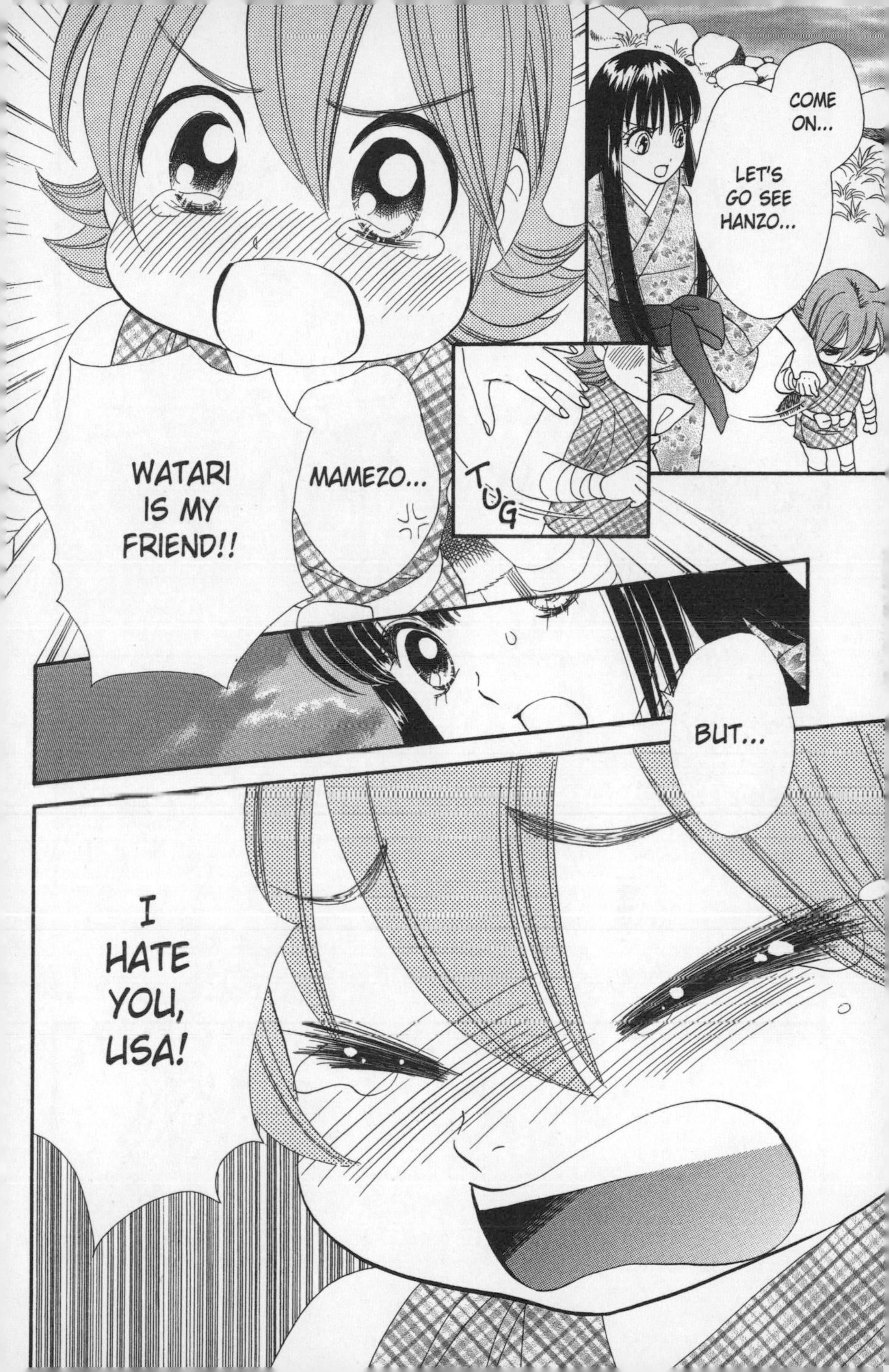
COME ON...
LET'S GO SEE HANZO...
TUG
MAMEZO...
WATARI IS MY FRIEND!!
BUT...
I HATE YOU, USA!

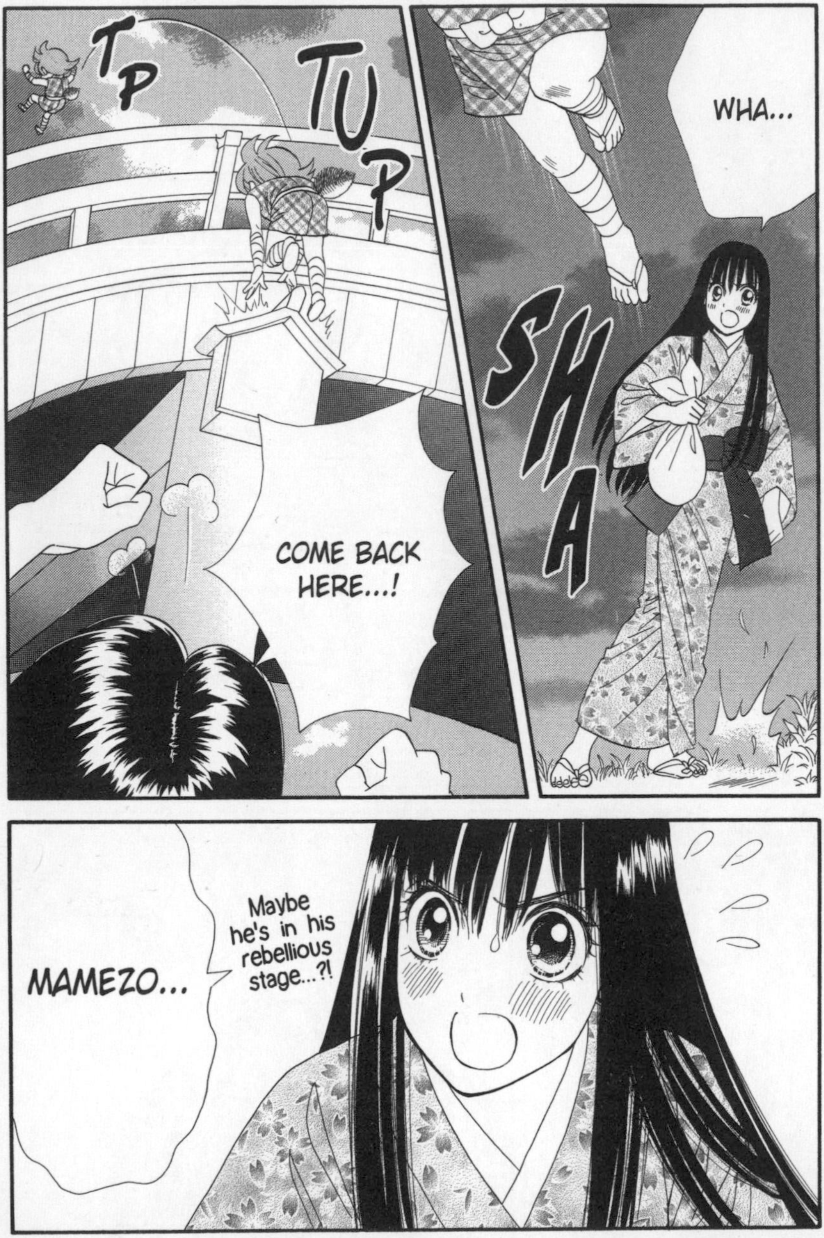
WHA...
SHA
TP
TUP
COME BACK HERE...!
Maybe he's in his rebellious stage...?!
MAMEZO...

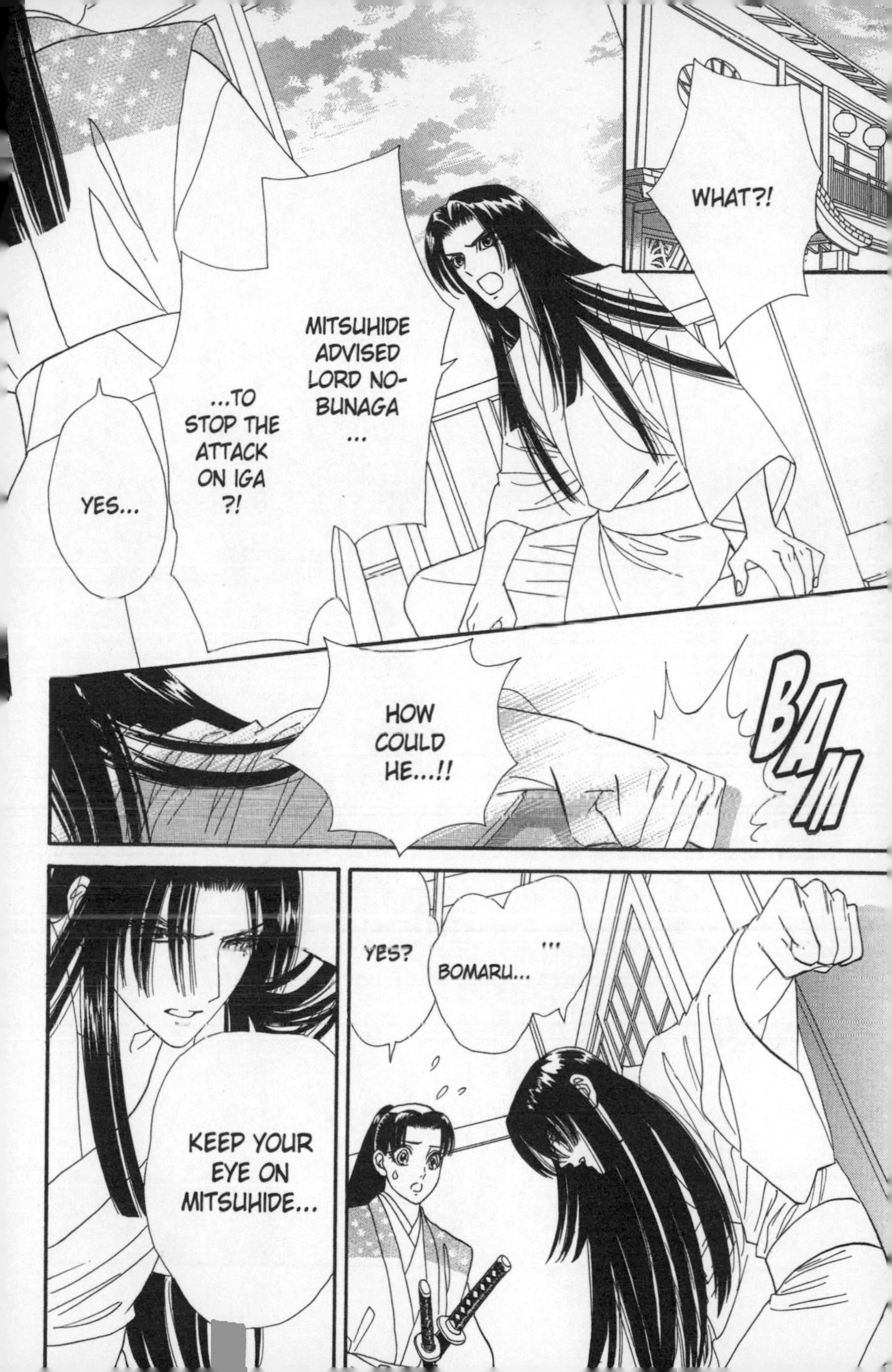
WHAT?!
MITSUHIDE ADVISED LORD NO-BUNAGA ...
...TO STOP THE ATTACK ON IGA ?!
YES...
BAM
HOW COULD HE...!!
...
BOMARU...
YES?
KEEP YOUR EYE ON MITSUHIDE...

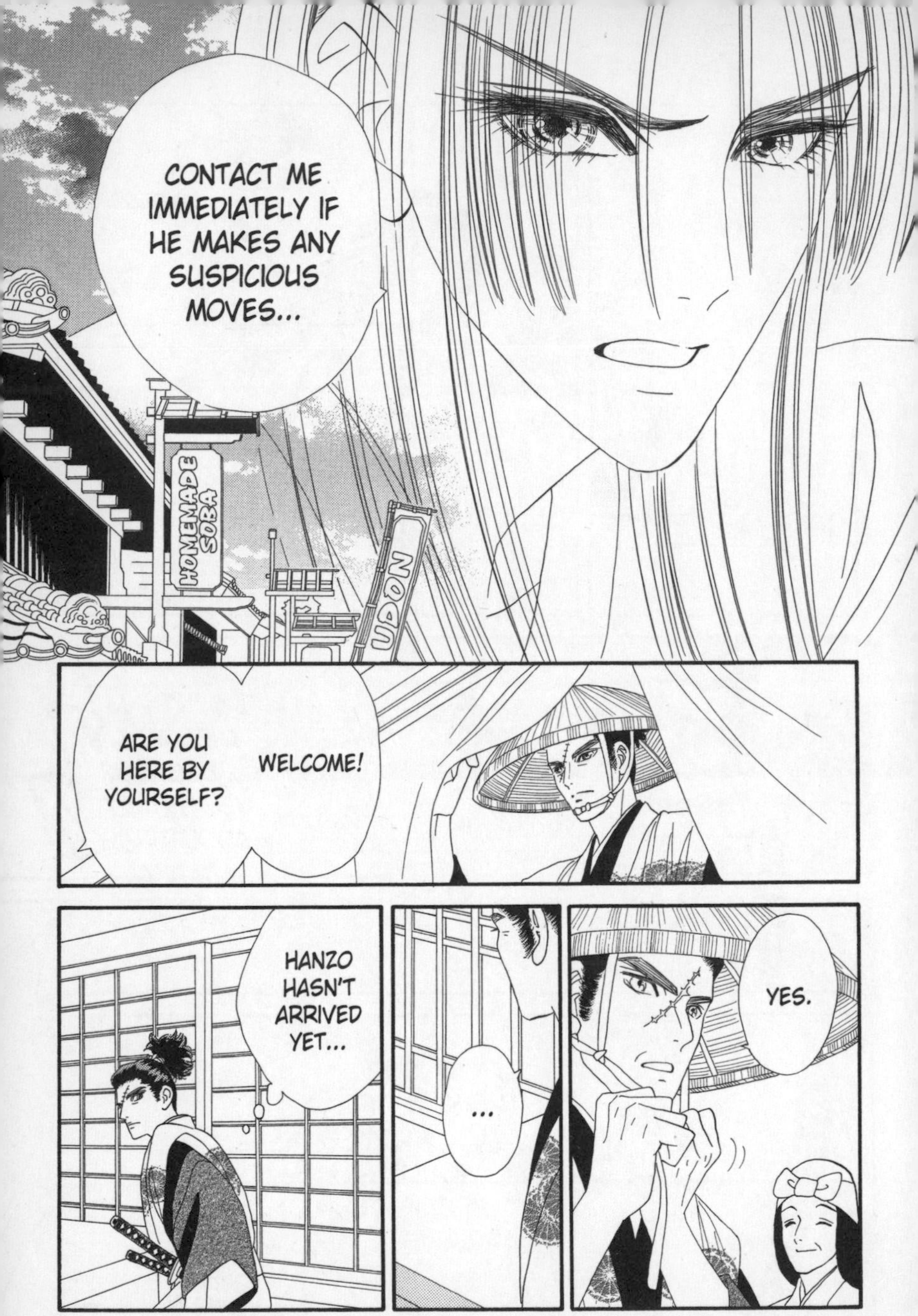
CONTACT ME IMMEDIATELY IF HE MAKES ANY SUSPICIOUS MOVES...
HOMEMADE SOBA
UDON
WELCOME!
ARE YOU HERE BY YOURSELF?
YES.
...
HANZO HASN'T ARRIVED YET...

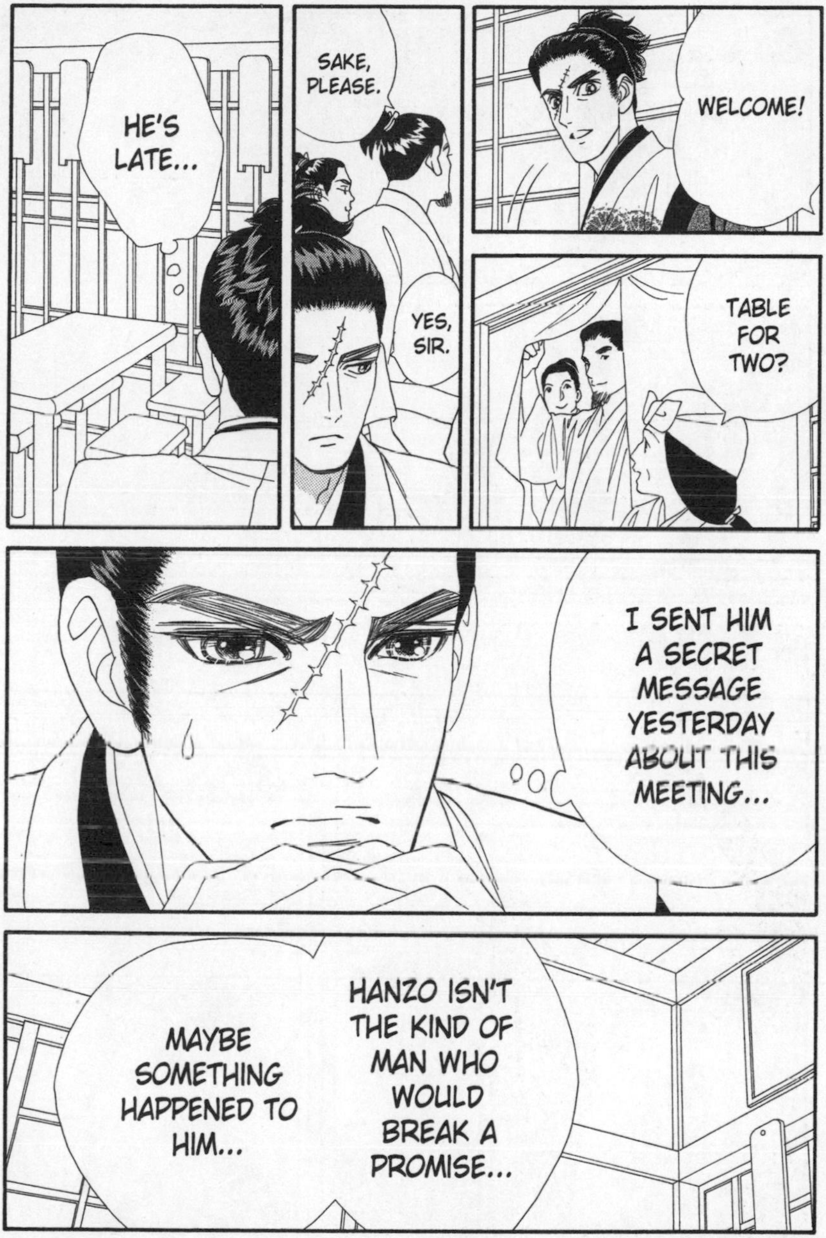
WELCOME!
TABLE FOR TWO?
SAKE, PLEASE.
YES, SIR.
HE'S LATE...
I SENT HIM A SECRET MESSAGE YESTERDAY ABOUT THIS MEETING...
HANZO ISN'T THE KIND OF MAN WHO WOULD BREAK A PROMISE...
MAYBE SOMETHING HAPPENED TO HIM...

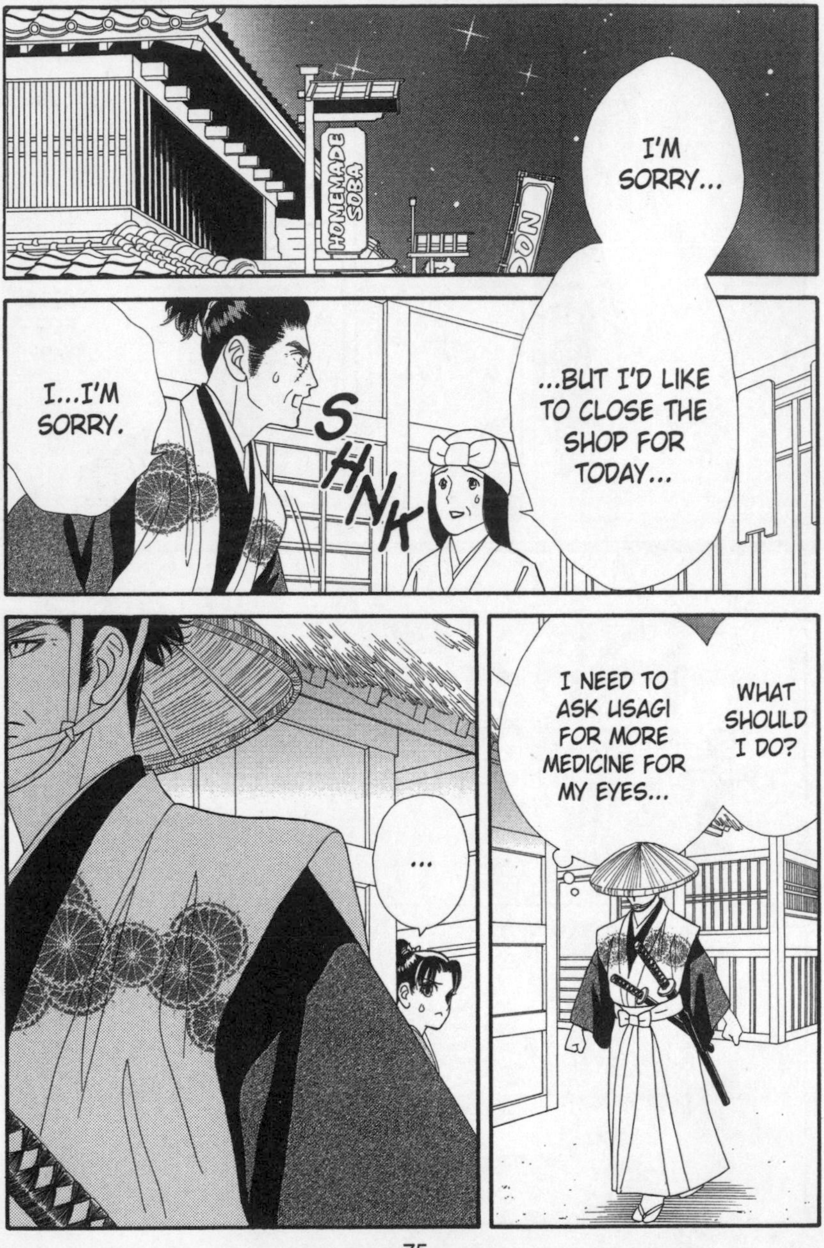
HOMEMADE SOBA
I'M SORRY...
...BUT I'D LIKE TO CLOSE THE SHOP FOR TODAY...
SHNK
I...I'M SORRY.
WHAT SHOULD I DO?
I NEED TO ASK USAGI FOR MORE MEDICINE FOR MY EYES...
...

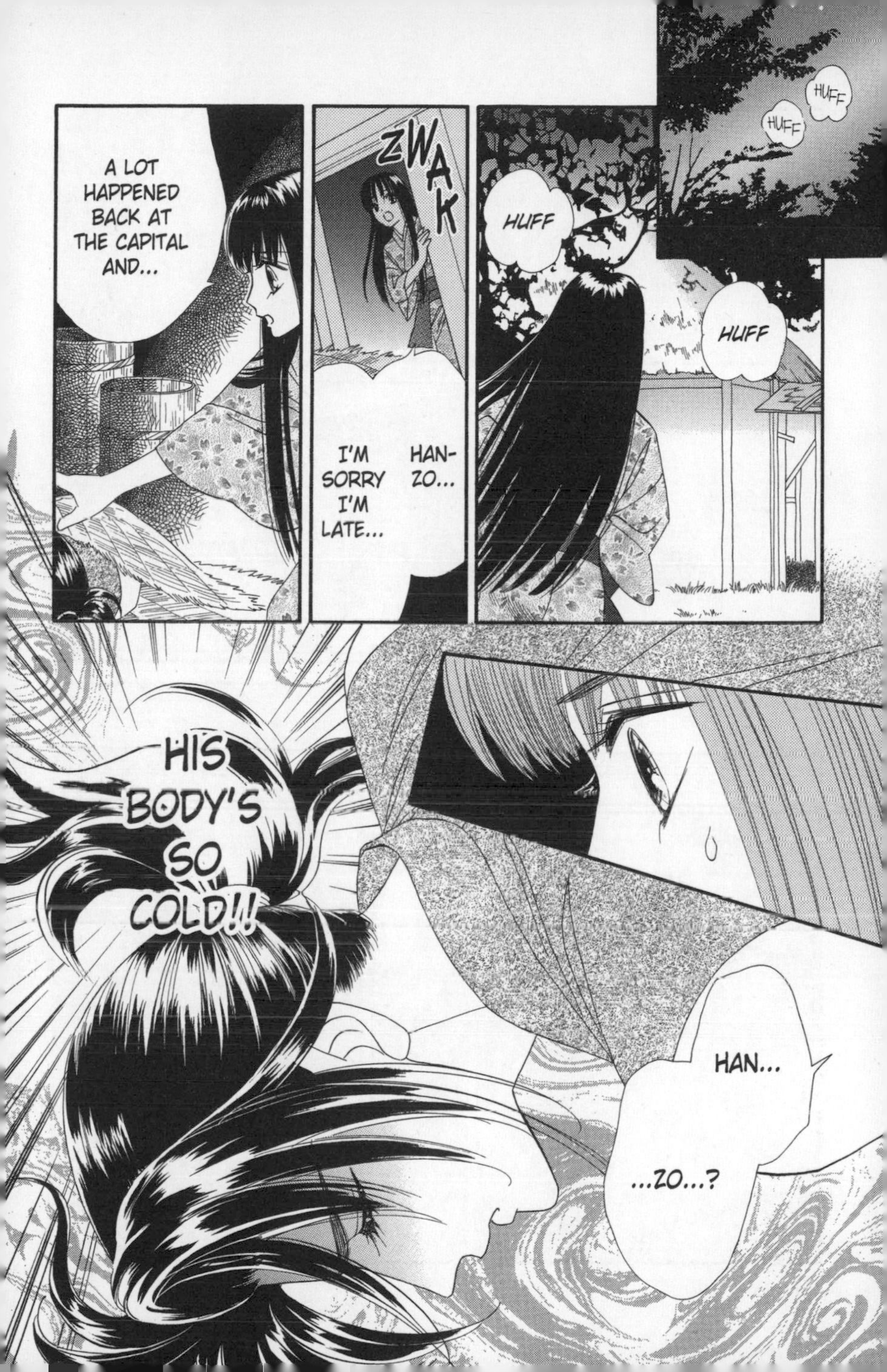
HUFF
HUFF
HUFF
HUFF
ZWAK
HAN-ZO...
I'M SORRY I'M LATE...
A LOT HAPPENED BACK AT THE CAPITAL AND...
HAN...
...ZO...?
HIS BODY'S SO COLD!!

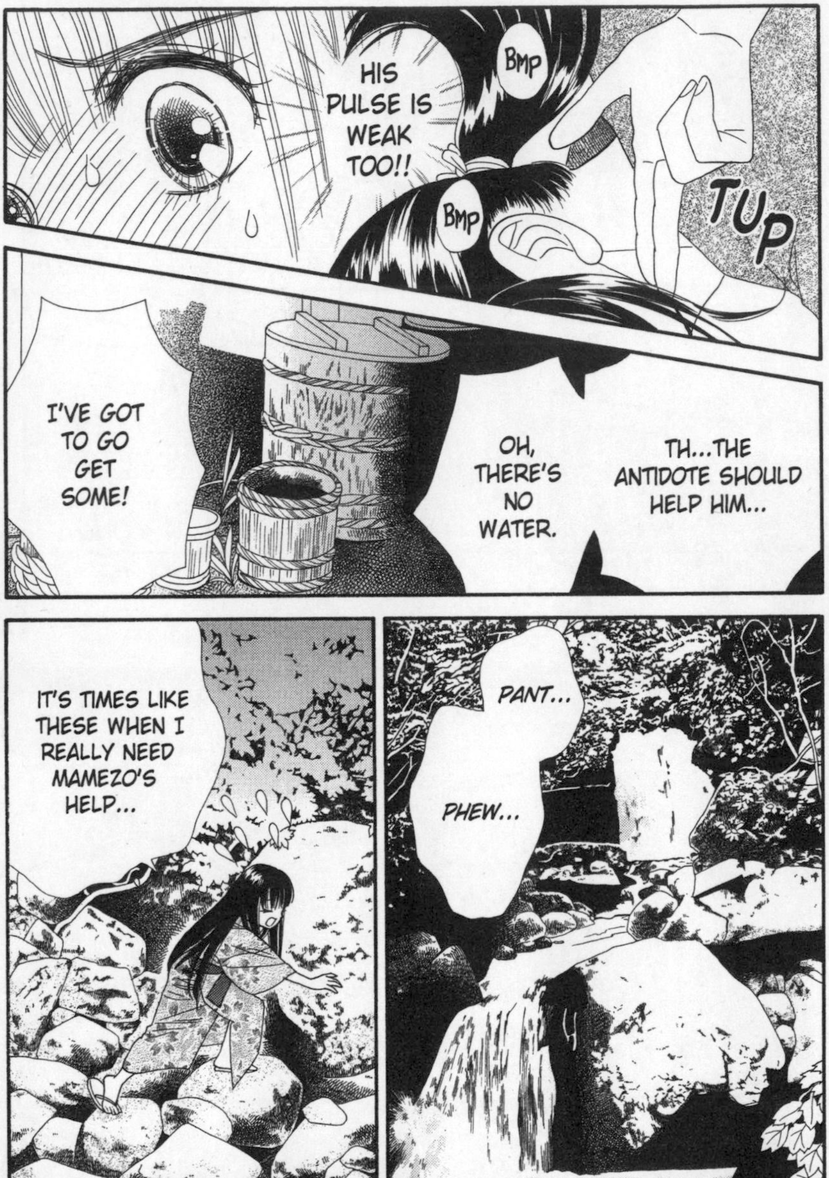
BMP
TUP
HIS PULSE IS WEAK TOO!!
BMP
TH...THE ANTIDOTE SHOULD HELP HIM...
OH, THERE'S NO WATER.
I'VE GOT TO GO GET SOME!
PANT...
PHEW...
IT'S TIMES LIKE THESE WHEN I REALLY NEED MAMEZO'S HELP...

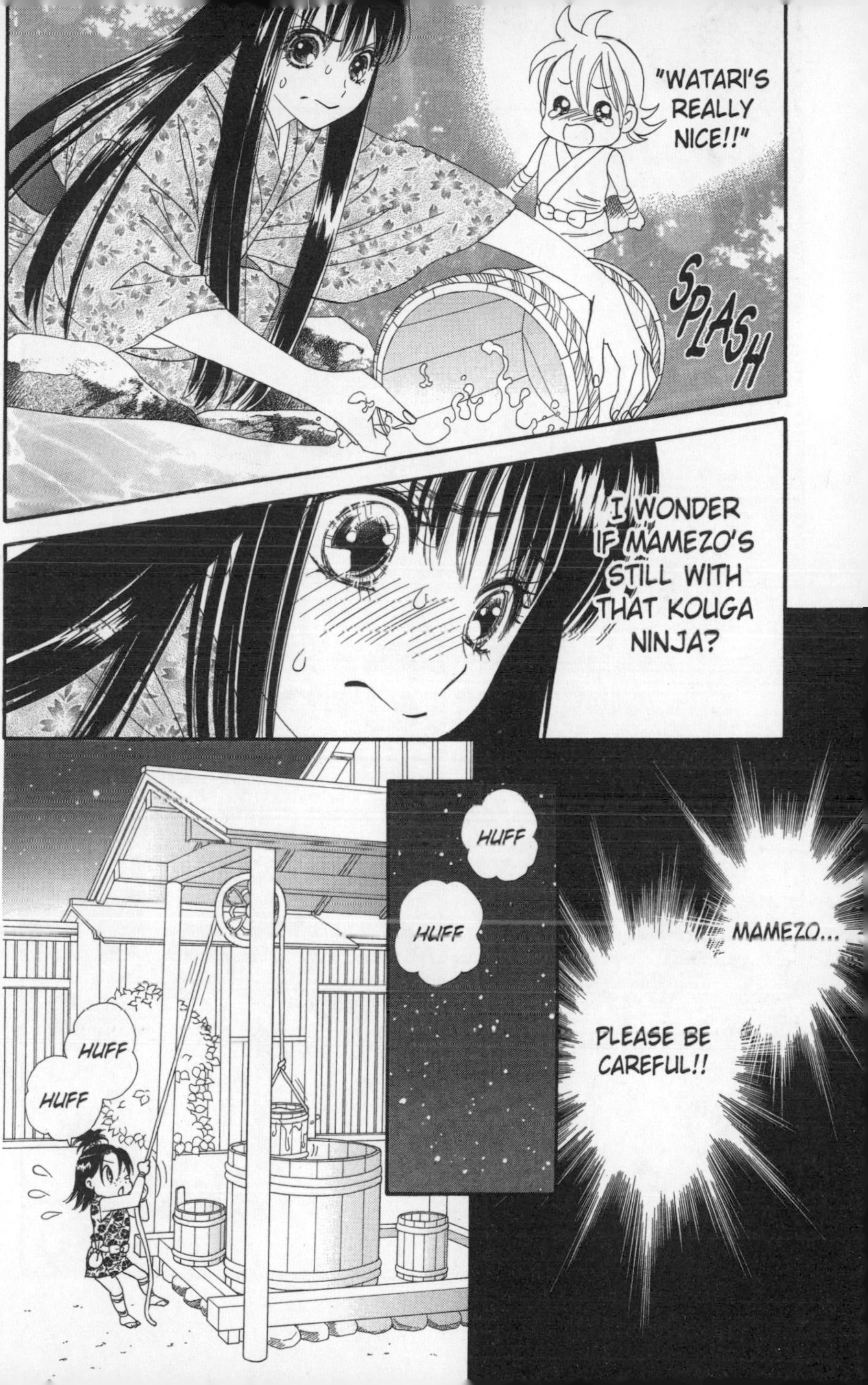
"WATARI'S REALLY NICE!!"
SPLASH
I WONDER IF MAMEZO'S STILL WITH THAT KOUGA NINJA?
MAMEZO...
PLEASE BE CAREFUL!!
HUFF
HUFF
HUFF
HUFF

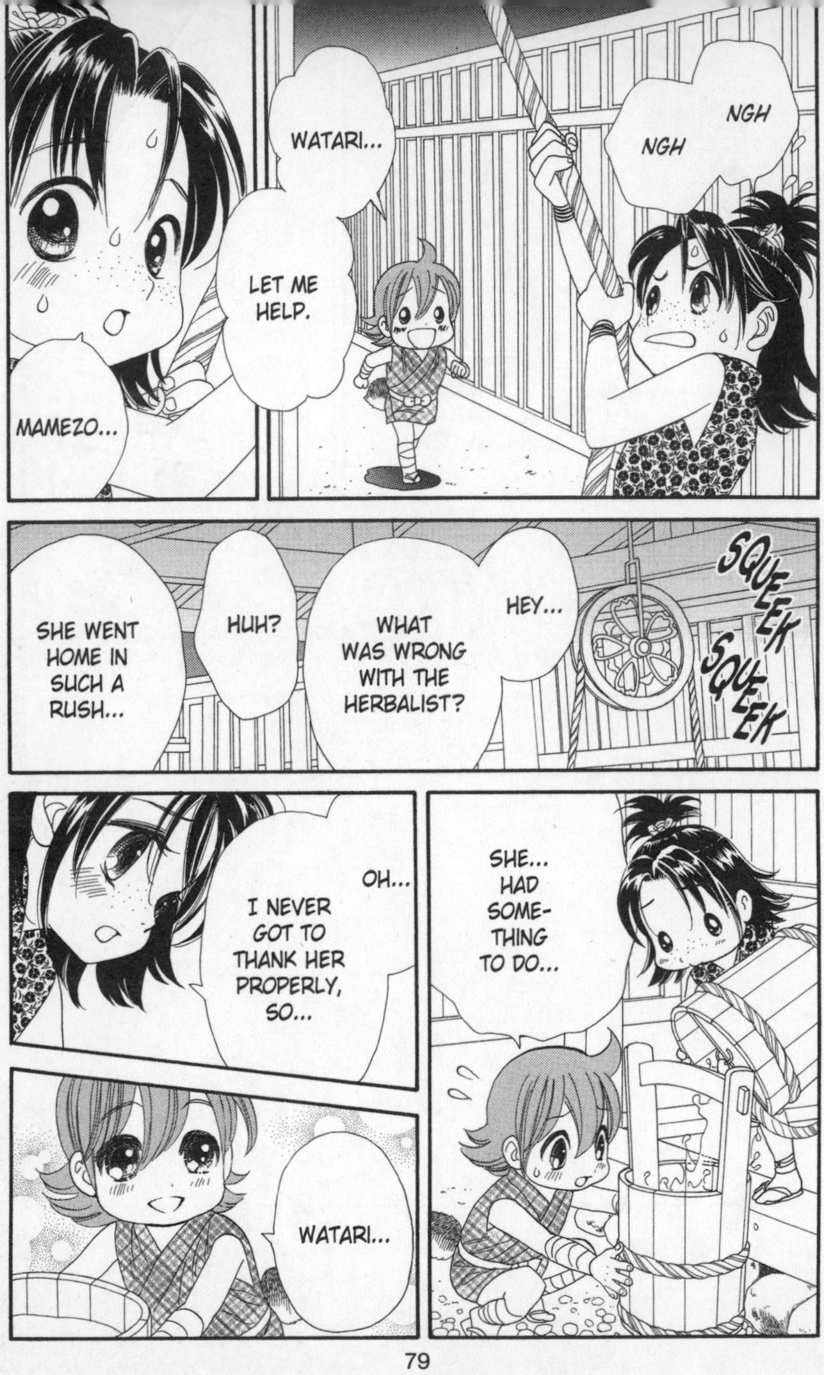
NGH
NGH
WATARI...
LET ME HELP.
MAMEZO...
SQUEEK
SQUEEK
HEY...
WHAT WAS WRONG WITH THE HERBALIST?
HUH?
SHE WENT HOME IN SUCH A RUSH...
SHE... HAD SOME-THING TO DO...
OH...
I NEVER GOT TO THANK HER PROPERLY, SO...
WATARI...

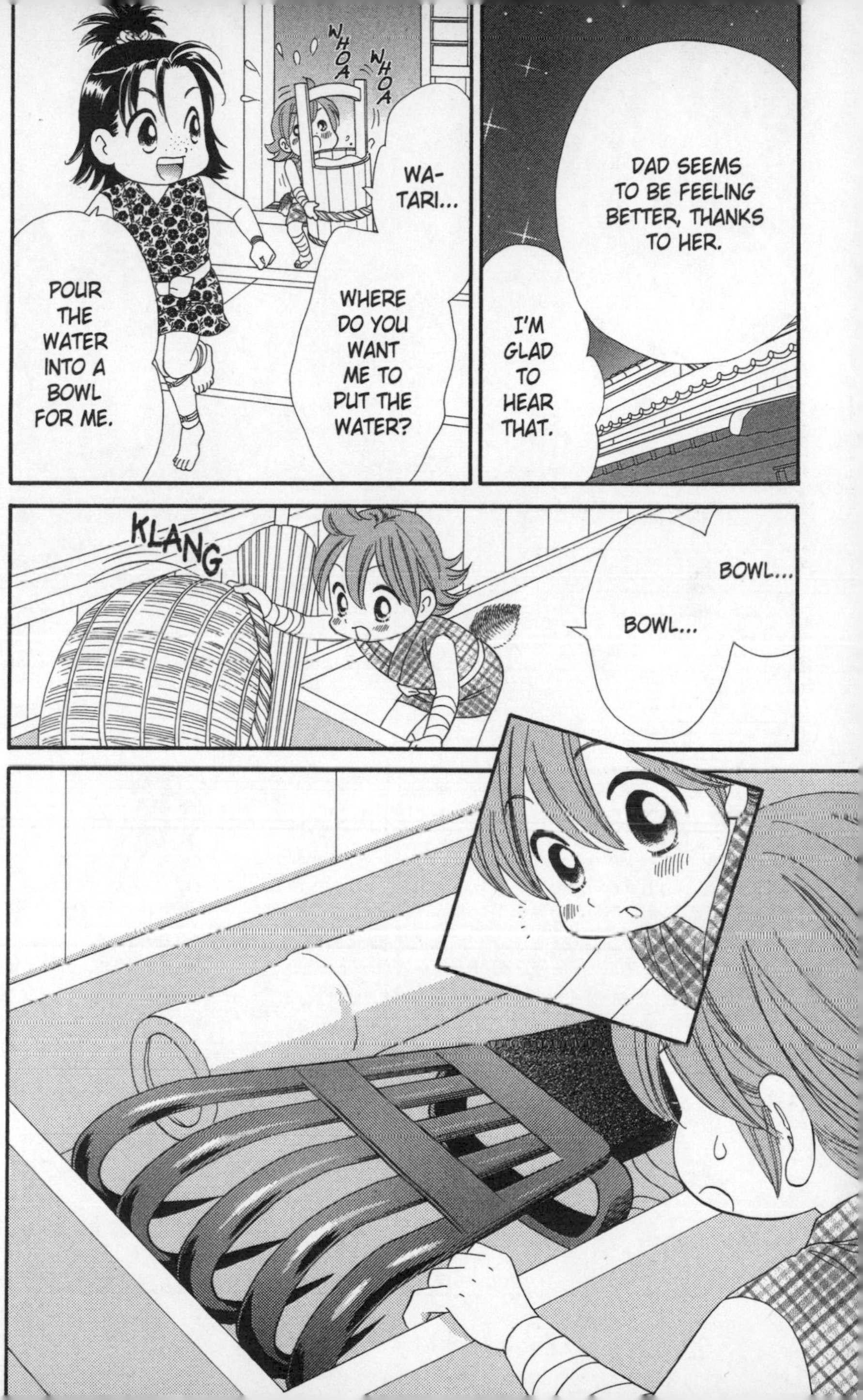
DAD SEEMS TO BE FEELING BETTER, THANKS TO HER.
I'M GLAD TO HEAR THAT.
WHOA WHOA
WA-TARI...
WHERE DO YOU WANT ME TO PUT THE WATER?
POUR THE WATER INTO A BOWL FOR ME.
BOWL...
BOWL...
KLANG

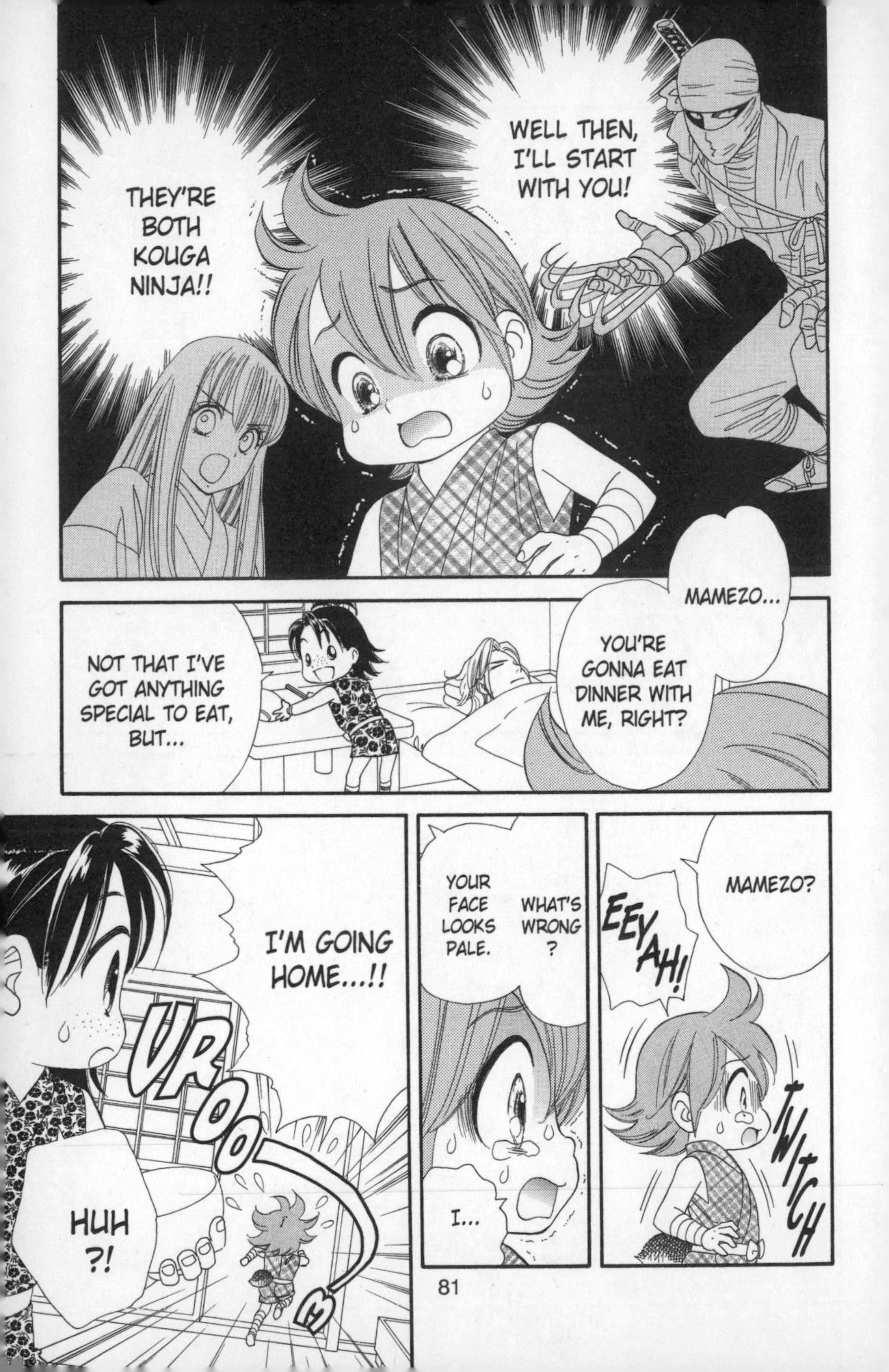
WELL THEN, I'LL START WITH YOU!
THEY'RE BOTH KOUGA NINJA!!
MAMEZO...
YOU'RE GONNA EAT DINNER WITH ME, RIGHT?
NOT THAT I'VE GOT ANYTHING SPECIAL TO EAT, BUT...
MAMEZO?
EEYAH!
TWITCH
WHAT'S WRONG?
YOUR FACE LOOKS PALE.
I...
I'M GOING HOME...!!
VROOOOM
HUH ?!

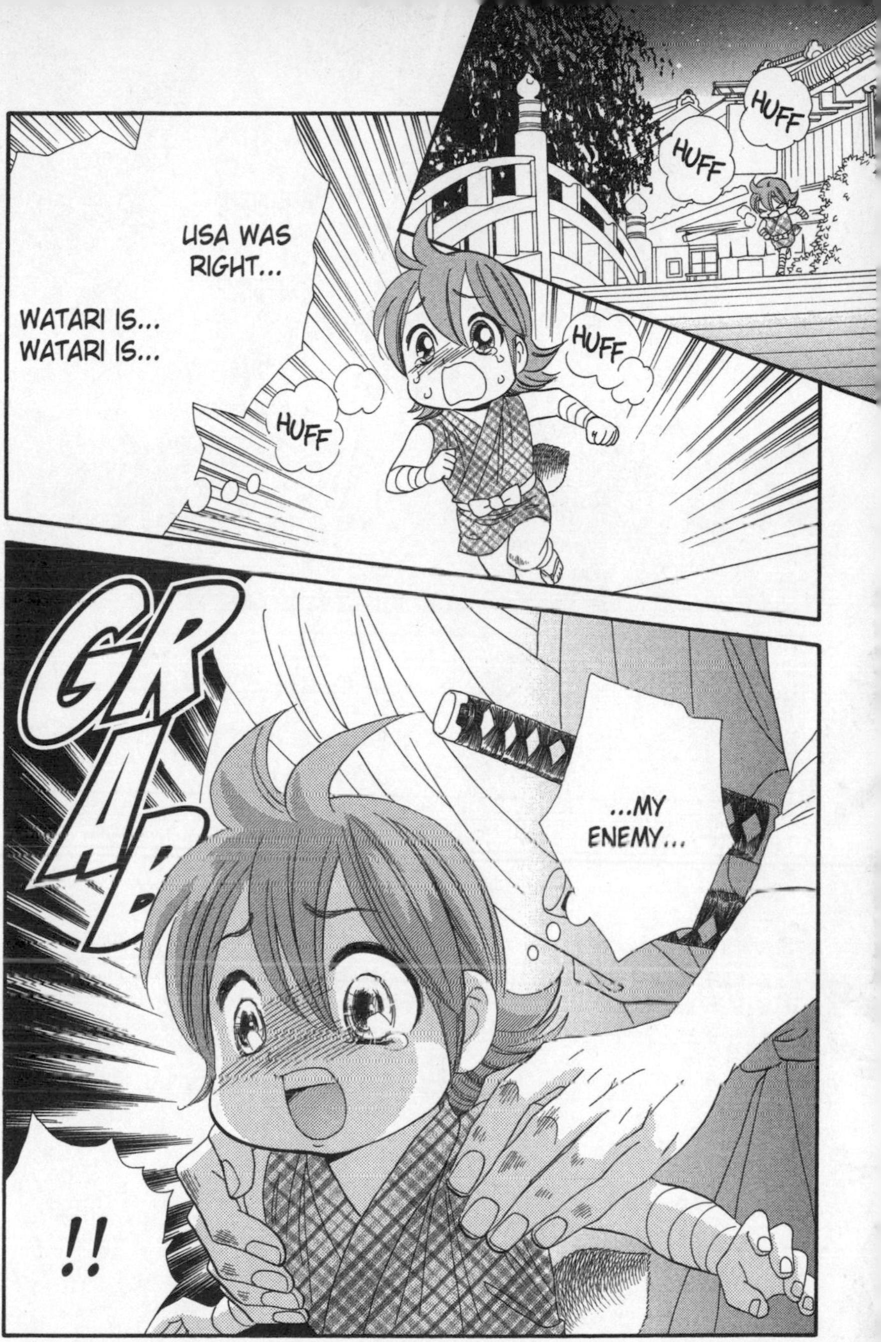
HUFF
HUFF
HUFF
USA WAS RIGHT...
WATARI IS... WATARI IS...
HUFF
...MY ENEMY...
GRAB
!!

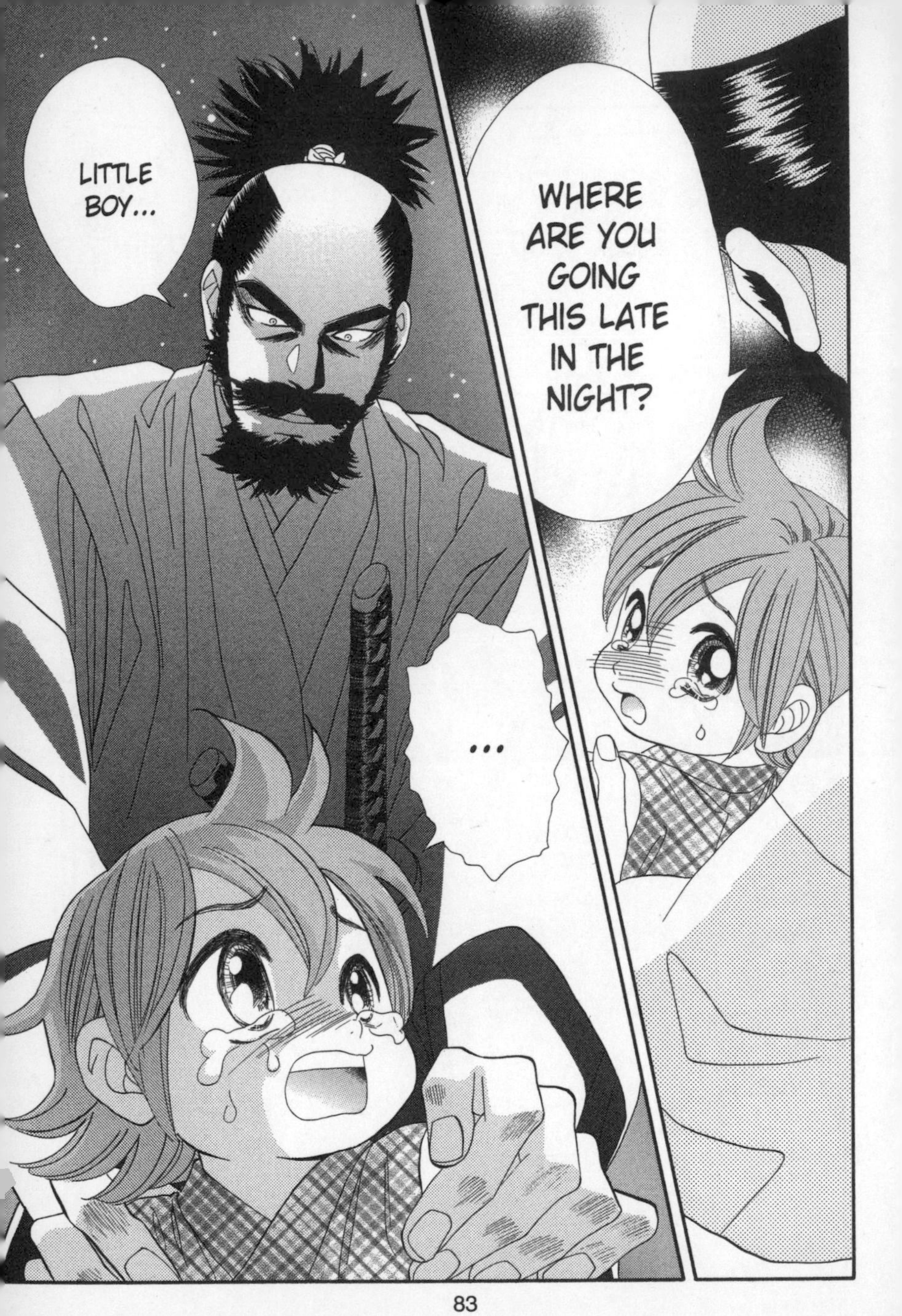
WHERE ARE YOU GOING THIS LATE IN THE NIGHT?
LITTLE BOY...
...

TAIL OF THE MOON EXTRA: TODAY'S MISSION

"I WANT TO SEE HANZOU IN RAZOR RAMON HG'S OUTFIT!"

-AZUSA YAMAMOTO, NARA PREFECTURE

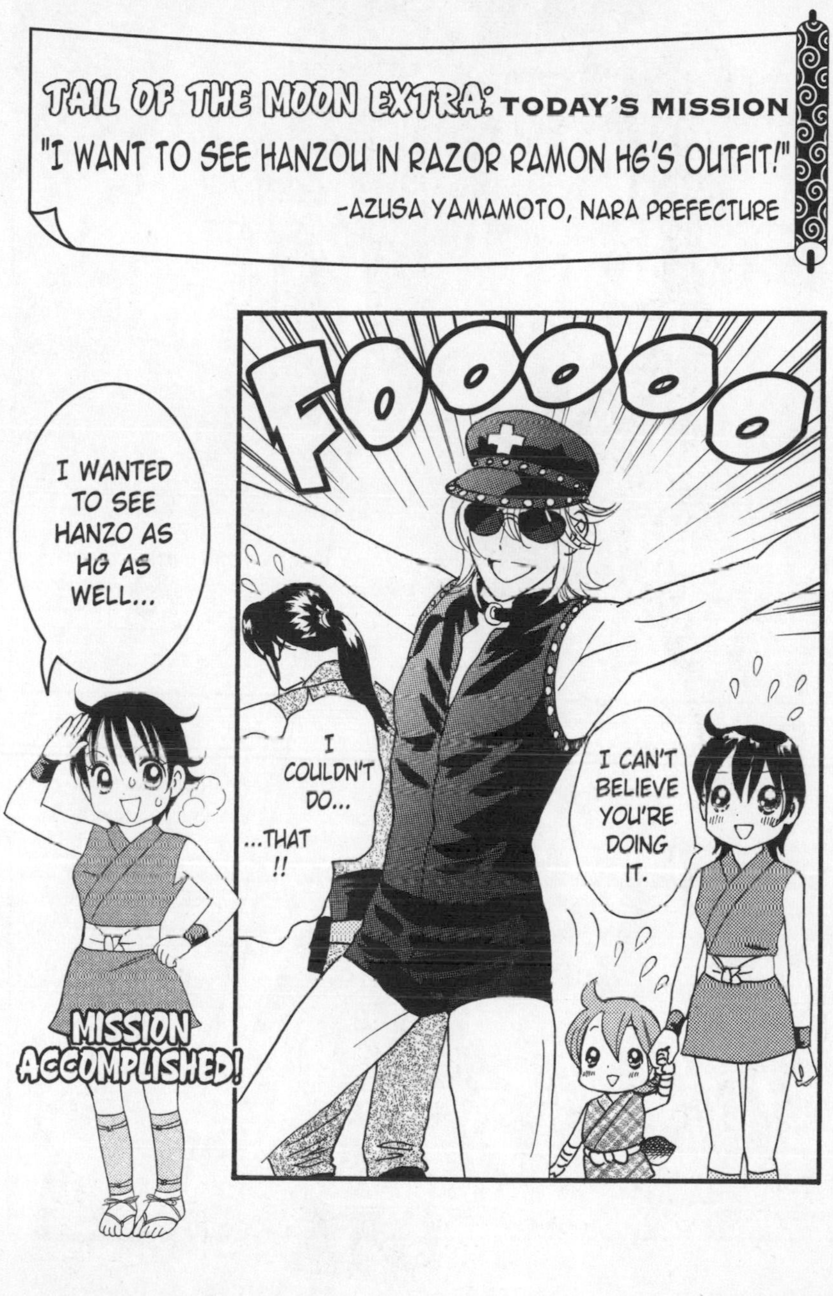
FOOOOOO
I CAN'T BELIEVE YOU'RE DOING IT.
I COULDN'T DO...
...THAT!!
I WANTED TO SEE HANZO AS HG AS WELL...
MISSION ACCOMPLISHED!

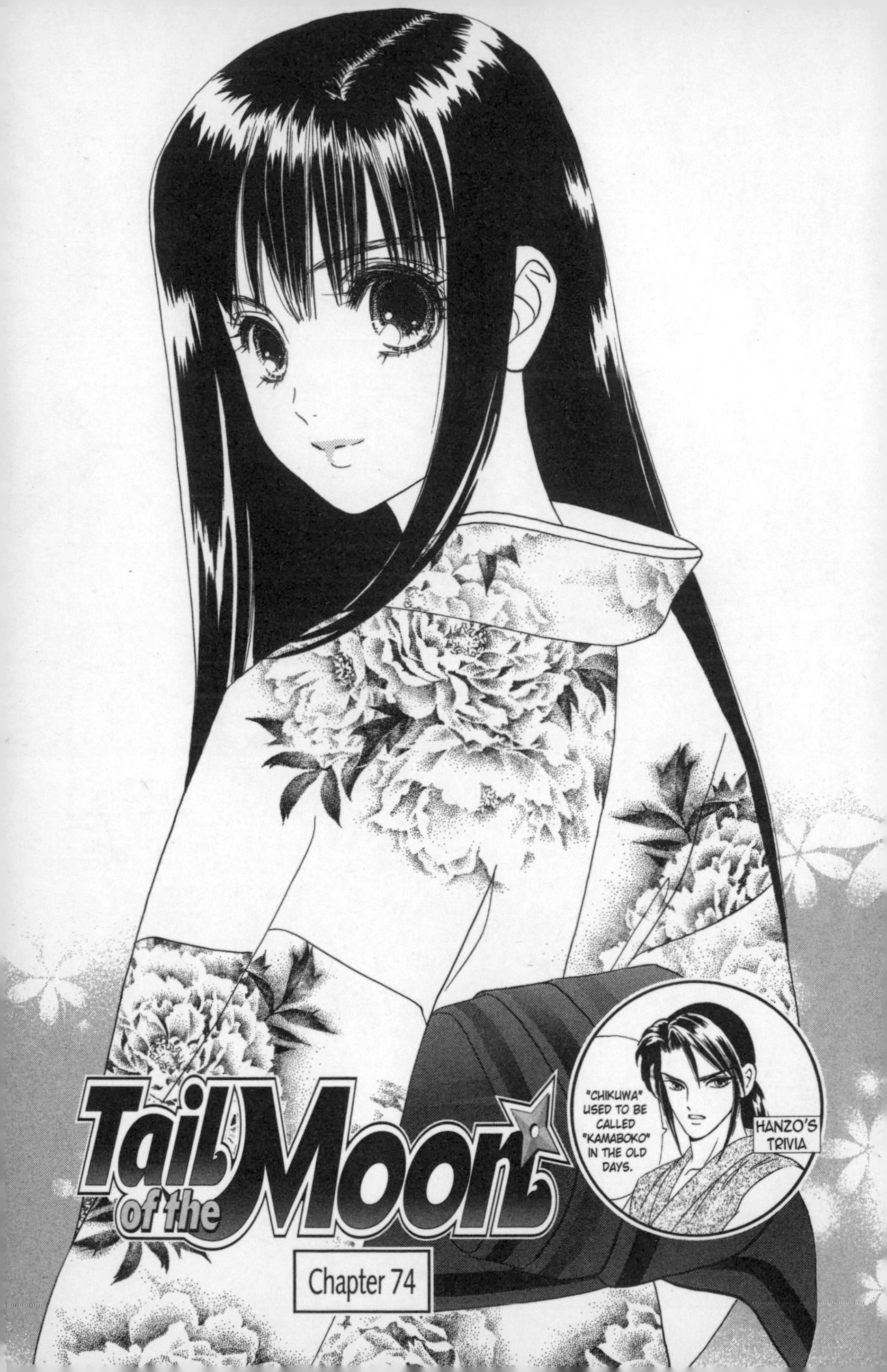
Tail of the Moon
Chapter 74
"CHIKUWA" USED TO BE CALLED "KAMABOKO" IN THE OLD DAYS.
HANZO'S TRIVIA

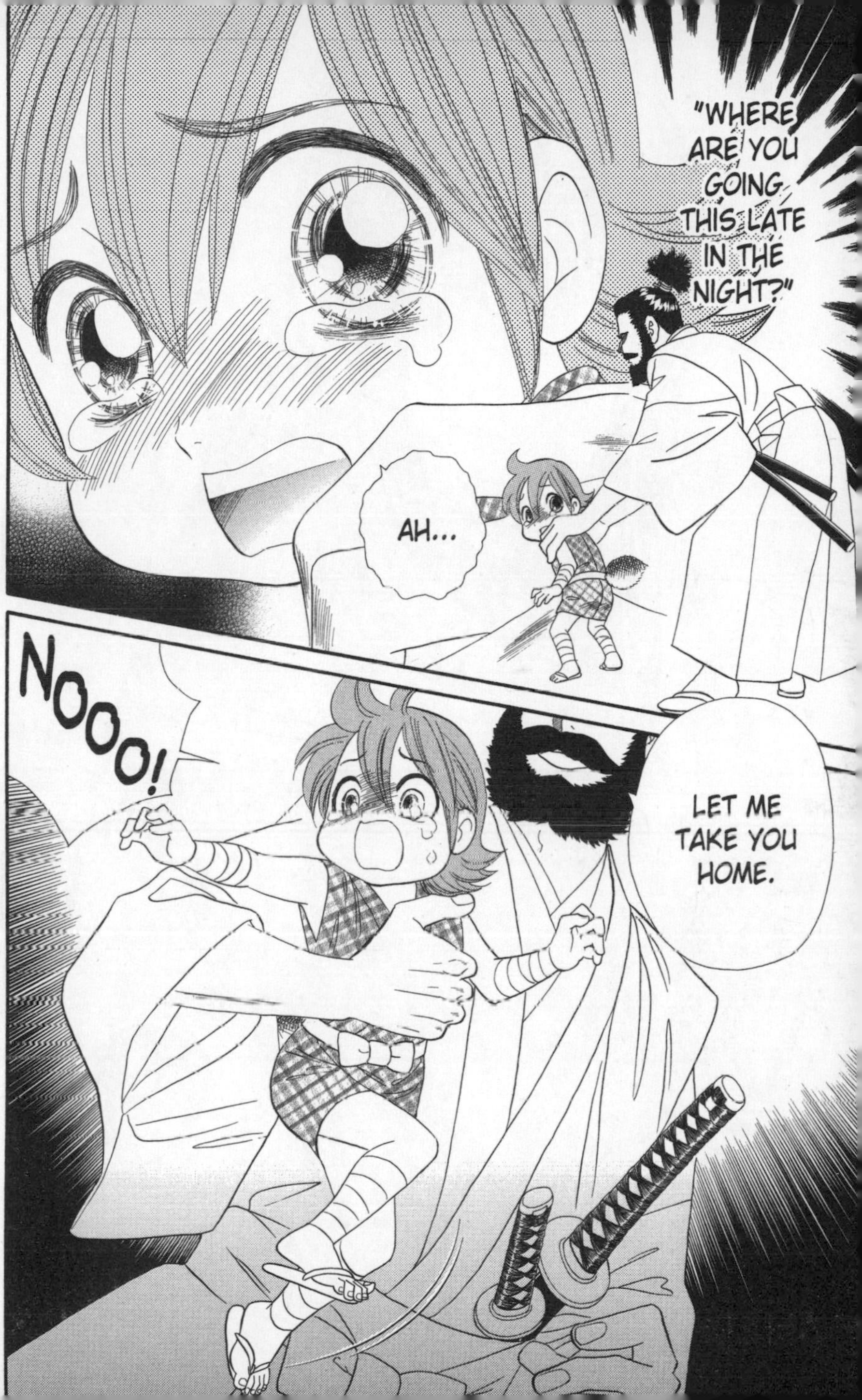
"WHERE ARE YOU GOING THIS LATE IN THE NIGHT?"
AH...
LET ME TAKE YOU HOME.
NOOO!

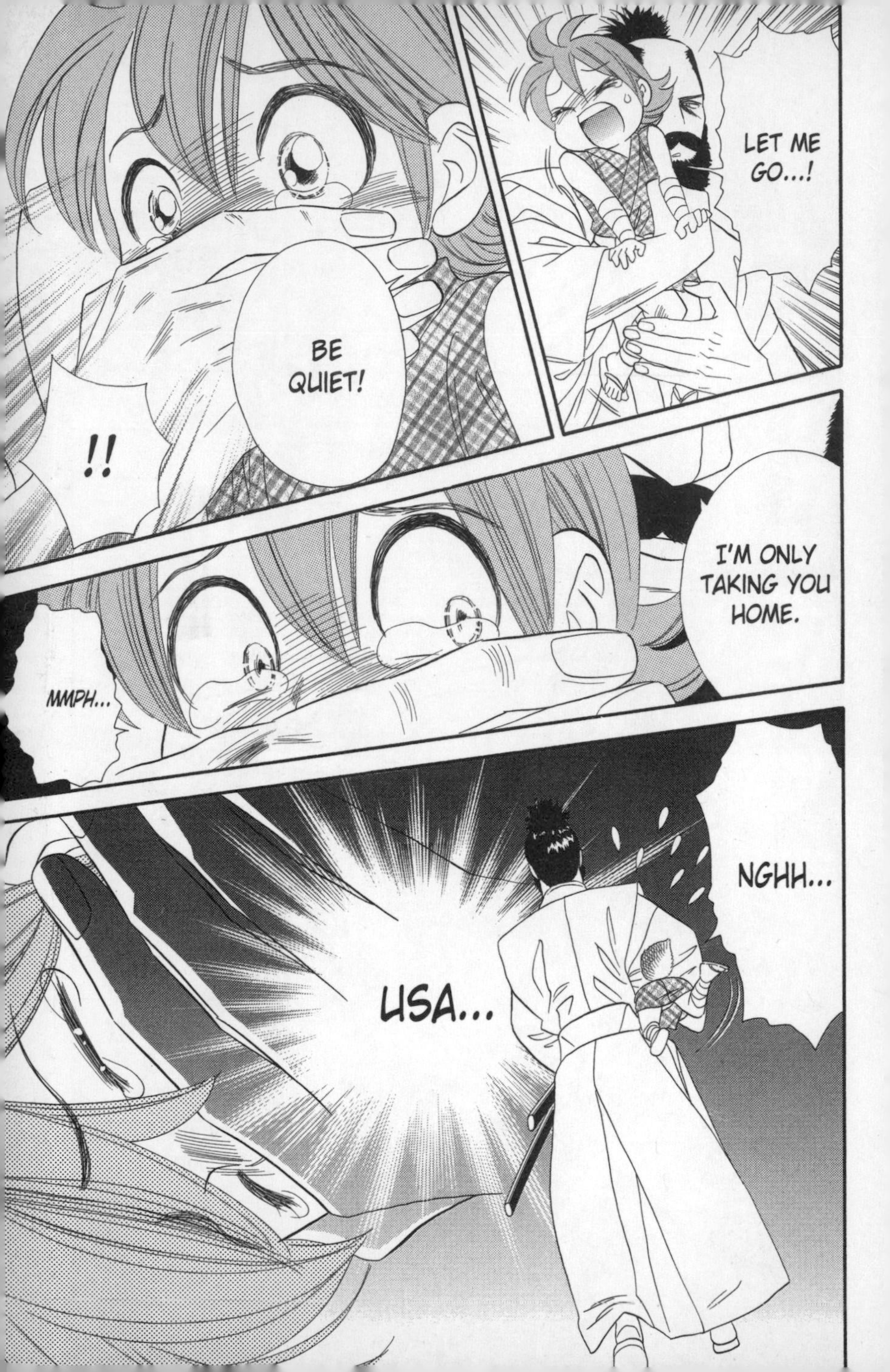
LET ME GO...!
BE QUIET!
!!
I'M ONLY TAKING YOU HOME.
MMPH...
NGHH...
USA...

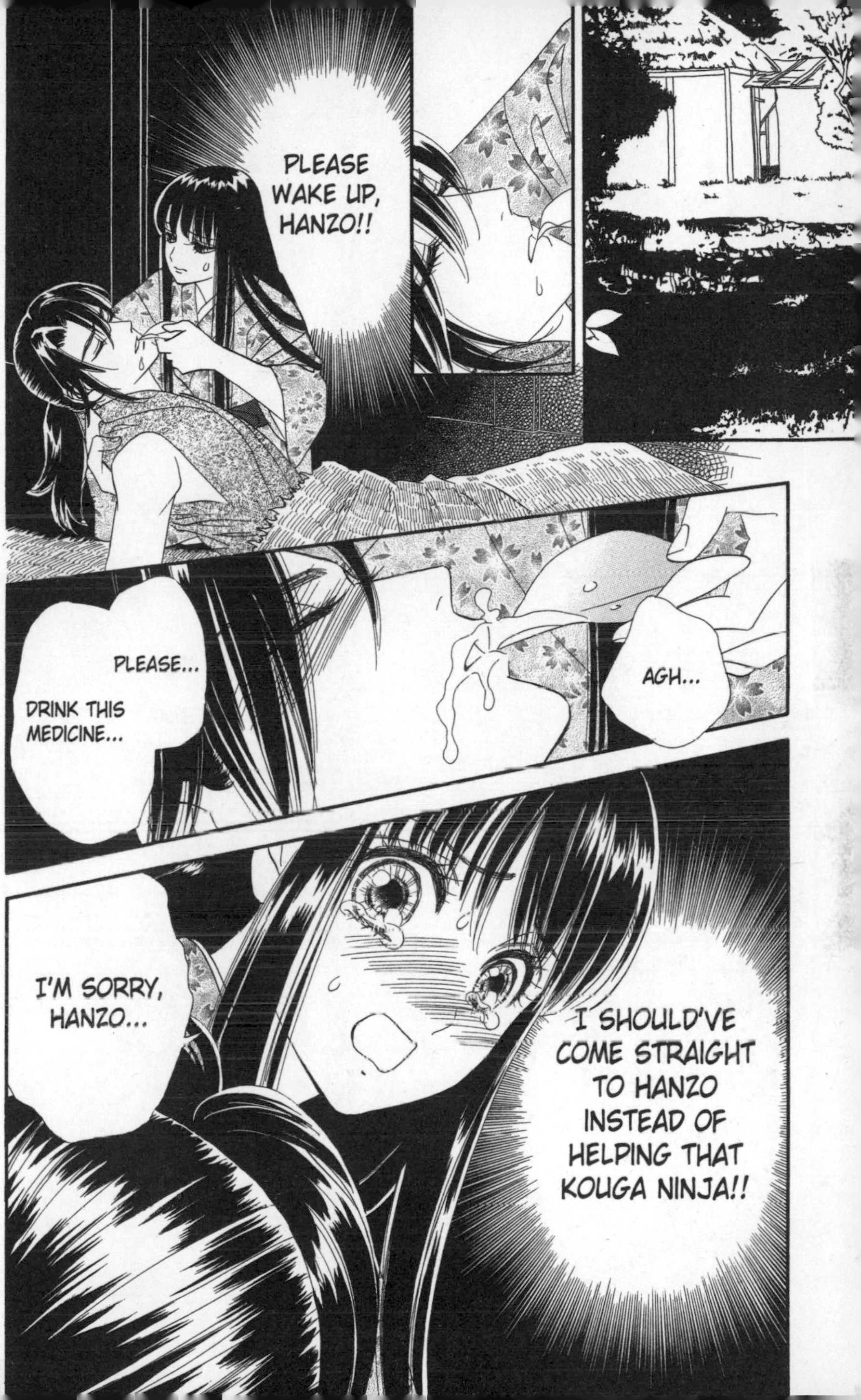
PLEASE WAKE UP, HANZO!!
AGH...
PLEASE...
DRINK THIS MEDICINE...
I SHOULD'VE COME STRAIGHT TO HANZO INSTEAD OF HELPING THAT KOUGA NINJA!!
I'M SORRY, HANZO...

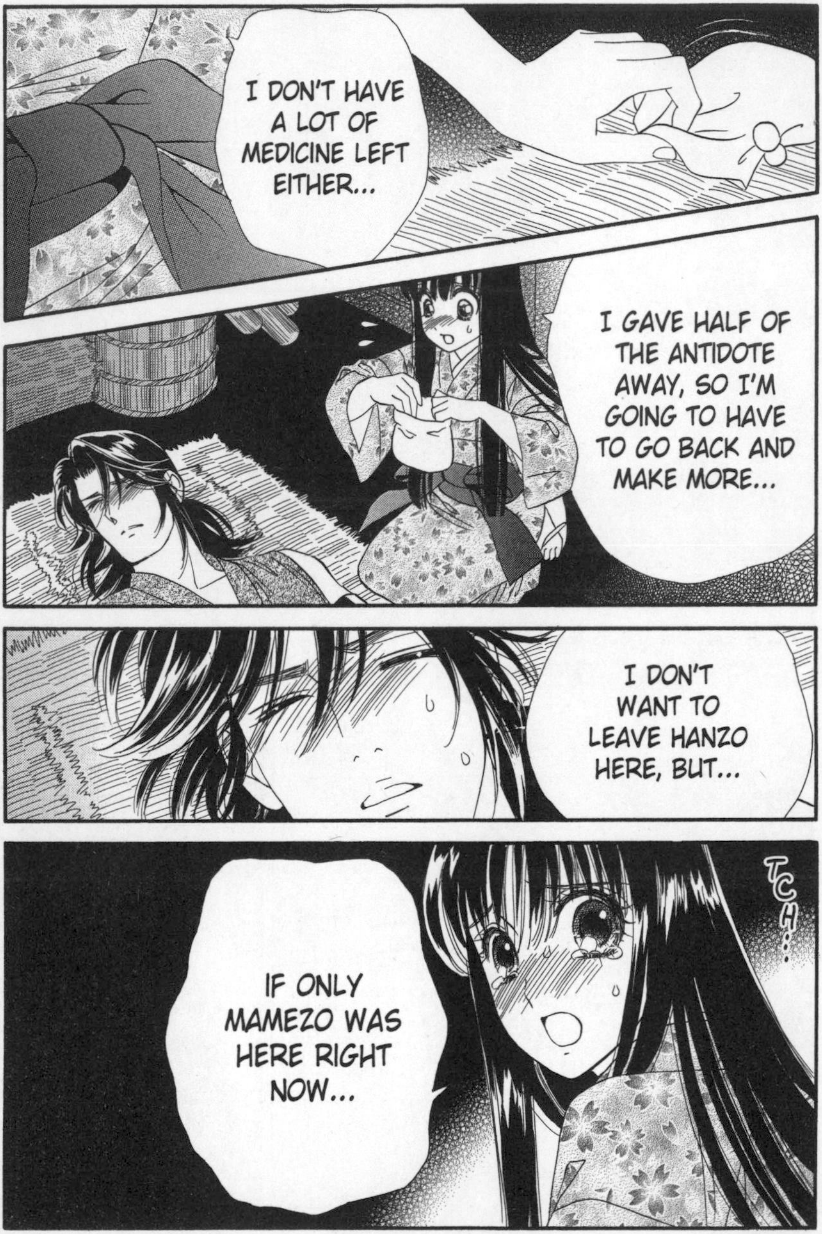
I DON'T HAVE A LOT OF MEDICINE LEFT EITHER...
I GAVE HALF OF THE ANTIDOTE AWAY, SO I'M GOING TO HAVE TO GO BACK AND MAKE MORE...
I DON'T WANT TO LEAVE HANZO HERE, BUT...
TCH...
IF ONLY MAMEZO WAS HERE RIGHT NOW...

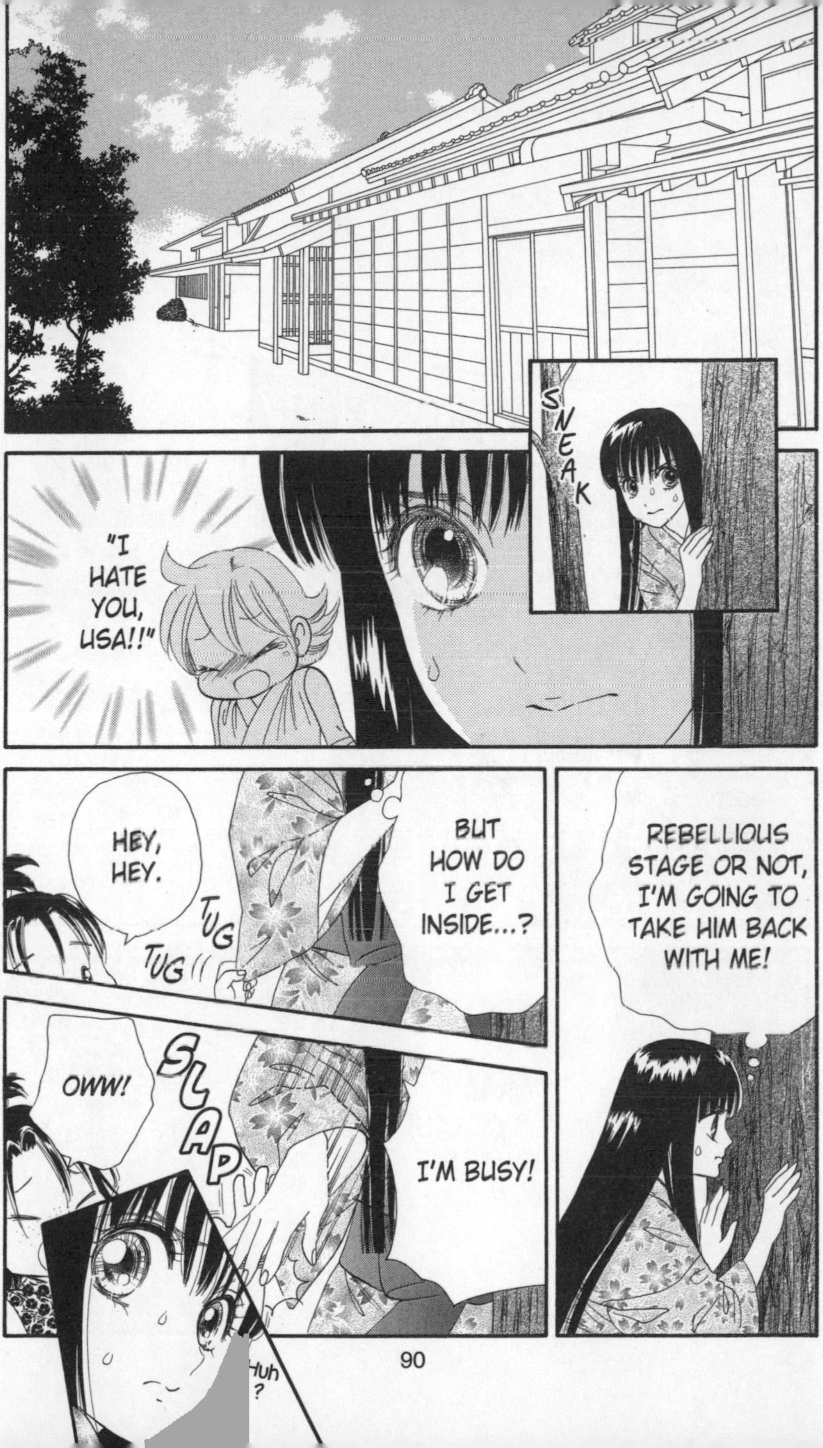
SNEAK
"I HATE YOU, USA!!"
REBELLIOUS STAGE OR NOT, I'M GOING TO TAKE HIM BACK WITH ME!
BUT HOW DO I GET INSIDE...?
HEY, HEY.
TUG TUG
I'M BUSY!
SLAP
OWW!
Huh?

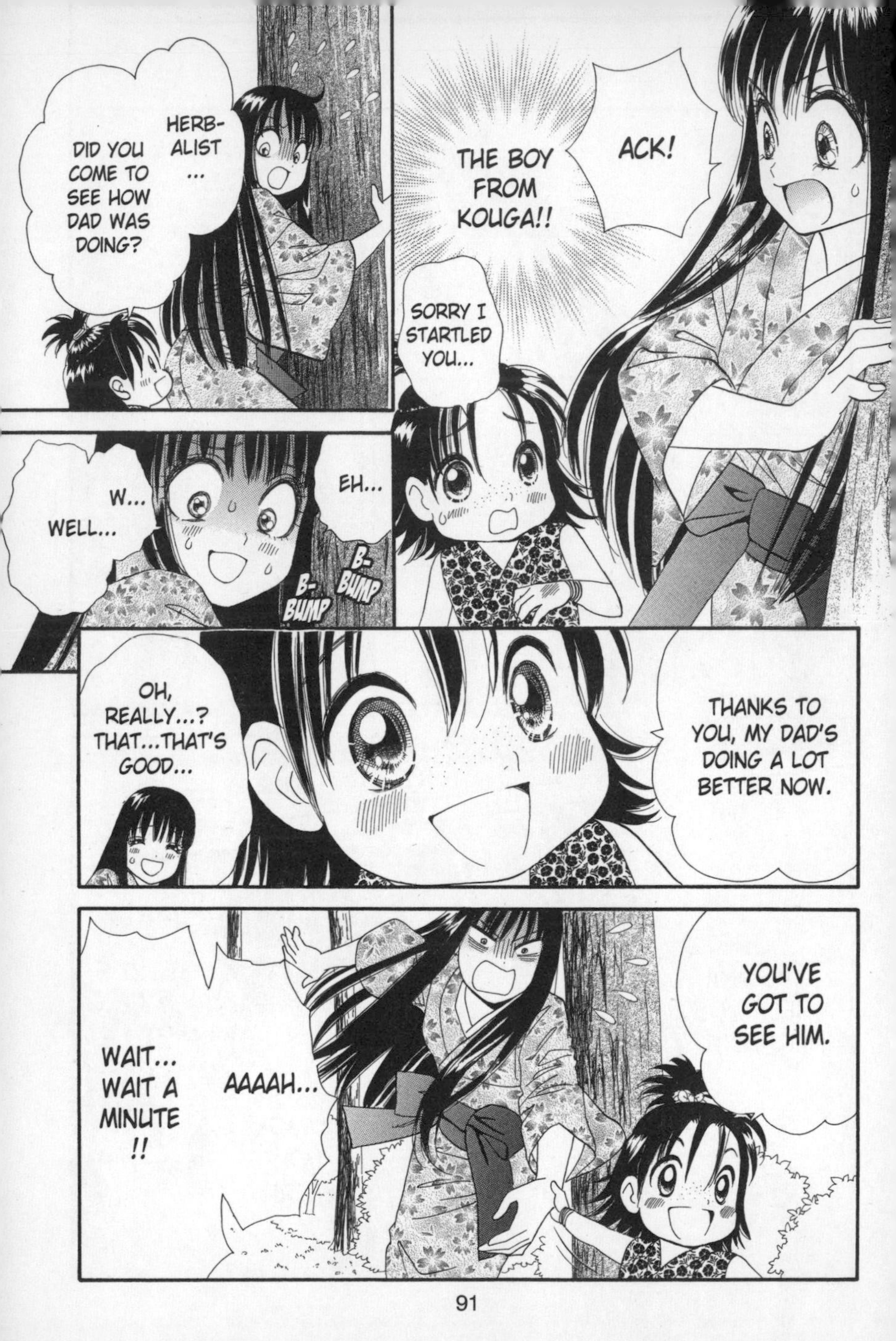
ACK!
THE BOY FROM KOUGA!!
SORRY I STARTLED YOU...
HERB-ALIST ...
DID YOU COME TO SEE HOW DAD WAS DOING?
EH...
W... WELL...
B-BUMP
B-BUMP
THANKS TO YOU, MY DAD'S DOING A LOT BETTER NOW.
OH, REALLY...? THAT...THAT'S GOOD...
YOU'VE GOT TO SEE HIM.
AAAAH...
WAIT... WAIT A MINUTE !!

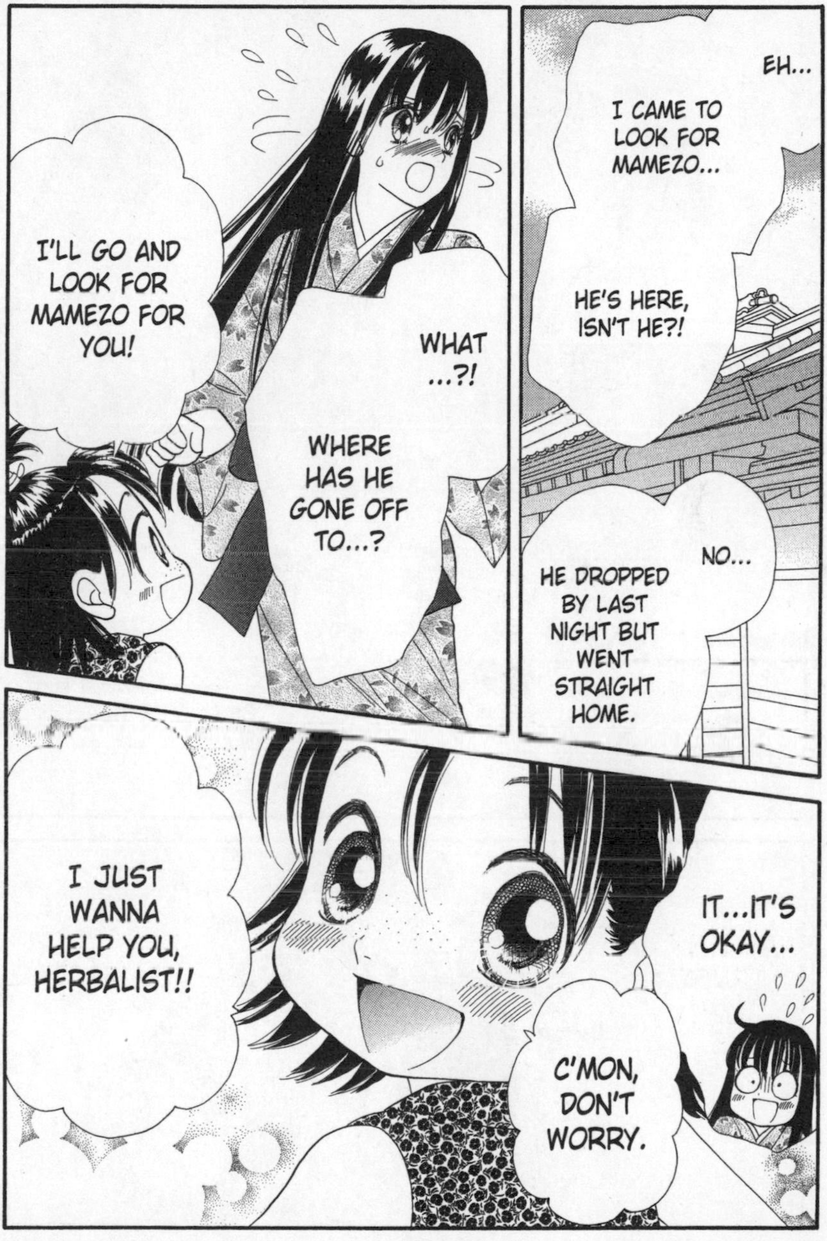
EH...
I CAME TO LOOK FOR MAMEZO...
HE'S HERE, ISN'T HE?!
NO...
HE DROPPED BY LAST NIGHT BUT WENT STRAIGHT HOME.
WHAT ...?!
WHERE HAS HE GONE OFF TO...?
I'LL GO AND LOOK FOR MAMEZO FOR YOU!
IT...IT'S OKAY...
C'MON, DON'T WORRY.
I JUST WANNA HELP YOU, HERBALIST!!

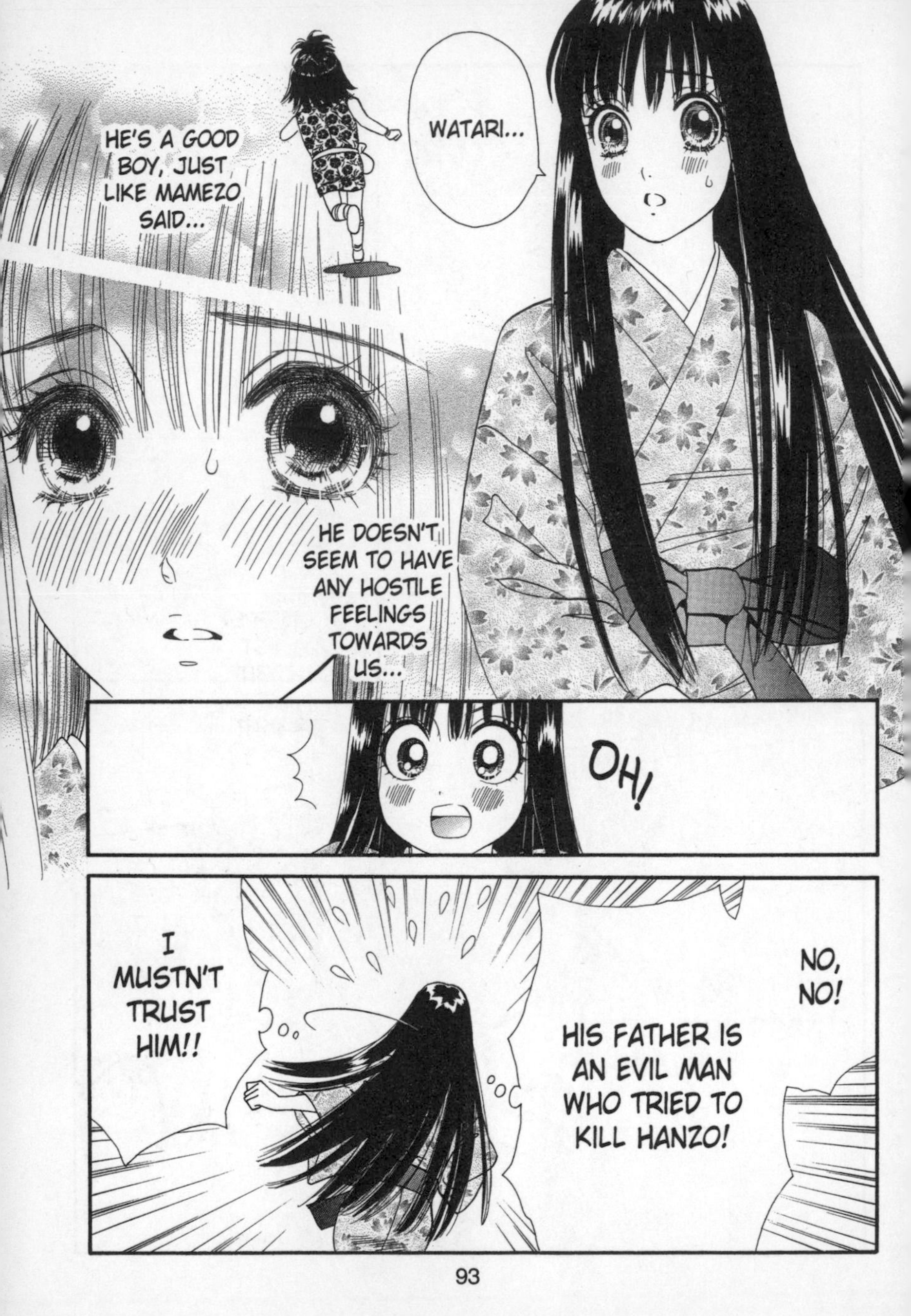
WATARI...
HE'S A GOOD BOY, JUST LIKE MAMEZO SAID...
HE DOESN'T SEEM TO HAVE ANY HOSTILE FEELINGS TOWARDS US...
OH!
NO, NO!
HIS FATHER IS AN EVIL MAN WHO TRIED TO KILL HANZO!
I MUSTN'T TRUST HIM!!

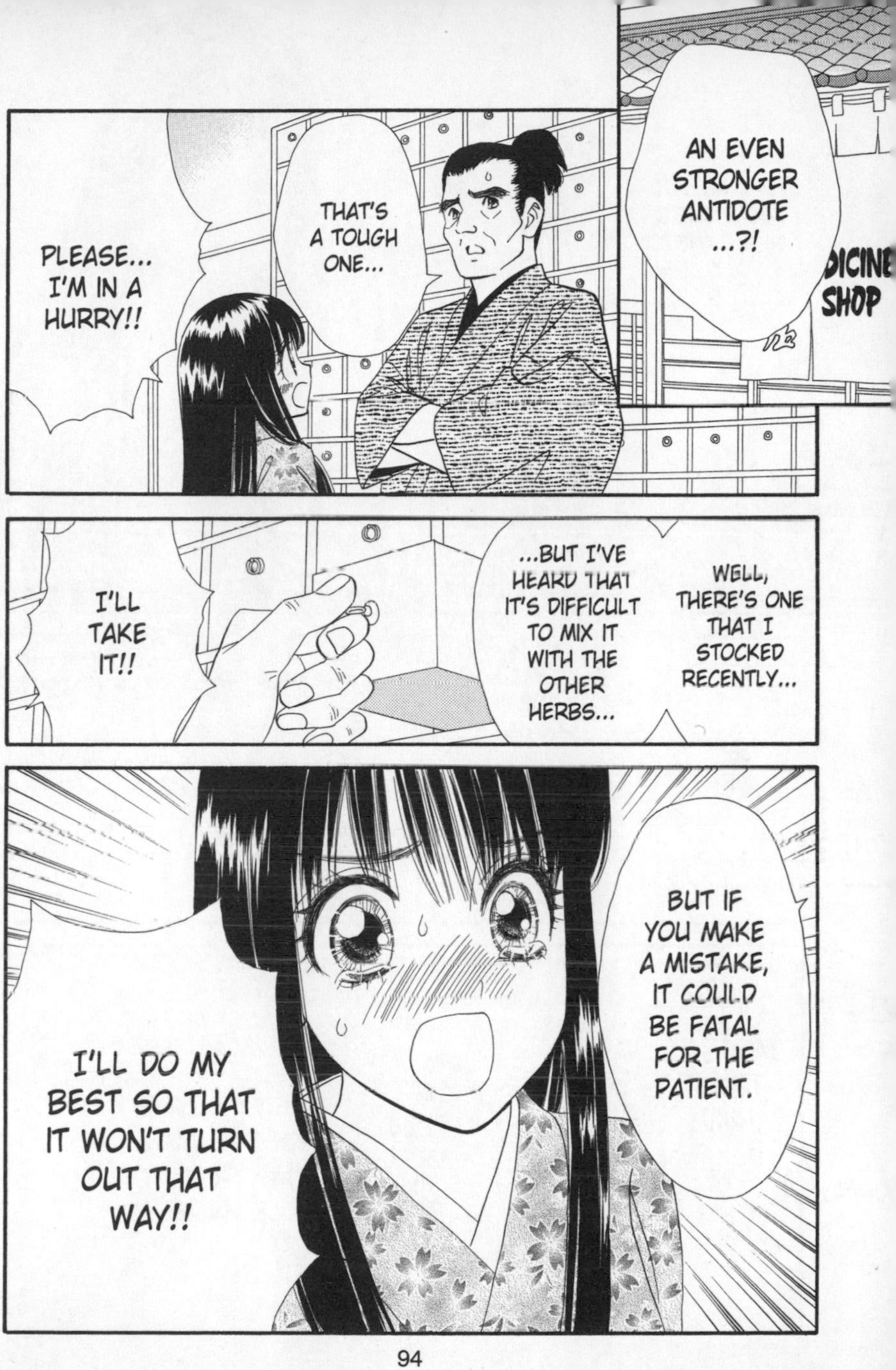
AN EVEN STRONGER ANTIDOTE ...?!
DICINE SHOP
THAT'S A TOUGH ONE...
PLEASE... I'M IN A HURRY!!
WELL, THERE'S ONE THAT I STOCKED RECENTLY...
...BUT I'VE HEARD THAT IT'S DIFFICULT TO MIX IT WITH THE OTHER HERBS...
I'LL TAKE IT!!
BUT IF YOU MAKE A MISTAKE, IT COULD BE FATAL FOR THE PATIENT.
I'LL DO MY BEST SO THAT IT WON'T TURN OUT THAT WAY!!

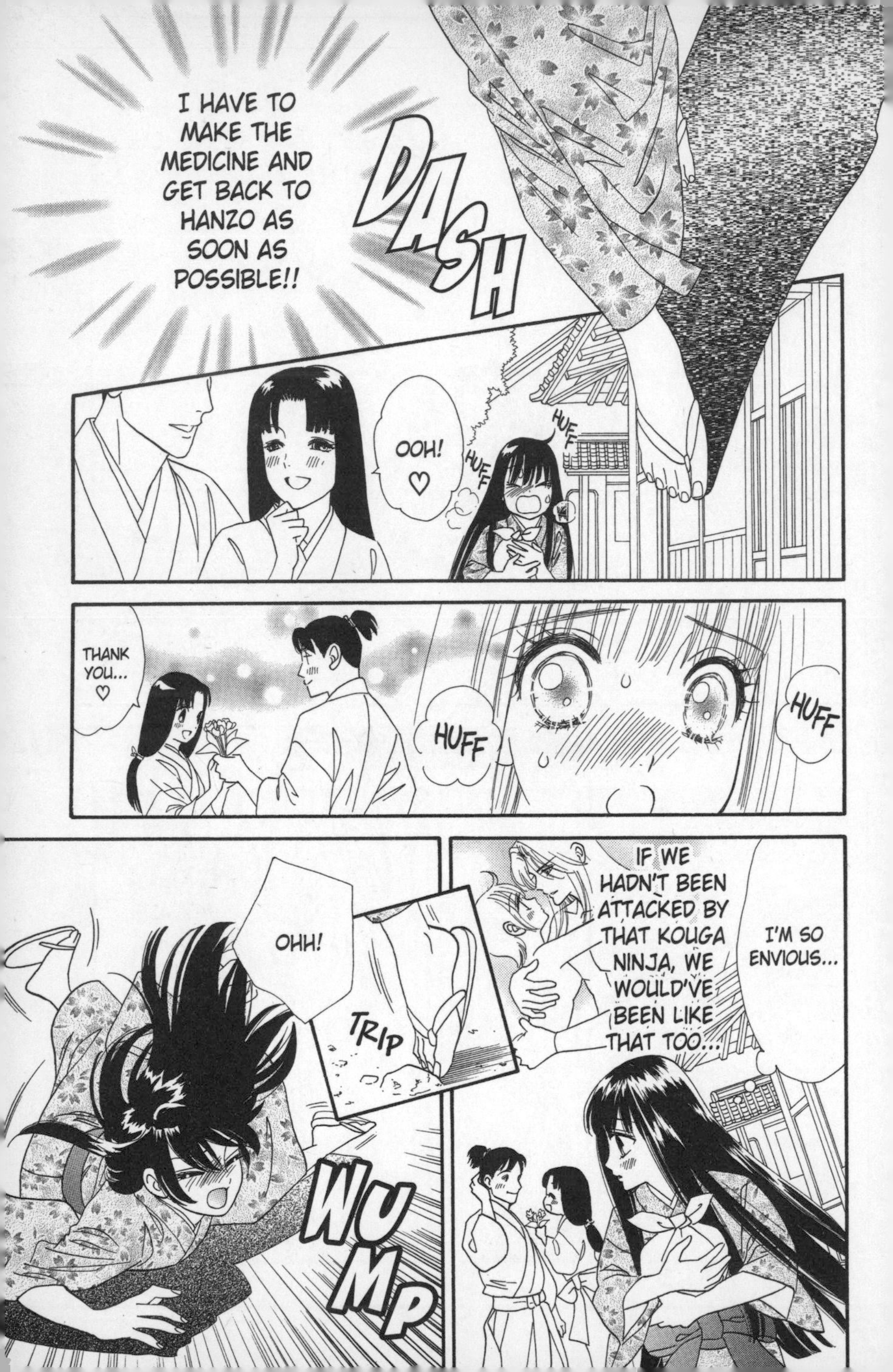

I HAVE TO MAKE THE MEDICINE AND GET BACK TO HANZO AS SOON AS POSSIBLE!!
DASH
HUFF
HUFF
OOH! ♡
HUFF
HUFF
THANK YOU... ♡
I'M SO ENVIOUS...
IF WE HADN'T BEEN ATTACKED BY THAT KOUGA NINJA, WE WOULD'VE BEEN LIKE THAT TOO...
OHH!
TRIP
WUMP

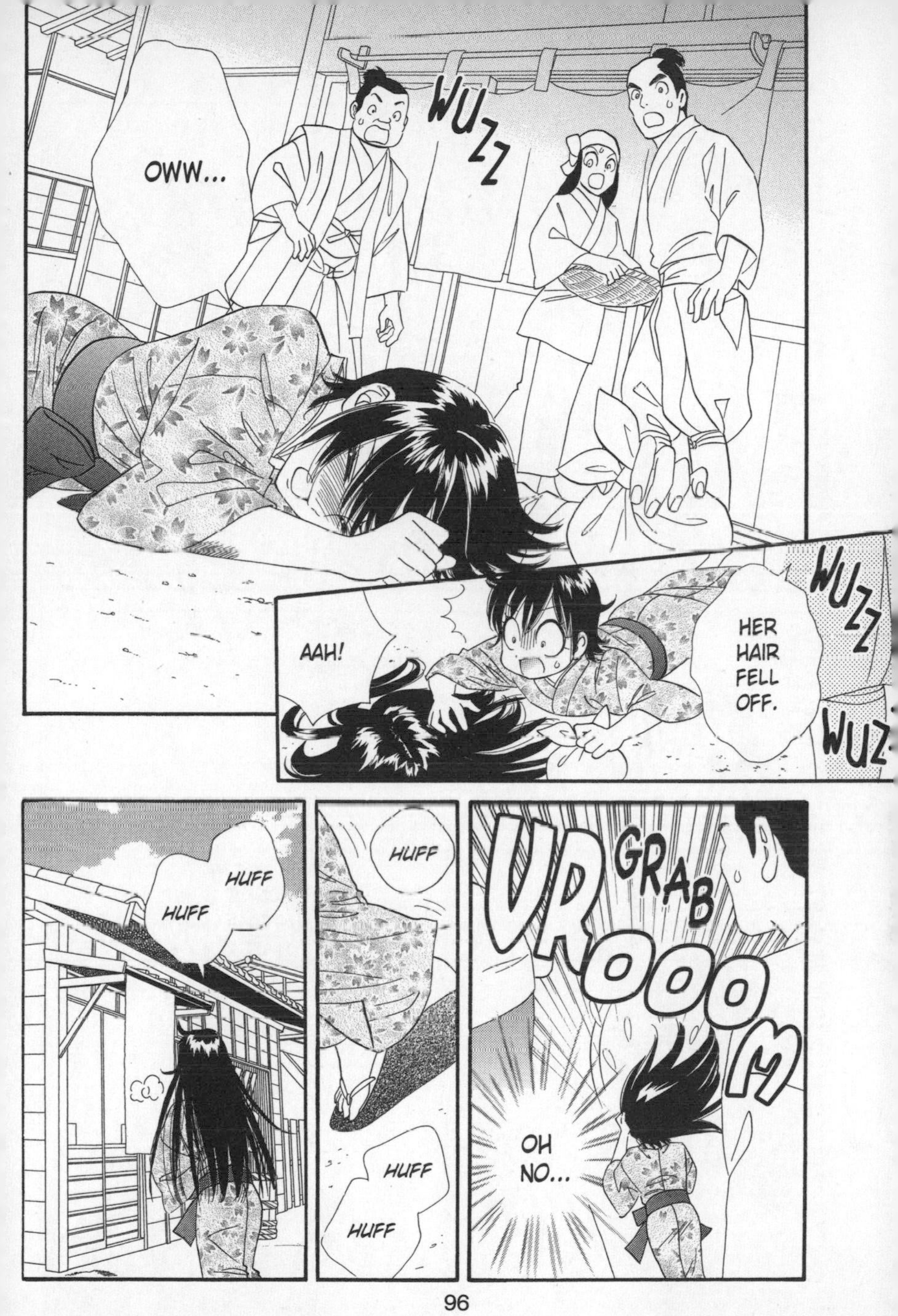
WUZZ
OWW...
WUZZ
HER HAIR FELL OFF.
WUZ
AAH!
UROOOOM
GRAB
OH NO...
HUFF
HUFF
HUFF
HUFF
HUFF

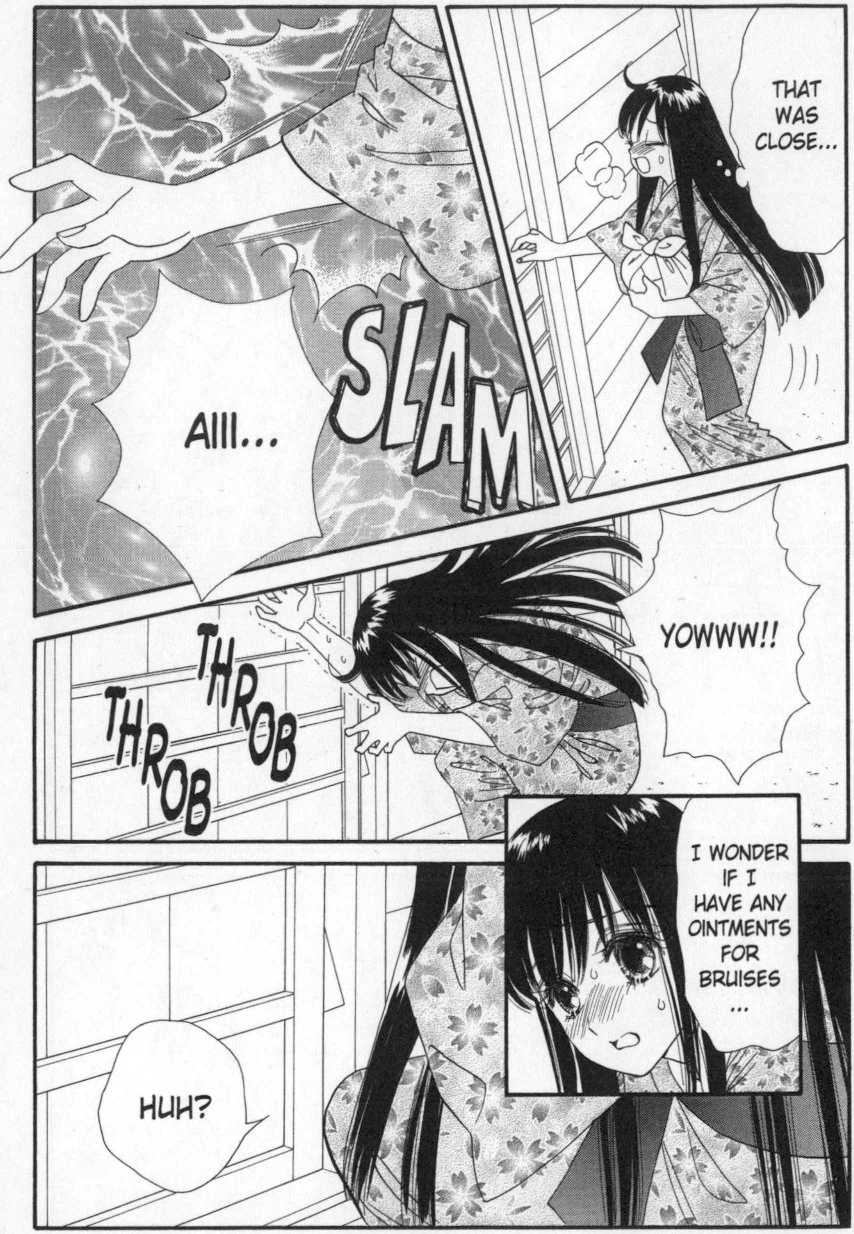
THAT WAS CLOSE...
SLAM
AIII...
YOWWW!!
THROB
THROB
I WONDER IF I HAVE ANY OINTMENTS FOR BRUISES ...
HUH?

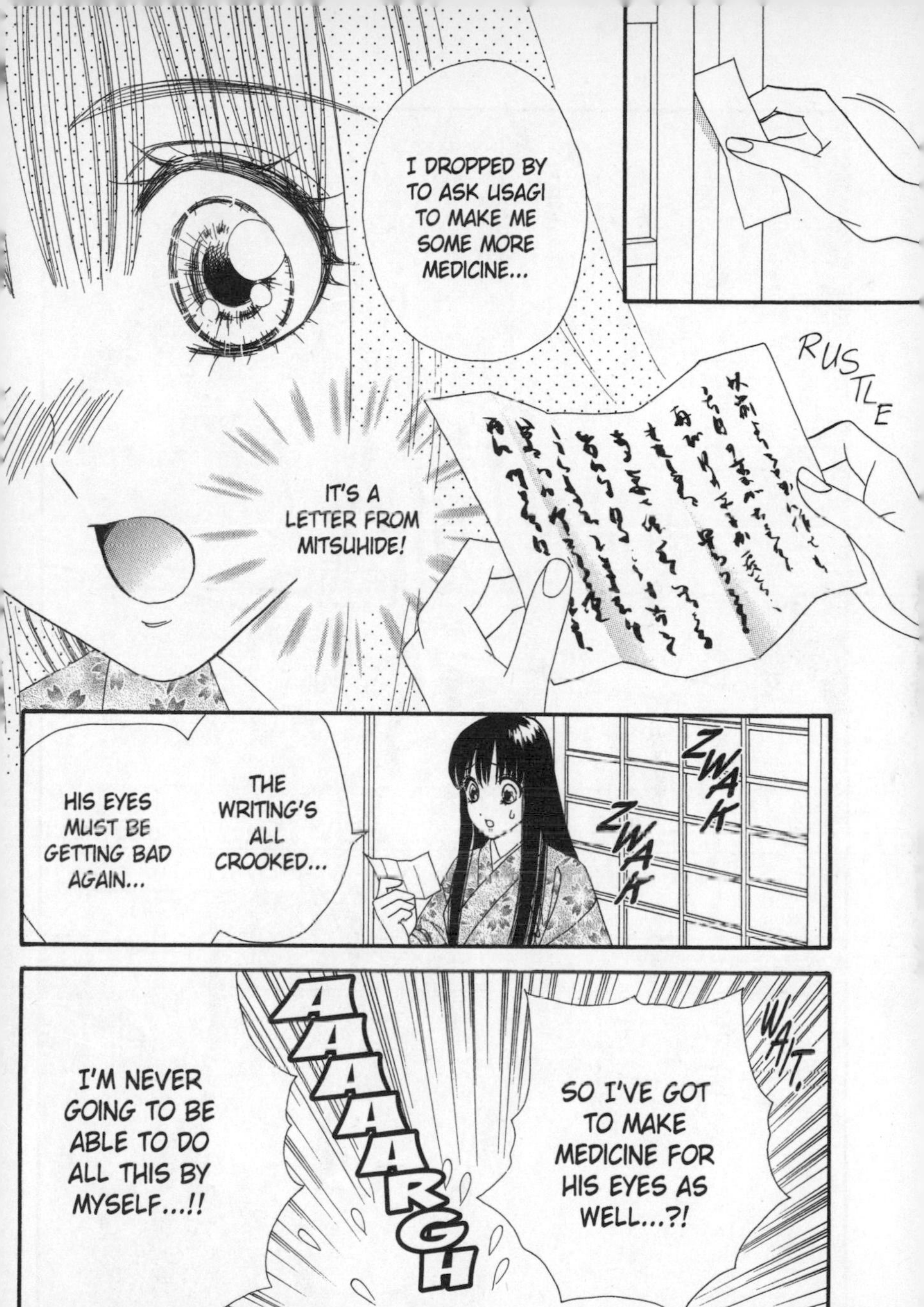

I DROPPED BY TO ASK USAGI TO MAKE ME SOME MORE MEDICINE...
RUSTLE
IT'S A LETTER FROM MITSUHIDE!
ZWAK ZWAK
THE WRITING'S ALL CROOKED...
HIS EYES MUST BE GETTING BAD AGAIN...
WAIT.
SO I'VE GOT TO MAKE MEDICINE FOR HIS EYES AS WELL...?!
AAAAARGH
I'M NEVER GOING TO BE ABLE TO DO ALL THIS BY MYSELF...!!

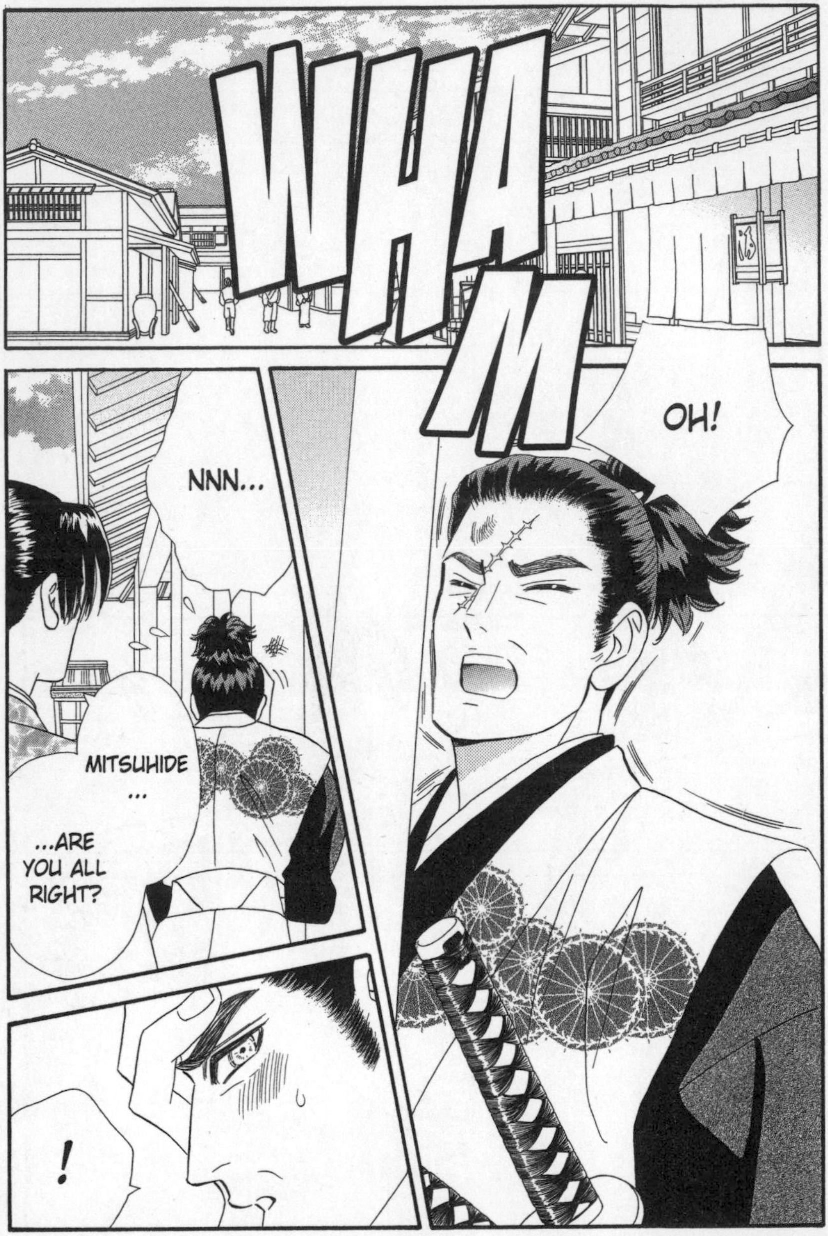
WHAM
OH!
NNN...
MITSUHIDE ...
...ARE YOU ALL RIGHT?
!

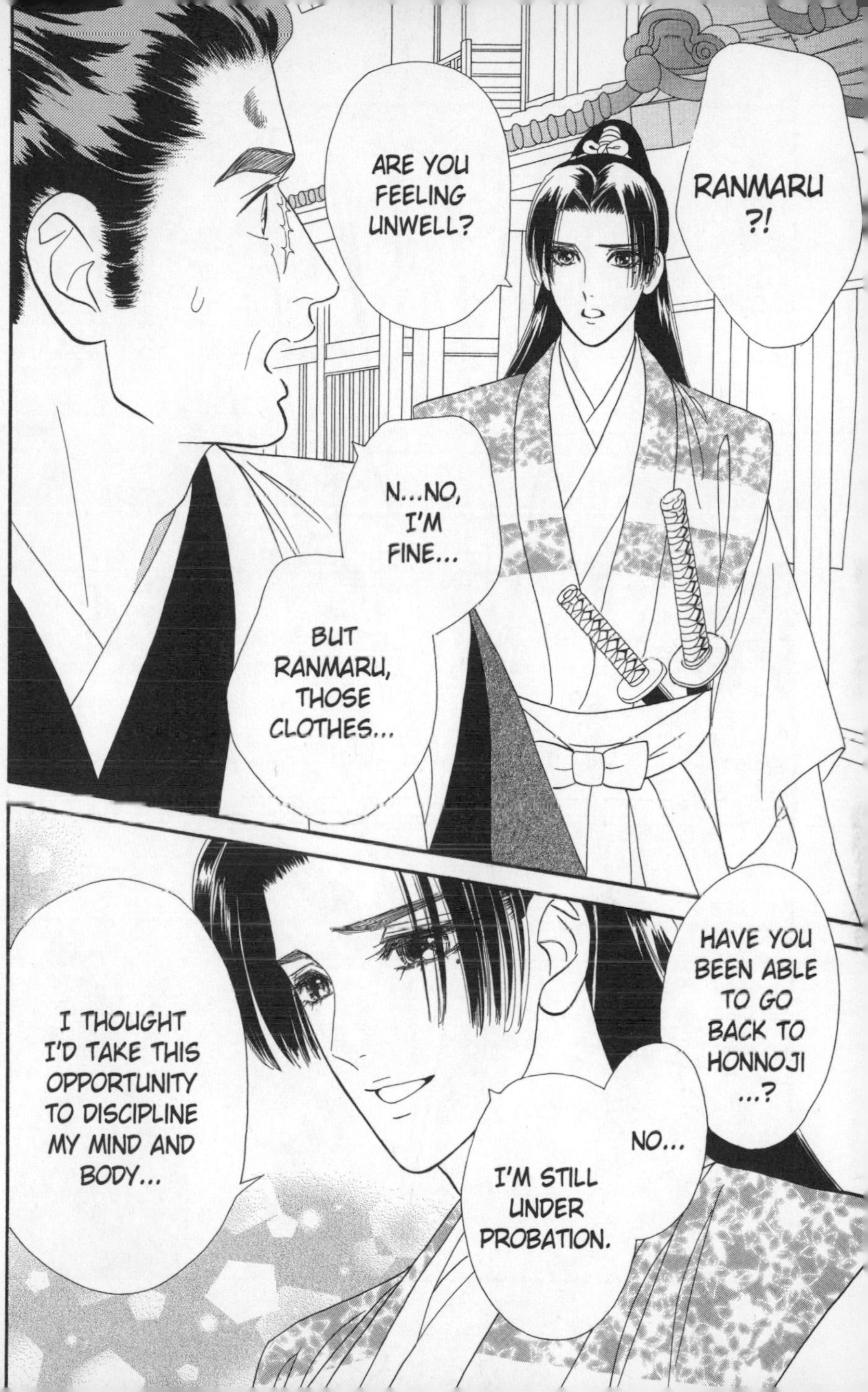
RANMARU ?!
ARE YOU FEELING UNWELL?
N...NO, I'M FINE...
BUT RANMARU, THOSE CLOTHES...
HAVE YOU BEEN ABLE TO GO BACK TO HONNOJI ...?
NO...
I'M STILL UNDER PROBATION.
I THOUGHT I'D TAKE THIS OPPORTUNITY TO DISCIPLINE MY MIND AND BODY...

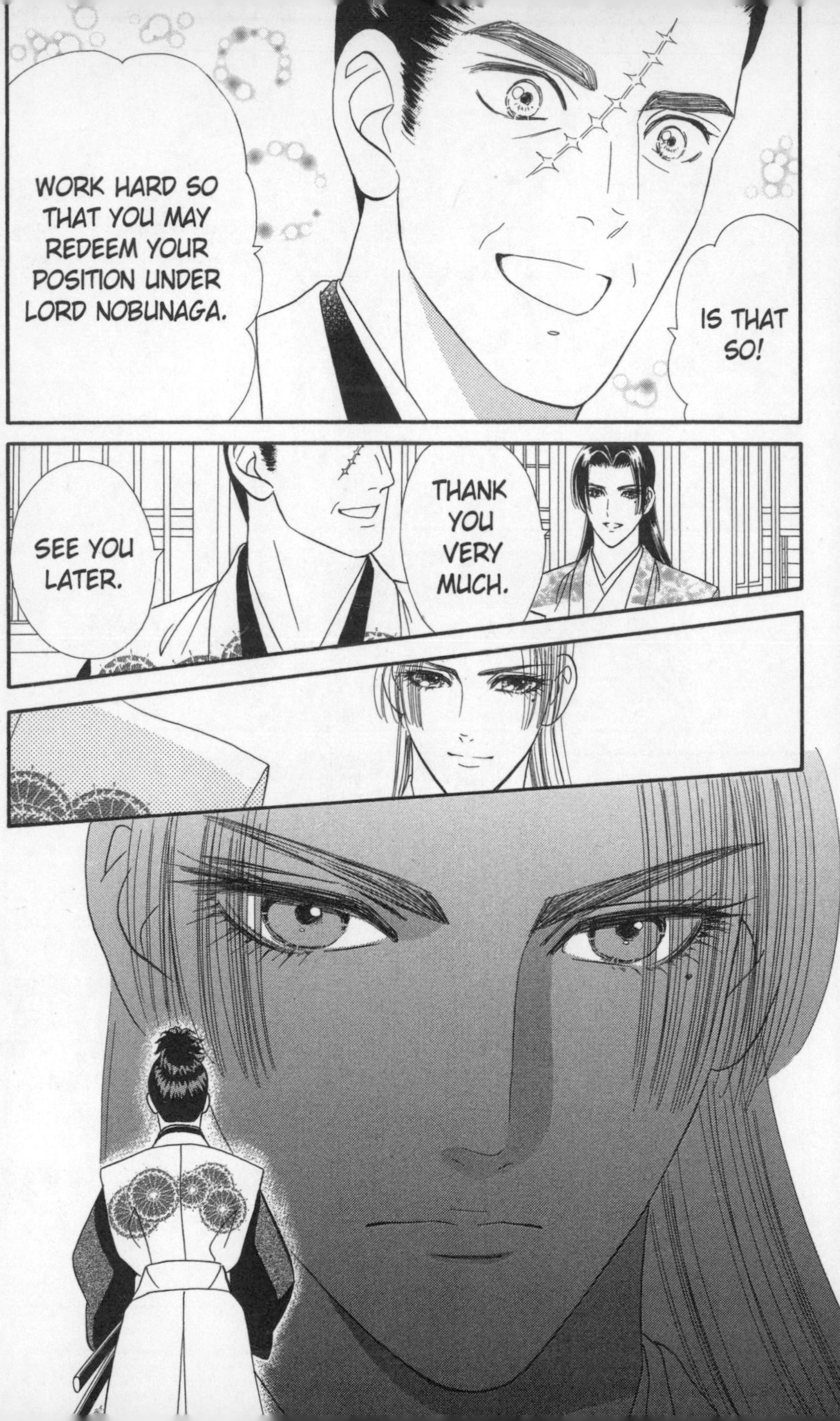
WORK HARD SO THAT YOU MAY REDEEM YOUR POSITION UNDER LORD NOBUNAGA.
IS THAT SO!
THANK YOU VERY MUCH.
SEE YOU LATER.

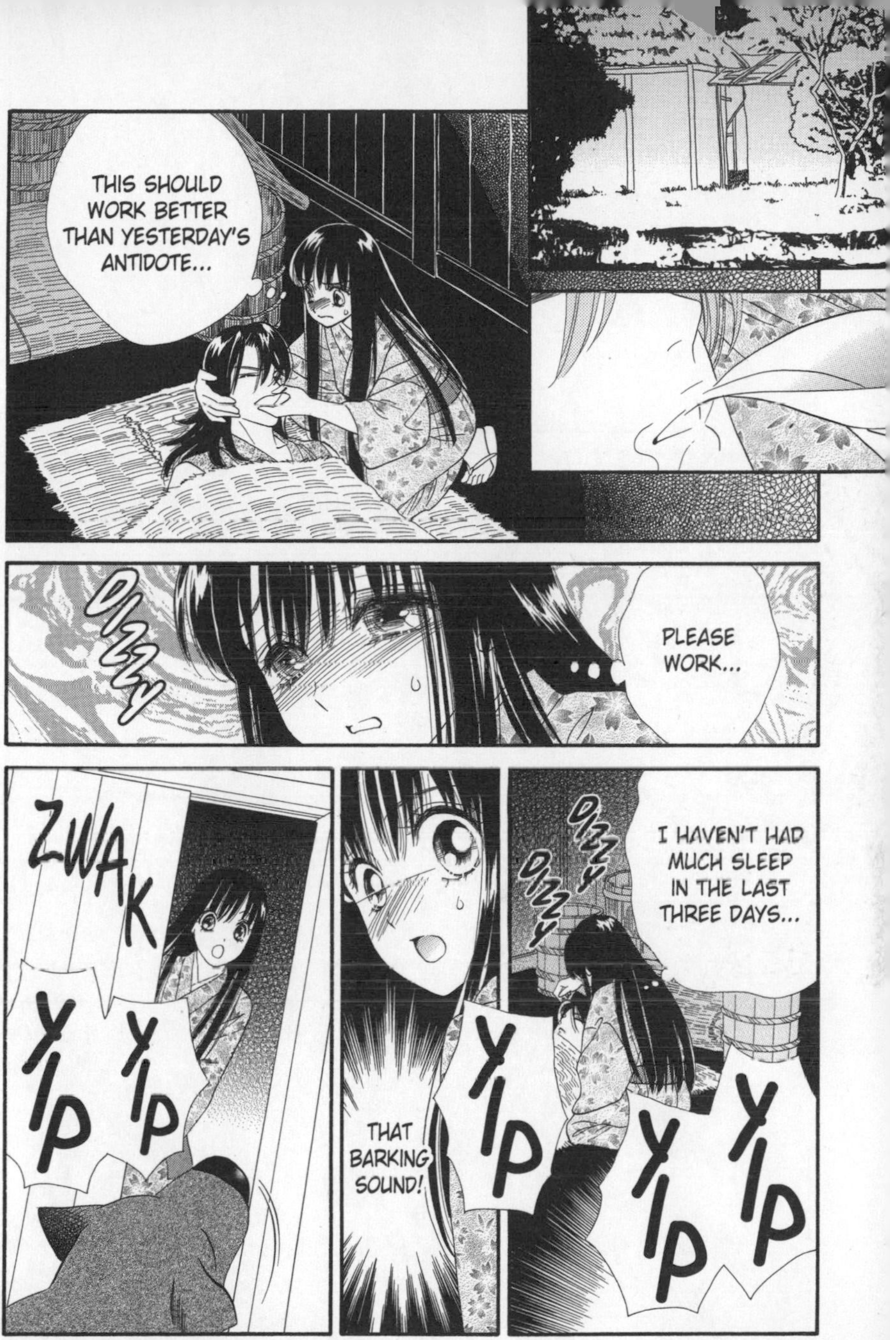
THIS SHOULD WORK BETTER THAN YESTERDAY'S ANTIDOTE...
PLEASE WORK...
DIZZY
I HAVEN'T HAD MUCH SLEEP IN THE LAST THREE DAYS...
DIZZY
DIZZY
YIP
YIP
YIP
YIP
THAT BARKING SOUND!
ZWAK
YIP
YIP

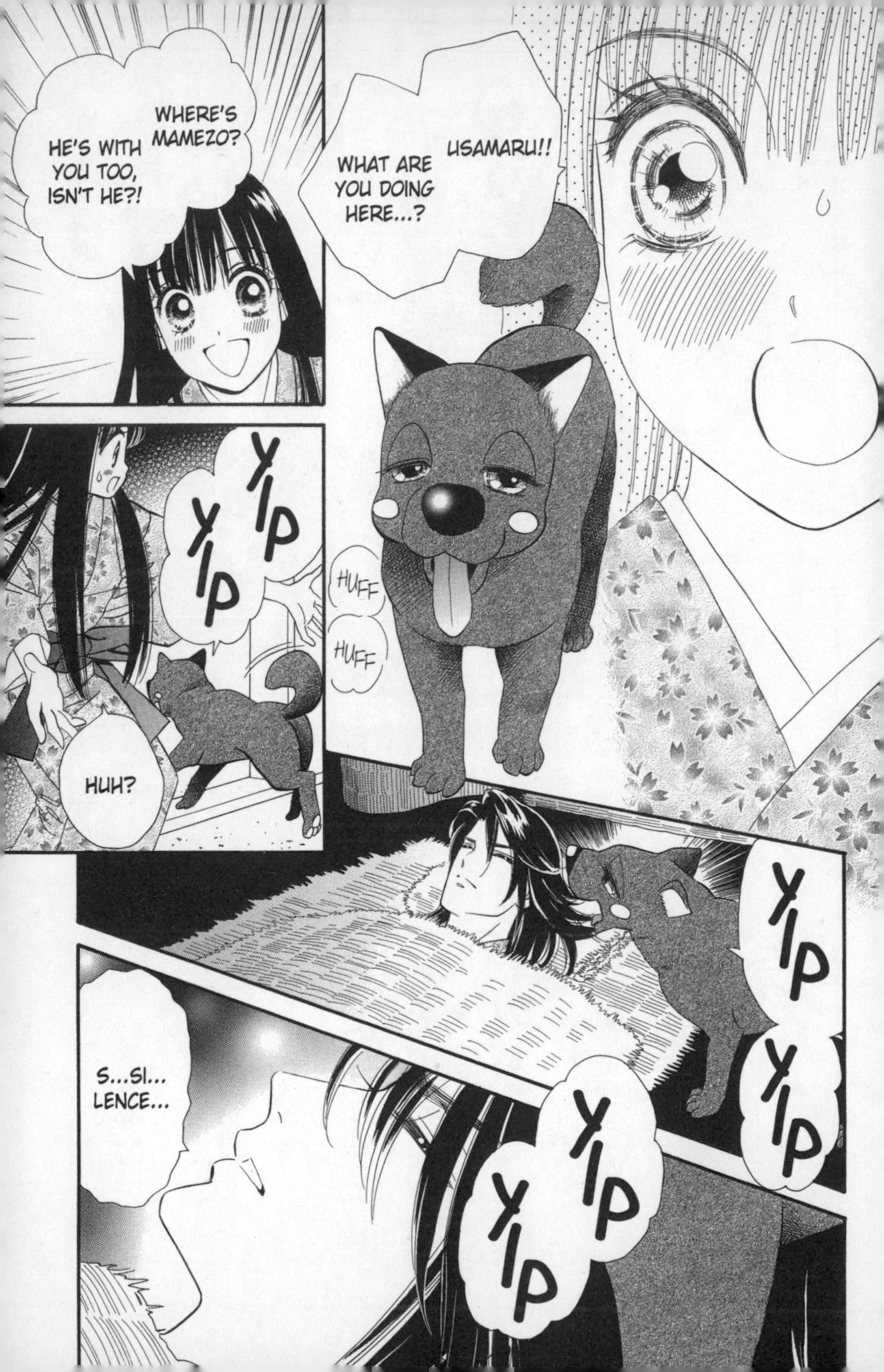
USAMARU!!
WHAT ARE YOU DOING HERE...?
HUFF
HUFF
WHERE'S MAMEZO?
HE'S WITH YOU TOO, ISN'T HE?!
YIP YIP
HUH?
YIP YIP
YIP YIP
S...SI... LENCE...

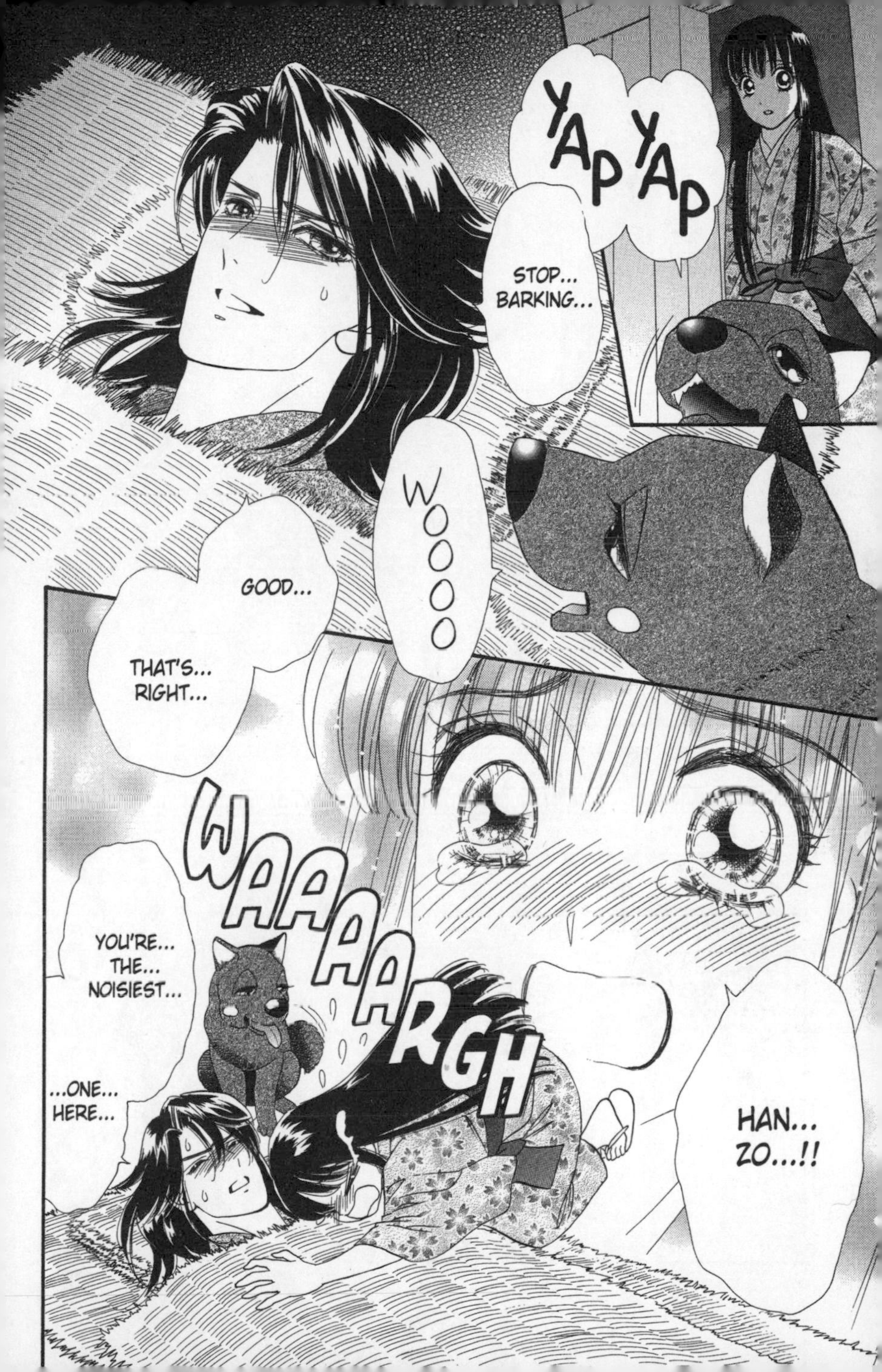
YAP YAP
STOP... BARKING...
WOOOOO
GOOD...
THAT'S... RIGHT...
HAN... ZO...!!
WAAAAARGH
YOU'RE... THE... NOISIEST...
...ONE... HERE...

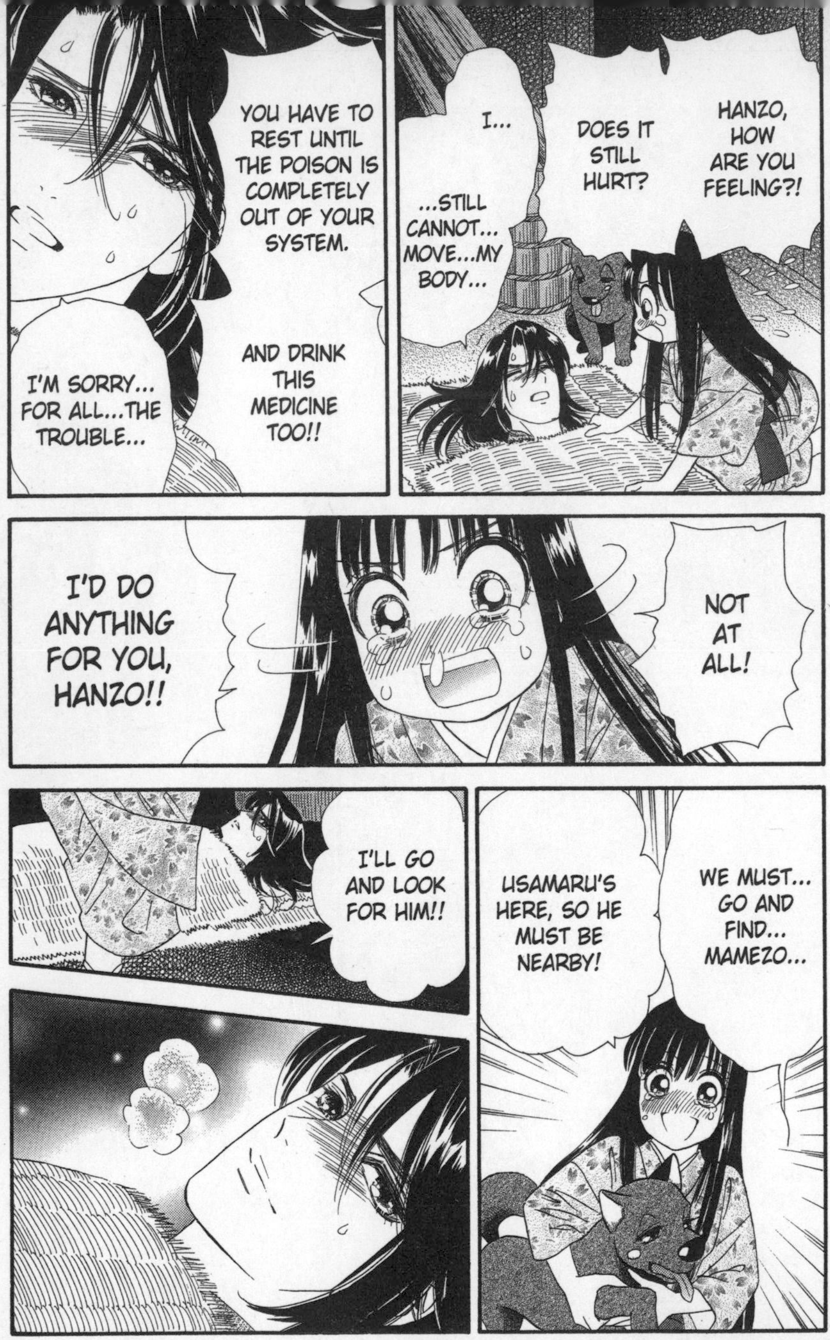
HANZO, HOW ARE YOU FEELING?!
DOES IT STILL HURT?
I...
...STILL CANNOT... MOVE...MY BODY...
YOU HAVE TO REST UNTIL THE POISON IS COMPLETELY OUT OF YOUR SYSTEM.
AND DRINK THIS MEDICINE TOO!!
I'M SORRY... FOR ALL...THE TROUBLE...
NOT AT ALL!
I'D DO ANYTHING FOR YOU, HANZO!!
WE MUST... GO AND FIND... MAMEZO...
USAMARU'S HERE, SO HE MUST BE NEARBY!
I'LL GO AND LOOK FOR HIM!!

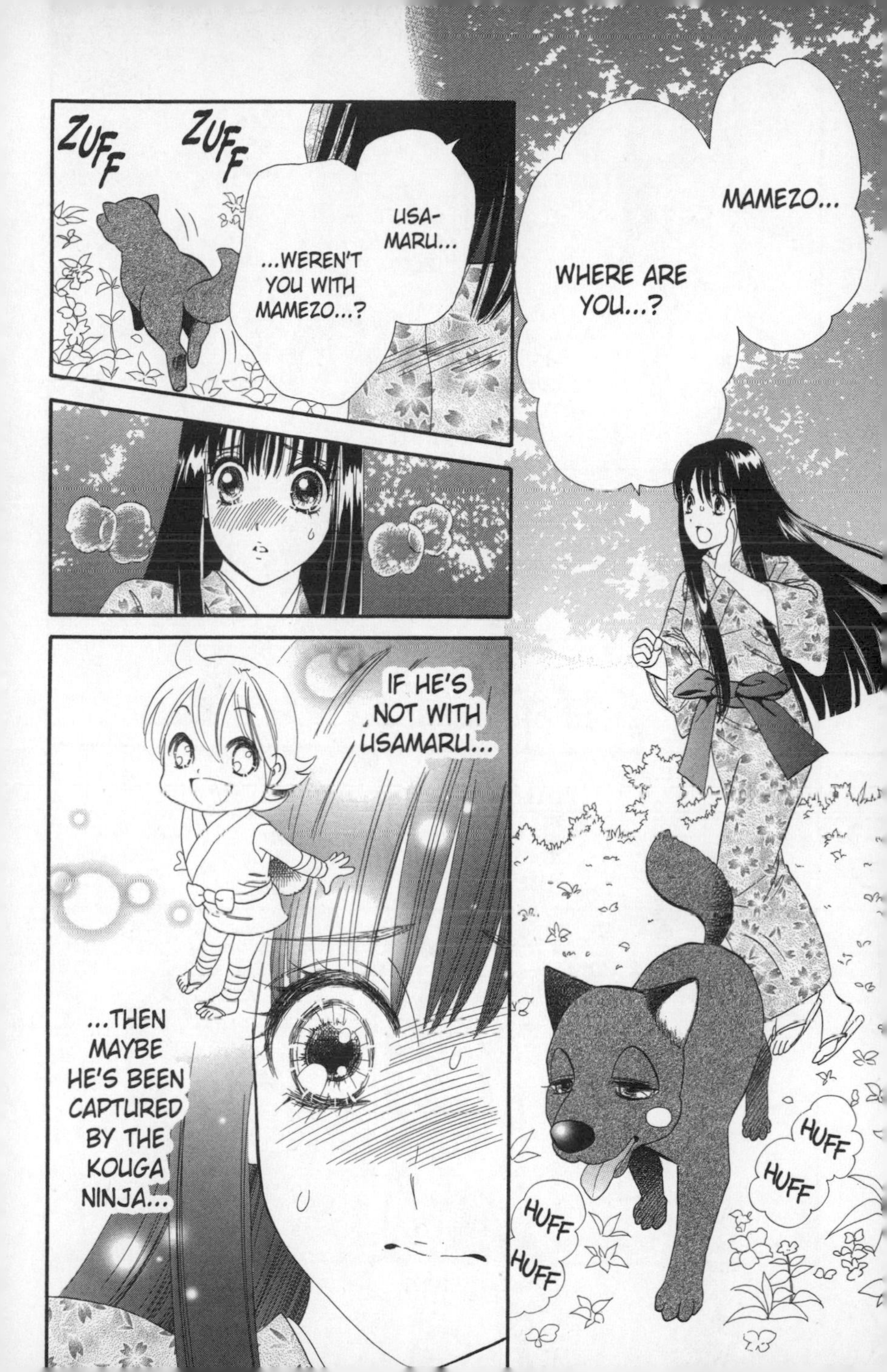
MAMEZO...
WHERE ARE YOU...?
HUFF
HUFF
HUFF
HUFF
ZUFF
ZUFF
USA-MARU...
...WEREN'T YOU WITH MAMEZO...?
IF HE'S NOT WITH USAMARU...
...THEN MAYBE HE'S BEEN CAPTURED BY THE KOUGA NINJA...

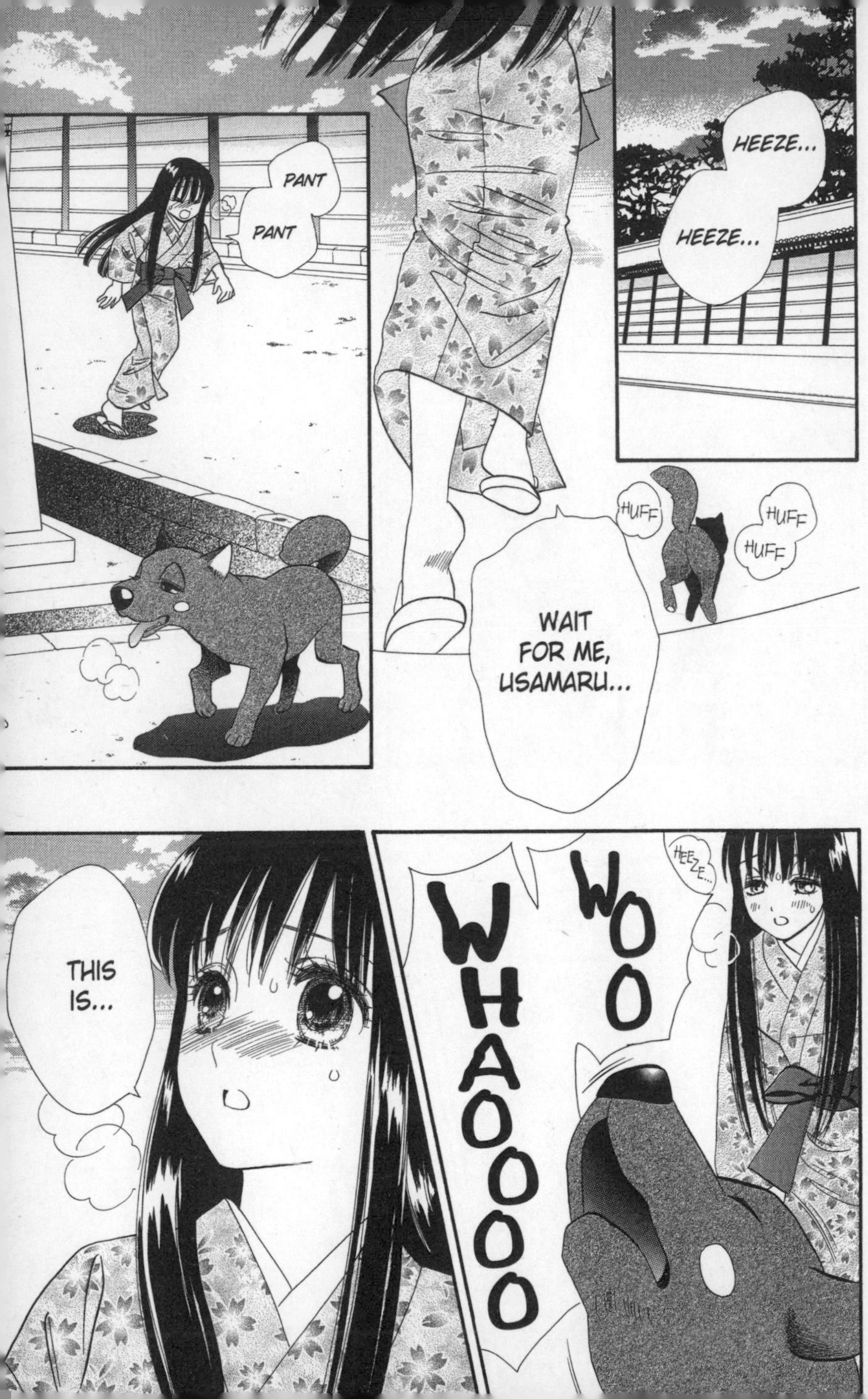
HEEZE...
HEEZE...
HUFF
HUFF
HUFF
WAIT FOR ME, USAMARU...
PANT
PANT
HEEZE...
WOO
WHAOOOOO
THIS IS...

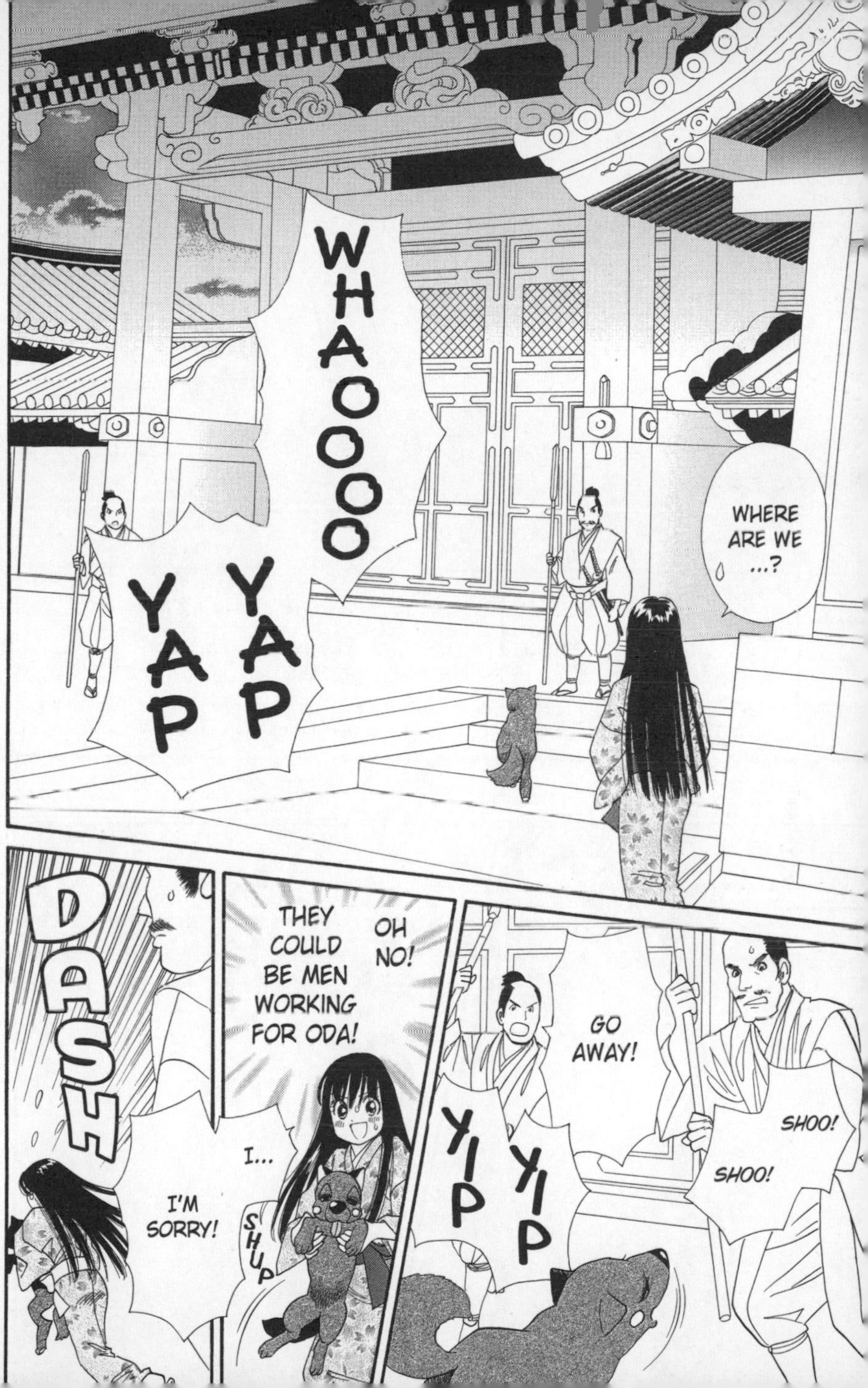
WHERE ARE WE ...?
WHAOOOO
YAP YAP
GO AWAY!
SHOO!
SHOO!
YIP YIP
OH NO!
THEY COULD BE MEN WORKING FOR ODA!
I...
I'M SORRY!
SHUP
DASH

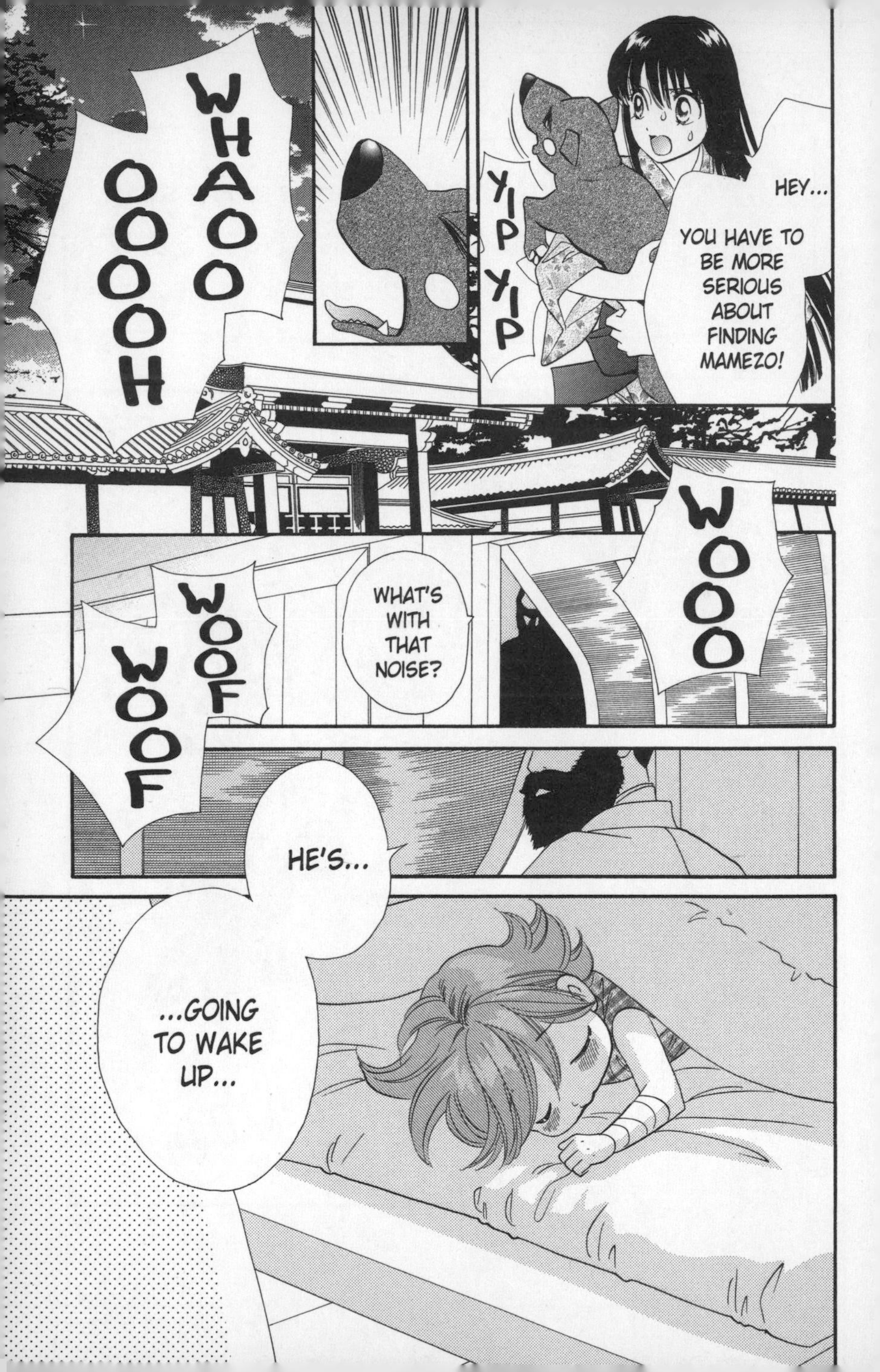
HEY...
YOU HAVE TO BE MORE SERIOUS ABOUT FINDING MAMEZO!
YIP YIP
WHAOOOOOOOH
WOOO
WHAT'S WITH THAT NOISE?
WOOF WOOF
HE'S...
...GOING TO WAKE UP...

TAIL OF THE MOON EXTRA: TODAY'S MISSION

"I WANT TO SEE USAGI AND HANZO'S VALENTINE'S DAY!"

-MICCHI, SHIZUOKA PREFECTURE

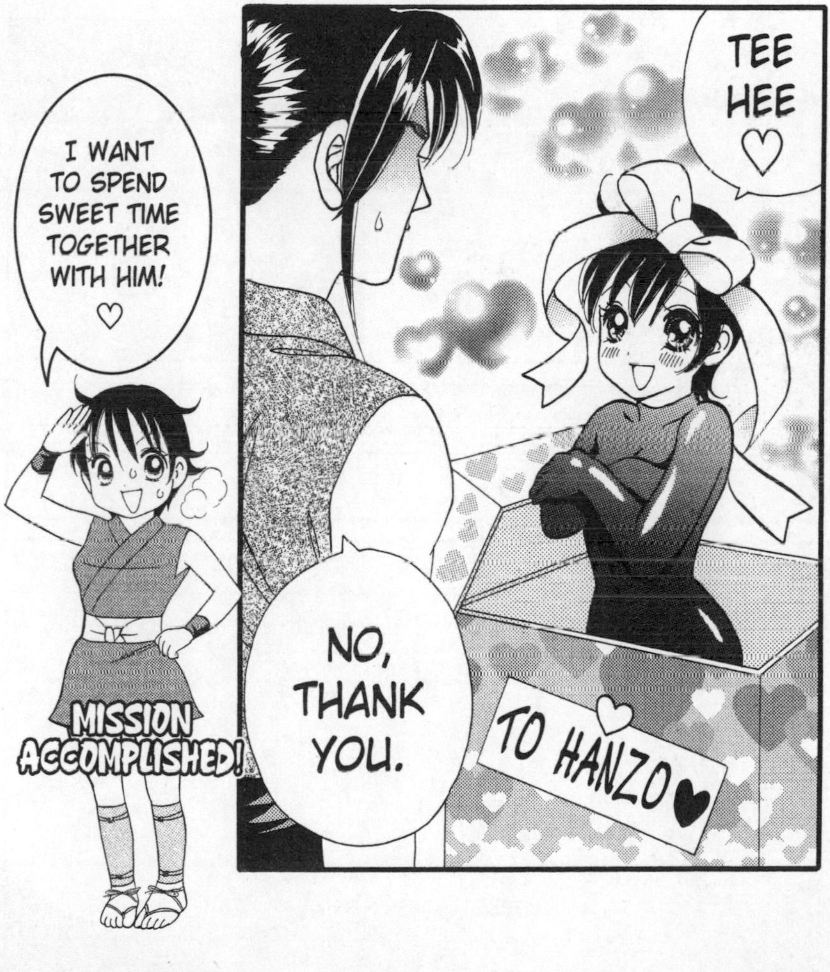
TEE HEE ♡
TO HANZO ♥
NO, THANK YOU.
I WANT TO SPEND SWEET TIME TOGETHER WITH HIM! ♡
MISSION ACCOMPLISHED!

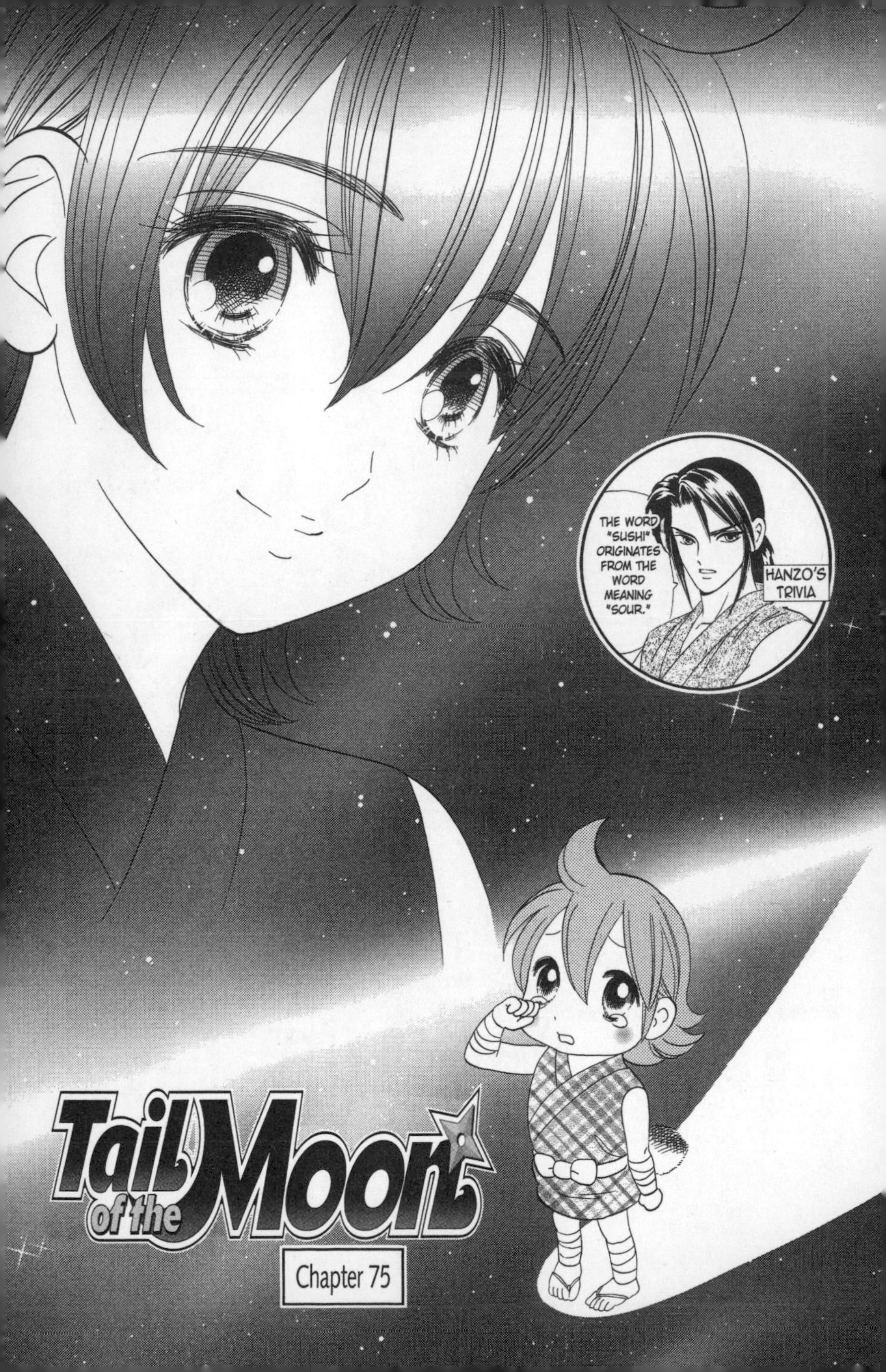
HANZO'S TRIVIA
THE WORD "SUSHI" ORIGINATES FROM THE WORD MEANING "SOUR."
Tail of the Moon
Chapter 75

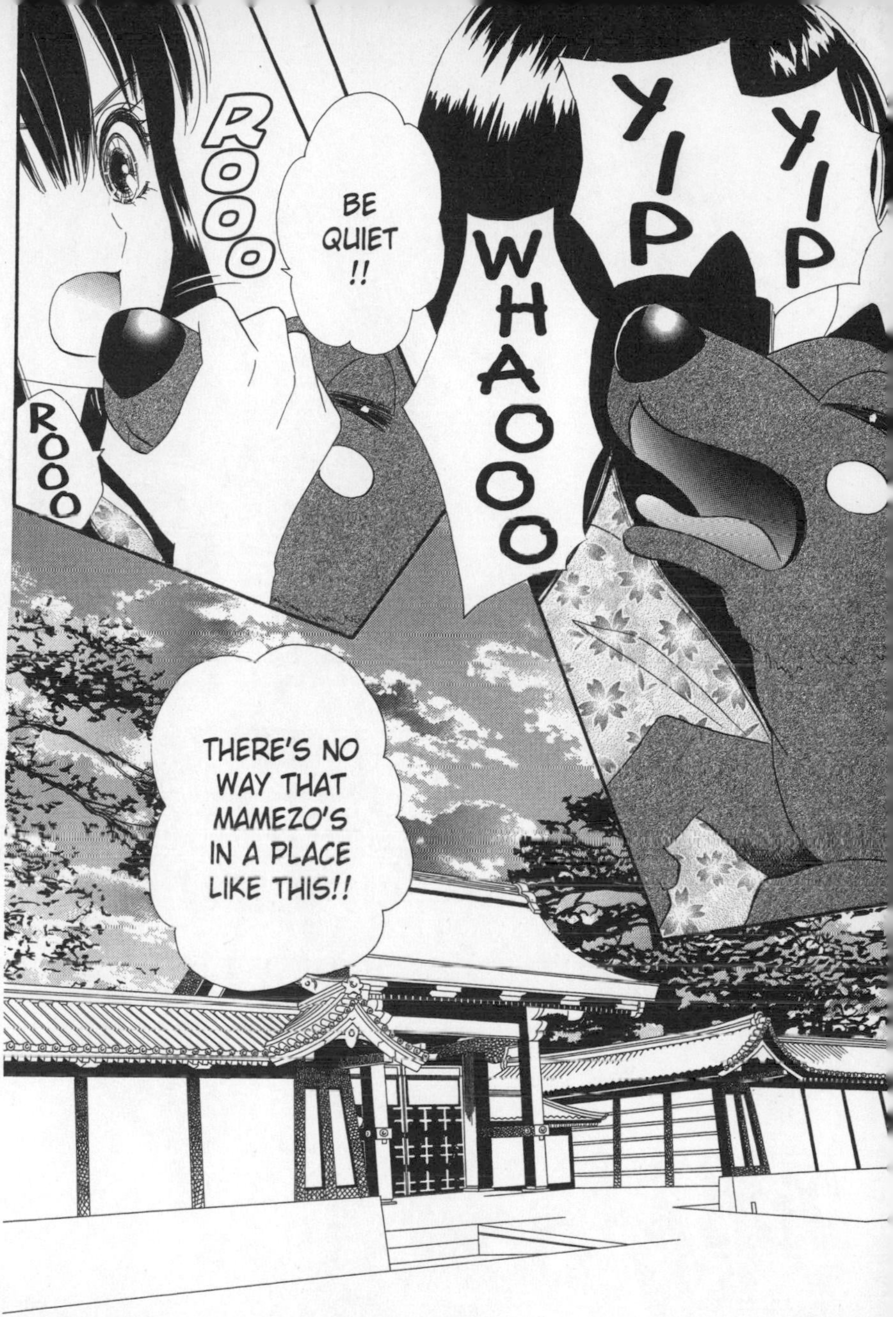
YIP YIP
WHAOOO
BE QUIET!!
ROOO
ROOO
THERE'S NO WAY THAT MAMEZO'S IN A PLACE LIKE THIS!!

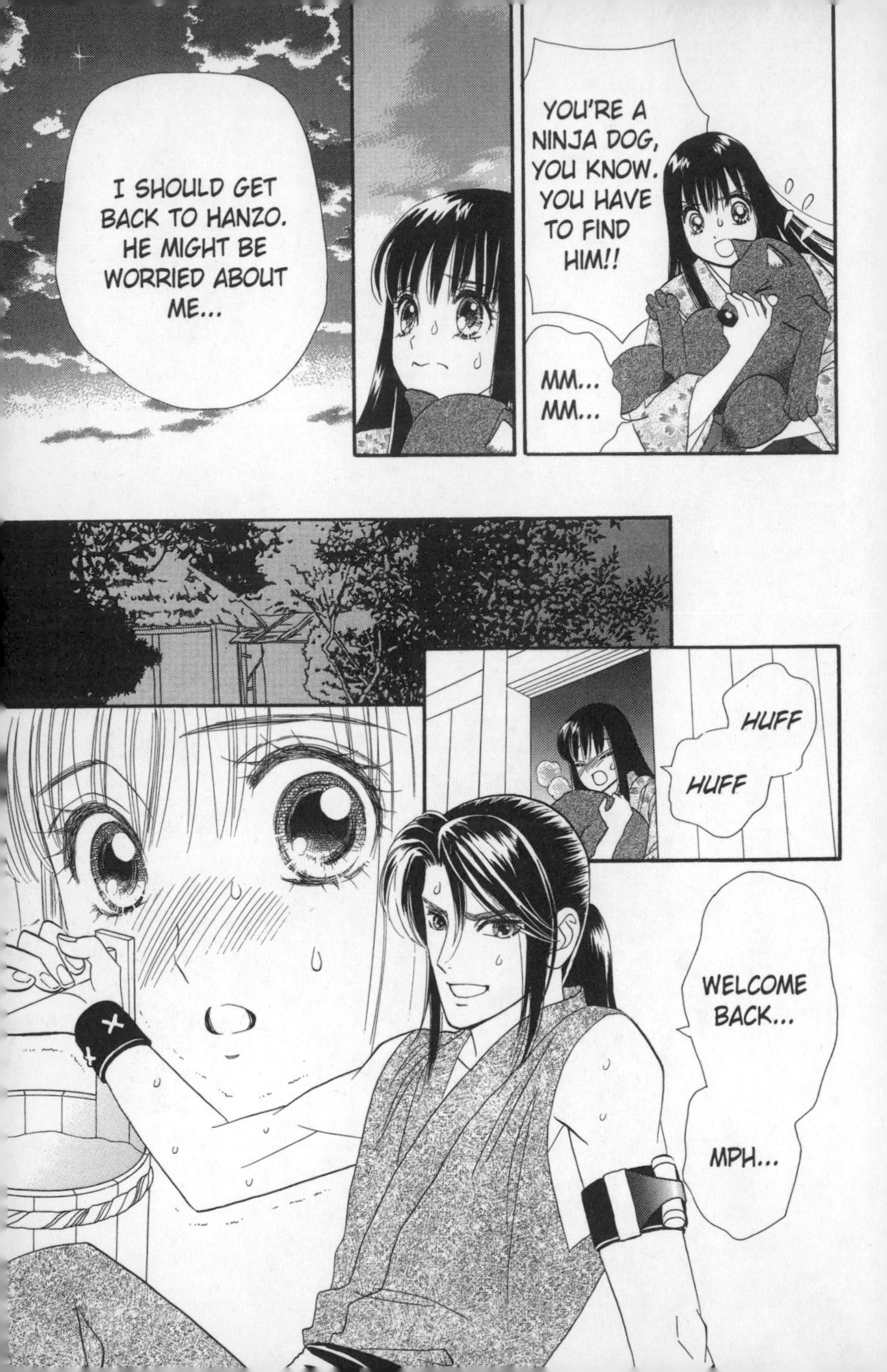
YOU'RE A NINJA DOG, YOU KNOW. YOU HAVE TO FIND HIM!!
MM... MM...
I SHOULD GET BACK TO HANZO. HE MIGHT BE WORRIED ABOUT ME...
HUFF
HUFF
WELCOME BACK...
MPH...

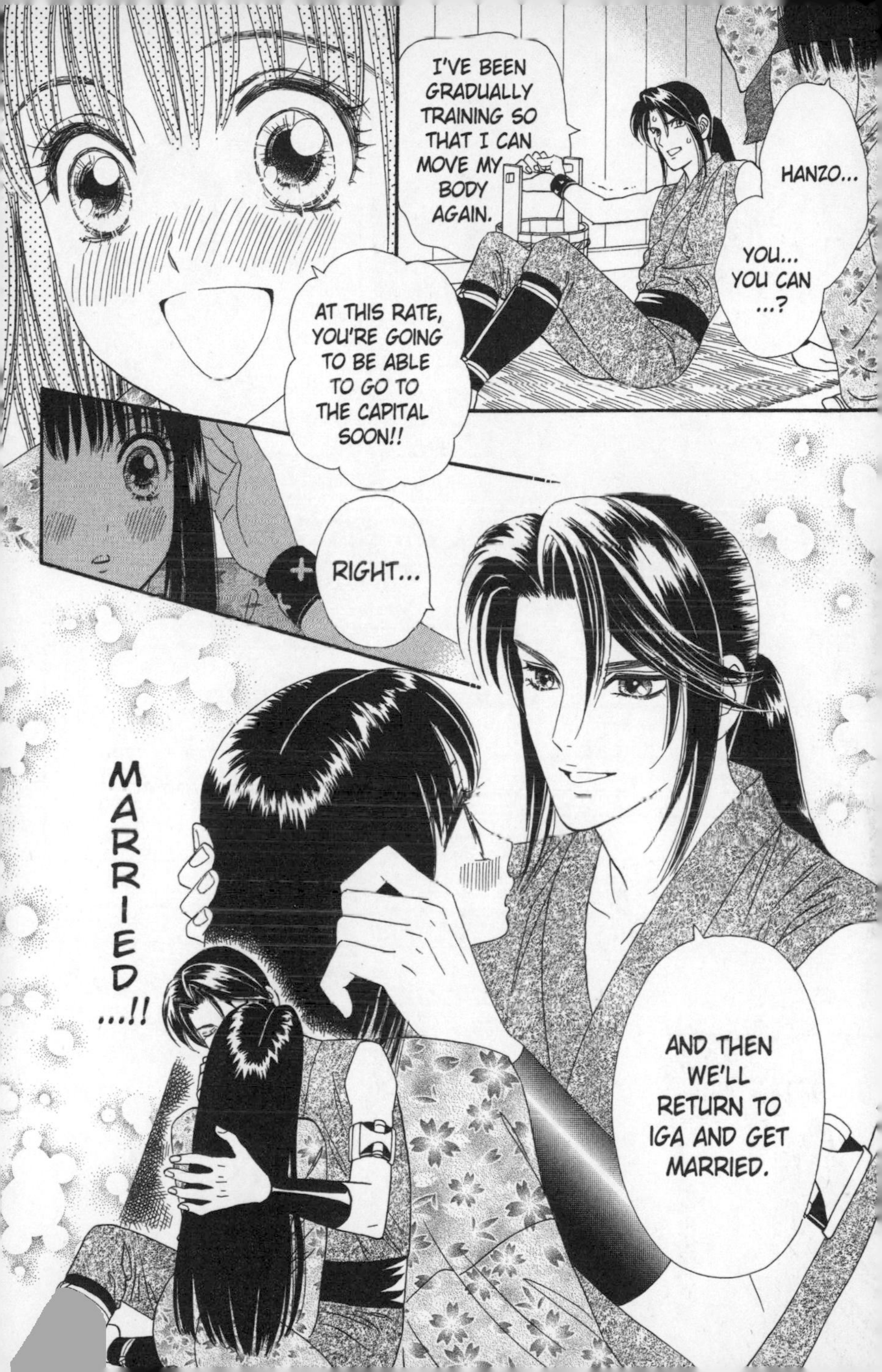
HANZO...
YOU... YOU CAN ...?
I'VE BEEN GRADUALLY TRAINING SO THAT I CAN MOVE MY BODY AGAIN.
AT THIS RATE, YOU'RE GOING TO BE ABLE TO GO TO THE CAPITAL SOON!!
RIGHT...
AND THEN WE'LL RETURN TO IGA AND GET MARRIED.
MARRIED ...!!

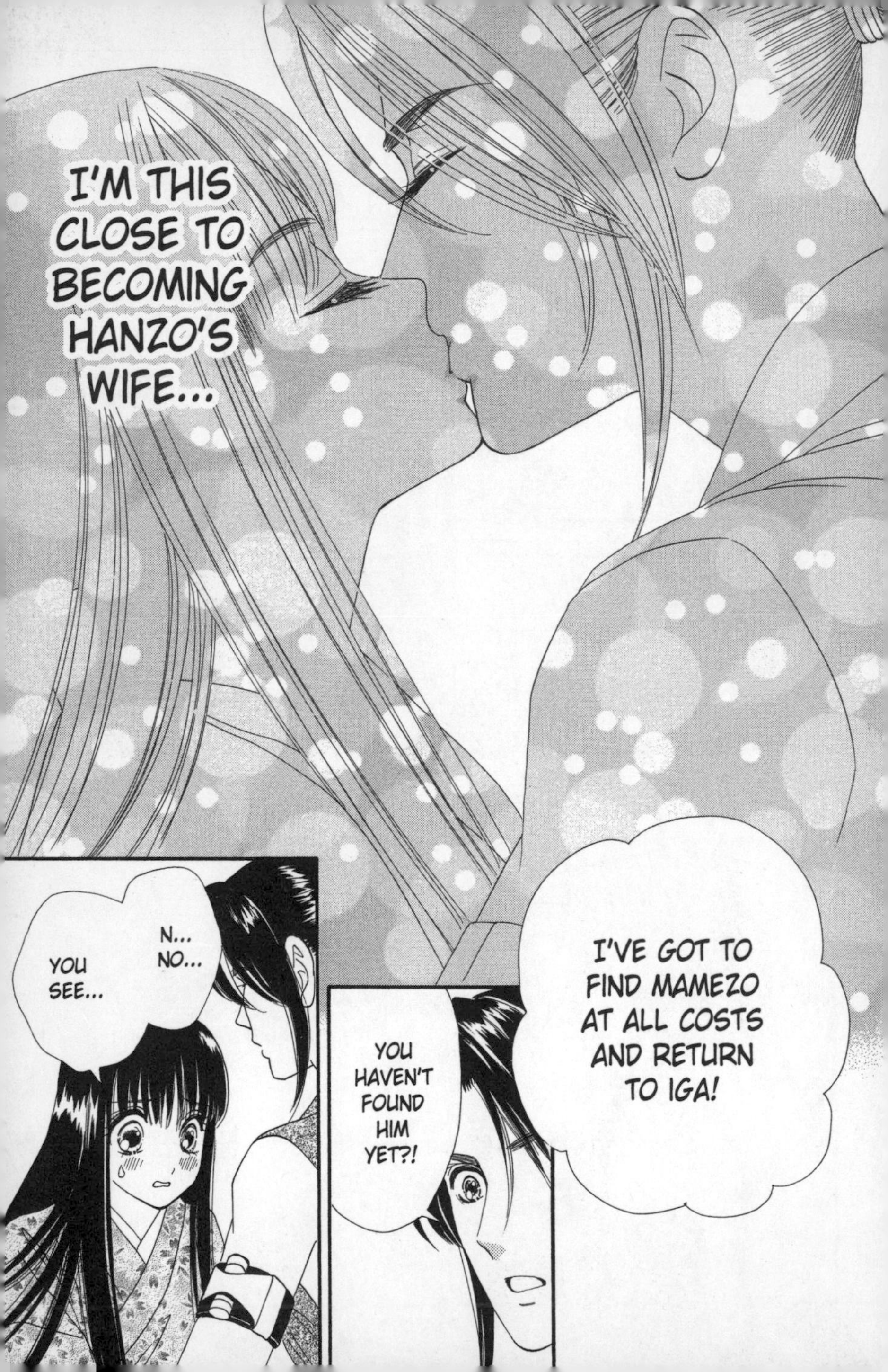
I'M THIS CLOSE TO BECOMING HANZO'S WIFE...
I'VE GOT TO FIND MAMEZO AT ALL COSTS AND RETURN TO IGA!
YOU HAVEN'T FOUND HIM YET?!
N... NO...
YOU SEE...

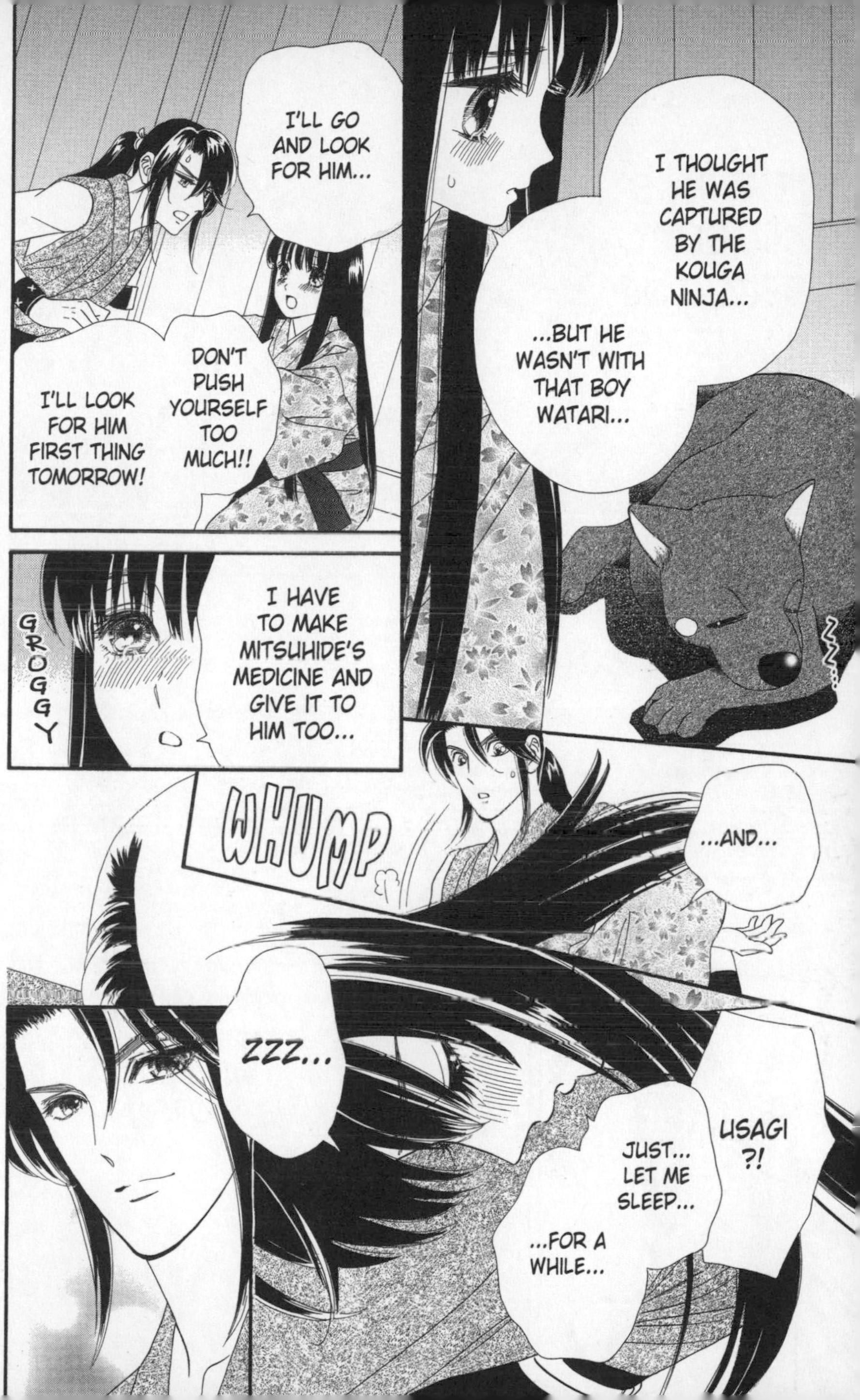
I THOUGHT HE WAS CAPTURED BY THE KOUGA NINJA...
...BUT HE WASN'T WITH THAT BOY WATARI...
I'LL GO AND LOOK FOR HIM...
DON'T PUSH YOURSELF TOO MUCH!!
I'LL LOOK FOR HIM FIRST THING TOMORROW!
GROGGY
I HAVE TO MAKE MITSUHIDE'S MEDICINE AND GIVE IT TO HIM TOO...
...AND...
WHUMP
USAGI ?!
JUST... LET ME SLEEP...
...FOR A WHILE...
ZZZ...

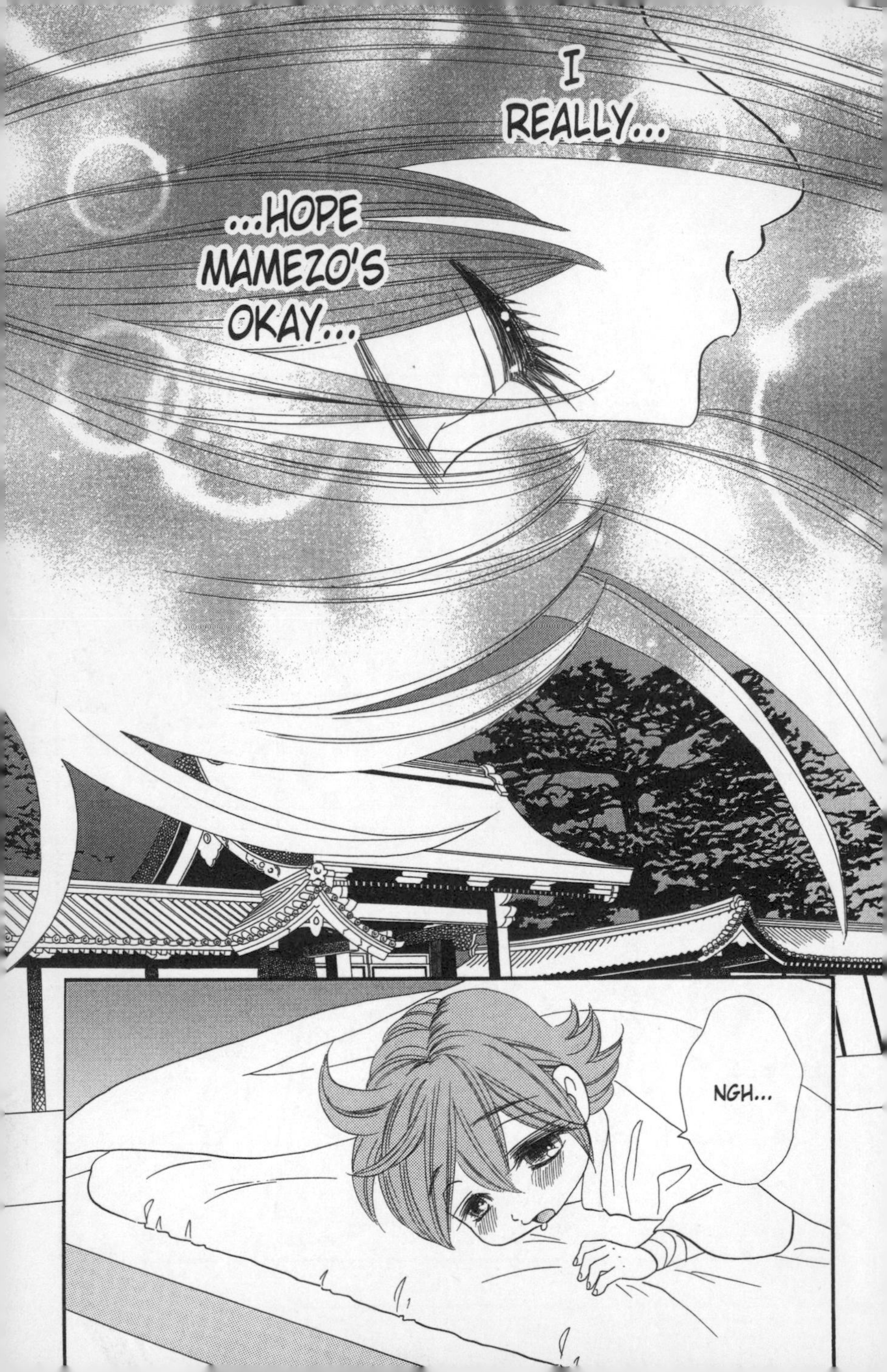
I REALLY...
...HOPE MAMEZO'S OKAY...
NGH...

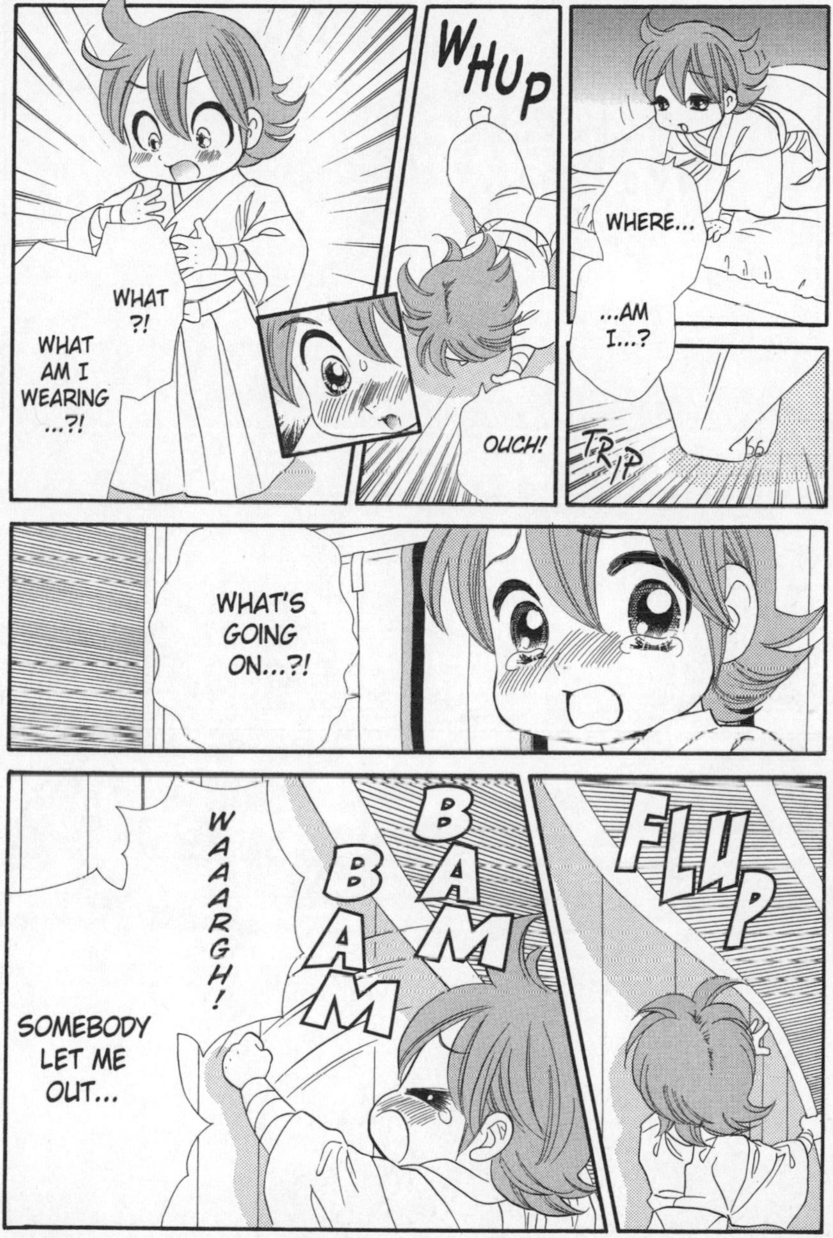
WHERE...
...AM I...?
TRIP
WHUP
OUCH!
WHAT?!
WHAT AM I WEARING...?!
WHAT'S GOING ON...?!
FLUP
BAM
BAM
WAAAARGH!
SOMEBODY LET ME OUT...

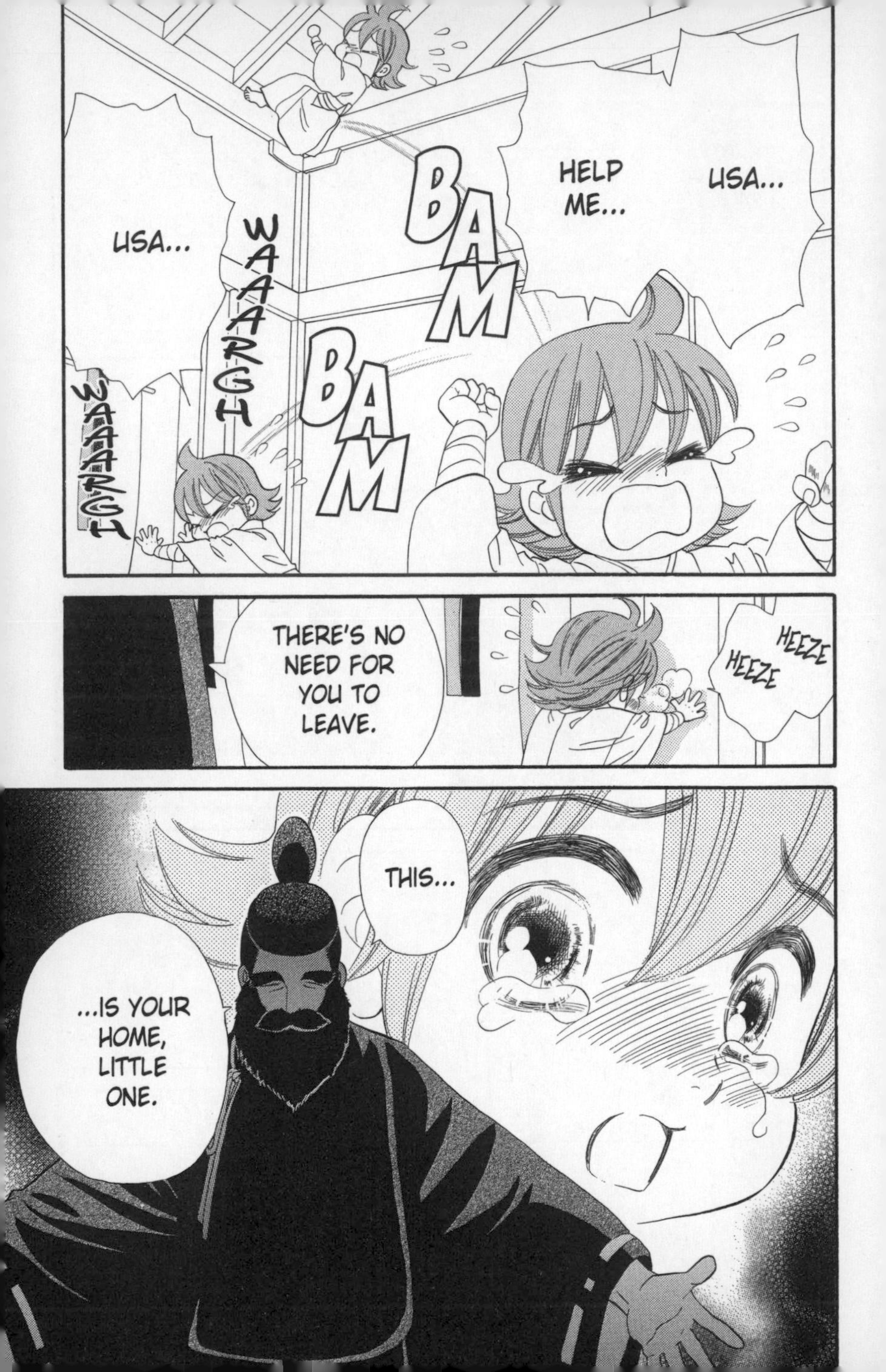
USA...
HELP ME...
BAM
BAM
USA...
WAAARGH
WAAARGH
HEEZE HEEZE
THERE'S NO NEED FOR YOU TO LEAVE.
THIS...
...IS YOUR HOME, LITTLE ONE.

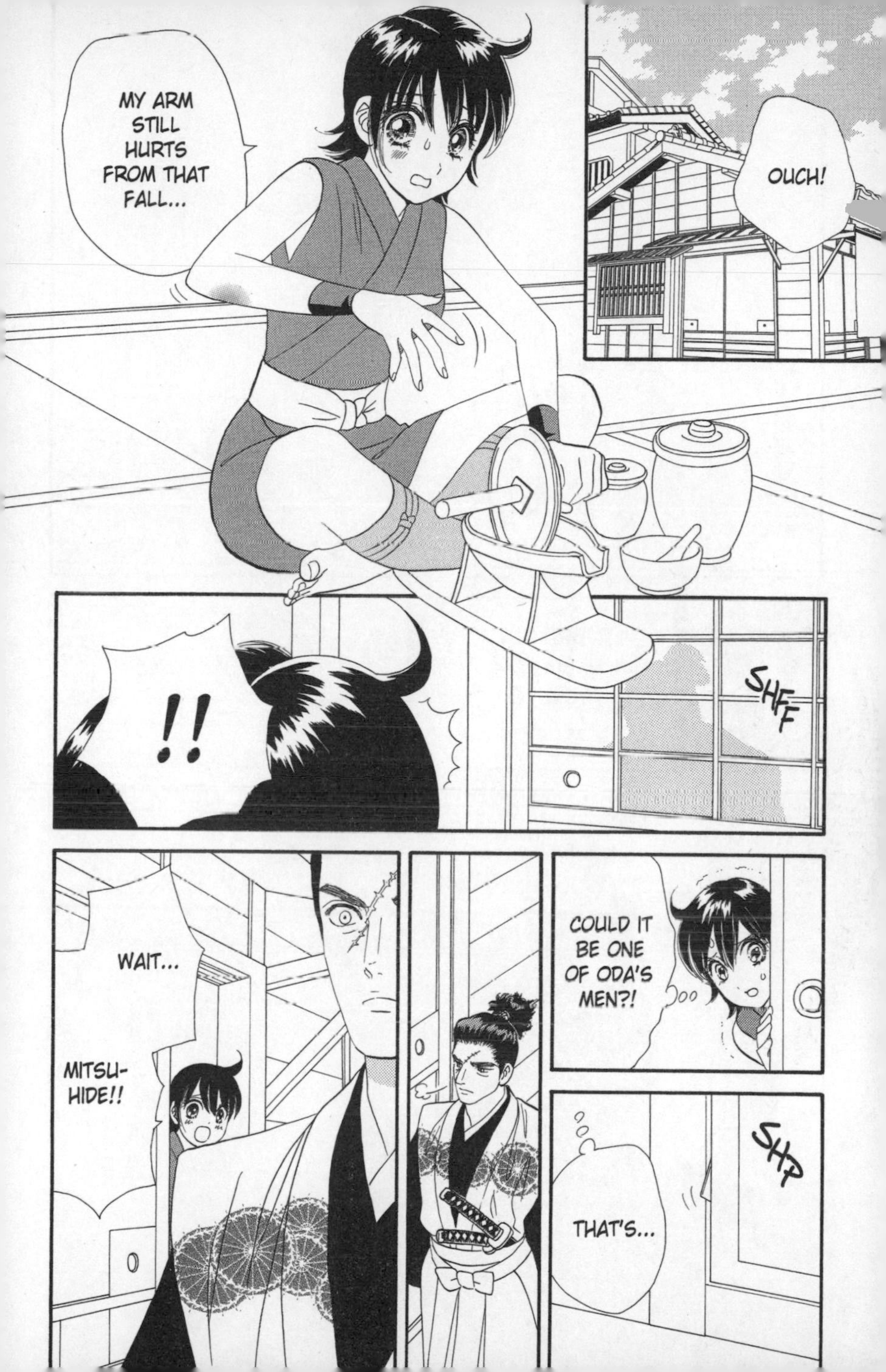
OUCH!
MY ARM STILL HURTS FROM THAT FALL...
SHFF
!!
COULD IT BE ONE OF ODA'S MEN?!
SHP
THAT'S...
WAIT...
MITSU-HIDE!!

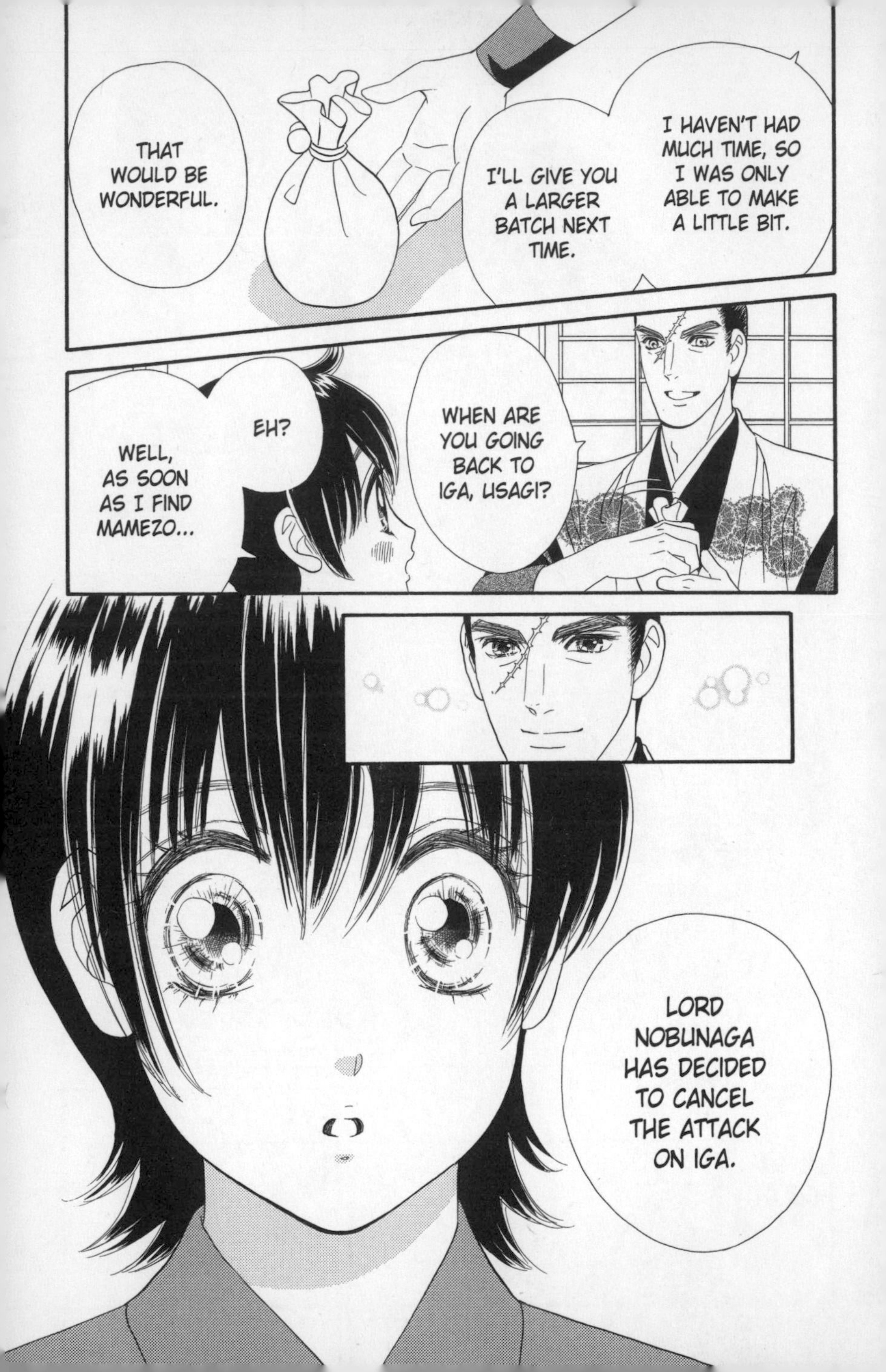
I HAVEN'T HAD MUCH TIME, SO I WAS ONLY ABLE TO MAKE A LITTLE BIT.
I'LL GIVE YOU A LARGER BATCH NEXT TIME.
THAT WOULD BE WONDERFUL.
WHEN ARE YOU GOING BACK TO IGA, USAGI?
EH?
WELL, AS SOON AS I FIND MAMEZO...
LORD NOBUNAGA HAS DECIDED TO CANCEL THE ATTACK ON IGA.

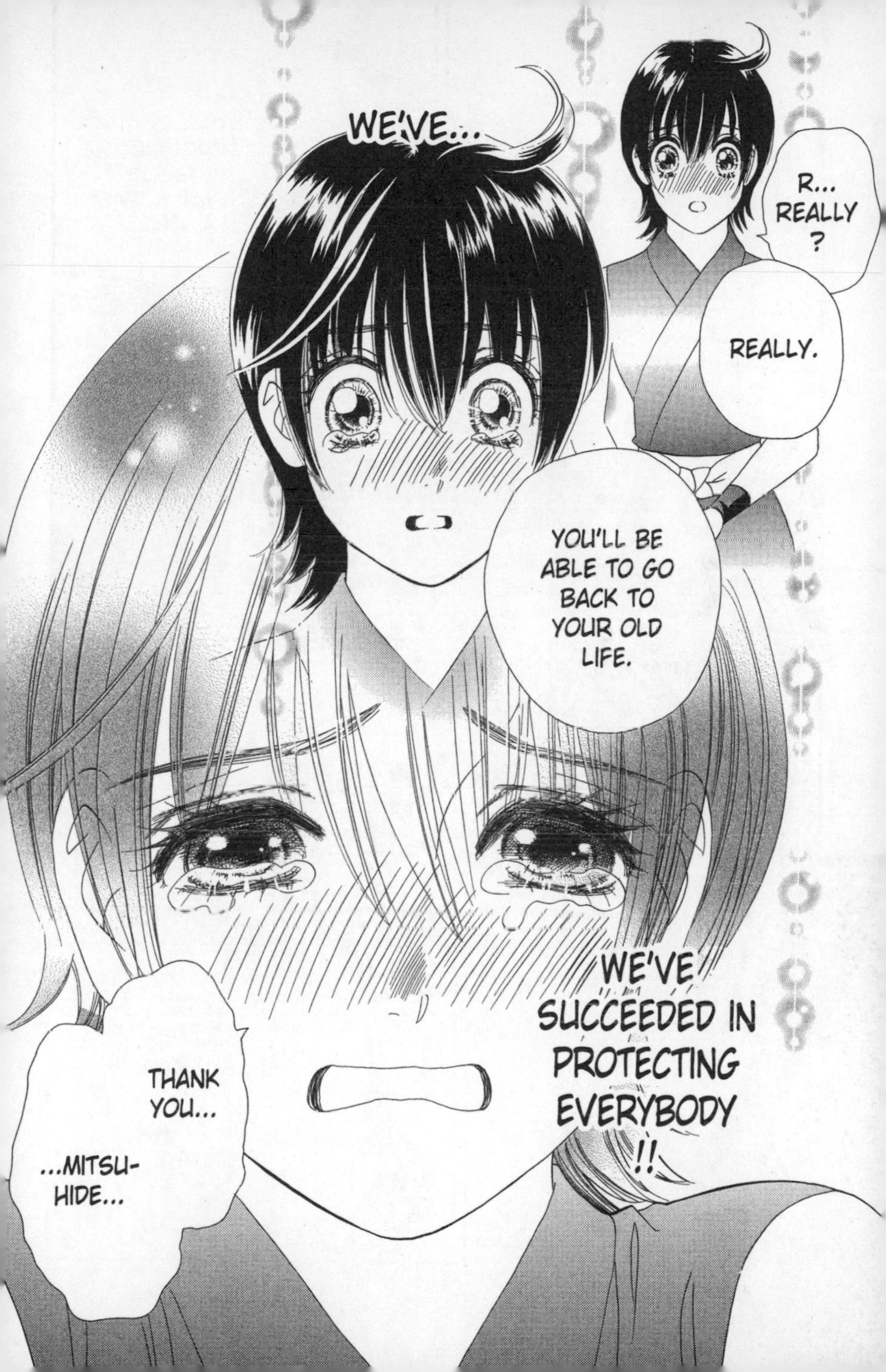
R... REALLY ?
REALLY.
YOU'LL BE ABLE TO GO BACK TO YOUR OLD LIFE.
WE'VE...
WE'VE SUCCEEDED IN PROTECTING EVERYBODY !!
THANK YOU...
...MITSU-HIDE...

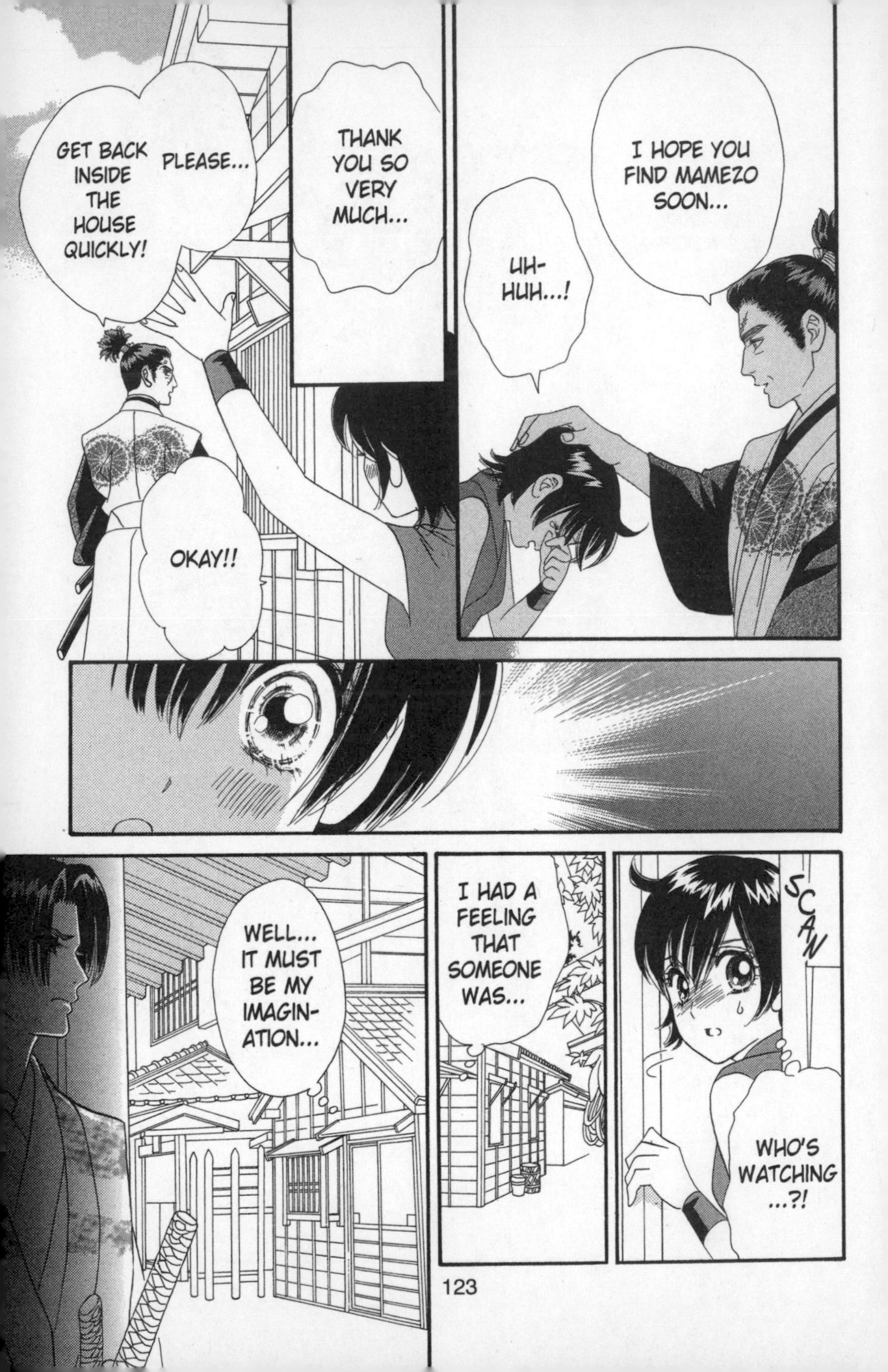
I HOPE YOU FIND MAMEZO SOON...
UH-HUH...!
THANK YOU SO VERY MUCH...
PLEASE...
GET BACK INSIDE THE HOUSE QUICKLY!
OKAY!!
SCAN
WHO'S WATCHING ...?!
I HAD A FEELING THAT SOMEONE WAS...
WELL... IT MUST BE MY IMAGINATION...

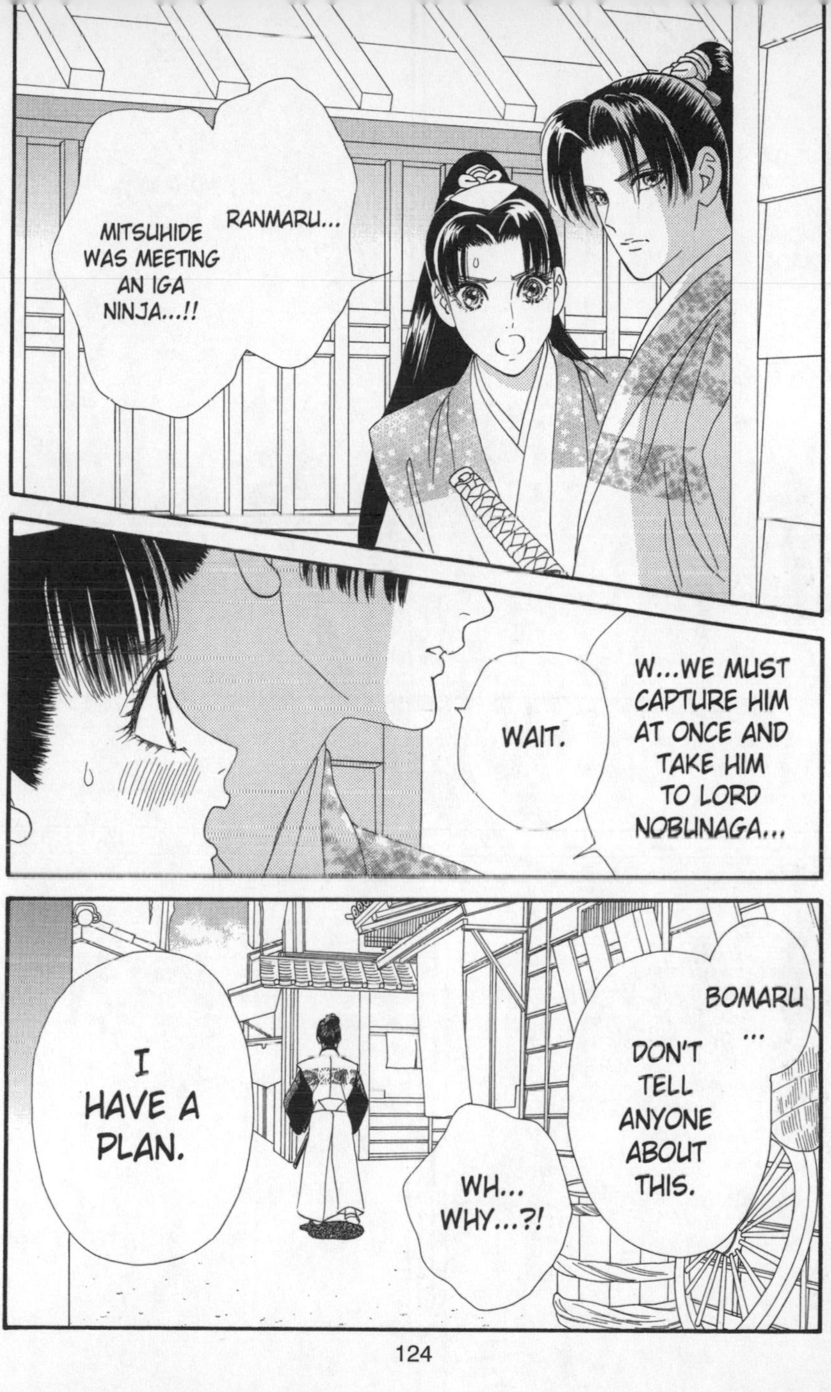
RANMARU...
MITSUHIDE WAS MEETING AN IGA NINJA...!!
W...WE MUST CAPTURE HIM AT ONCE AND TAKE HIM TO LORD NOBUNAGA...
WAIT.
BOMARU ...
DON'T TELL ANYONE ABOUT THIS.
WH... WHY...?!
I HAVE A PLAN.

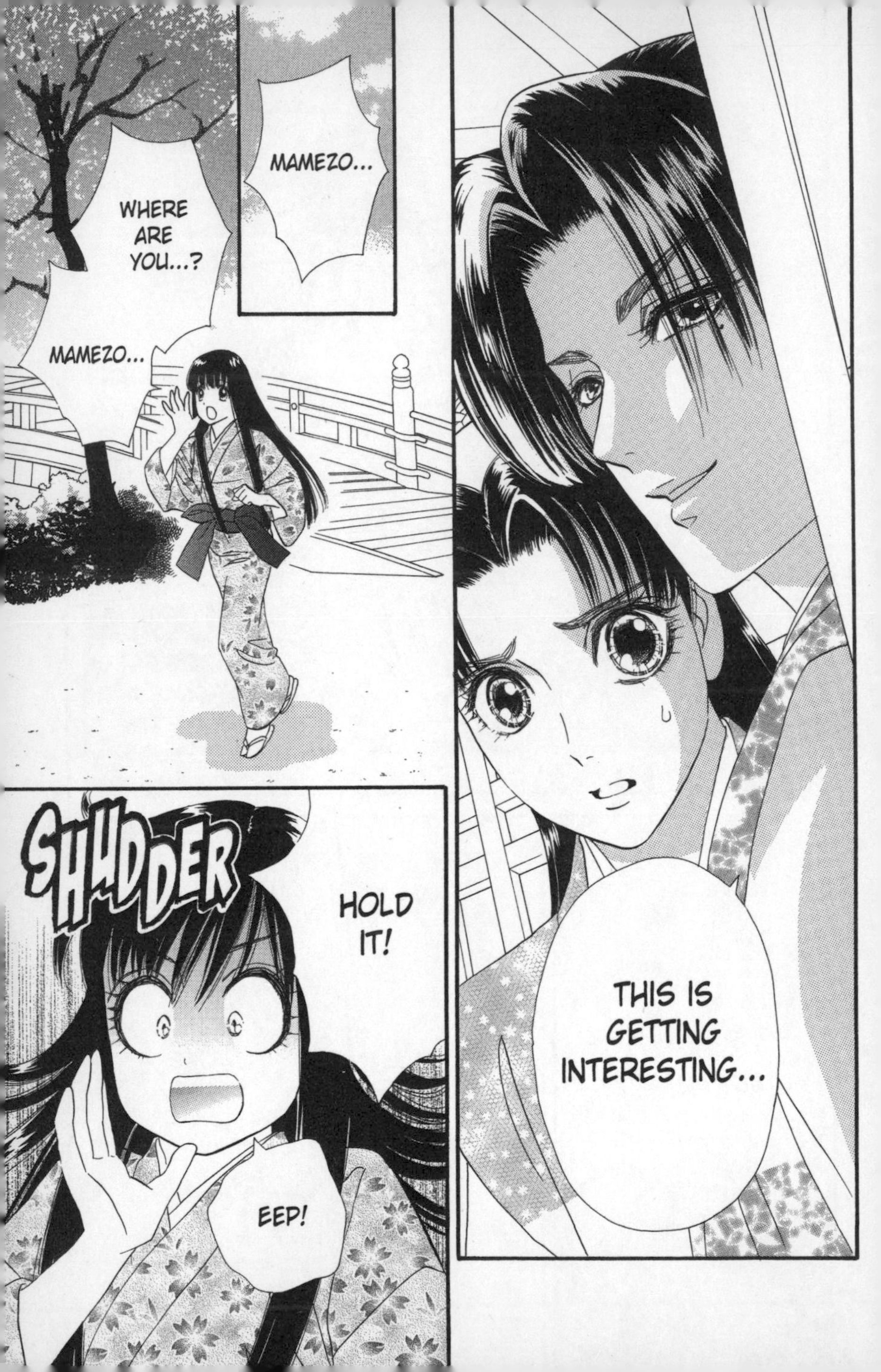
THIS IS GETTING INTERESTING...
MAMEZO...
WHERE ARE YOU...?
MAMEZO...
HOLD IT!
SHUDDER
EEP!

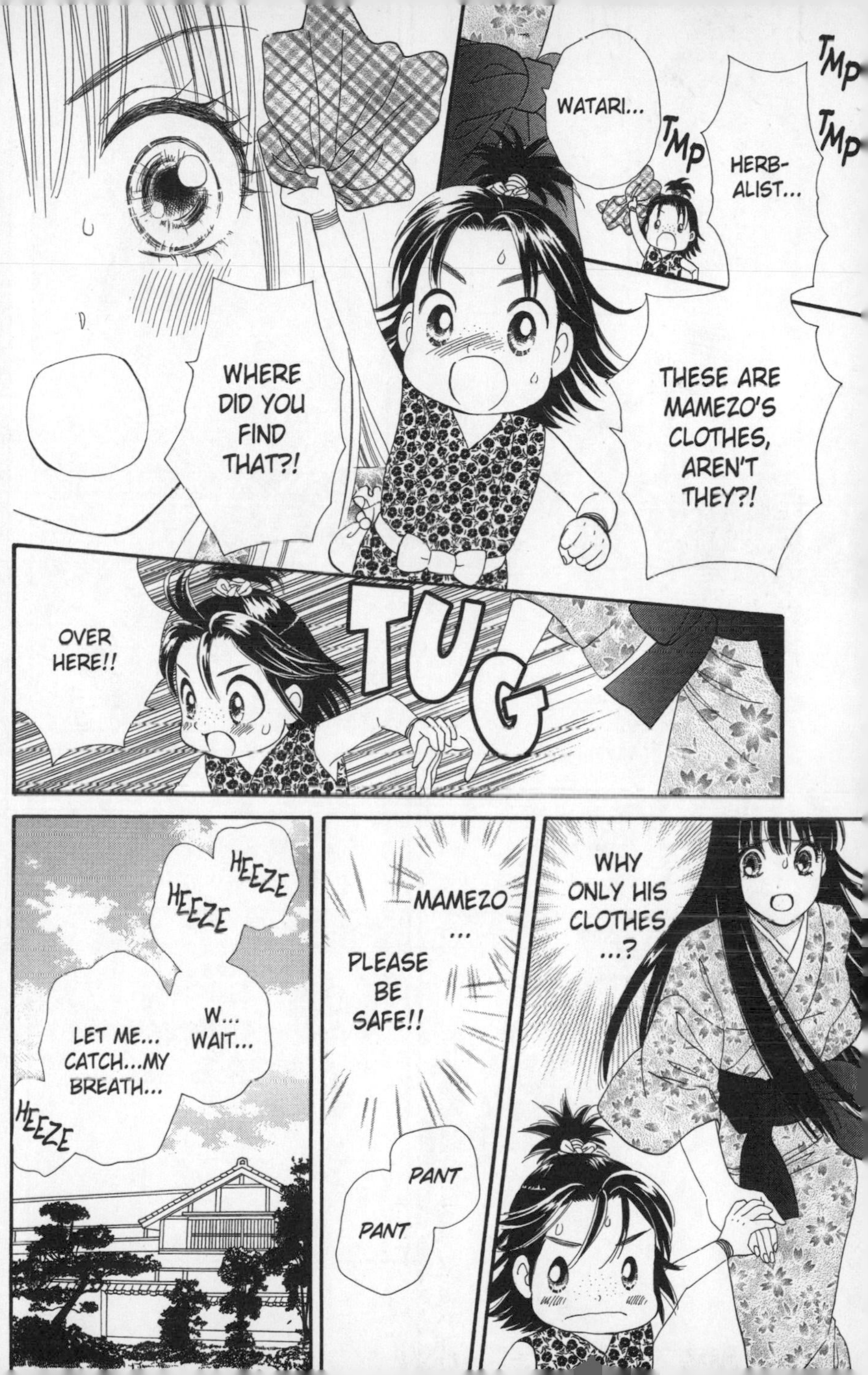
TMP
TMP
WATARI...
TMP
HERB-ALIST...
THESE ARE MAMEZO'S CLOTHES, AREN'T THEY?!
WHERE DID YOU FIND THAT?!
TUG
OVER HERE!!
WHY ONLY HIS CLOTHES ...?
MAMEZO ...
PLEASE BE SAFE!!
PANT
PANT
HEEZE
HEEZE
W... WAIT...
LET ME... CATCH...MY BREATH...
HEEZE

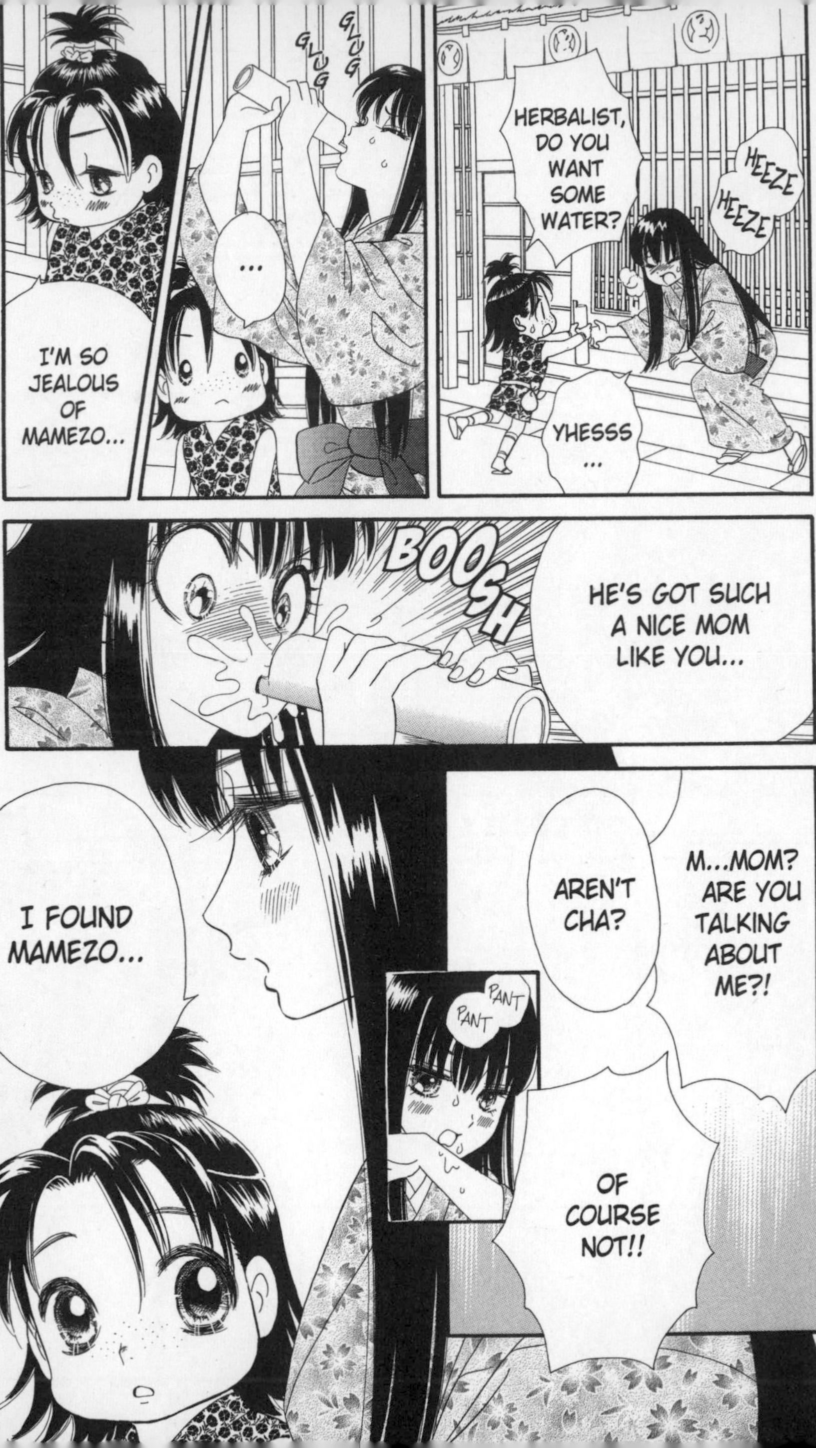
HERBALIST, DO YOU WANT SOME WATER?
HEEZE HEEZE
YHESSS ...
GLUG GLUG
...
I'M SO JEALOUS OF MAMEZO...
HE'S GOT SUCH A NICE MOM LIKE YOU...
BOOSH
M...MOM? ARE YOU TALKING ABOUT ME?!
AREN'T CHA?
PANT PANT
OF COURSE NOT!!
I FOUND MAMEZO...

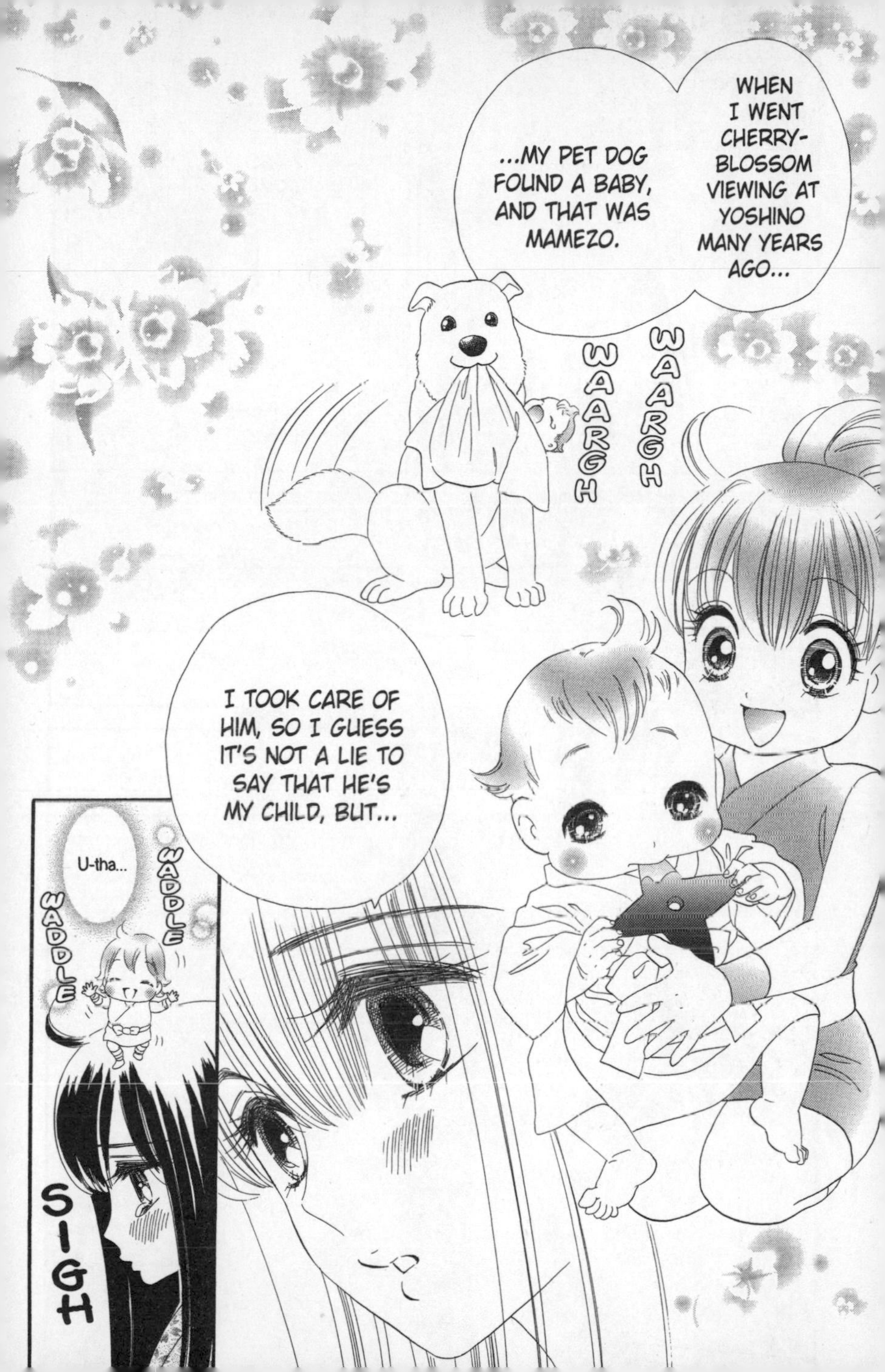
WHEN I WENT CHERRY-BLOSSOM VIEWING AT YOSHINO MANY YEARS AGO...
...MY PET DOG FOUND A BABY, AND THAT WAS MAMEZO.
WAARGH
WAARGH
I TOOK CARE OF HIM, SO I GUESS IT'S NOT A LIE TO SAY THAT HE'S MY CHILD, BUT...
WADDLE
U-tha...
WADDLE
SIGH

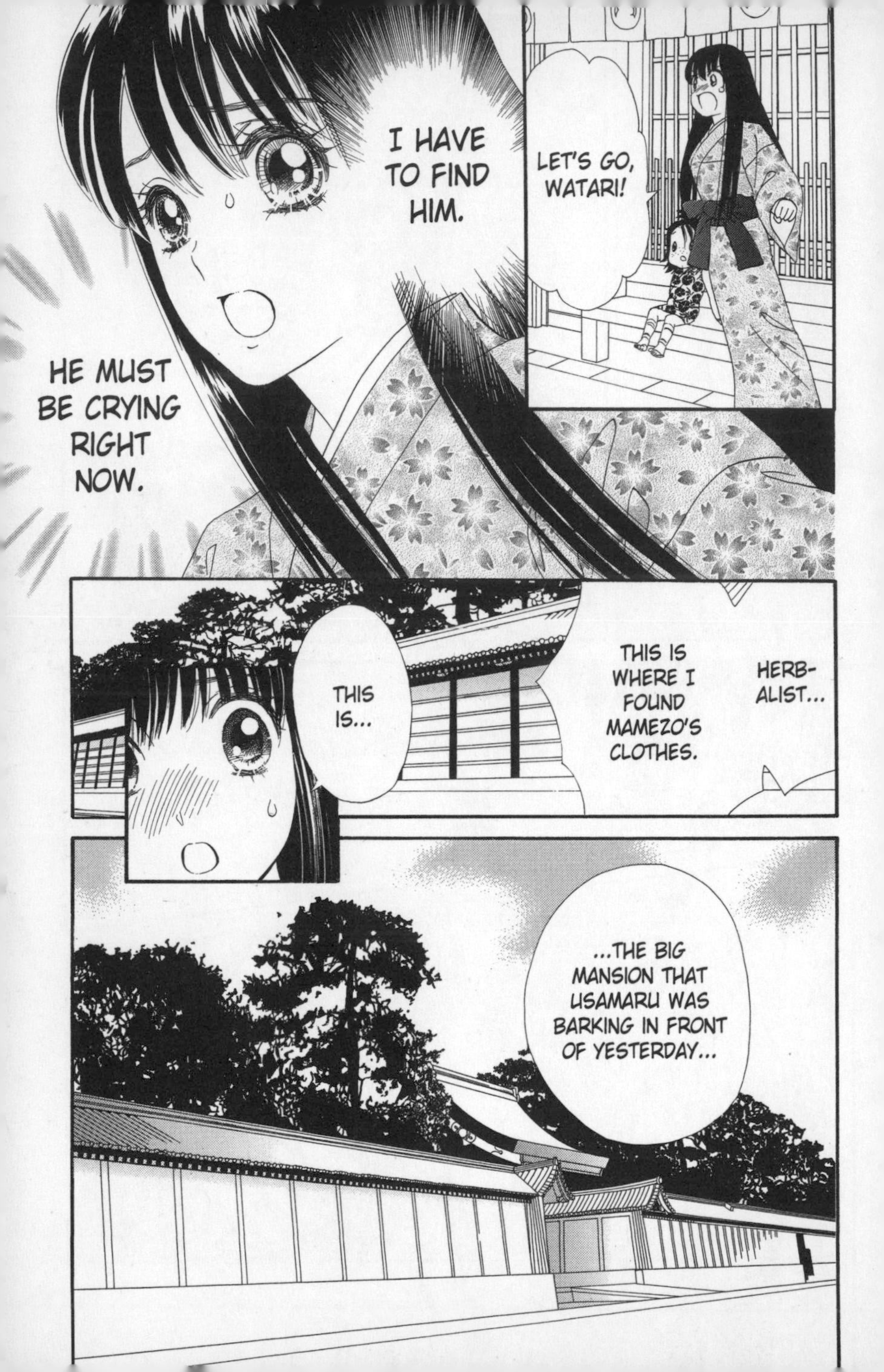
I HAVE TO FIND HIM.
HE MUST BE CRYING RIGHT NOW.
LET'S GO, WATARI!
HERB-ALIST...
THIS IS WHERE I FOUND MAMEZO'S CLOTHES.
THIS IS...
...THE BIG MANSION THAT USAMARU WAS BARKING IN FRONT OF YESTERDAY...

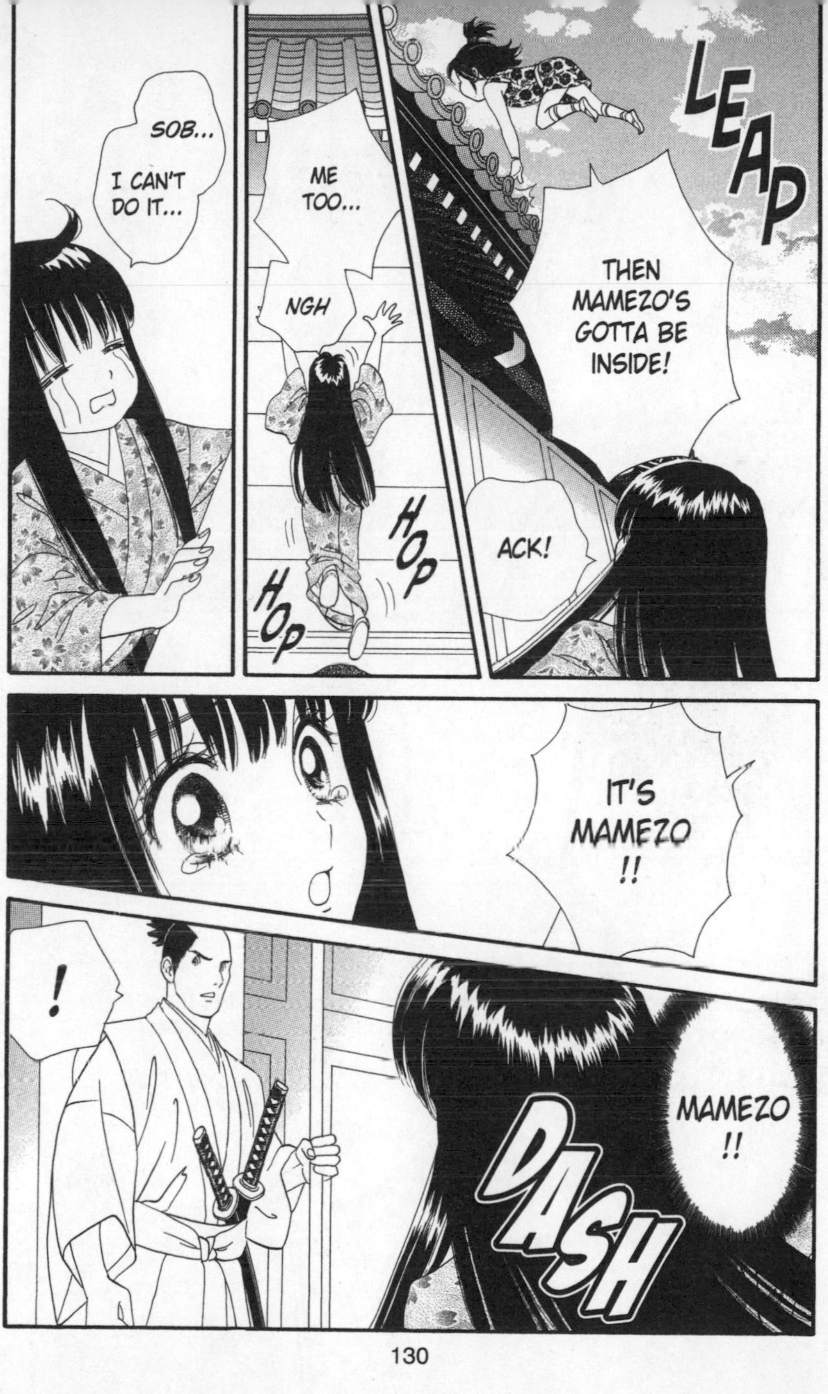
LEAP
THEN MAMEZO'S GOTTA BE INSIDE!
ACK!
ME TOO...
NGH
HOP
HOP
SOB...
I CAN'T DO IT...
IT'S MAMEZO !!
MAMEZO !!
DASH
!

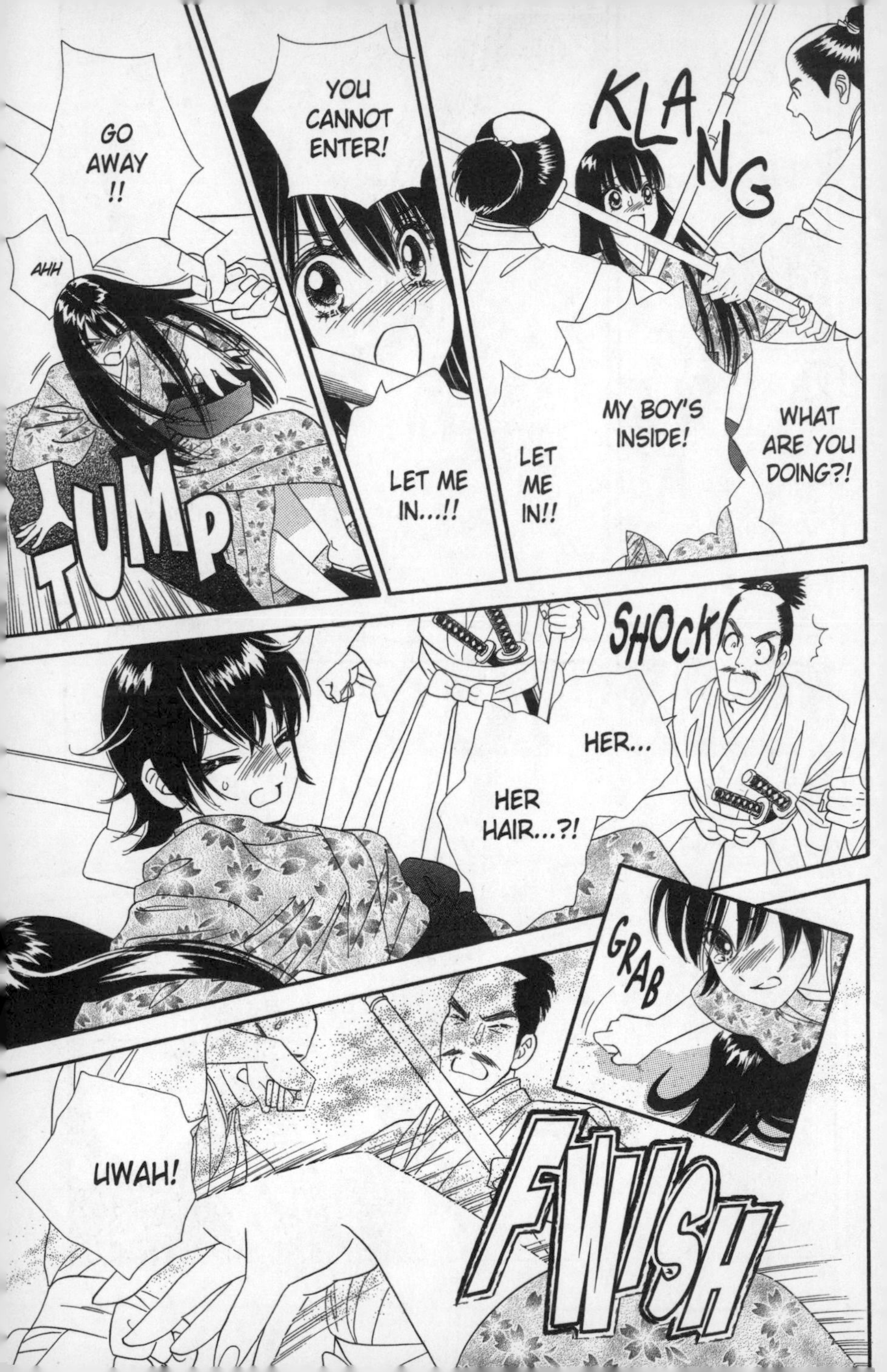
KLANG
WHAT ARE YOU DOING?!
MY BOY'S INSIDE!
LET ME IN!!
YOU CANNOT ENTER!
LET ME IN...!!
GO AWAY !!
AHH
TUMP
SHOCK
HER...
HER HAIR...?!
GRAB
FWISH
UWAH!

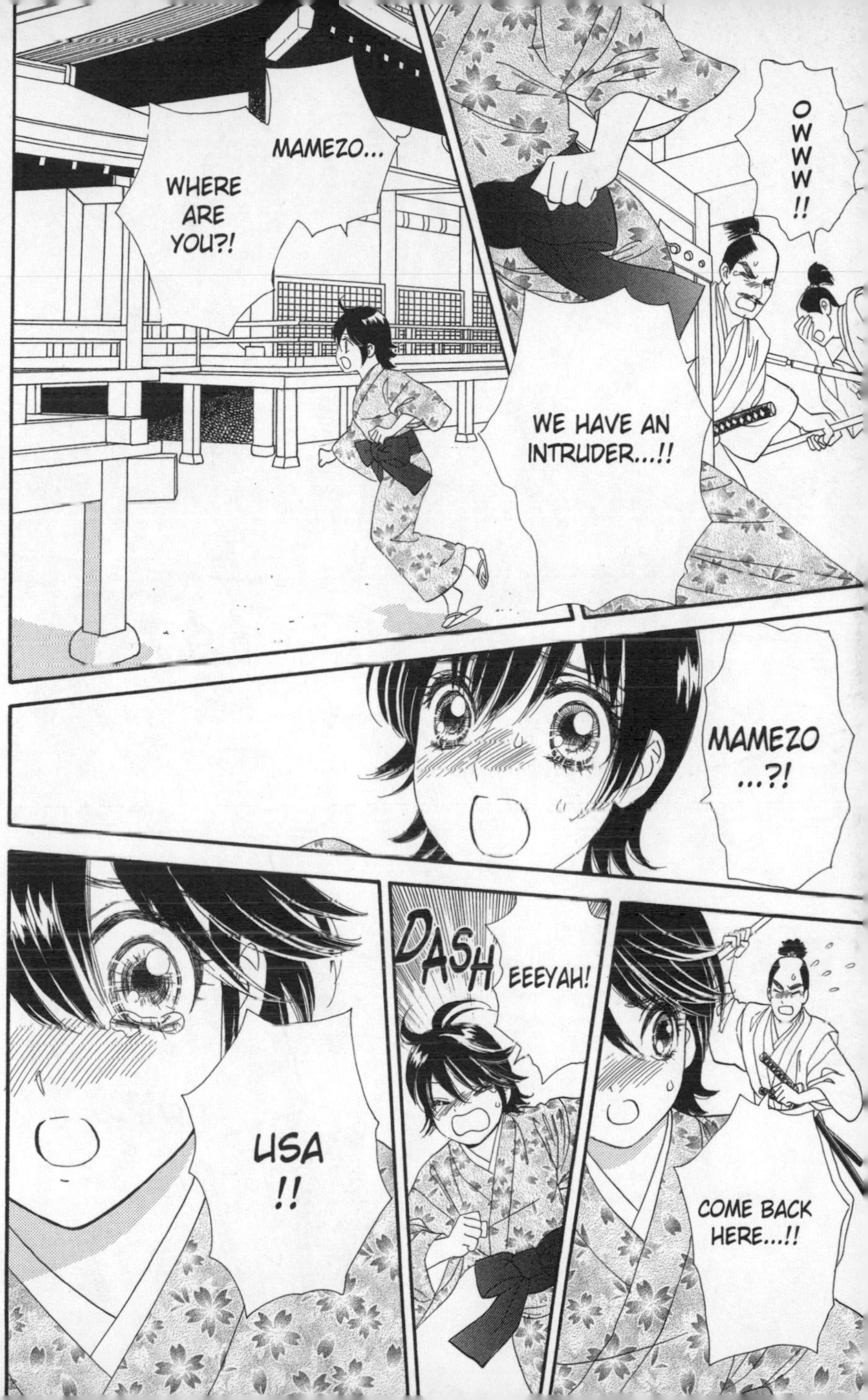
OWWW!!
WE HAVE AN INTRUDER...!!
MAMEZO...
WHERE ARE YOU?!
MAMEZO ...?!
COME BACK HERE...!!
DASH
EEEYAH!
USA !!

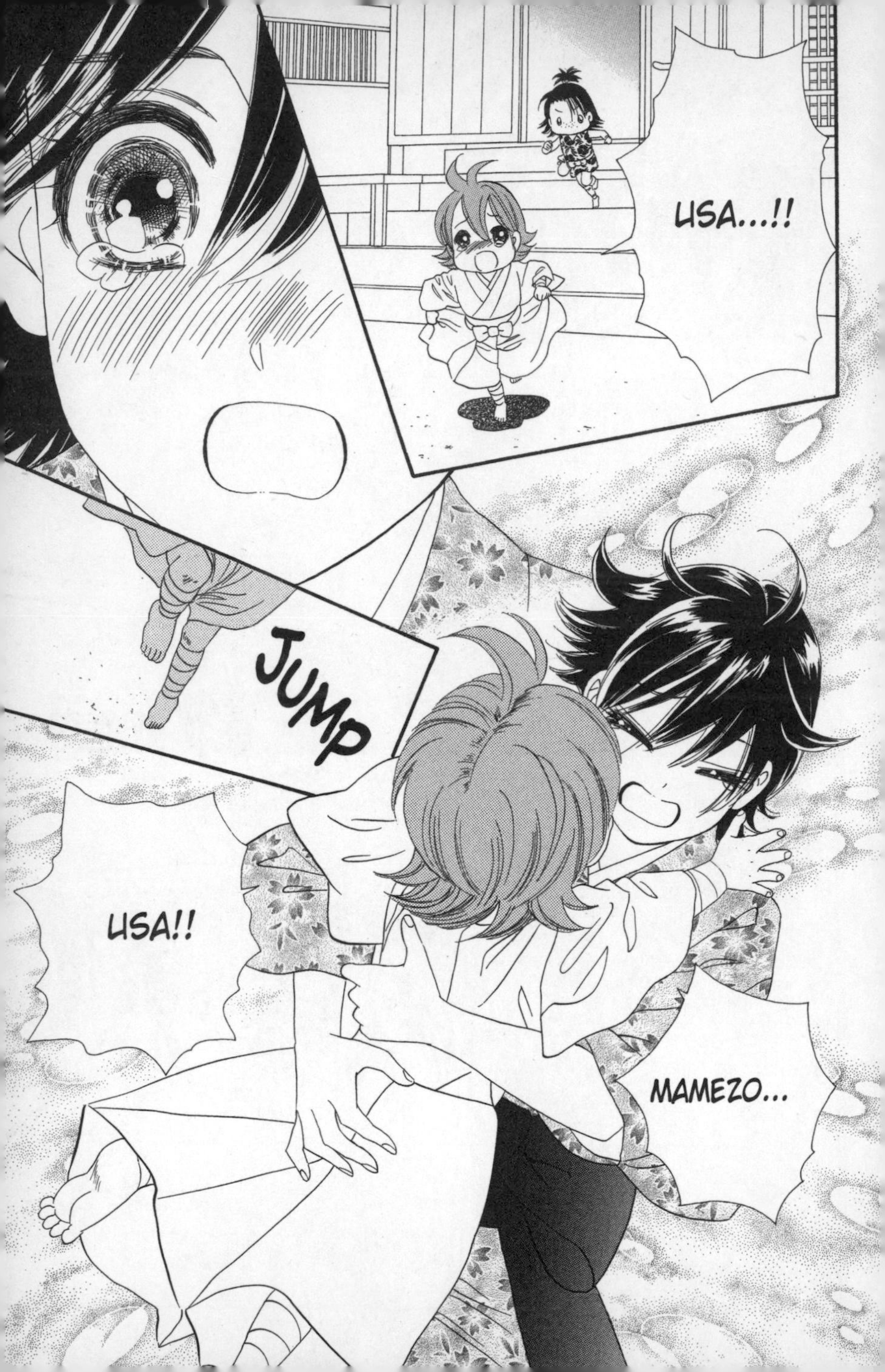
USA...!!
JUMP
USA!!
MAMEZO...

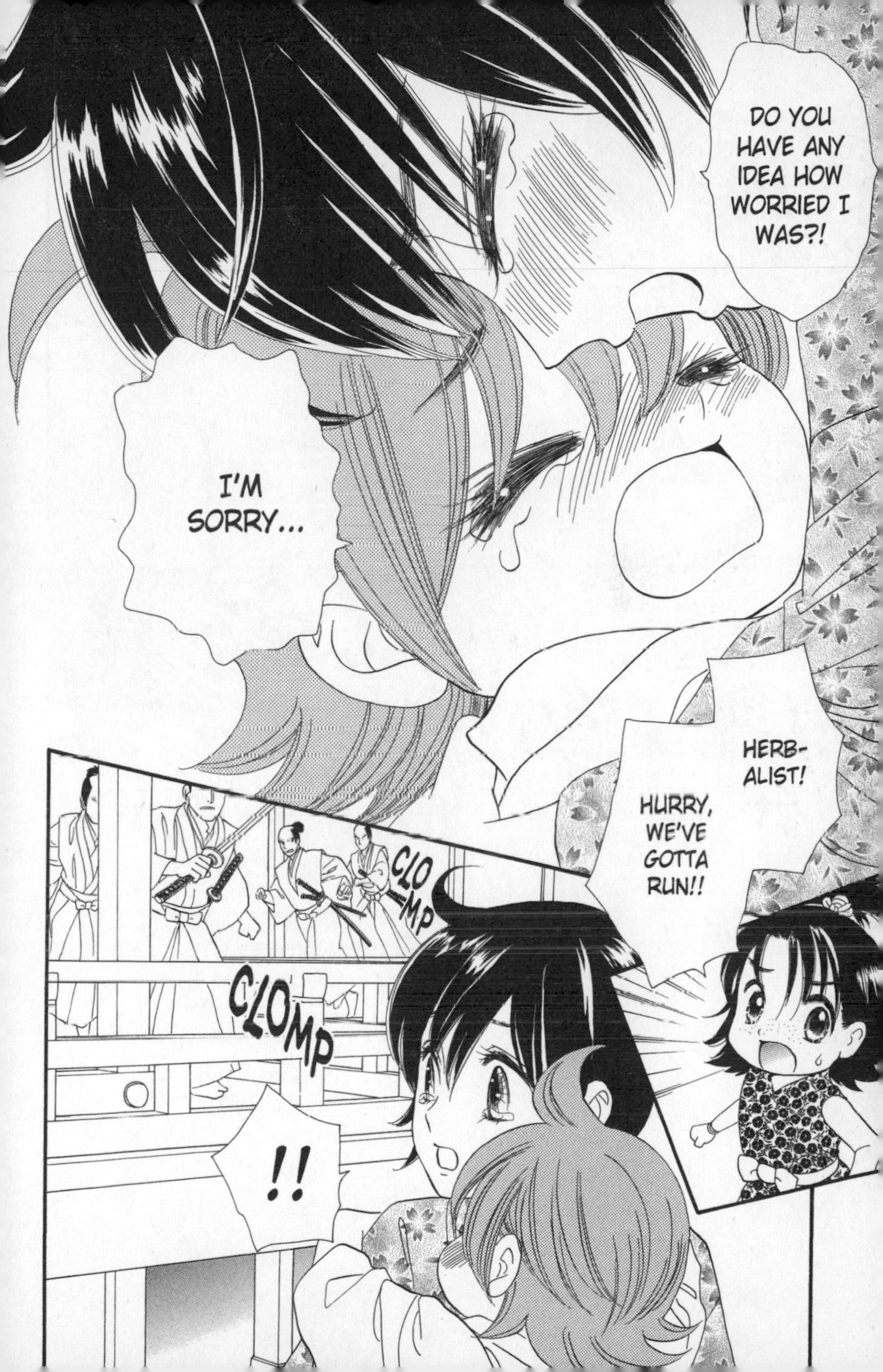
DO YOU HAVE ANY IDEA HOW WORRIED I WAS?!
I'M SORRY...
HERB-ALIST!
HURRY, WE'VE GOTTA RUN!!
CLOMP
CLOMP
!!

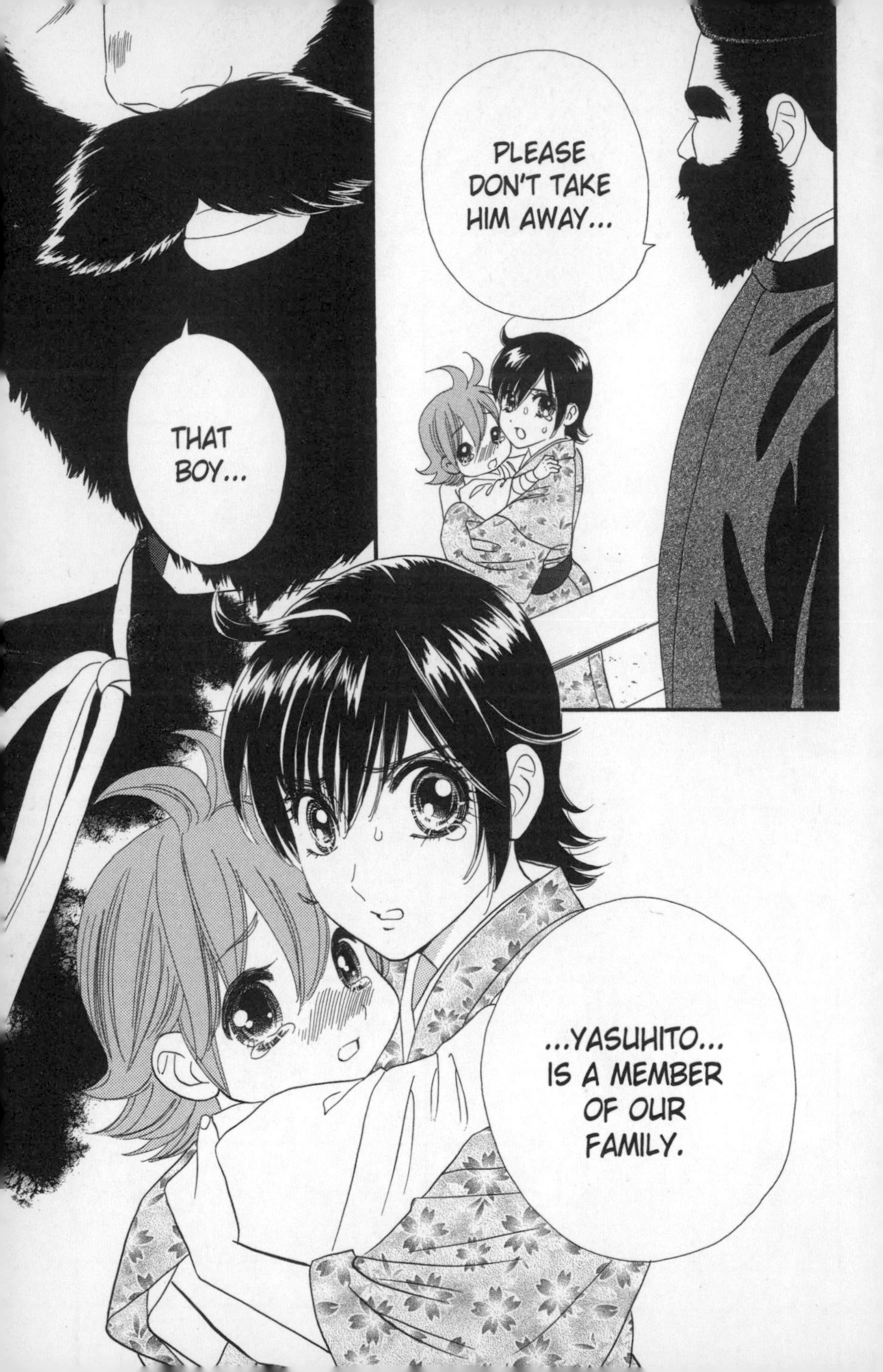
PLEASE DON'T TAKE HIM AWAY...
THAT BOY...
...YASUHITO... IS A MEMBER OF OUR FAMILY.

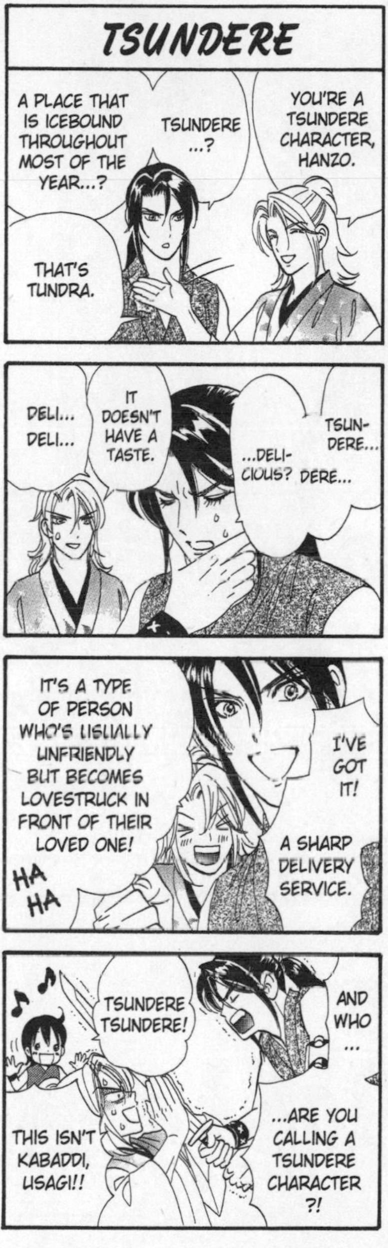
TSUNDERE
YOU'RE A TSUNDERE CHARACTER, HANZO.
TSUNDERE ...?
A PLACE THAT IS ICEBOUND THROUGHOUT MOST OF THE YEAR...?
THAT'S TUNDRA.
TSUN-DERE... DERE...
...DELI-CIOUS?
IT DOESN'T HAVE A TASTE.
DELI... DELI...
I'VE GOT IT!
IT'S A TYPE OF PERSON WHO'S USUALLY UNFRIENDLY BUT BECOMES LOVESTRUCK IN FRONT OF THEIR LOVED ONE!
A SHARP DELIVERY SERVICE.
HA HA
AND WHO ...
...ARE YOU CALLING A TSUNDERE CHARACTER ?!
TSUNDERE TSUNDERE!
THIS ISN'T KABADDI, USAGI!!

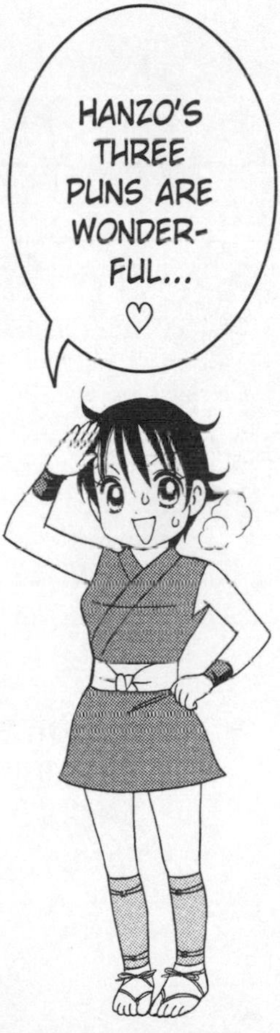
HANZO'S THREE PUNS ARE WONDER-FUL... ♡

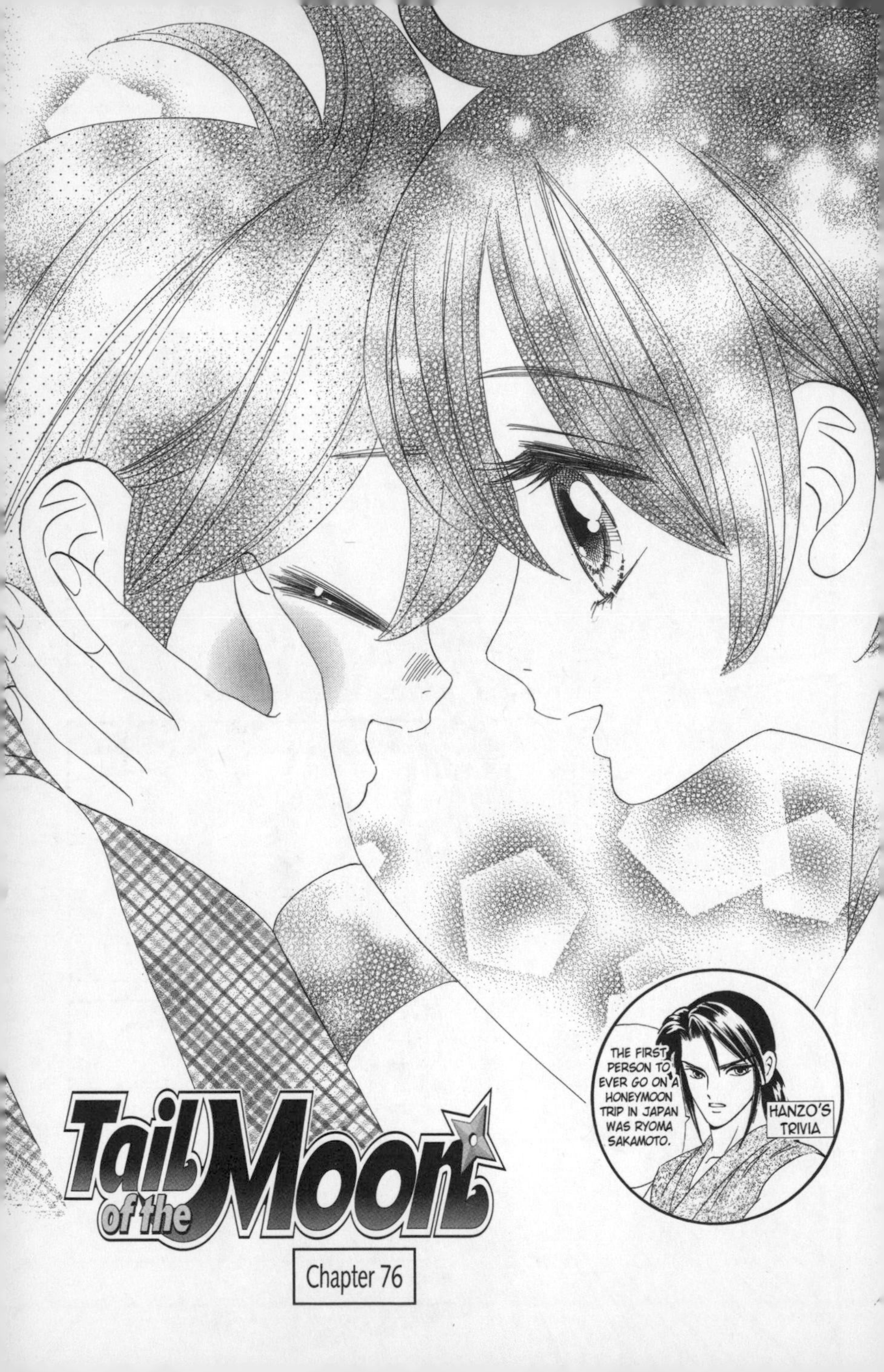
HANZO'S TRIVIA
THE FIRST PERSON TO EVER GO ON A HONEYMOON TRIP IN JAPAN WAS RYOMA SAKAMOTO.
Tail of the Moon
Chapter 76

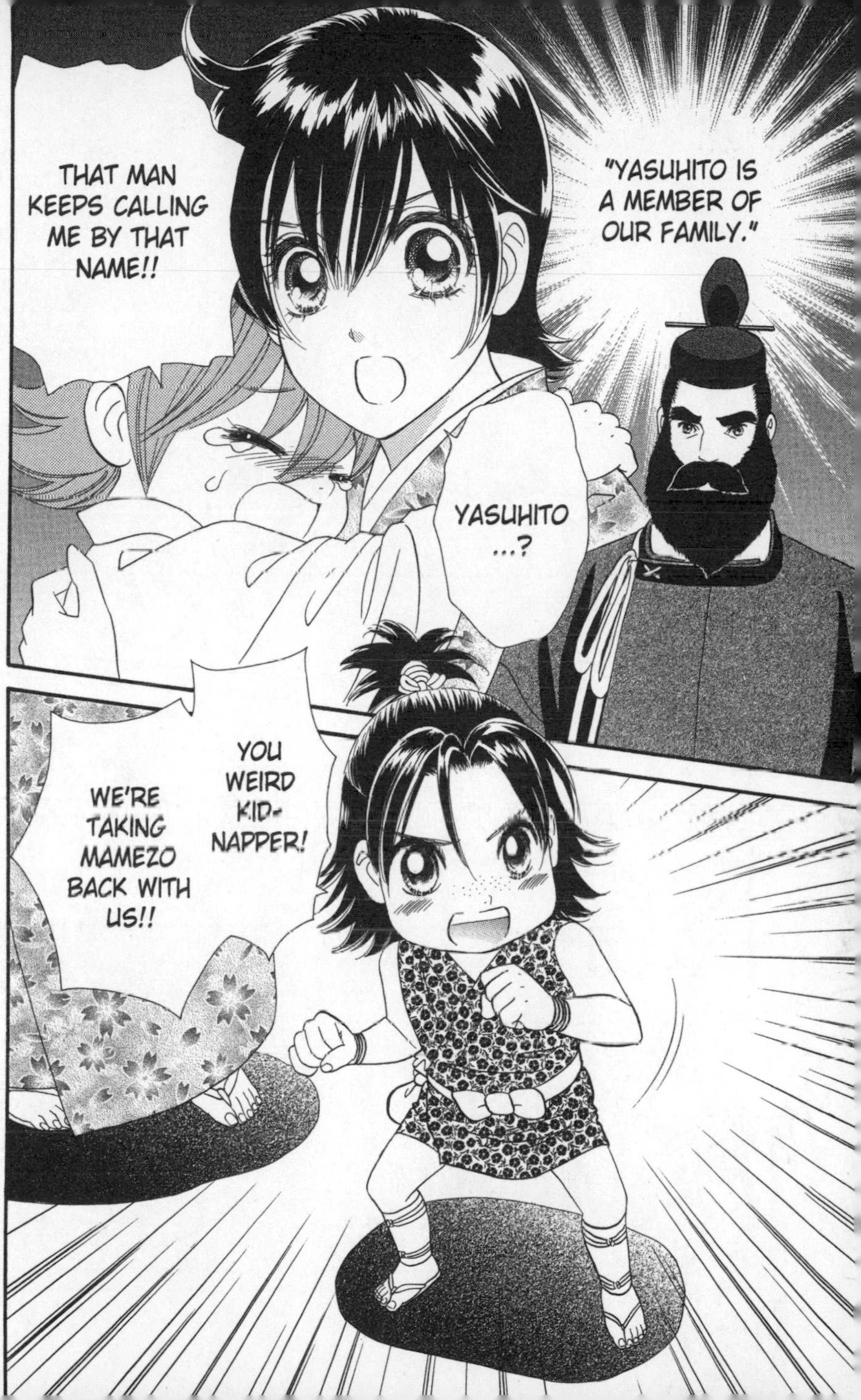
"YASUHITO IS A MEMBER OF OUR FAMILY."
THAT MAN KEEPS CALLING ME BY THAT NAME!!
YASUHITO ...?
YOU WEIRD KID-NAPPER!
WE'RE TAKING MAMEZO BACK WITH US!!

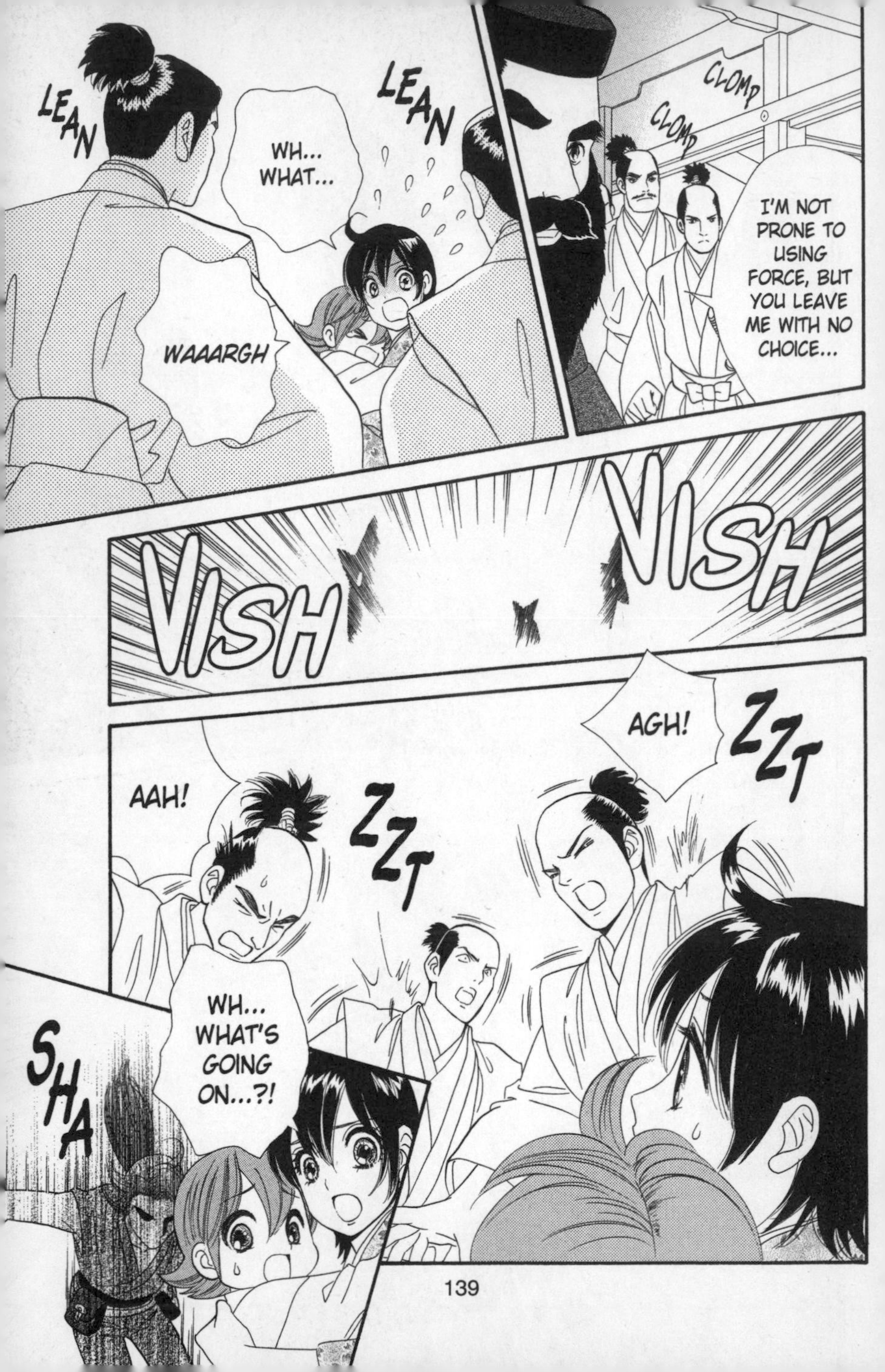

CLOMP
CLOMP
I'M NOT PRONE TO USING FORCE, BUT YOU LEAVE ME WITH NO CHOICE...
LEAN
WH... WHAT...
LEAN
WAAARGH
VISH
VISH
AGH!
ZZT
ZZT
AAH!
WH... WHAT'S GOING ON...?!
SHA

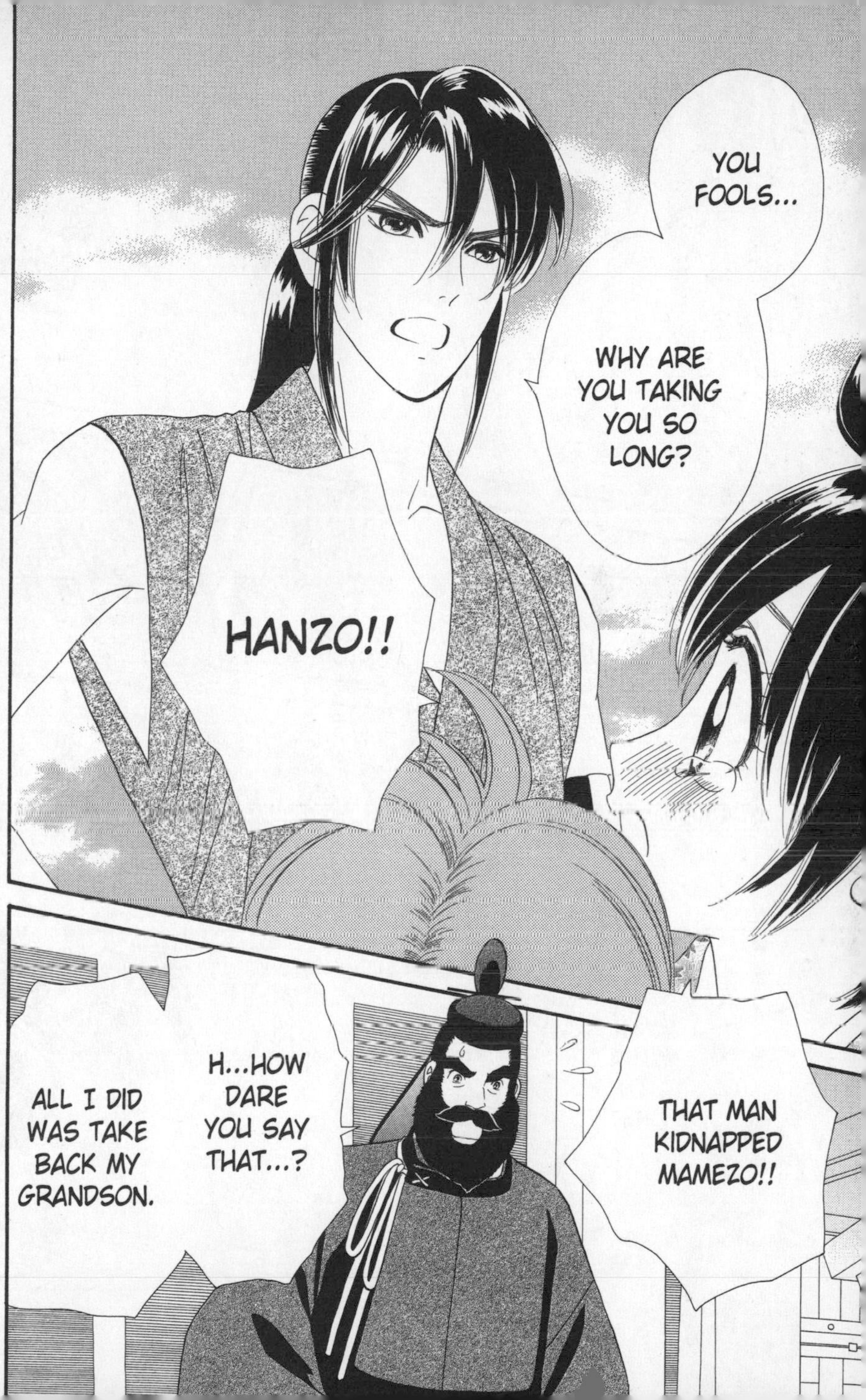
YOU FOOLS...
WHY ARE YOU TAKING YOU SO LONG?
HANZO!!
THAT MAN KIDNAPPED MAMEZO!!
H...HOW DARE YOU SAY THAT...?
ALL I DID WAS TAKE BACK MY GRANDSON.

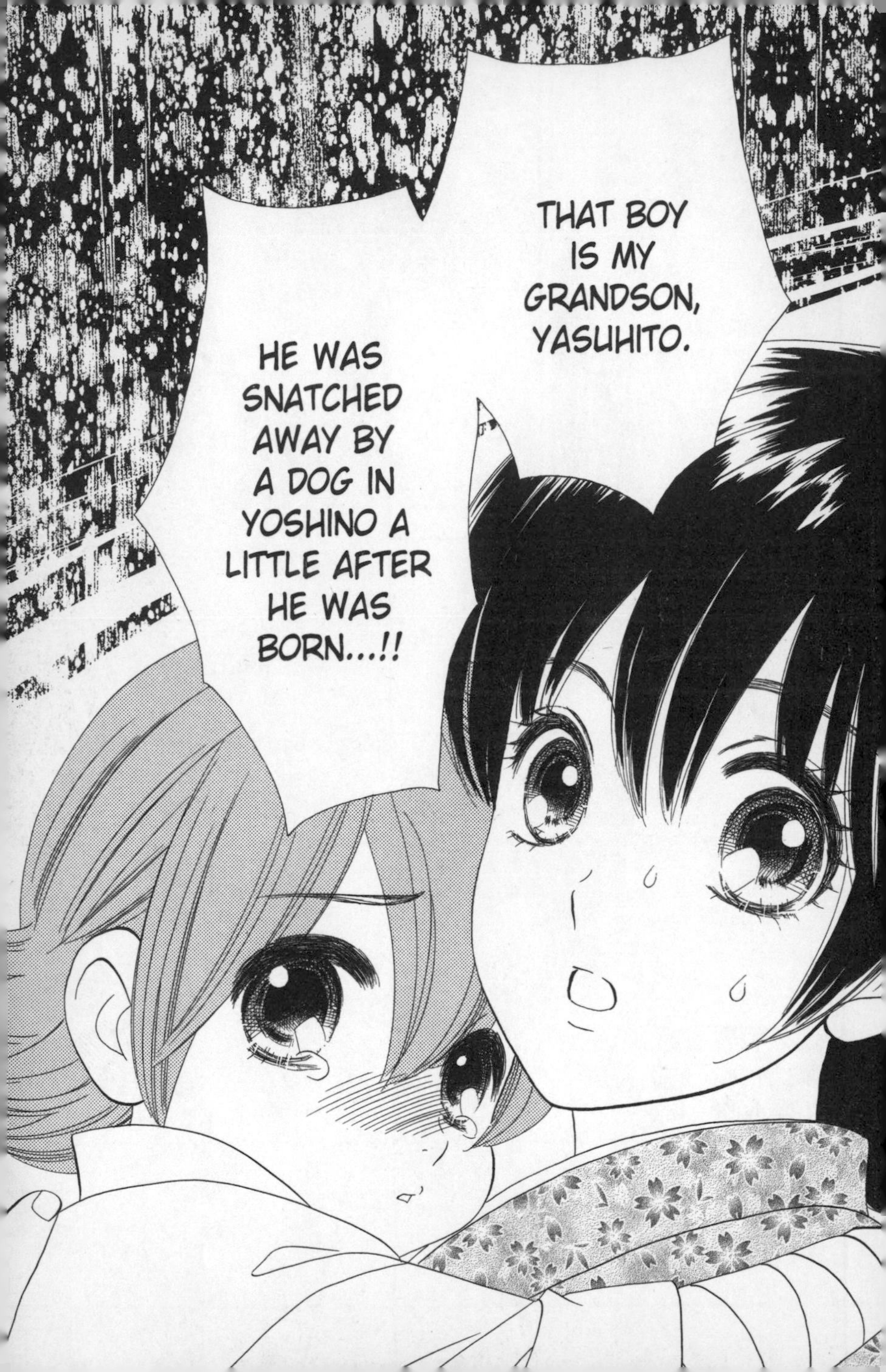
THAT BOY IS MY GRANDSON, YASUHITO.
HE WAS SNATCHED AWAY BY A DOG IN YOSHINO A LITTLE AFTER HE WAS BORN...!!

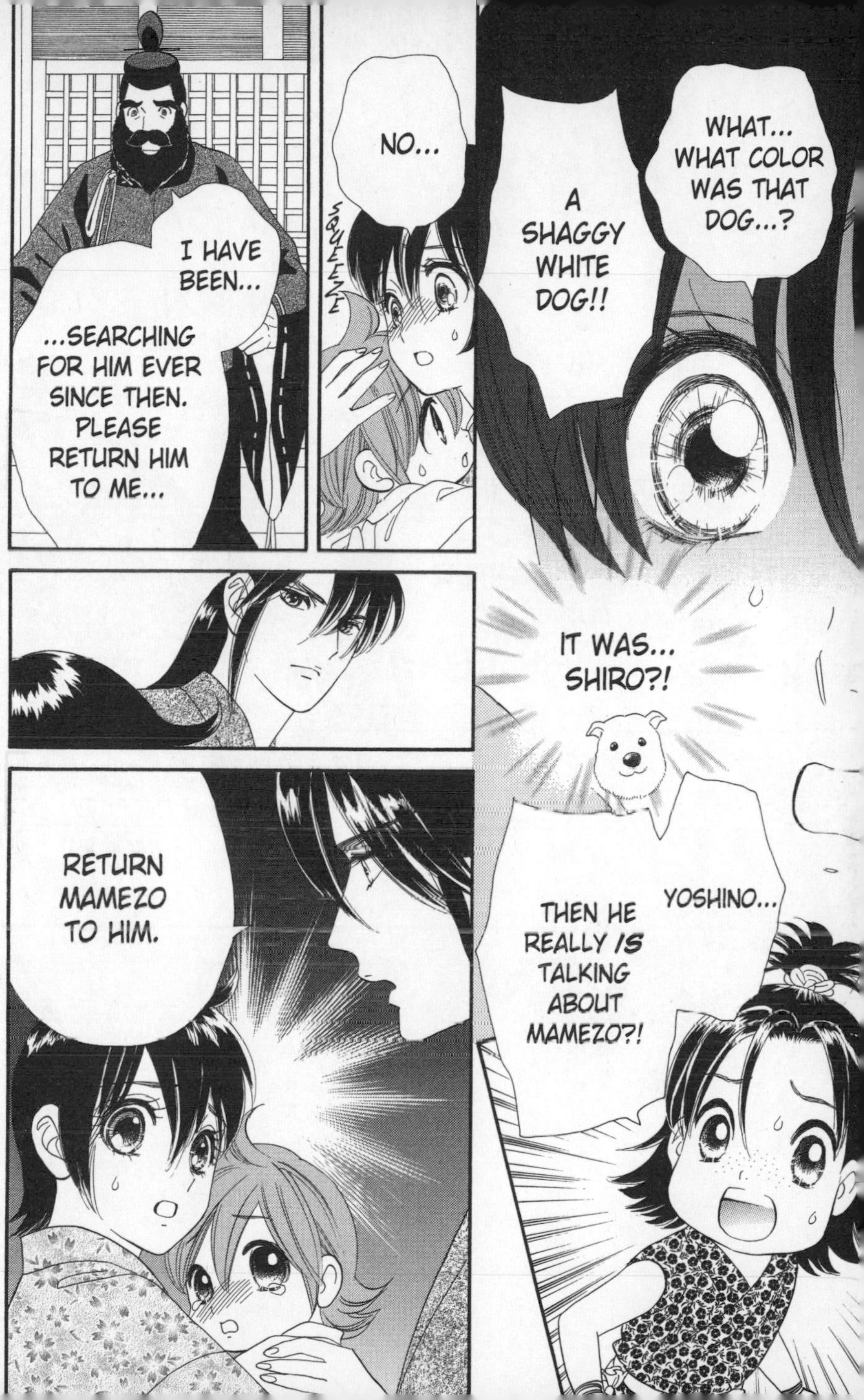
WHAT... WHAT COLOR WAS THAT DOG...?
A SHAGGY WHITE DOG!!
NO...
SQUEEZE
I HAVE BEEN...
...SEARCHING FOR HIM EVER SINCE THEN. PLEASE RETURN HIM TO ME...
IT WAS... SHIRO?!
YOSHINO...
THEN HE REALLY *IS* TALKING ABOUT MAMEZO?!
RETURN MAMEZO TO HIM.

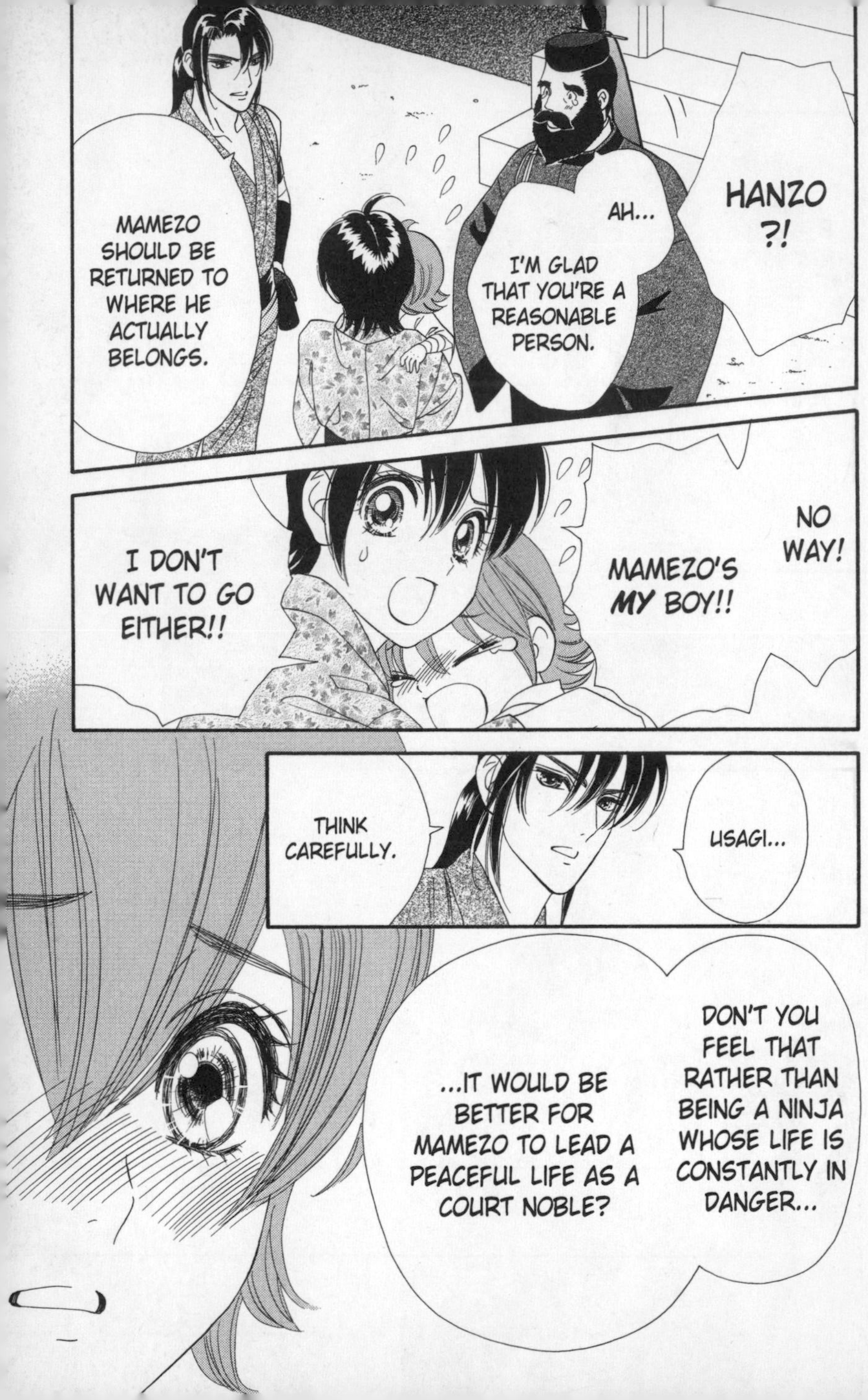
HANZO ?!
AH...
I'M GLAD THAT YOU'RE A REASONABLE PERSON.
MAMEZO SHOULD BE RETURNED TO WHERE HE ACTUALLY BELONGS.
NO WAY!
MAMEZO'S *MY* BOY!!
I DON'T WANT TO GO EITHER!!
USAGI...
THINK CAREFULLY.
DON'T YOU FEEL THAT RATHER THAN BEING A NINJA WHOSE LIFE IS CONSTANTLY IN DANGER...
...IT WOULD BE BETTER FOR MAMEZO TO LEAD A PEACEFUL LIFE AS A COURT NOBLE?

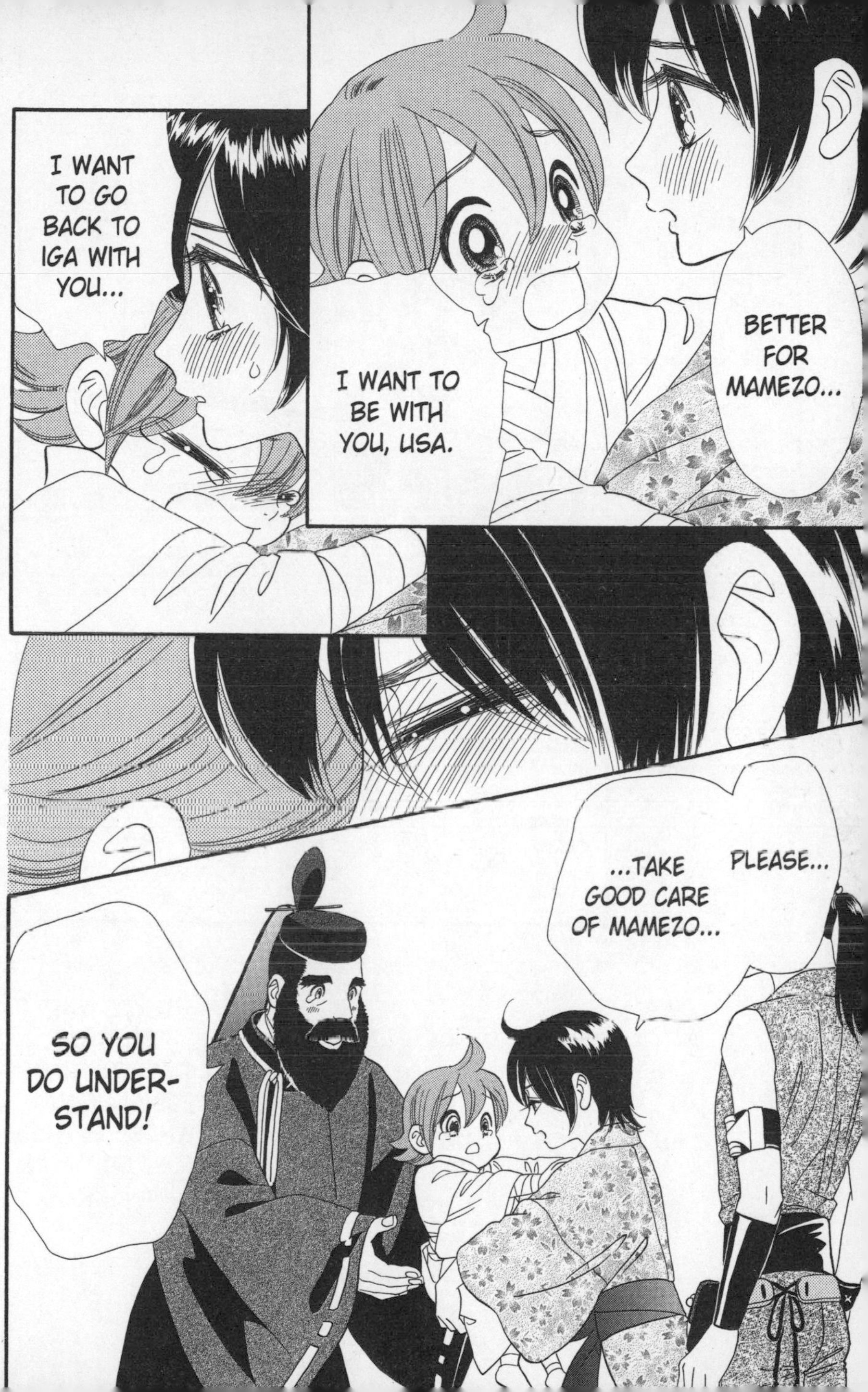
BETTER FOR MAMEZO...
I WANT TO BE WITH YOU, USA.
I WANT TO GO BACK TO IGA WITH YOU...
PLEASE...
...TAKE GOOD CARE OF MAMEZO...
SO YOU DO UNDER-STAND!

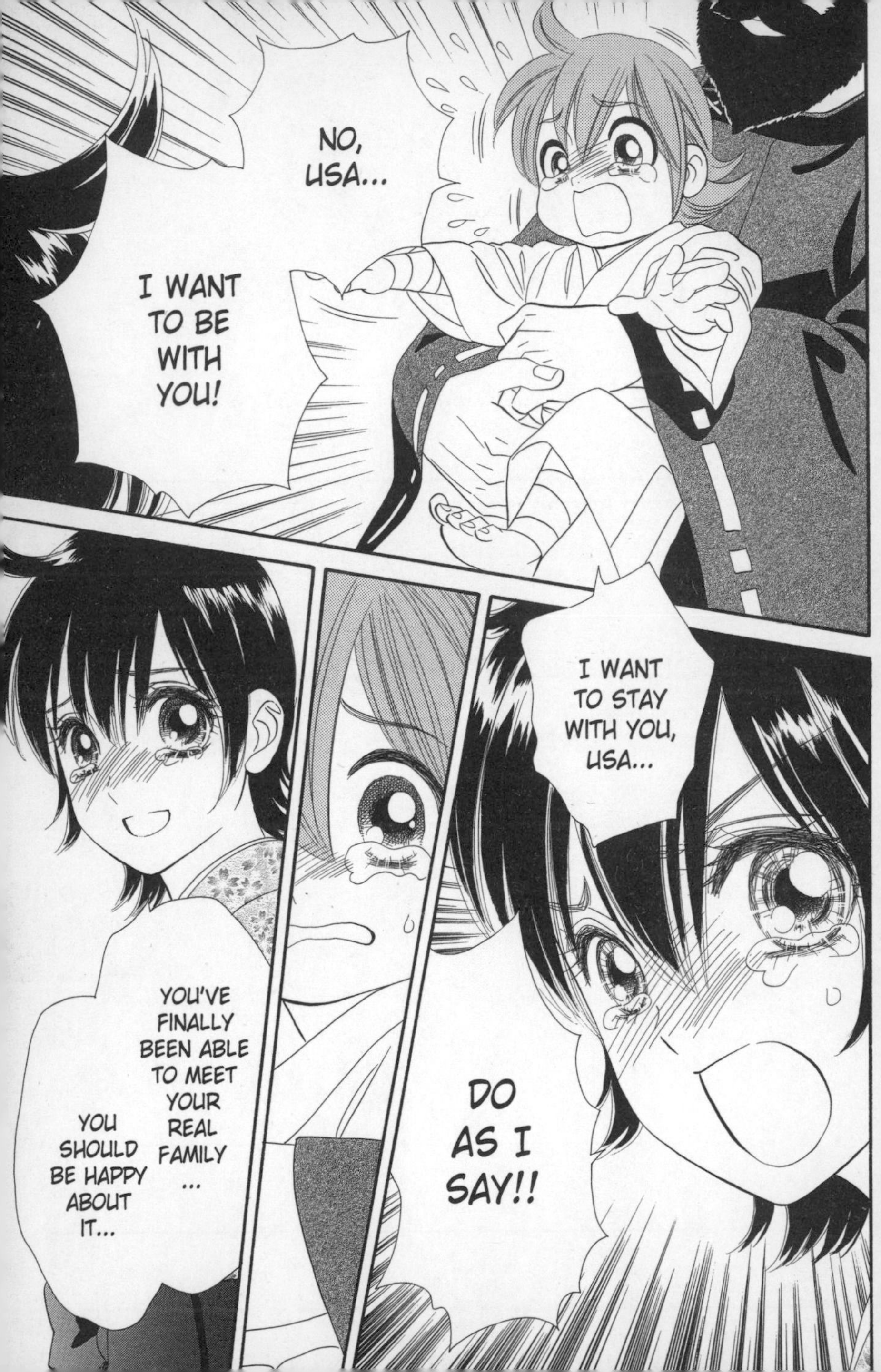
NO, USA...
I WANT TO BE WITH YOU!
I WANT TO STAY WITH YOU, USA...
DO AS I SAY!!
YOU'VE FINALLY BEEN ABLE TO MEET YOUR REAL FAMILY...
YOU SHOULD BE HAPPY ABOUT IT...

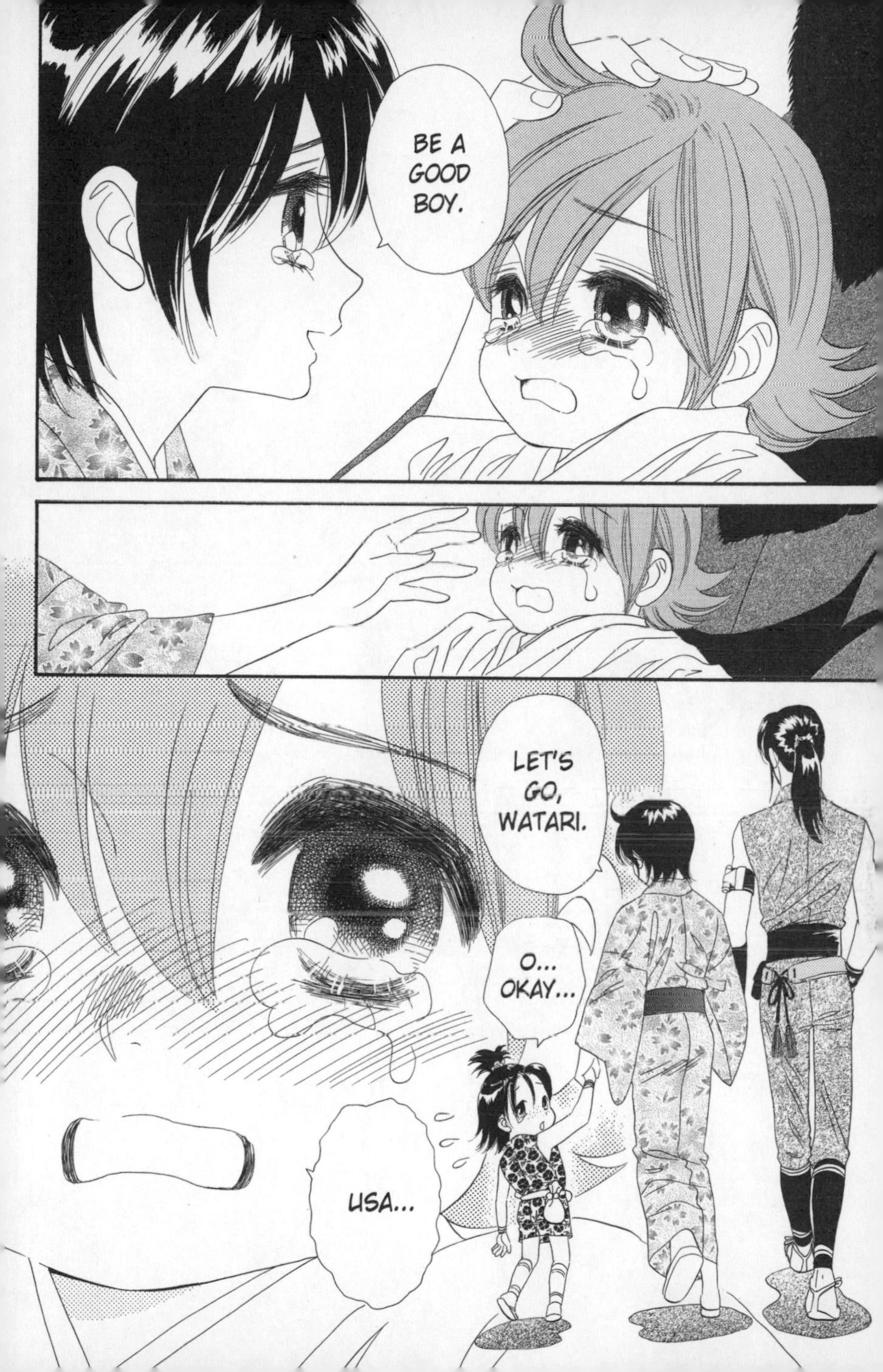
BE A GOOD BOY.
LET'S GO, WATARI.
O... OKAY...
USA...

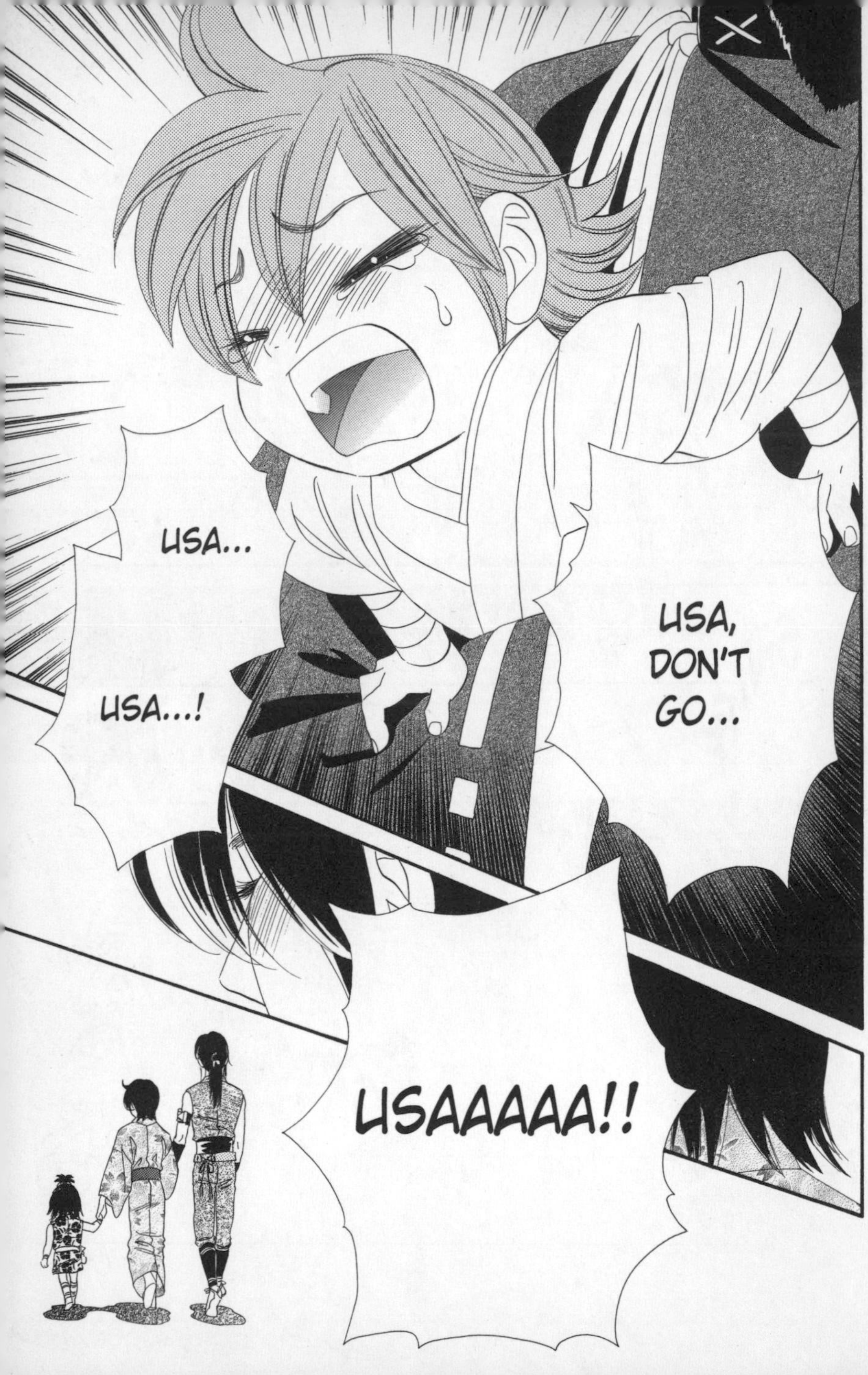
USA, DON'T GO...
USA...
USA...!
USAAAAAA!!

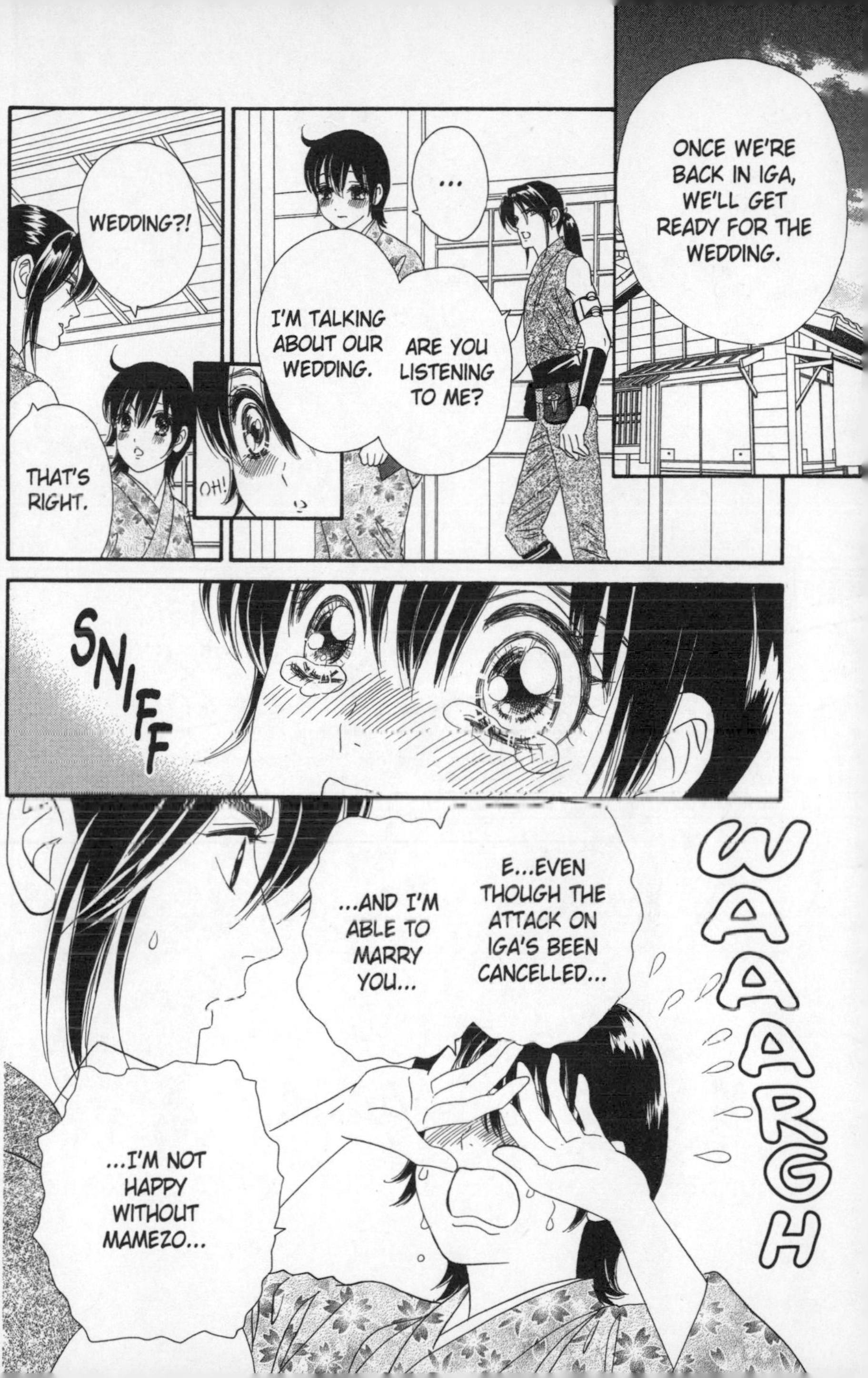
ONCE WE'RE BACK IN IGA, WE'LL GET READY FOR THE WEDDING.
...
I'M TALKING ABOUT OUR WEDDING.
ARE YOU LISTENING TO ME?
WEDDING?!
OH!
THAT'S RIGHT.
SNIFF
WAAARGH
E...EVEN THOUGH THE ATTACK ON IGA'S BEEN CANCELLED...
...AND I'M ABLE TO MARRY YOU...
...I'M NOT HAPPY WITHOUT MAMEZO...

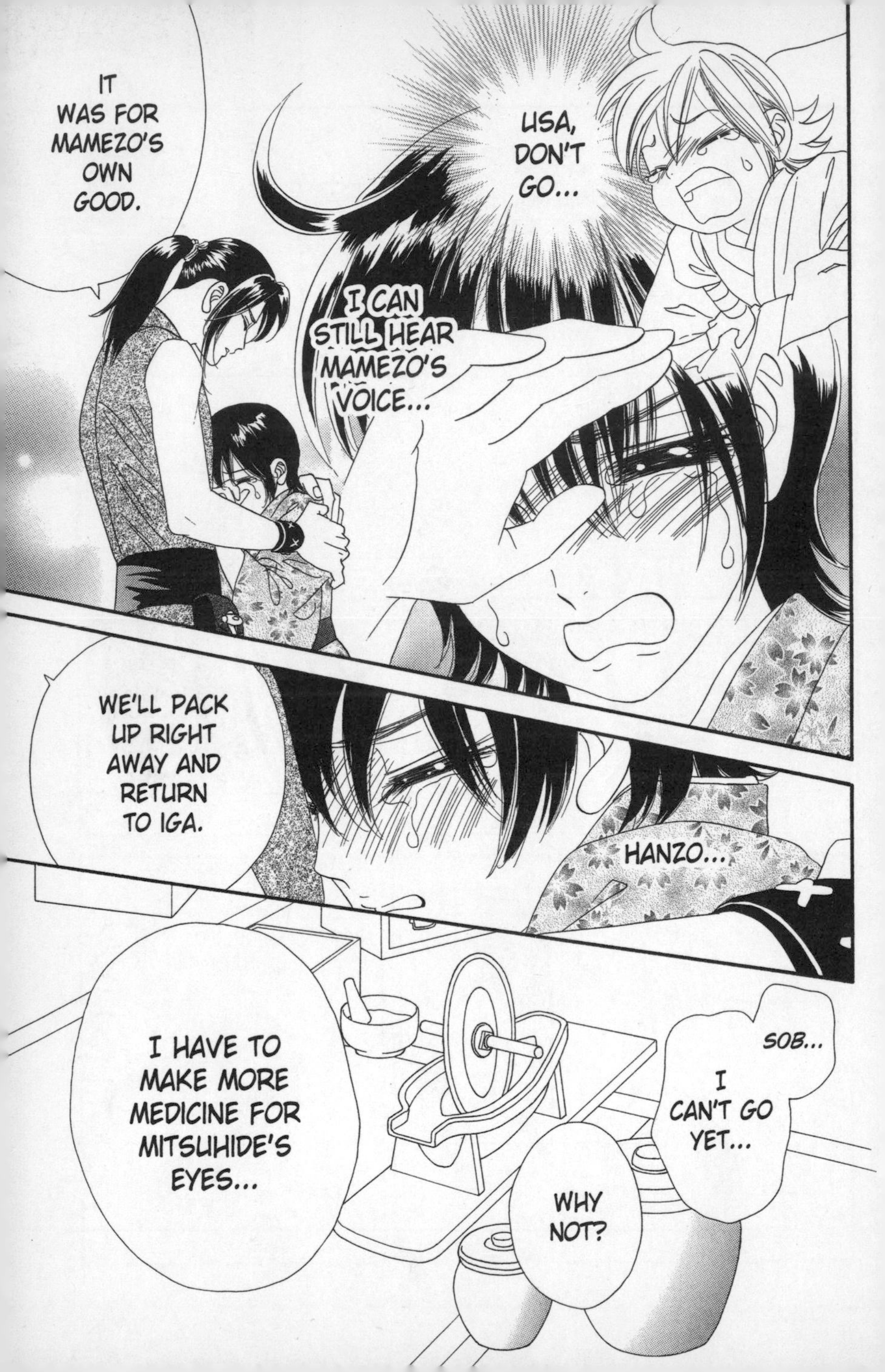
USA, DON'T GO...
I CAN STILL HEAR MAMEZO'S VOICE...
IT WAS FOR MAMEZO'S OWN GOOD.
HANZO...
WE'LL PACK UP RIGHT AWAY AND RETURN TO IGA.
SOB...
I CAN'T GO YET...
WHY NOT?
I HAVE TO MAKE MORE MEDICINE FOR MITSUHIDE'S EYES...

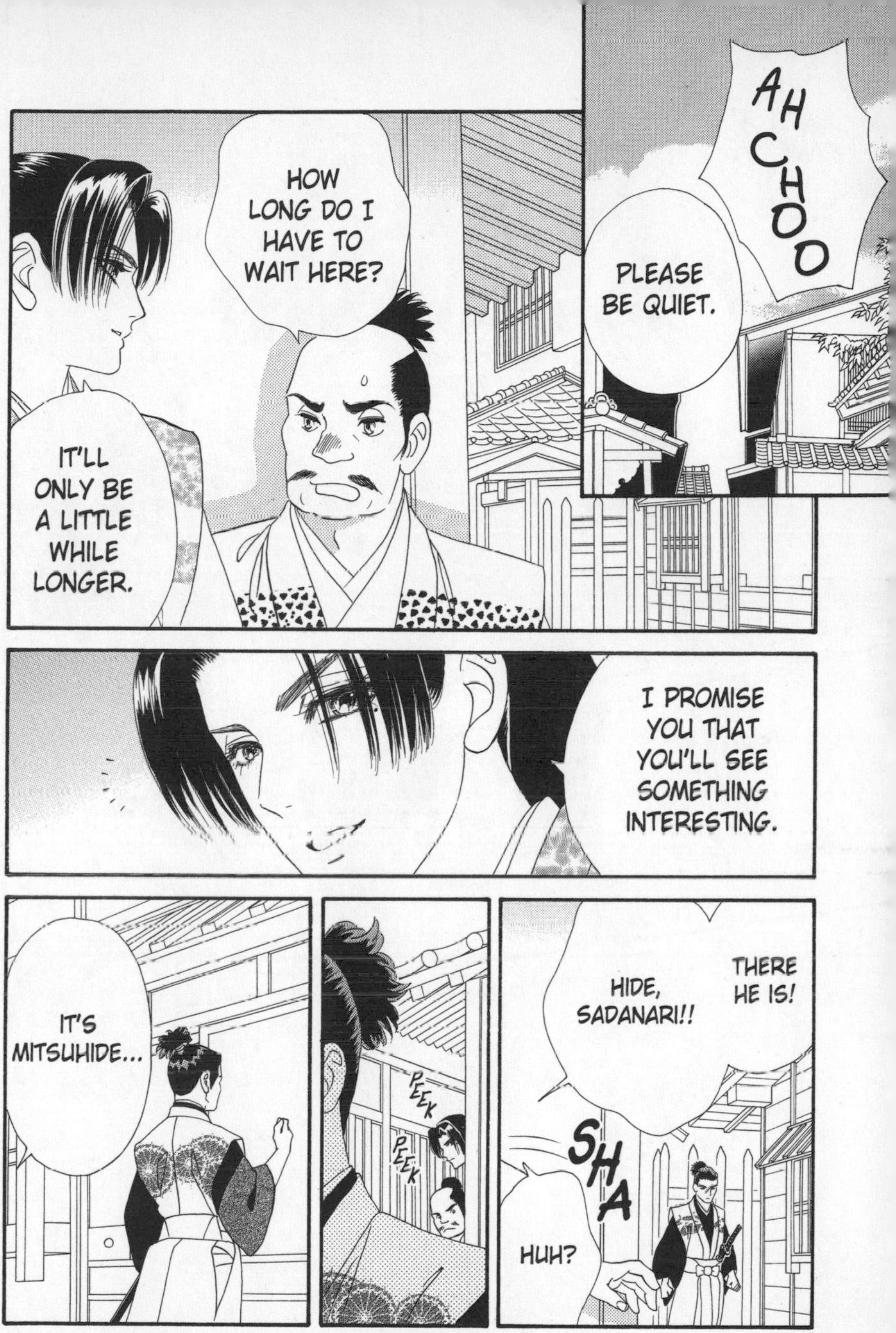
AH CHOO
PLEASE BE QUIET.
HOW LONG DO I HAVE TO WAIT HERE?
IT'LL ONLY BE A LITTLE WHILE LONGER.
I PROMISE YOU THAT YOU'LL SEE SOMETHING INTERESTING.
THERE HE IS!
HIDE, SADANARI!!
SHA
HUH?
PEEK
PEEK
IT'S MITSUHIDE...

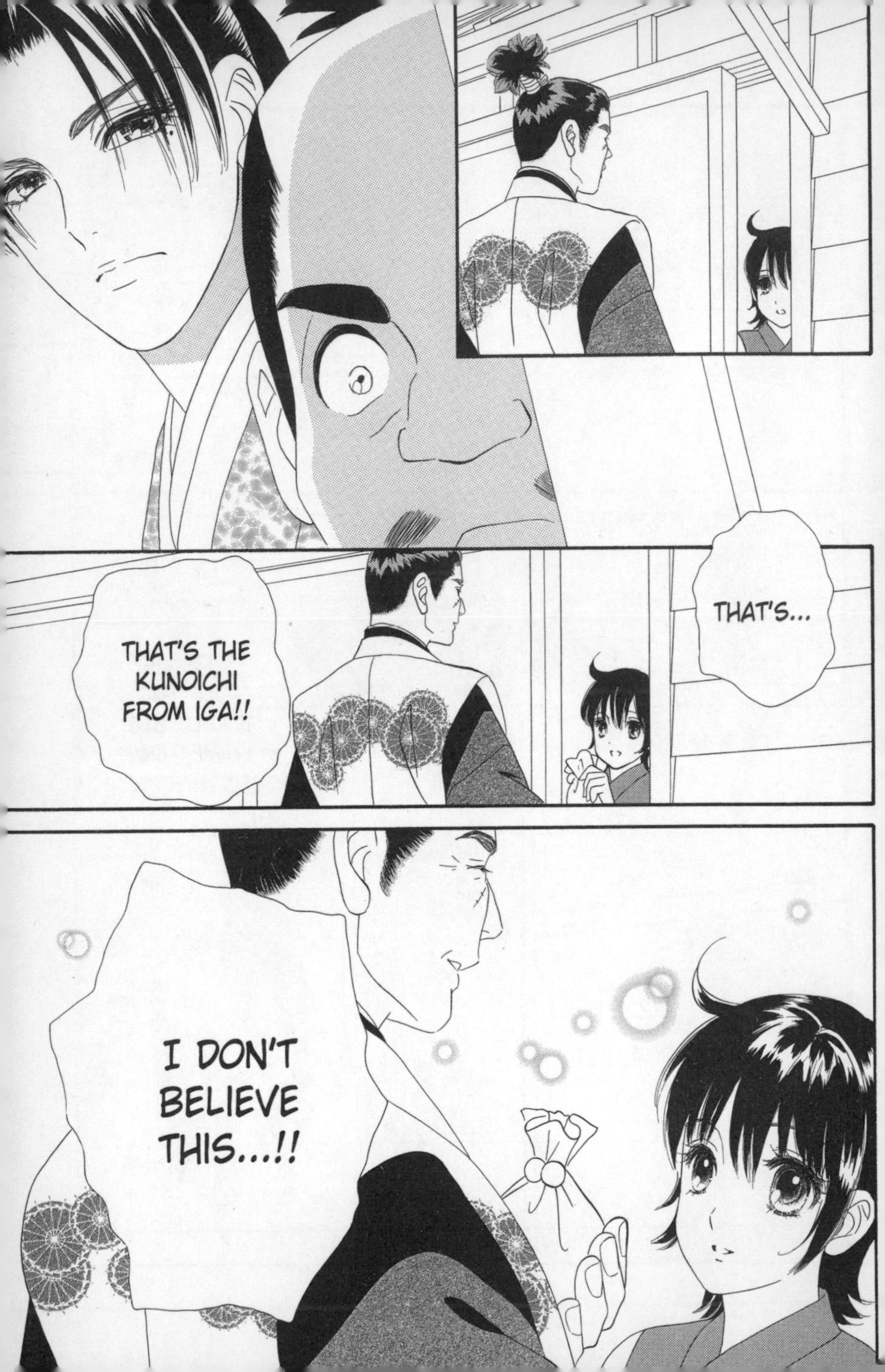
THAT'S...
THAT'S THE KUNOICHI FROM IGA!!
I DON'T BELIEVE THIS...!!

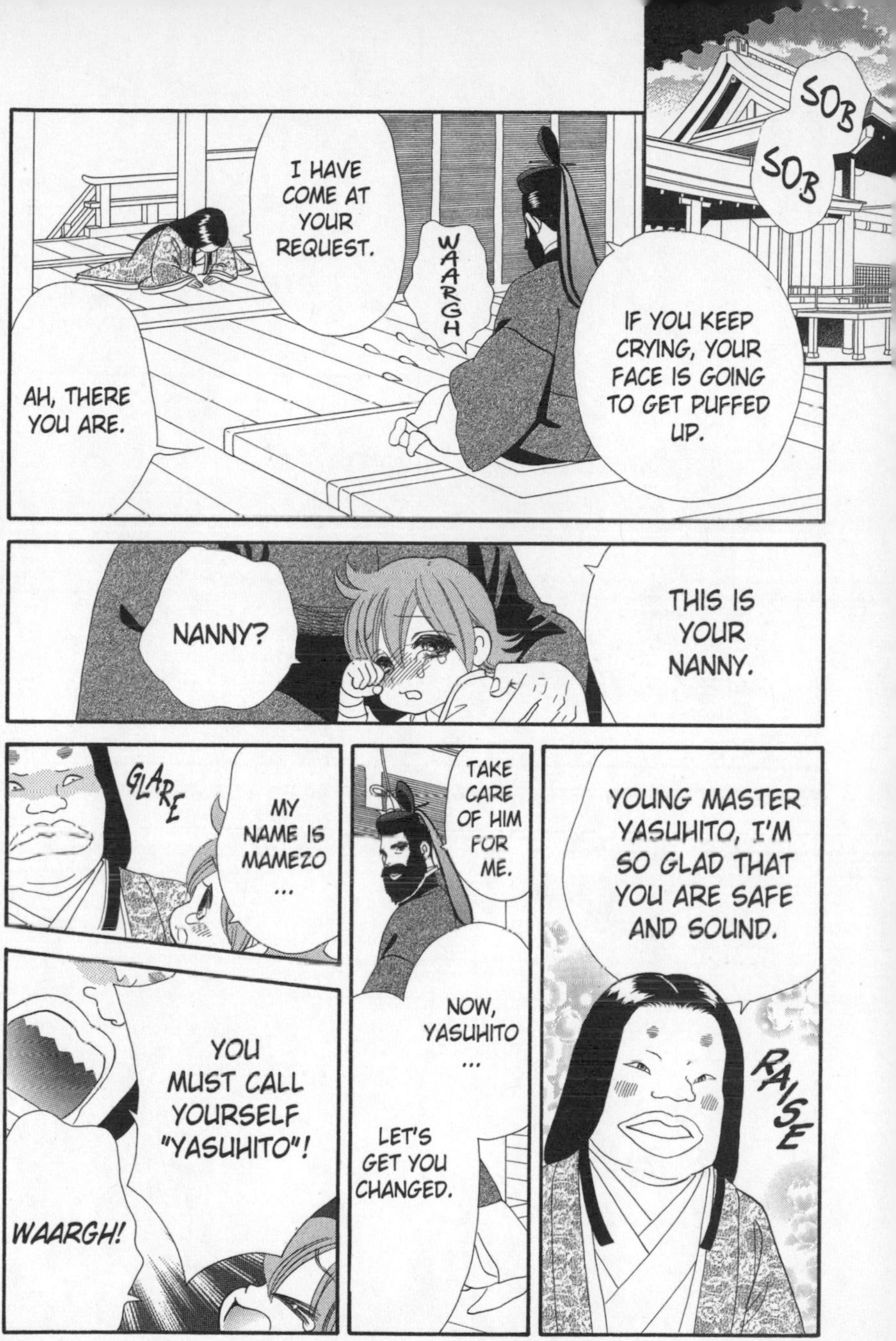
SOB
SOB
IF YOU KEEP CRYING, YOUR FACE IS GOING TO GET PUFFED UP.
WAARGH
I HAVE COME AT YOUR REQUEST.
AH, THERE YOU ARE.
THIS IS YOUR NANNY.
NANNY?
YOUNG MASTER YASUHITO, I'M SO GLAD THAT YOU ARE SAFE AND SOUND.
RAISE
TAKE CARE OF HIM FOR ME.
NOW, YASUHITO...
LET'S GET YOU CHANGED.
MY NAME IS MAMEZO...
GLARE
YOU MUST CALL YOURSELF "YASUHITO"!
WAARGH!

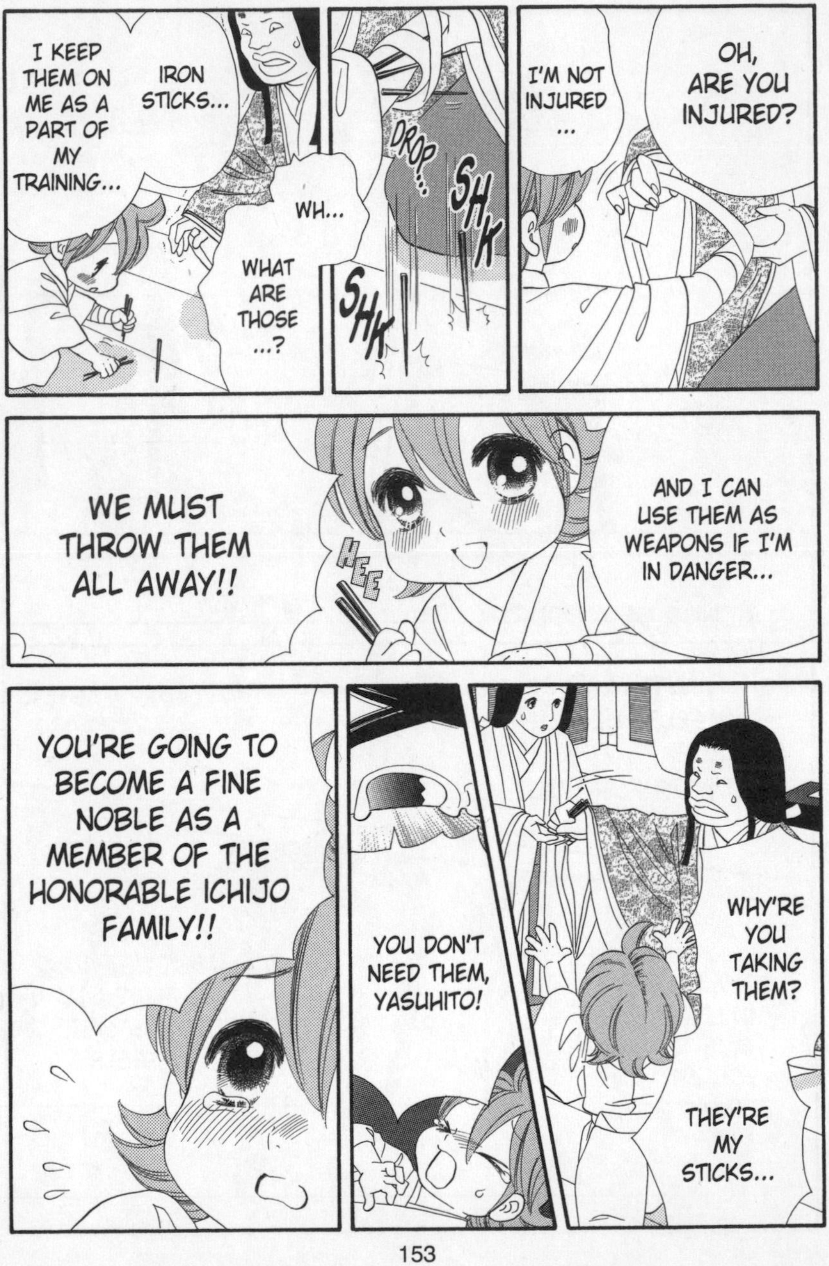
OH, ARE YOU INJURED?
I'M NOT INJURED ...
SHK
DROP...
SHK
WH...
WHAT ARE THOSE ...?
IRON STICKS...
I KEEP THEM ON ME AS A PART OF MY TRAINING...
AND I CAN USE THEM AS WEAPONS IF I'M IN DANGER...
HEE
WE MUST THROW THEM ALL AWAY!!
WHY'RE YOU TAKING THEM?
THEY'RE MY STICKS...
YOU DON'T NEED THEM, YASUHITO!
YOU'RE GOING TO BECOME A FINE NOBLE AS A MEMBER OF THE HONORABLE ICHIJO FAMILY!!

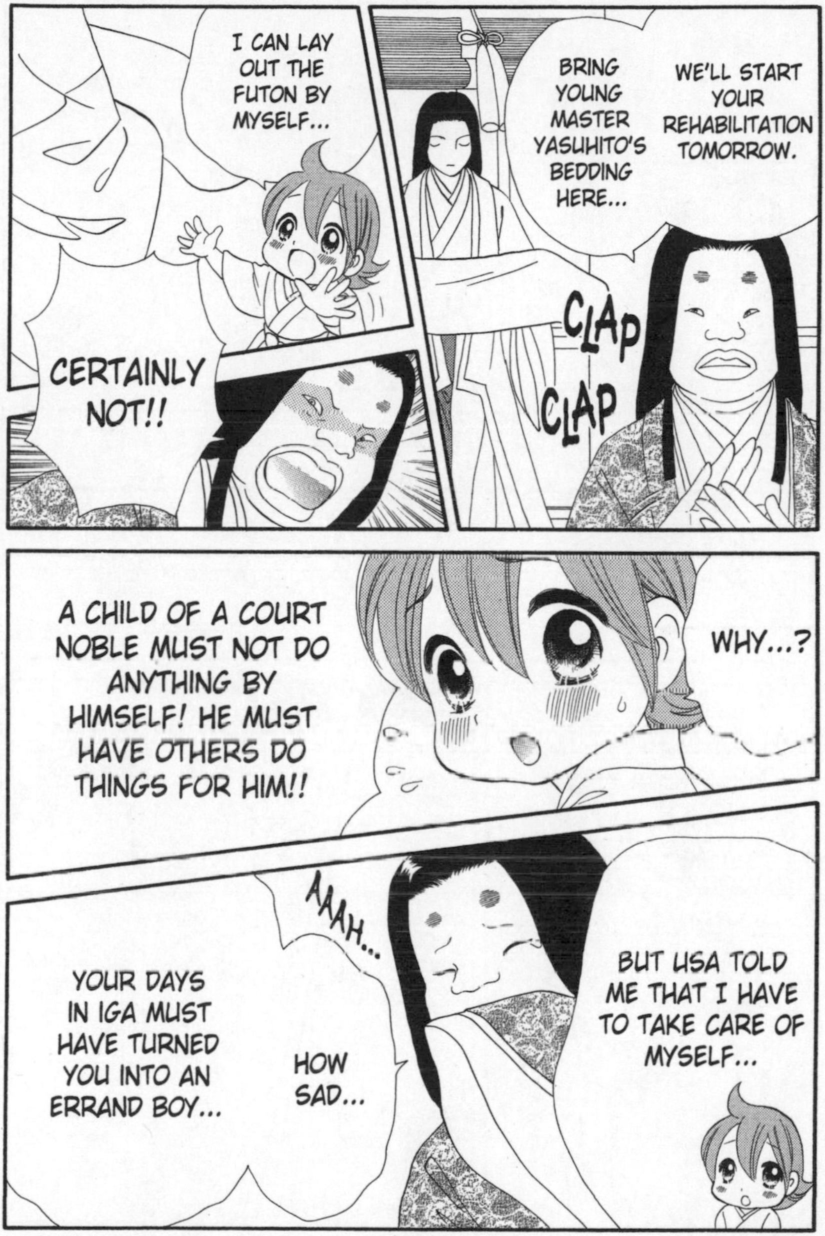
WE'LL START YOUR REHABILITATION TOMORROW.
BRING YOUNG MASTER YASUHITO'S BEDDING HERE...
CLAP
CLAP
I CAN LAY OUT THE FUTON BY MYSELF...
CERTAINLY NOT!!
WHY...?
A CHILD OF A COURT NOBLE MUST NOT DO ANYTHING BY HIMSELF! HE MUST HAVE OTHERS DO THINGS FOR HIM!!
BUT USA TOLD ME THAT I HAVE TO TAKE CARE OF MYSELF...
AAAH...
HOW SAD...
YOUR DAYS IN IGA MUST HAVE TURNED YOU INTO AN ERRAND BOY...

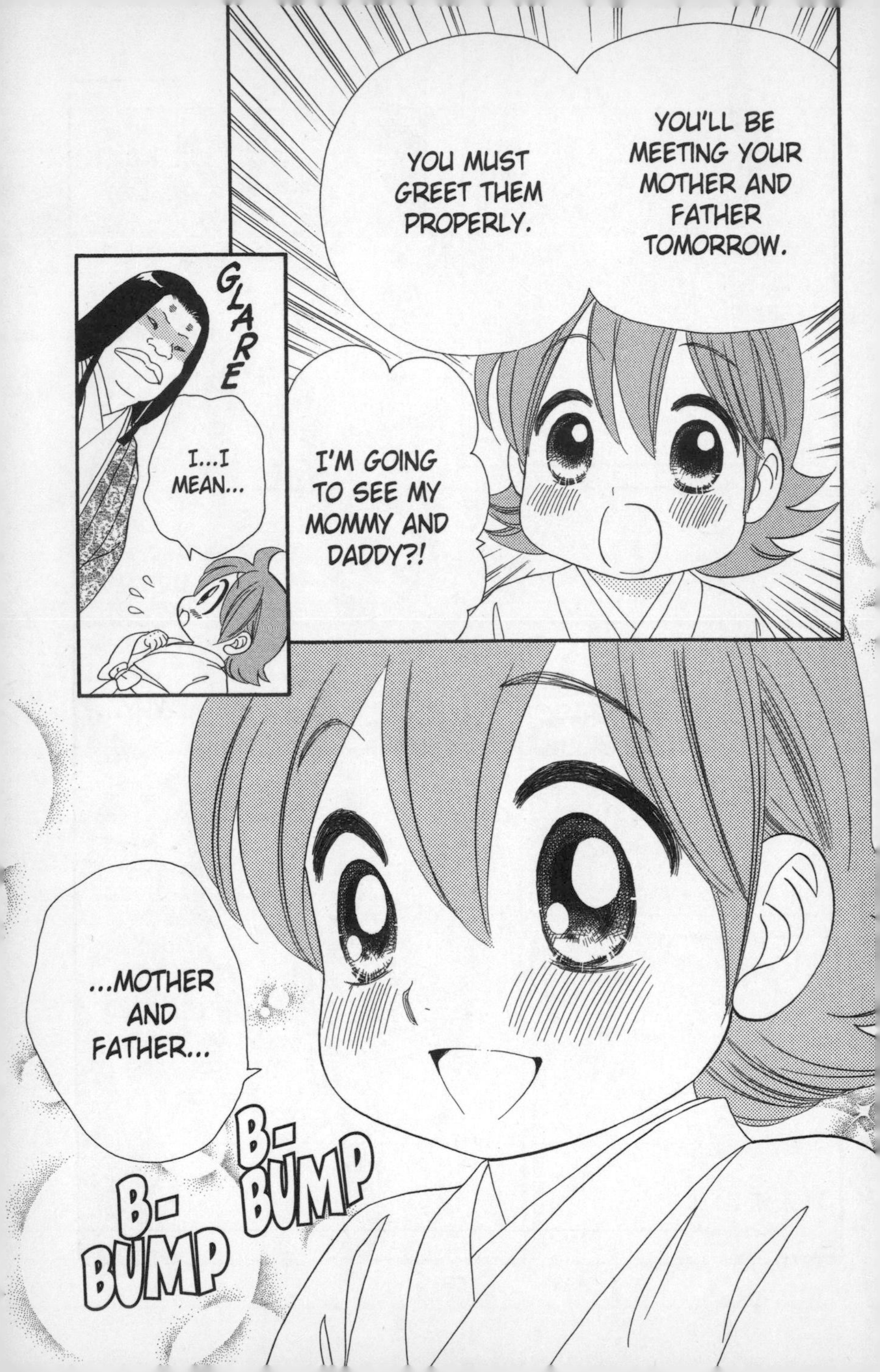
YOU'LL BE MEETING YOUR MOTHER AND FATHER TOMORROW.
YOU MUST GREET THEM PROPERLY.
I'M GOING TO SEE MY MOMMY AND DADDY?!
GLARE
I...I MEAN...
...MOTHER AND FATHER...
B-BUMP
B-BUMP

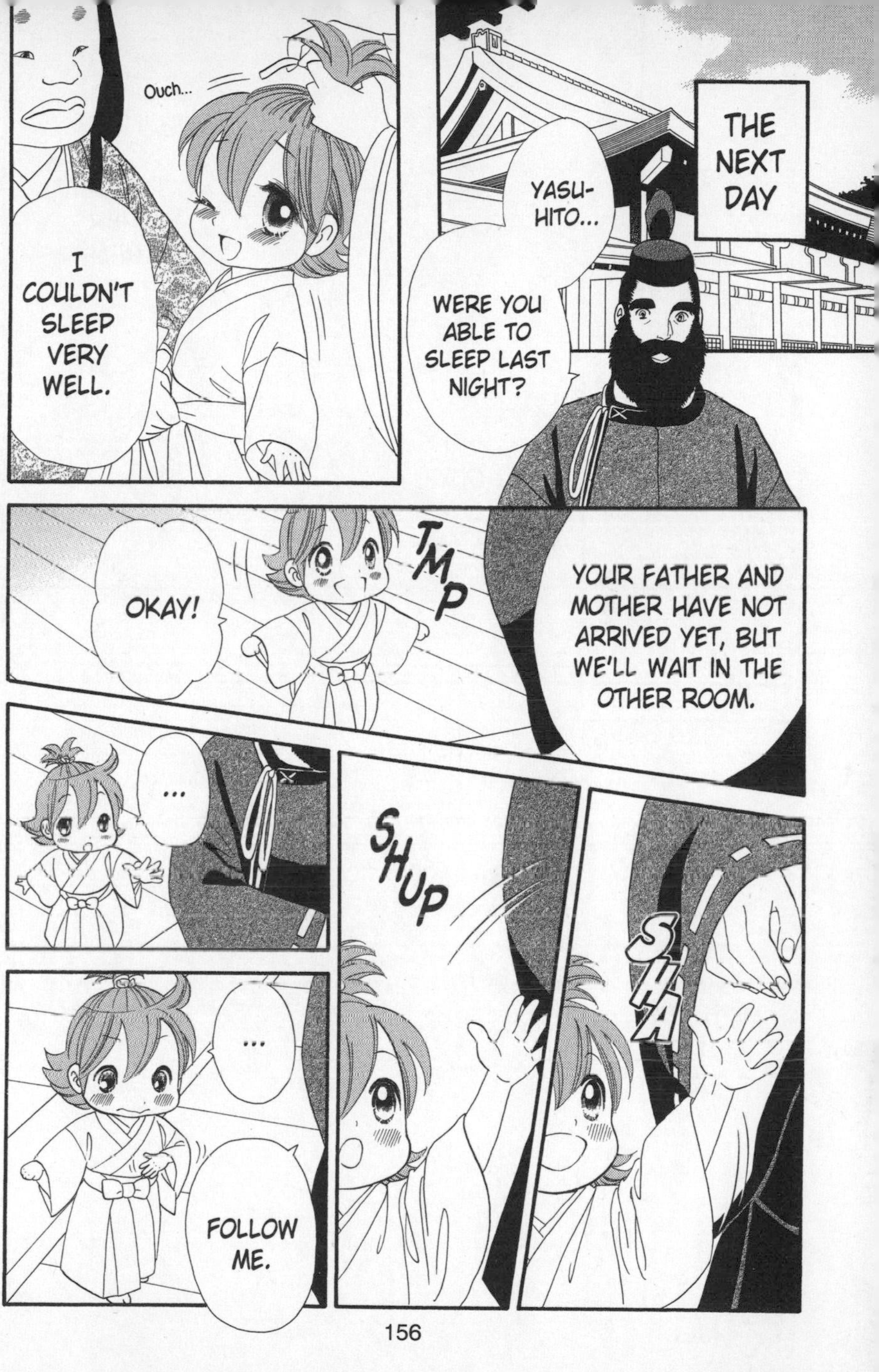
THE NEXT DAY
YASU-HITO...
WERE YOU ABLE TO SLEEP LAST NIGHT?
Ouch...
I COULDN'T SLEEP VERY WELL.
YOUR FATHER AND MOTHER HAVE NOT ARRIVED YET, BUT WE'LL WAIT IN THE OTHER ROOM.
TMP
OKAY!
SHA
SHUP
...
...
FOLLOW ME.

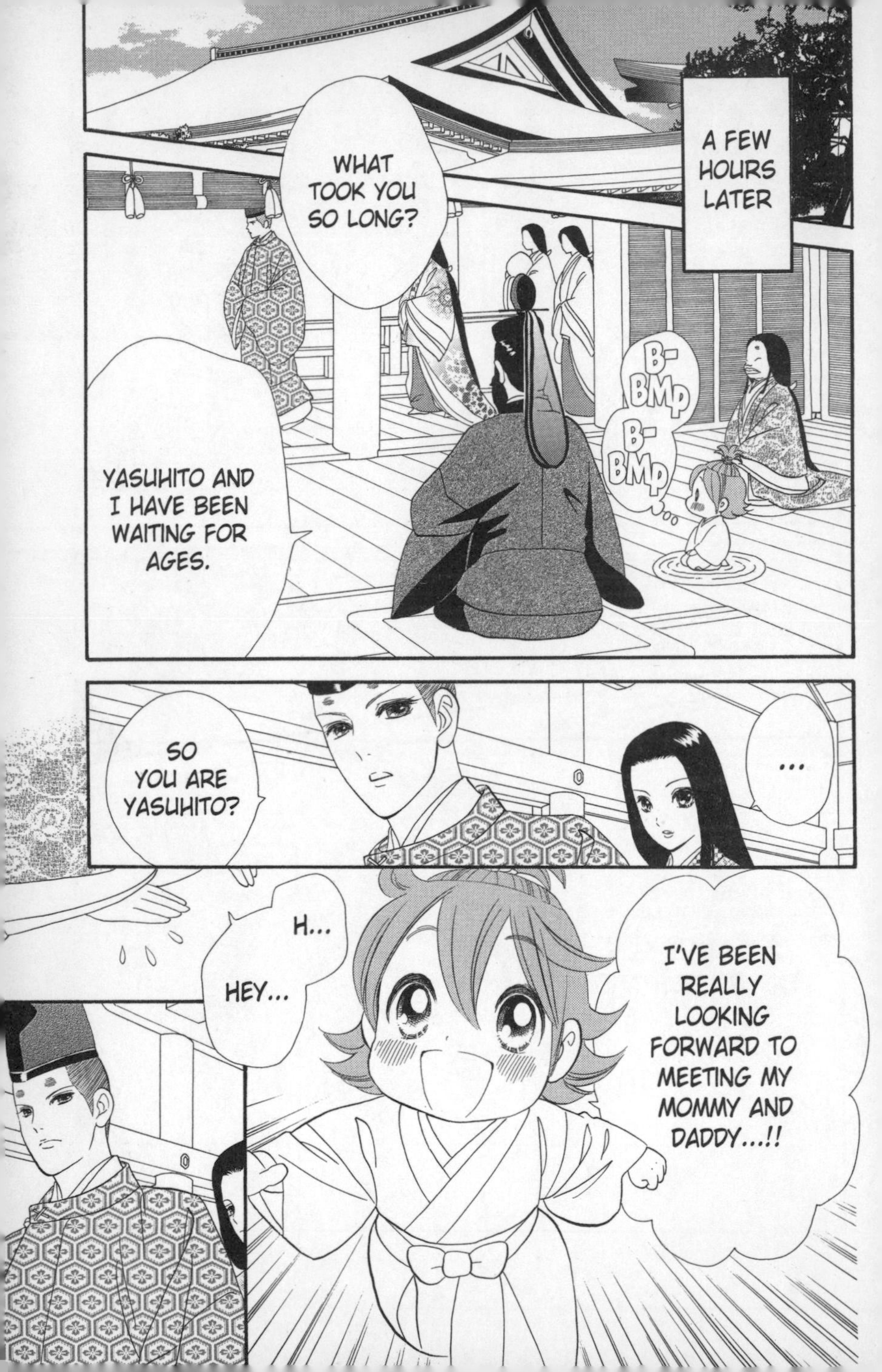
A FEW HOURS LATER
WHAT TOOK YOU SO LONG?
B-BMP
B-BMP...
YASUHITO AND I HAVE BEEN WAITING FOR AGES.
...
SO YOU ARE YASUHITO?
I'VE BEEN REALLY LOOKING FORWARD TO MEETING MY MOMMY AND DADDY...!!
H...
HEY...

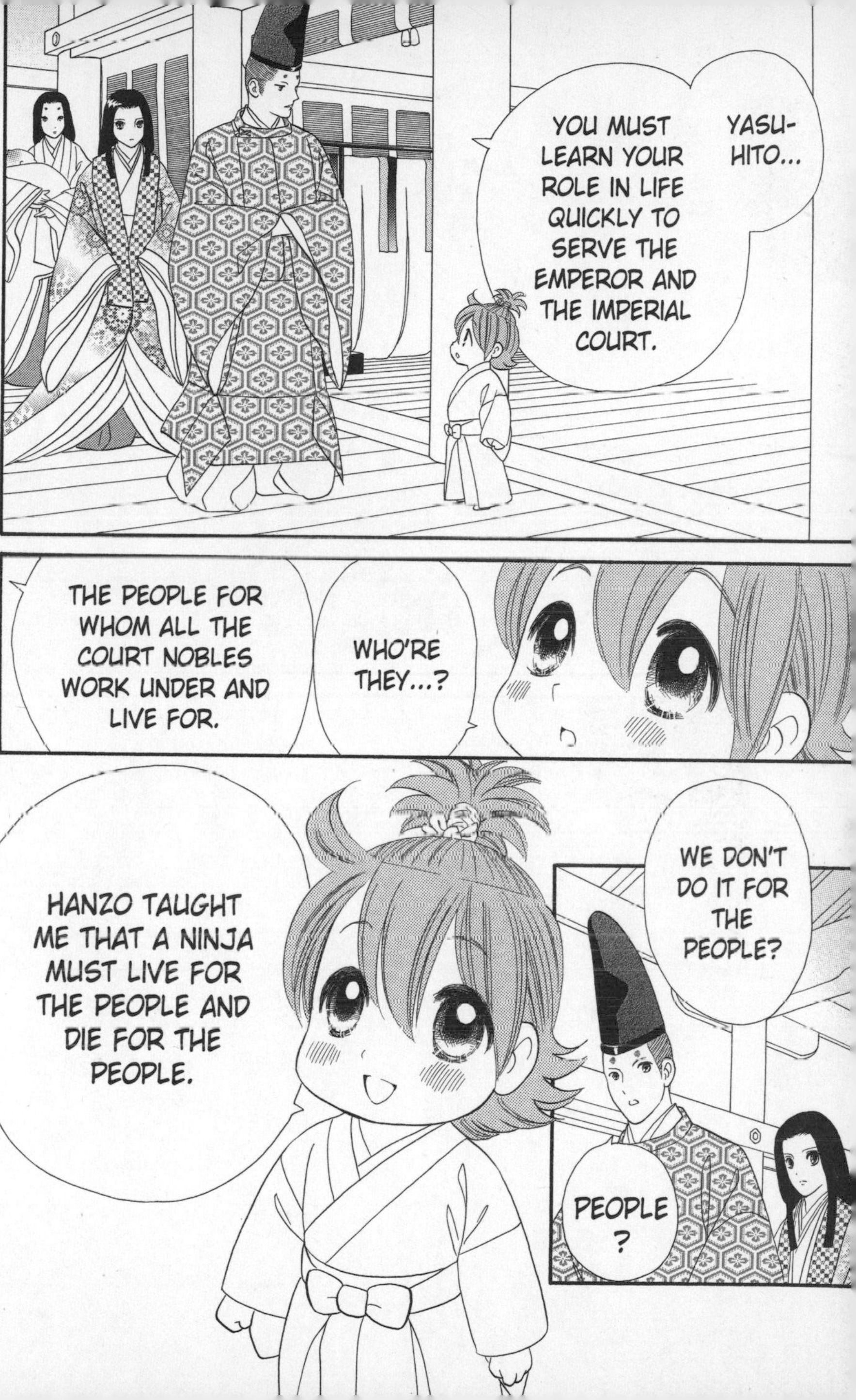
YASU-HITO...
YOU MUST LEARN YOUR ROLE IN LIFE QUICKLY TO SERVE THE EMPEROR AND THE IMPERIAL COURT.
WHO'RE THEY...?
THE PEOPLE FOR WHOM ALL THE COURT NOBLES WORK UNDER AND LIVE FOR.
WE DON'T DO IT FOR THE PEOPLE?
PEOPLE ?
HANZO TAUGHT ME THAT A NINJA MUST LIVE FOR THE PEOPLE AND DIE FOR THE PEOPLE.

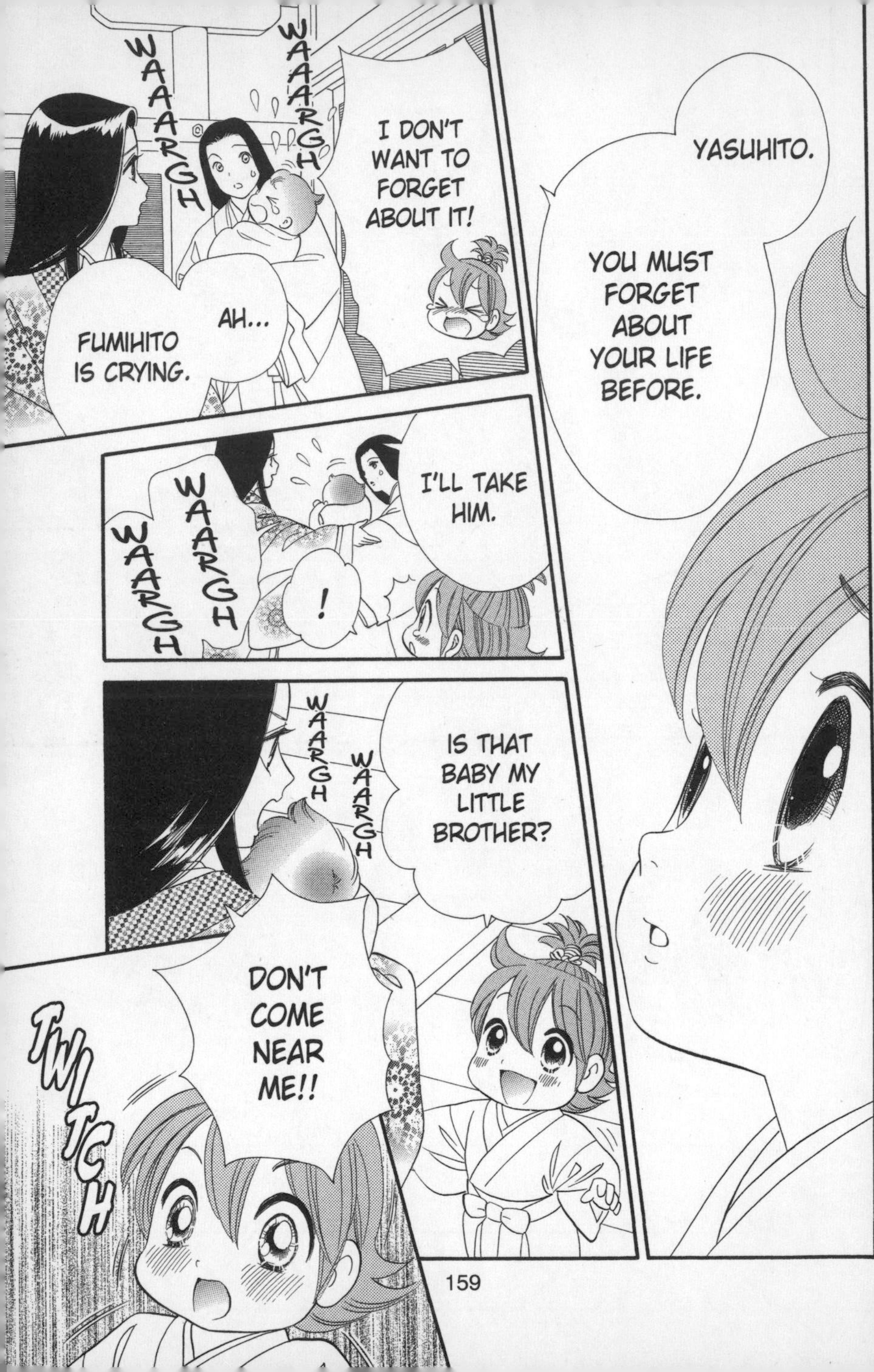
YASUHITO.
YOU MUST FORGET ABOUT YOUR LIFE BEFORE.
I DON'T WANT TO FORGET ABOUT IT!
WAAAARGH
WAAARGH
AH...
FUMIHITO IS CRYING.
I'LL TAKE HIM.
WAARGH
WAARGH
!
IS THAT BABY MY LITTLE BROTHER?
WAARGH
WAARGH
DON'T COME NEAR ME!!
TWITCH

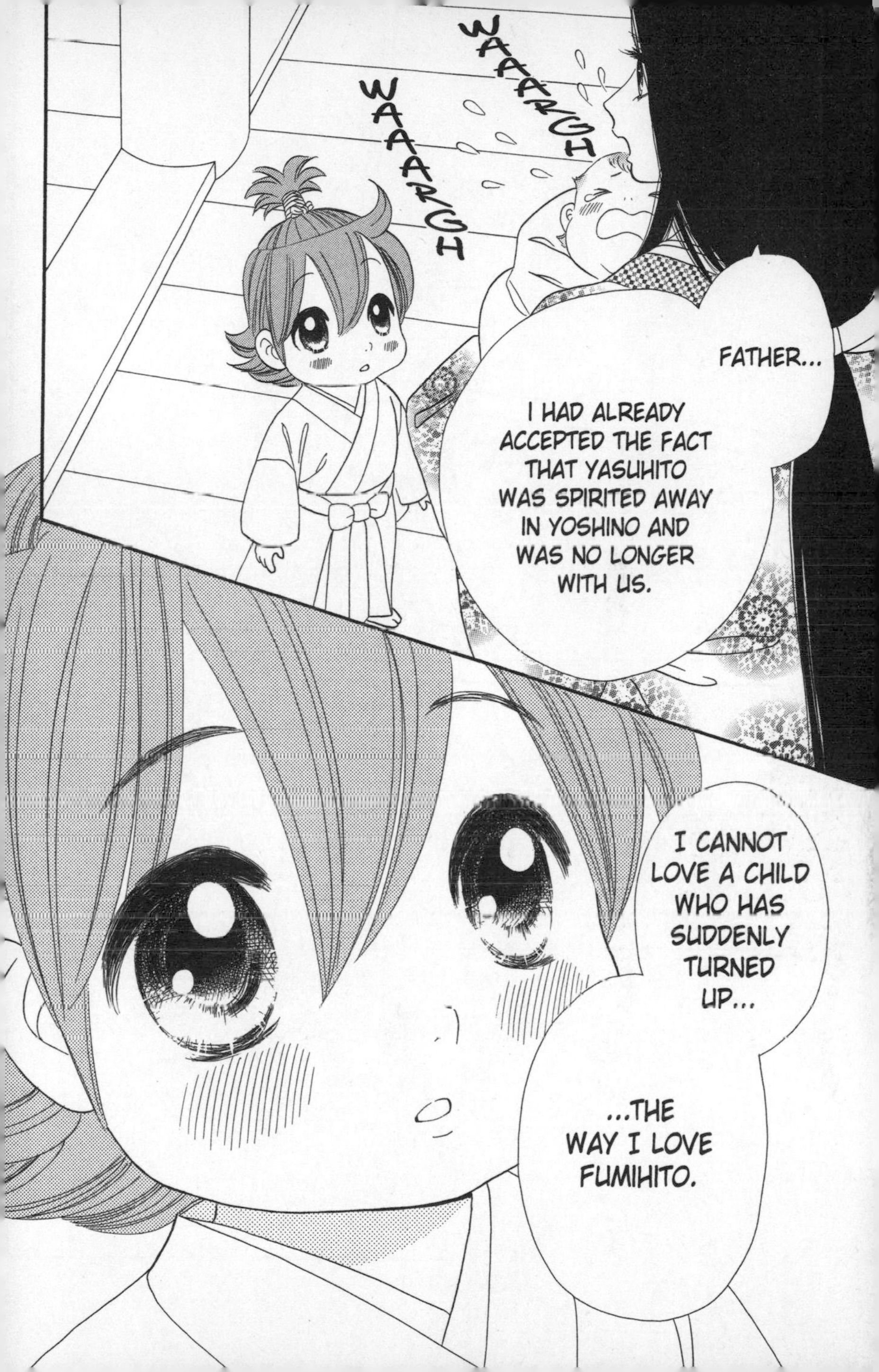
WAAAARGH
WAAAARGH
FATHER...
I HAD ALREADY ACCEPTED THE FACT THAT YASUHITO WAS SPIRITED AWAY IN YOSHINO AND WAS NO LONGER WITH US.
I CANNOT LOVE A CHILD WHO HAS SUDDENLY TURNED UP...
...THE WAY I LOVE FUMIHITO.

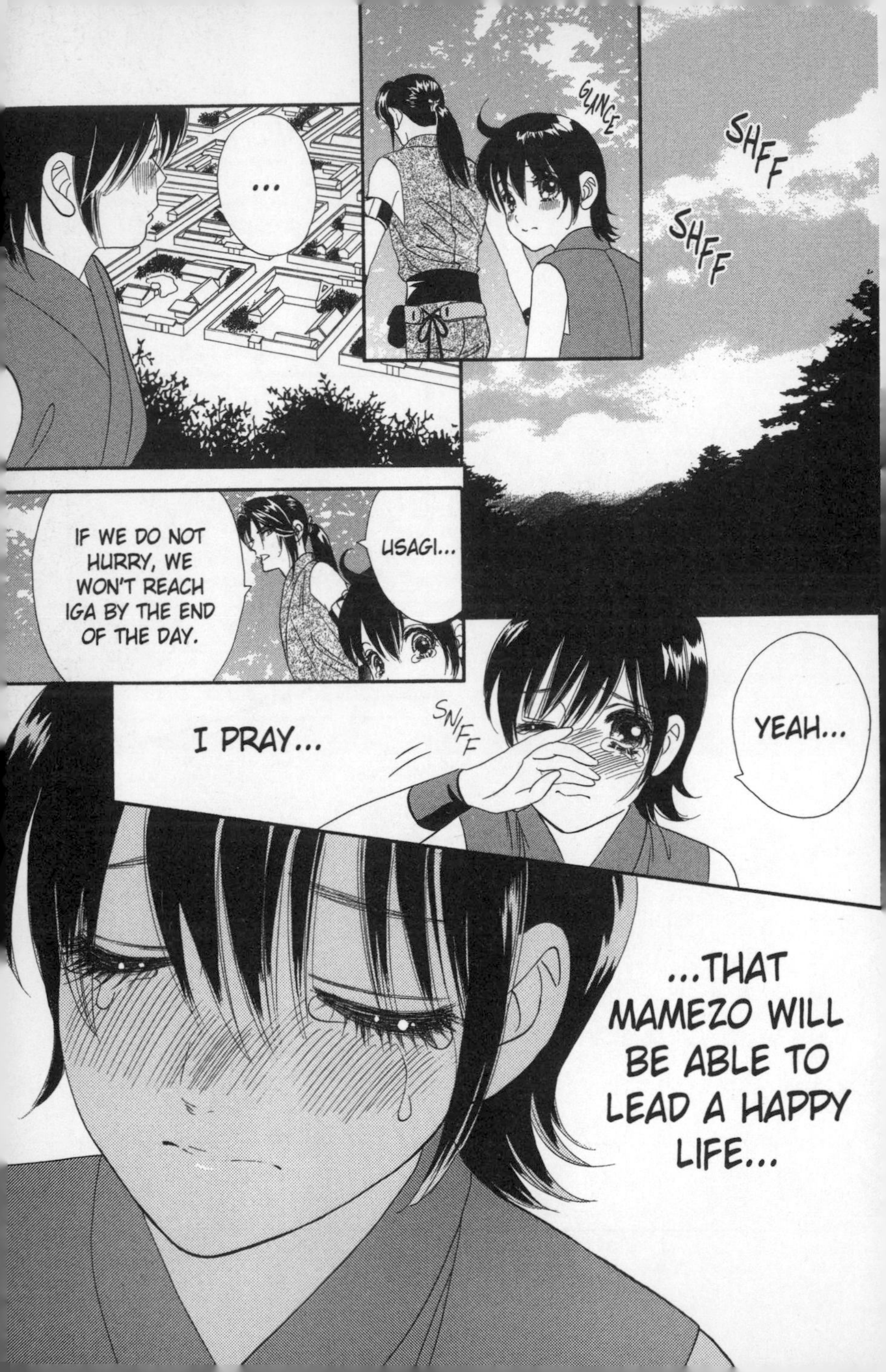
SHFF
SHFF
GLANCE
...
USAGI...
IF WE DO NOT HURRY, WE WON'T REACH IGA BY THE END OF THE DAY.
YEAH...
SNIFF
I PRAY...
...THAT MAMEZO WILL BE ABLE TO LEAD A HAPPY LIFE...

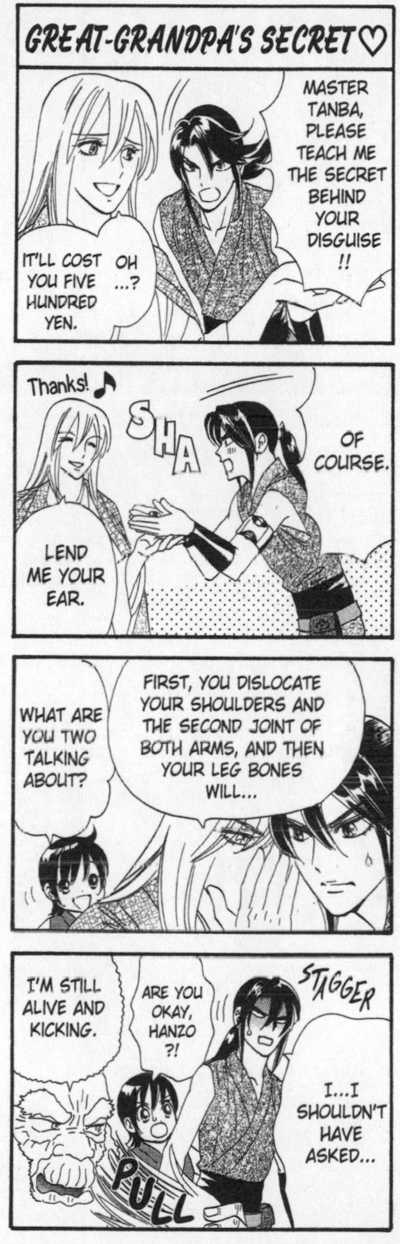
GREAT-GRANDPA'S SECRET♡
MASTER TANBA, PLEASE TEACH ME THE SECRET BEHIND YOUR DISGUISE!!
OH ...?
IT'LL COST YOU FIVE HUNDRED YEN.
OF COURSE.
SHA
Thanks! ♪
LEND ME YOUR EAR.
FIRST, YOU DISLOCATE YOUR SHOULDERS AND THE SECOND JOINT OF BOTH ARMS, AND THEN YOUR LEG BONES WILL...
WHAT ARE YOU TWO TALKING ABOUT?
STAGGER
I...I SHOULDN'T HAVE ASKED...
ARE YOU OKAY, HANZO ?!
I'M STILL ALIVE AND KICKING.
PULL

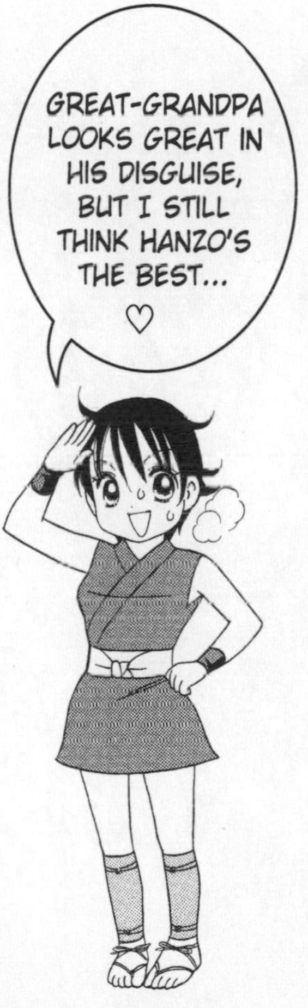
GREAT-GRANDPA LOOKS GREAT IN HIS DISGUISE, BUT I STILL THINK HANZO'S THE BEST... ♡

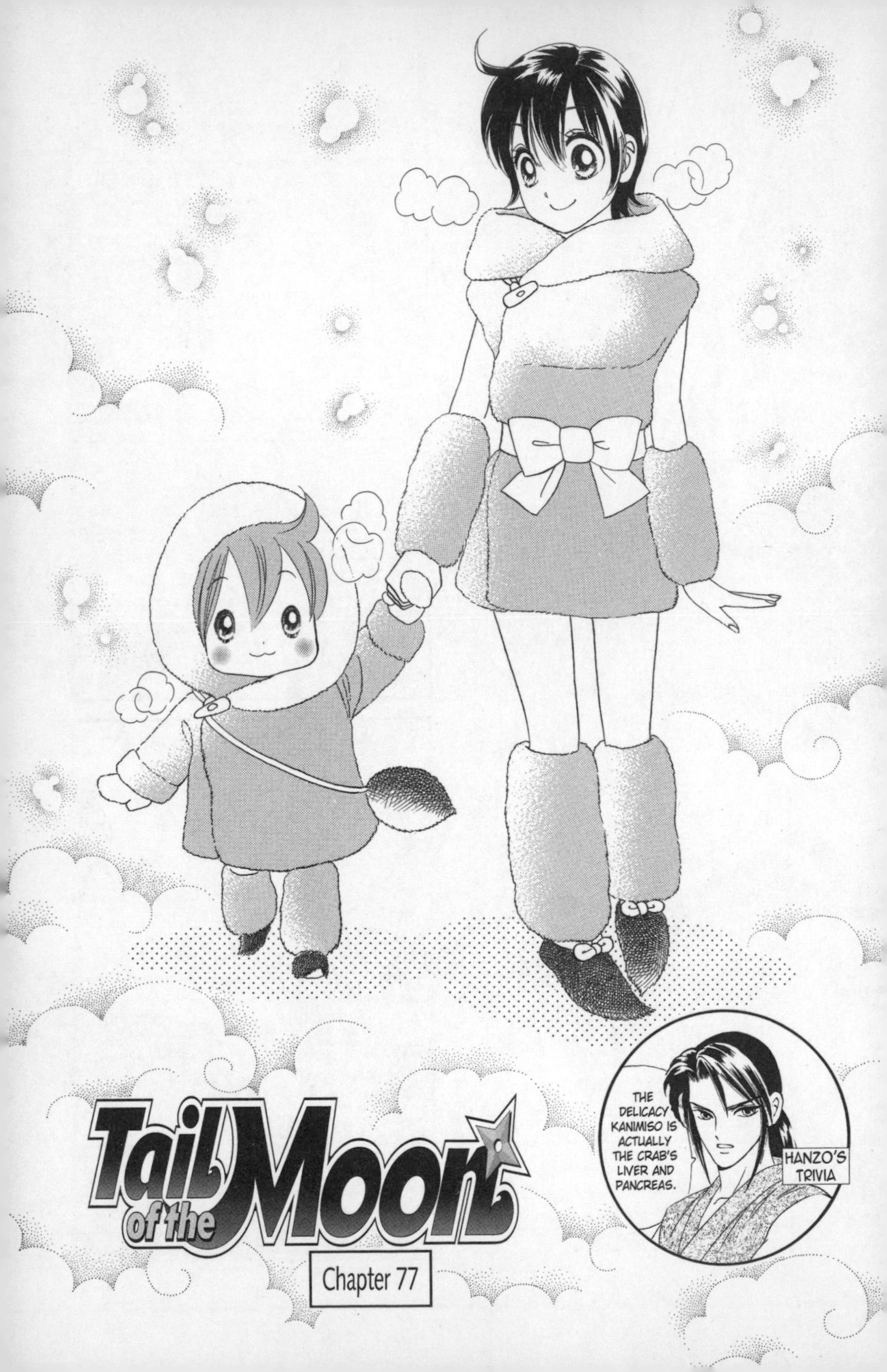
Tail of the Moon
Chapter 77
THE DELICACY KANIMISO IS ACTUALLY THE CRAB'S LIVER AND PANCREAS.
HANZO'S TRIVIA

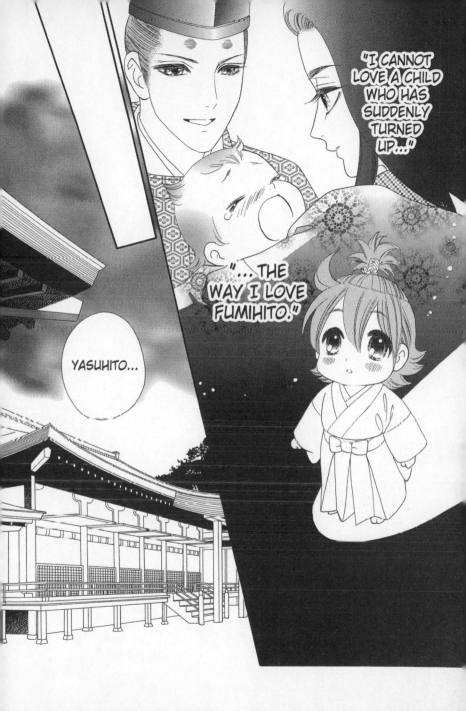

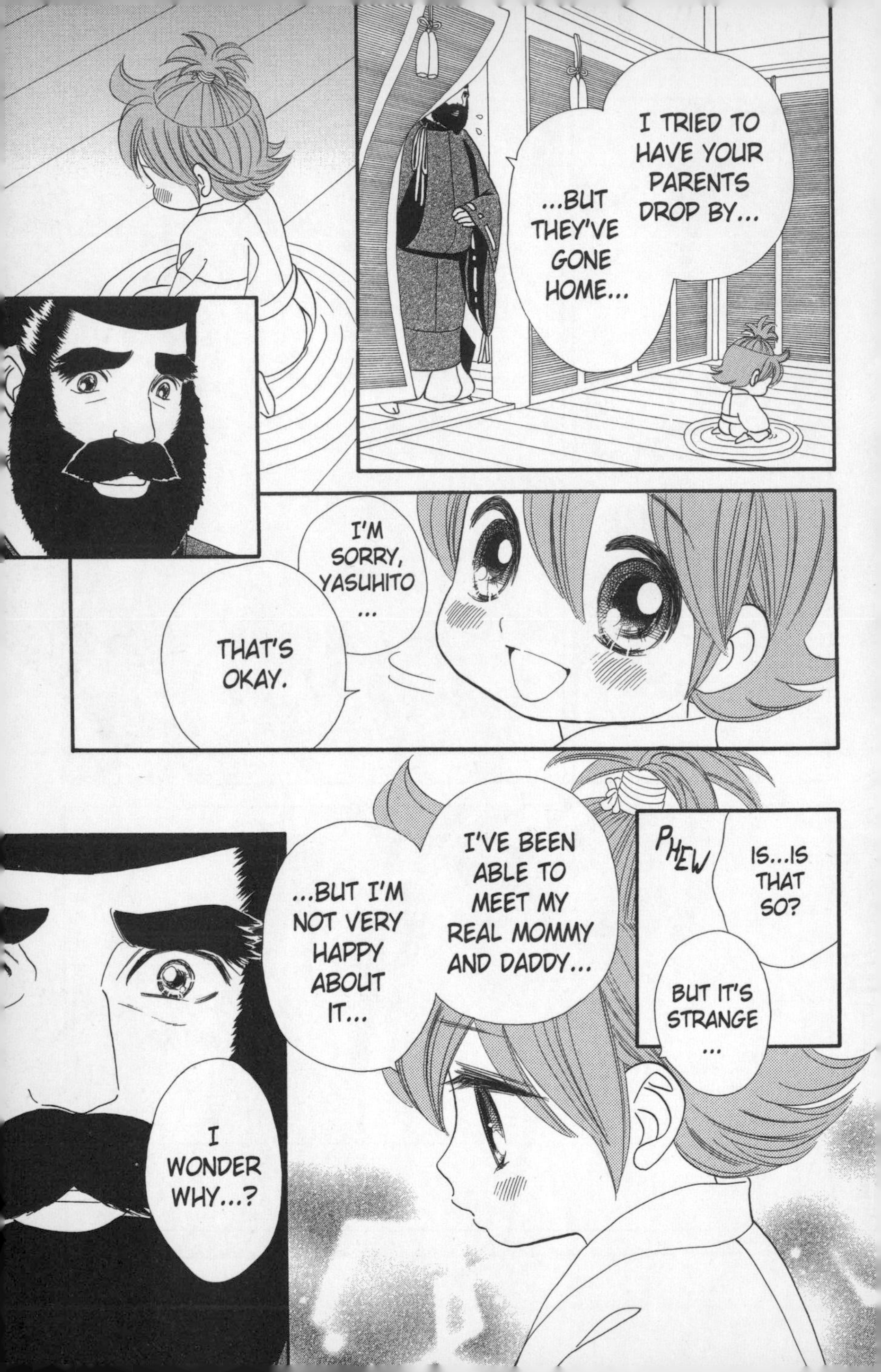
I TRIED TO HAVE YOUR PARENTS DROP BY...
...BUT THEY'VE GONE HOME...
I'M SORRY, YASUHITO...
THAT'S OKAY.
PHEW
IS...IS THAT SO?
BUT IT'S STRANGE...
I'VE BEEN ABLE TO MEET MY REAL MOMMY AND DADDY...
...BUT I'M NOT VERY HAPPY ABOUT IT...
I WONDER WHY...?

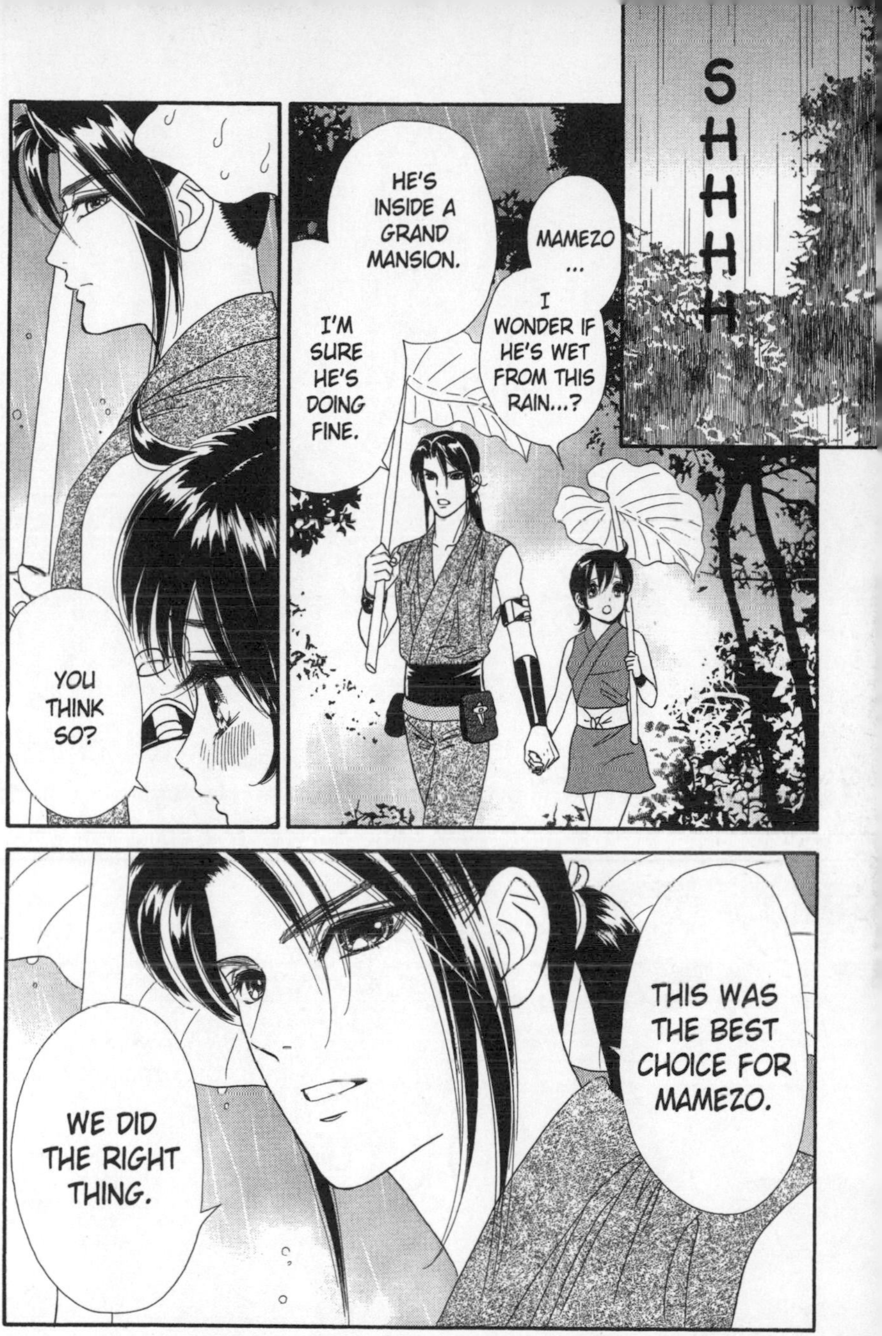
SHHHH
MAMEZO ...
I WONDER IF HE'S WET FROM THIS RAIN...?
HE'S INSIDE A GRAND MANSION.
I'M SURE HE'S DOING FINE.
YOU THINK SO?
THIS WAS THE BEST CHOICE FOR MAMEZO.
WE DID THE RIGHT THING.

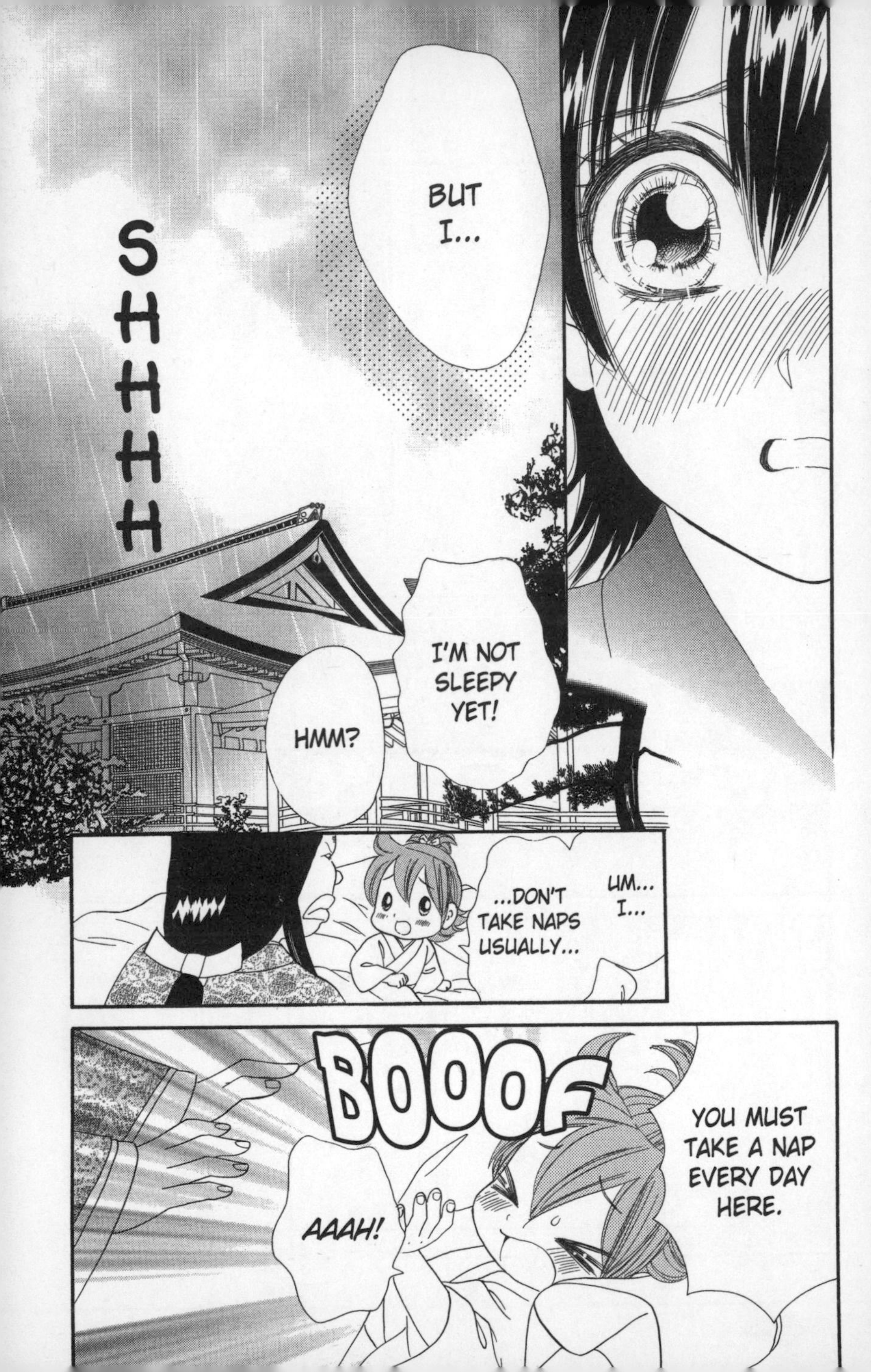
BUT I...
SHHHH
I'M NOT SLEEPY YET!
HMM?
UM... I...
...DON'T TAKE NAPS USUALLY...
YOU MUST TAKE A NAP EVERY DAY HERE.
BOOOF
AAAH!

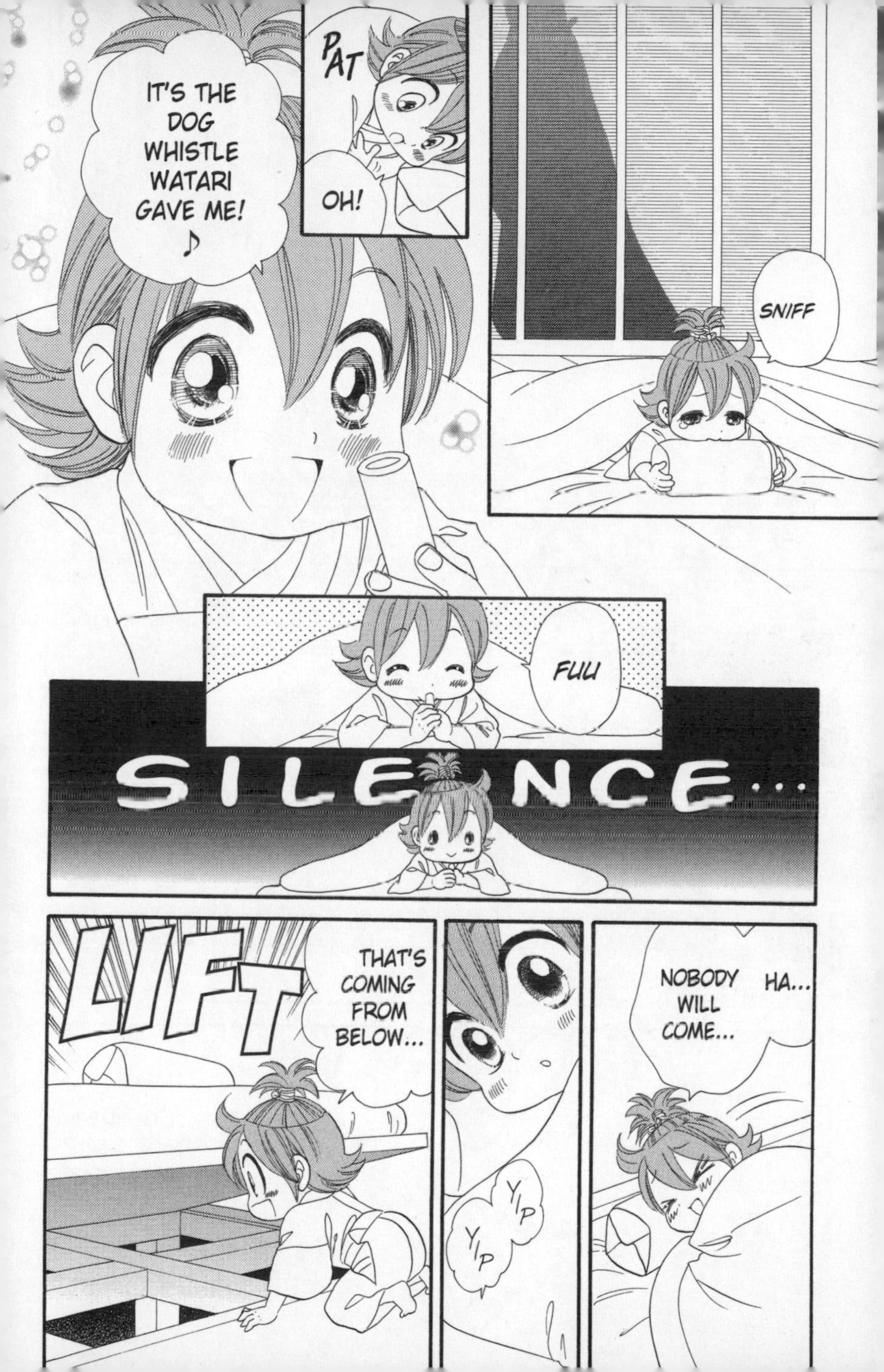
SNIFF
PAT
OH!
IT'S THE DOG WHISTLE WATARI GAVE ME! ♪
FUU
SILENCE...
HA...
NOBODY WILL COME...
YIP
YIP
YIP
LIFT
THAT'S COMING FROM BELOW...

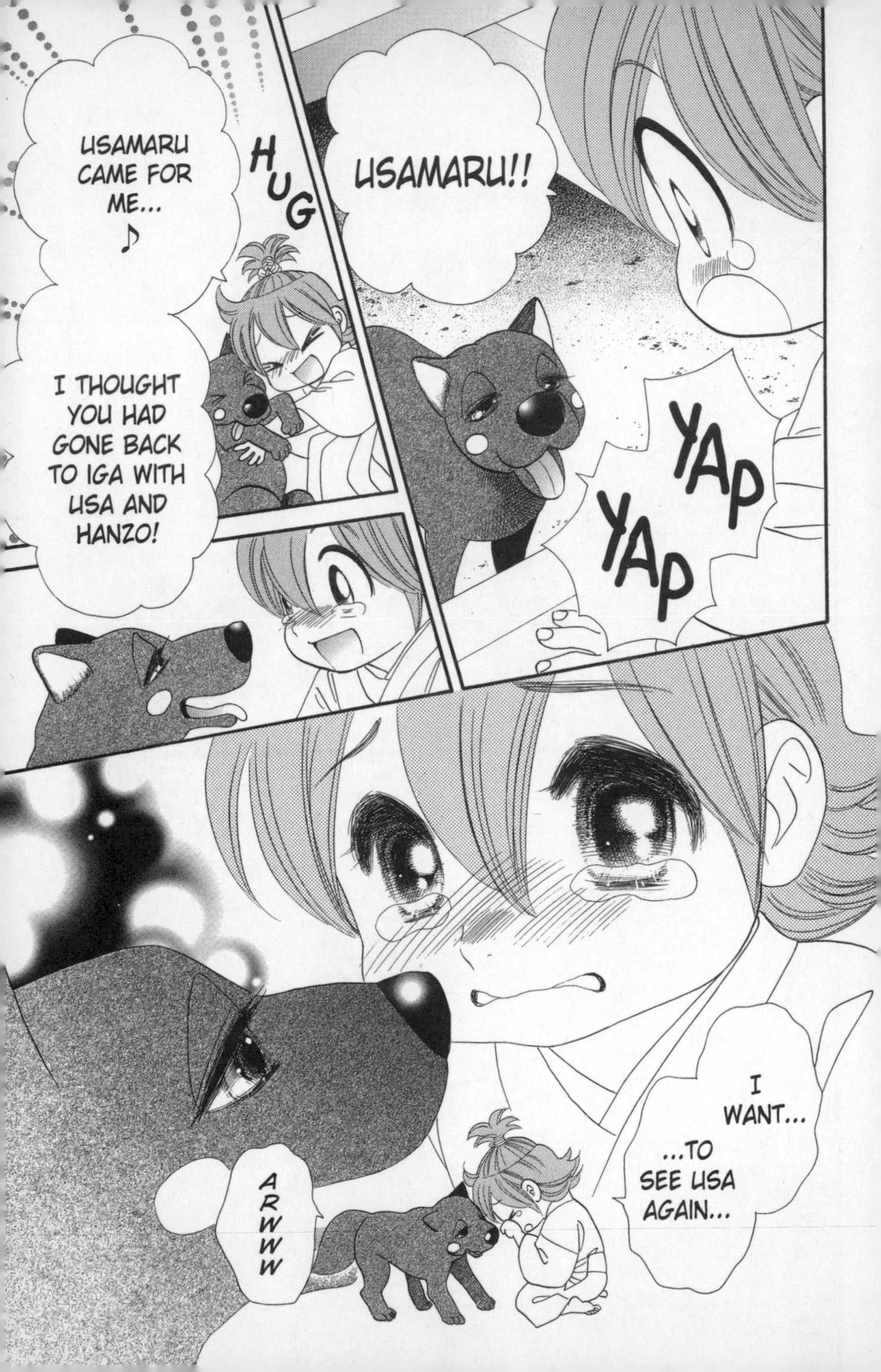
USAMARU!!
YAP YAP
HUG
USAMARU CAME FOR ME... ♪
I THOUGHT YOU HAD GONE BACK TO IGA WITH USA AND HANZO!
I WANT...
...TO SEE USA AGAIN...
ARWWW

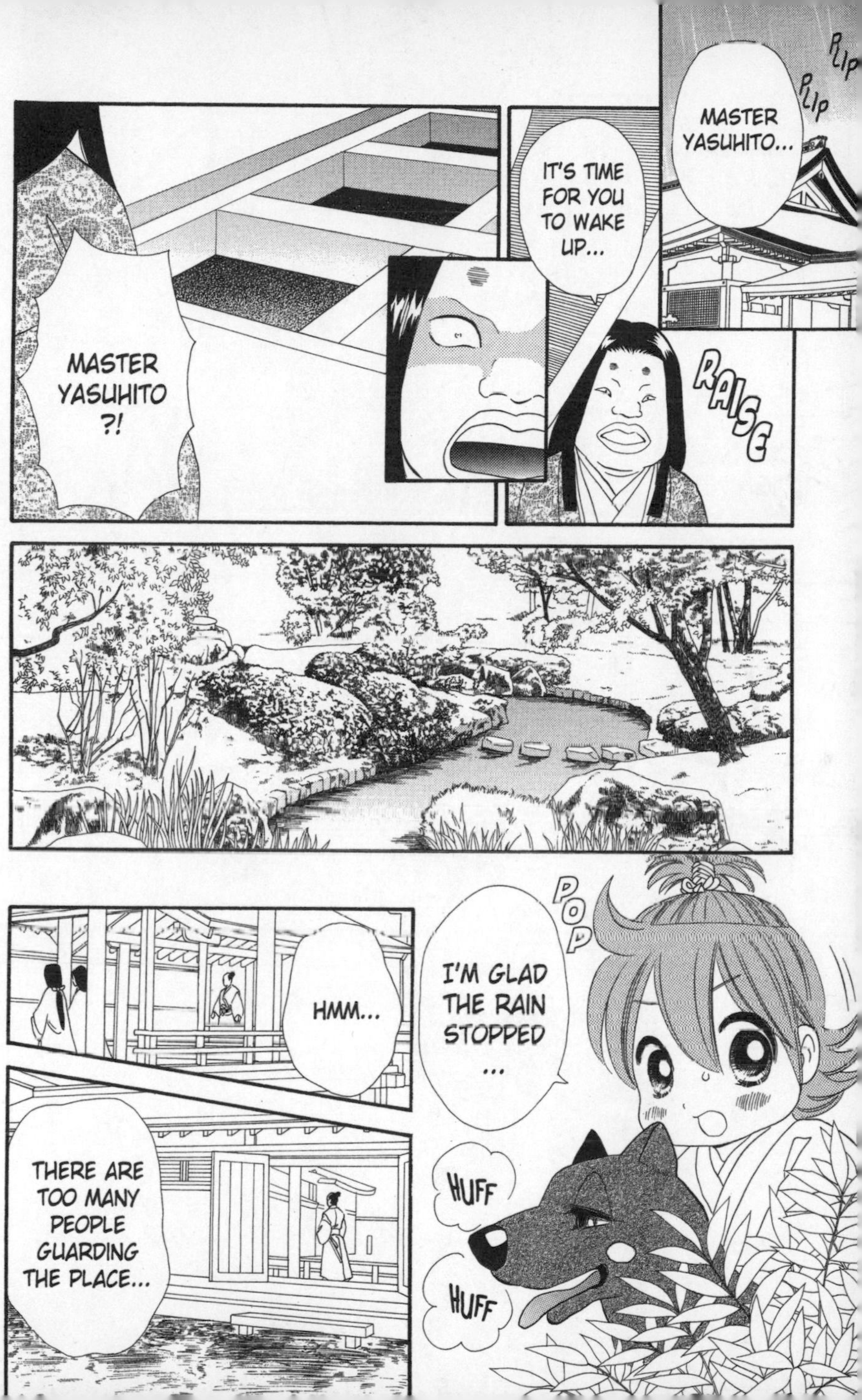
PLIP
PLIP
MASTER YASUHITO...
IT'S TIME FOR YOU TO WAKE UP...
RAISE
MASTER YASUHITO ?!
POP
I'M GLAD THE RAIN STOPPED ...
HUFF
HUFF
HMM...
THERE ARE TOO MANY PEOPLE GUARDING THE PLACE...

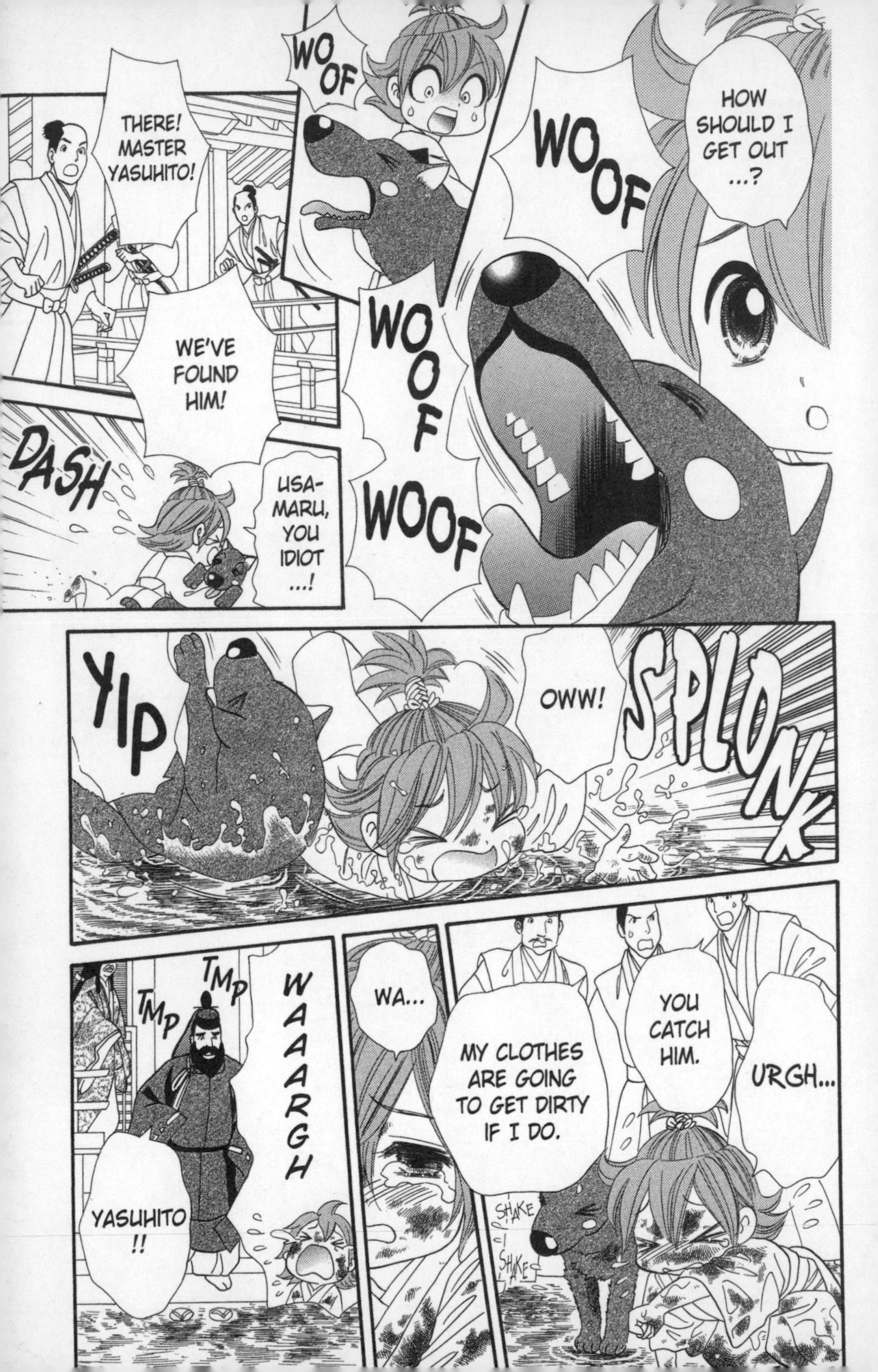
HOW SHOULD I GET OUT ...?
WOOF
WOOF
WOOF
WOOF
WOOF
THERE! MASTER YASUHITO!
WE'VE FOUND HIM!
USA-MARU, YOU IDIOT ...!
DASH
SPLONK
OWW!
YIP
URGH...
YOU CATCH HIM.
MY CLOTHES ARE GOING TO GET DIRTY IF I DO.
SHAKE
SHAKE
WA...
WAAAARGH
TMP
TMP
YASUHITO !!

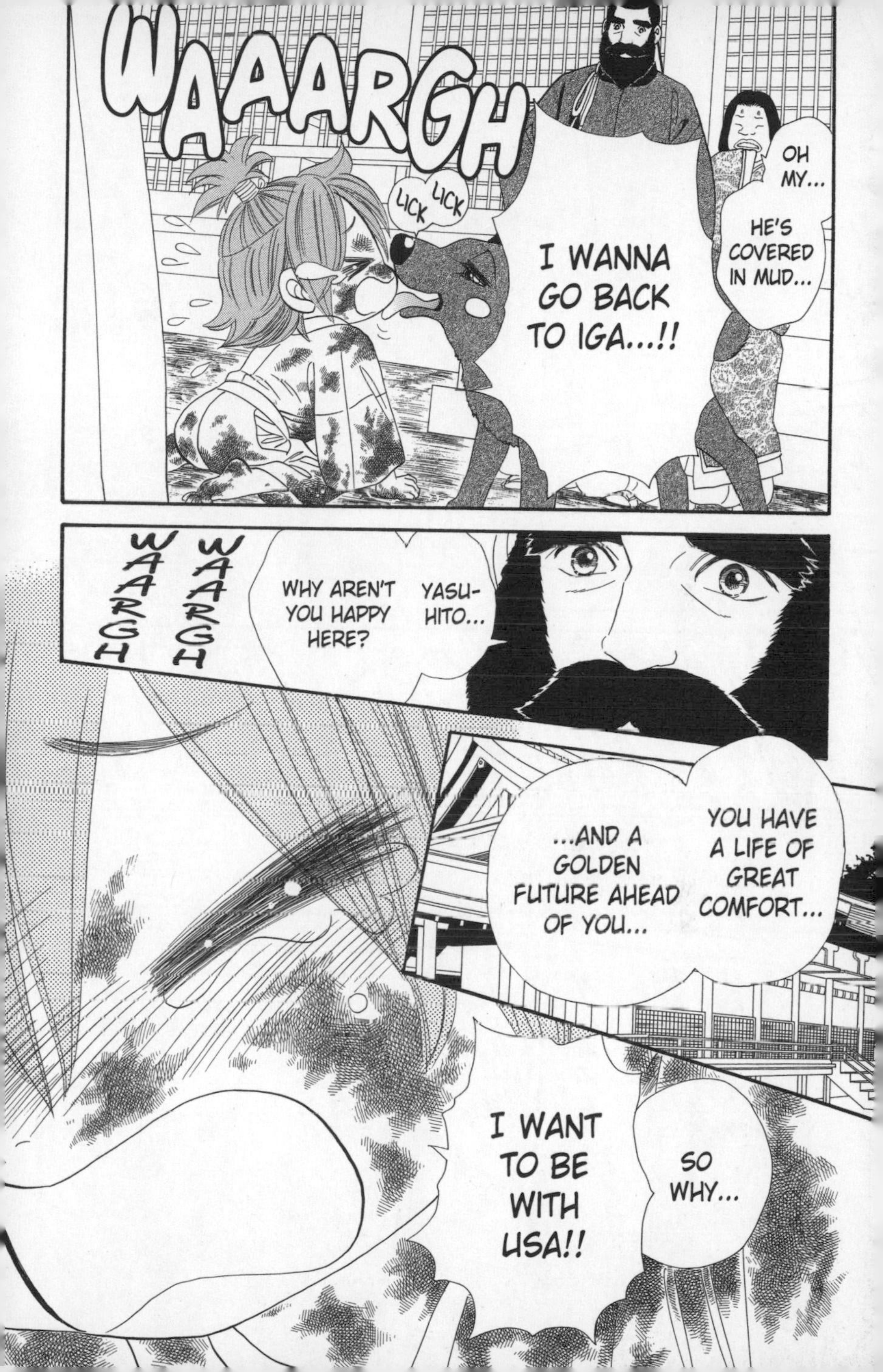
OH MY...
HE'S COVERED IN MUD...
I WANNA GO BACK TO IGA...!!
LICK LICK
WAAARGH
YASU-HITO...
WHY AREN'T YOU HAPPY HERE?
WAARGH WAARGH
YOU HAVE A LIFE OF GREAT COMFORT...
...AND A GOLDEN FUTURE AHEAD OF YOU...
SO WHY...
I WANT TO BE WITH USA!!

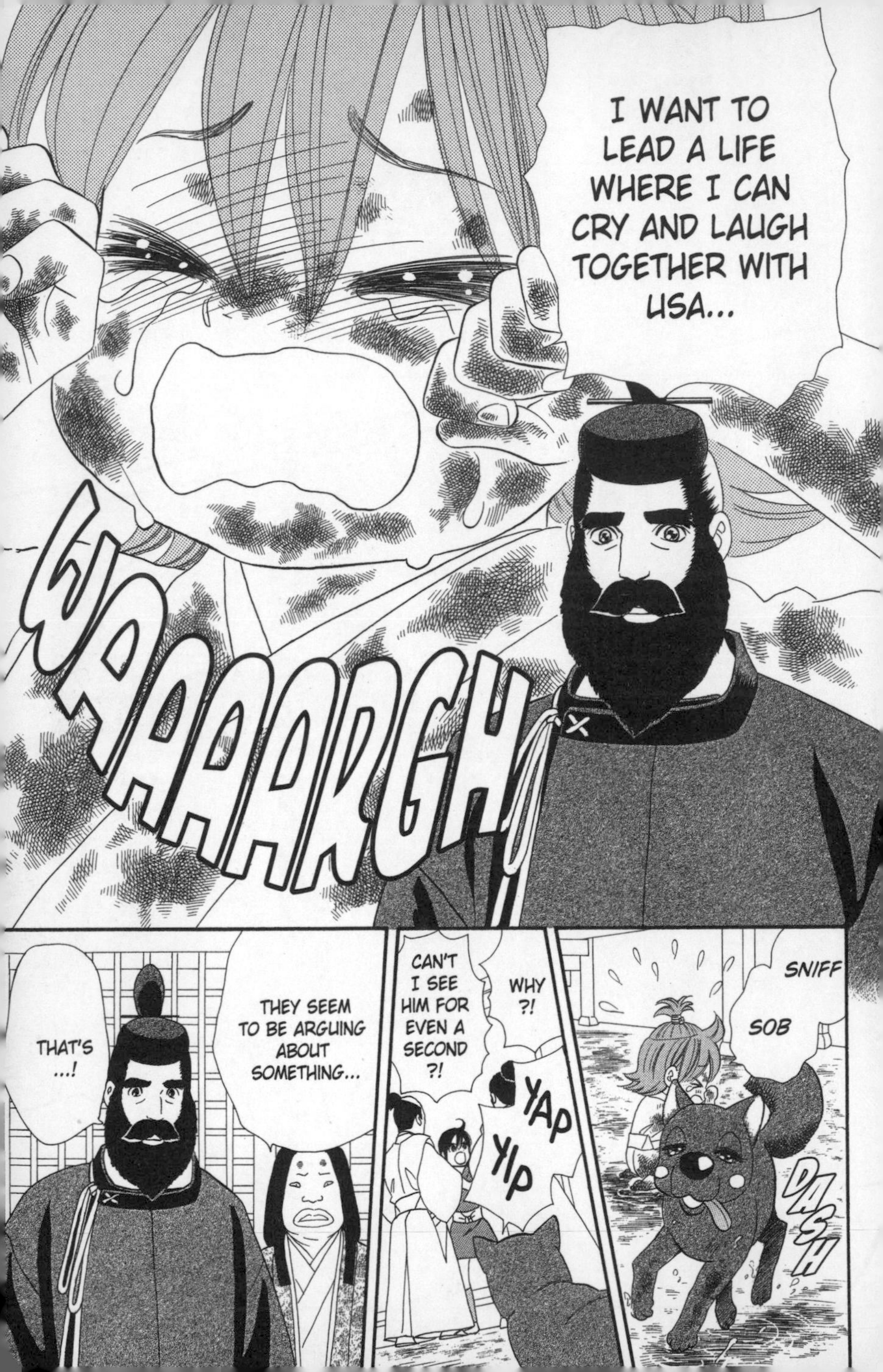
I WANT TO LEAD A LIFE WHERE I CAN CRY AND LAUGH TOGETHER WITH USA...
WAAAARGH
SNIFF
SOB
DASH
WHY?!
CAN'T I SEE HIM FOR EVEN A SECOND?!
YAP
YIP
THEY SEEM TO BE ARGUING ABOUT SOMETHING...
THAT'S ...!

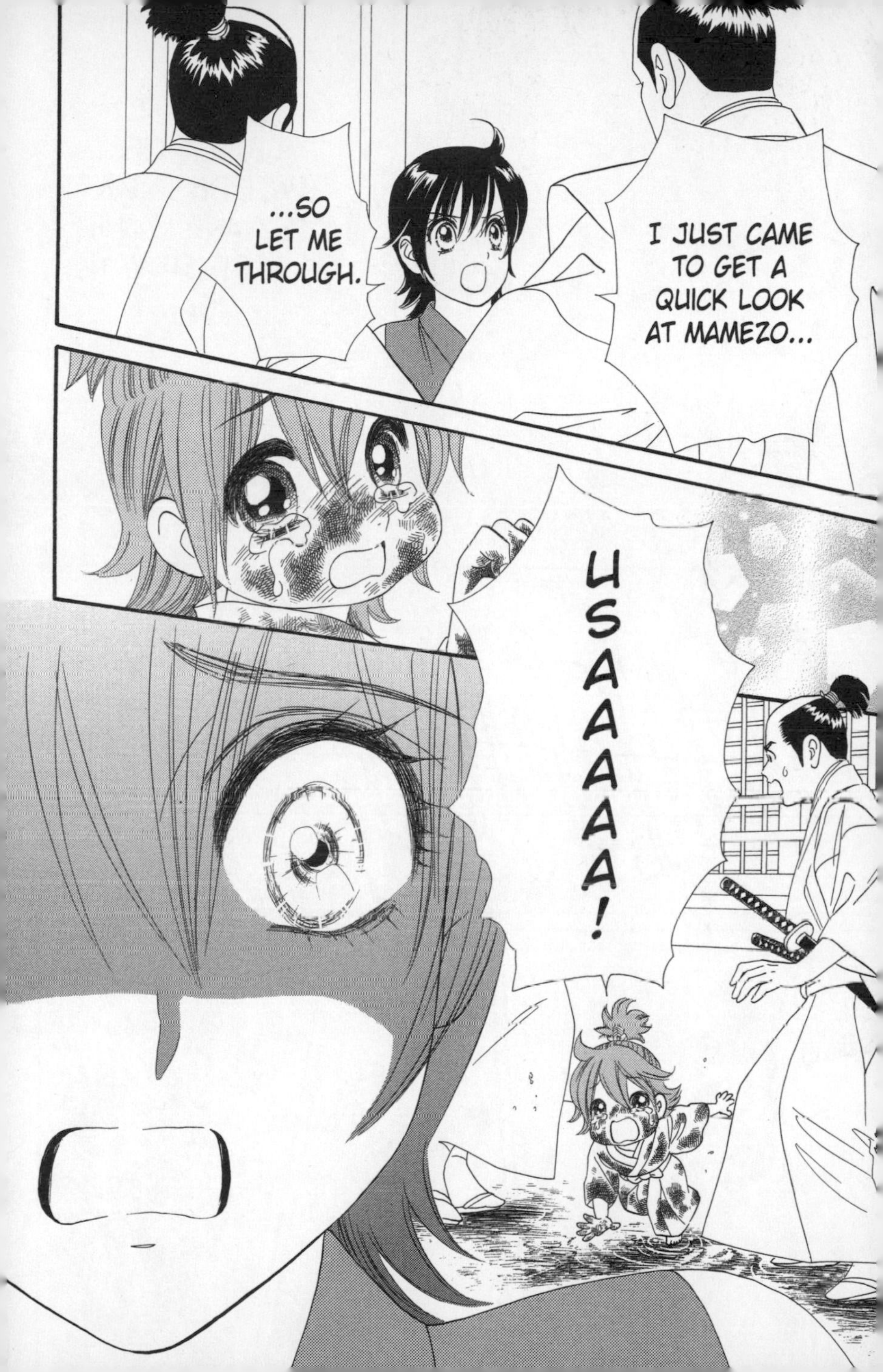
I JUST CAME TO GET A QUICK LOOK AT MAMEZO...
...SO LET ME THROUGH.
USAAAAA!

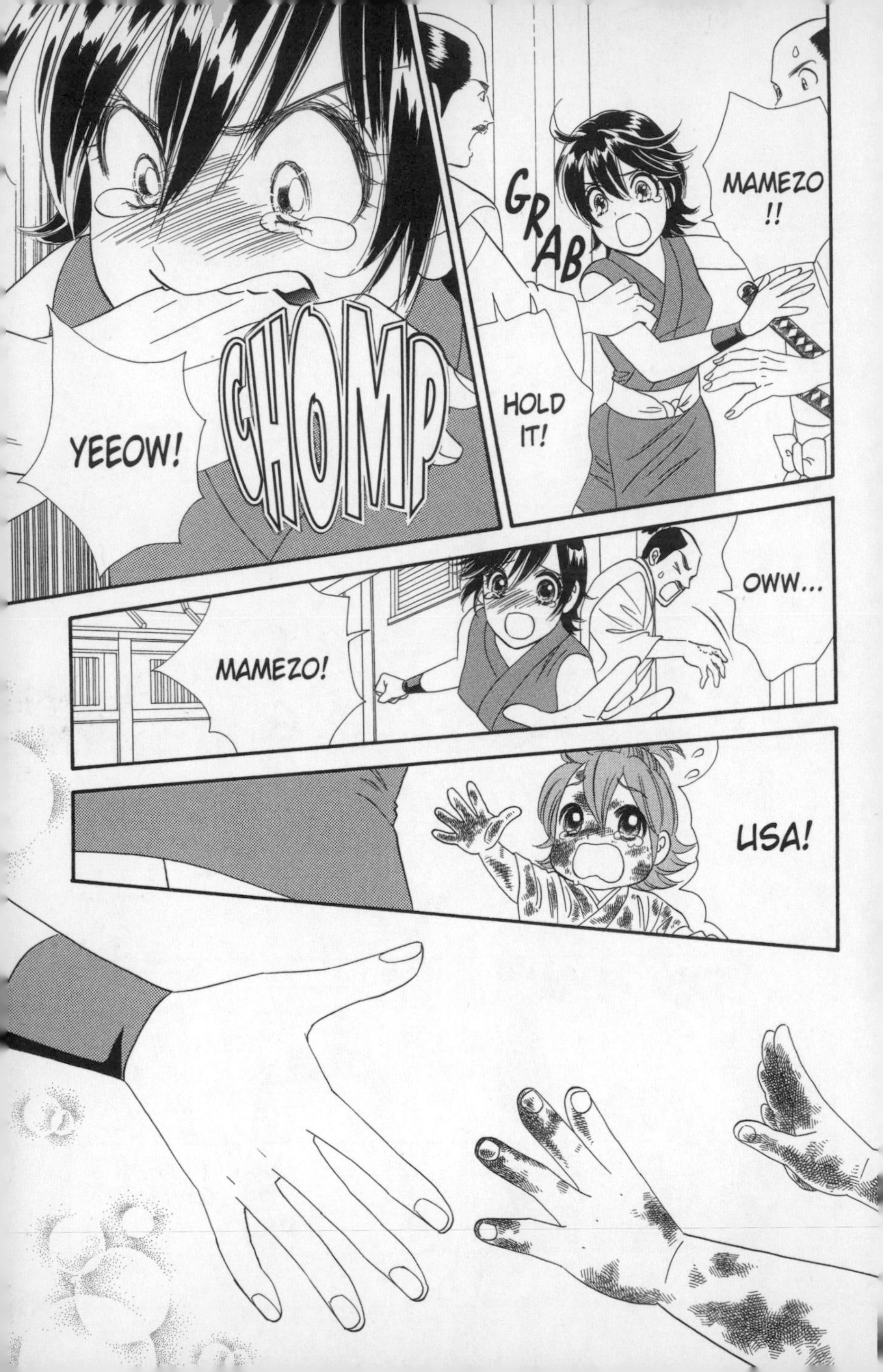
MAMEZO !!
GRAB
HOLD IT!
CHOMP
YEEOW!
OWW...
MAMEZO!
USA!

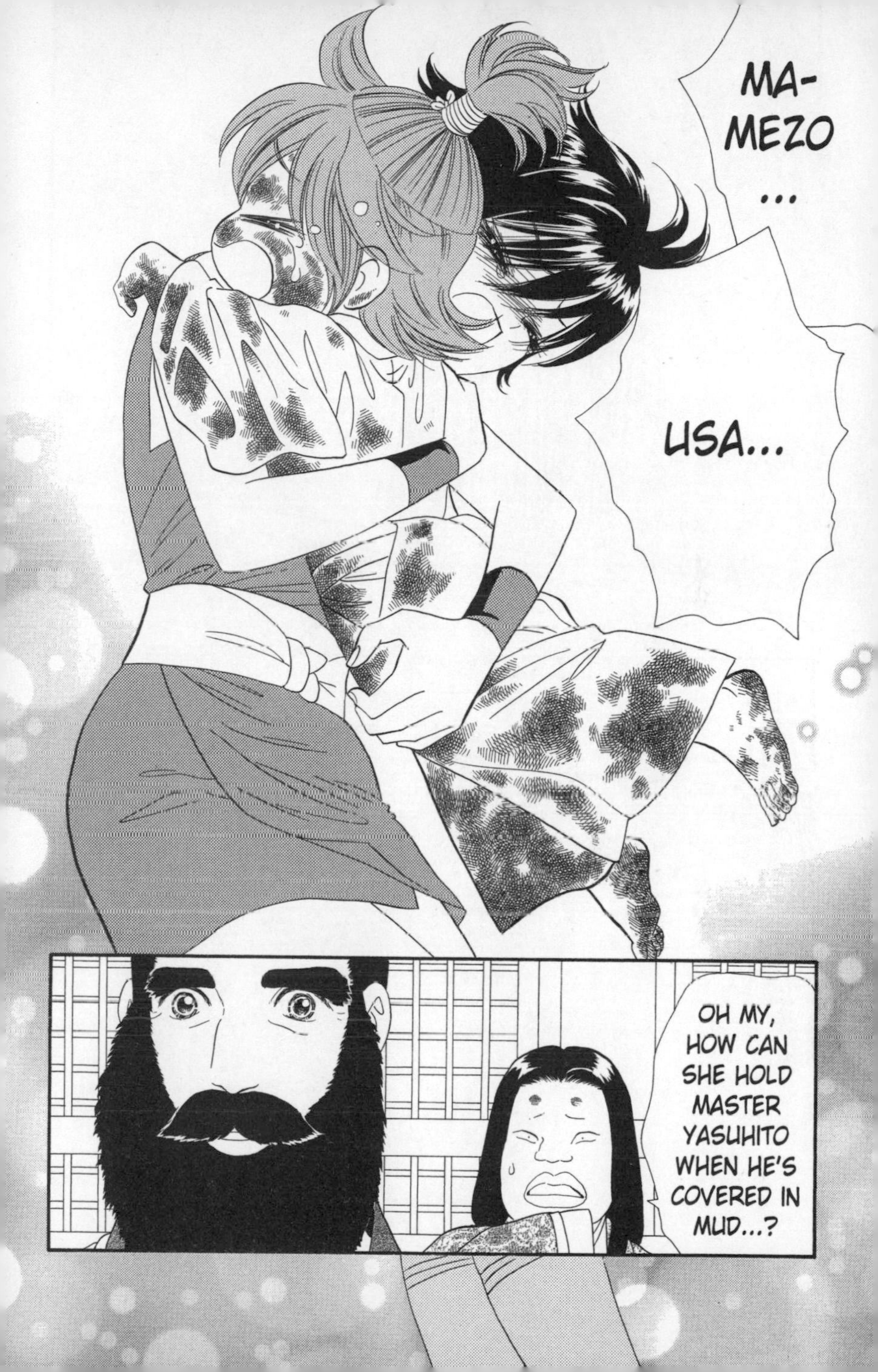
MA-MEZO...
USA...
OH MY, HOW CAN SHE HOLD MASTER YASUHITO WHEN HE'S COVERED IN MUD...?

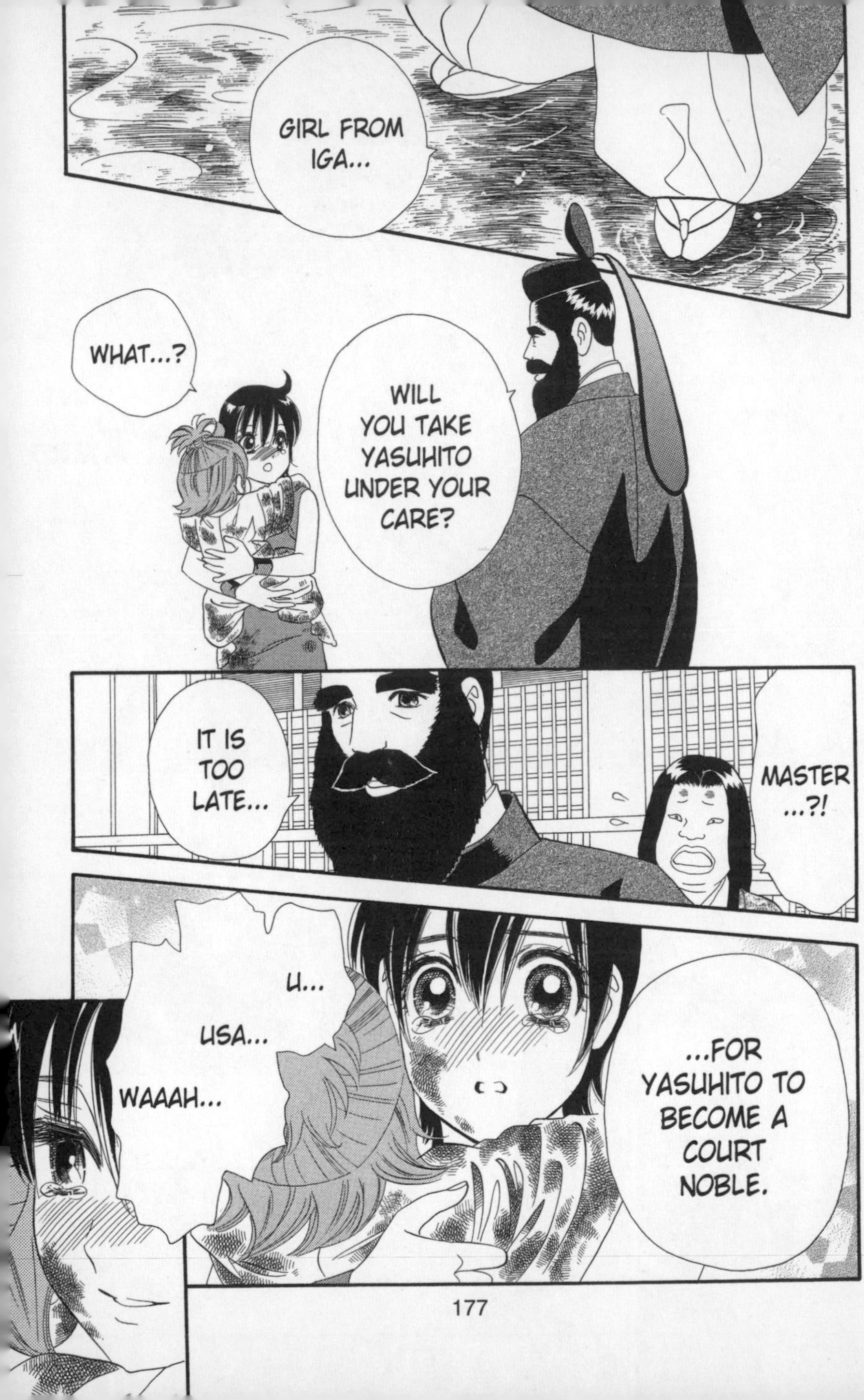
GIRL FROM IGA...
WILL YOU TAKE YASUHITO UNDER YOUR CARE?
WHAT...?
MASTER ...?!
IT IS TOO LATE...
...FOR YASUHITO TO BECOME A COURT NOBLE.
U...
USA...
WAAAH...

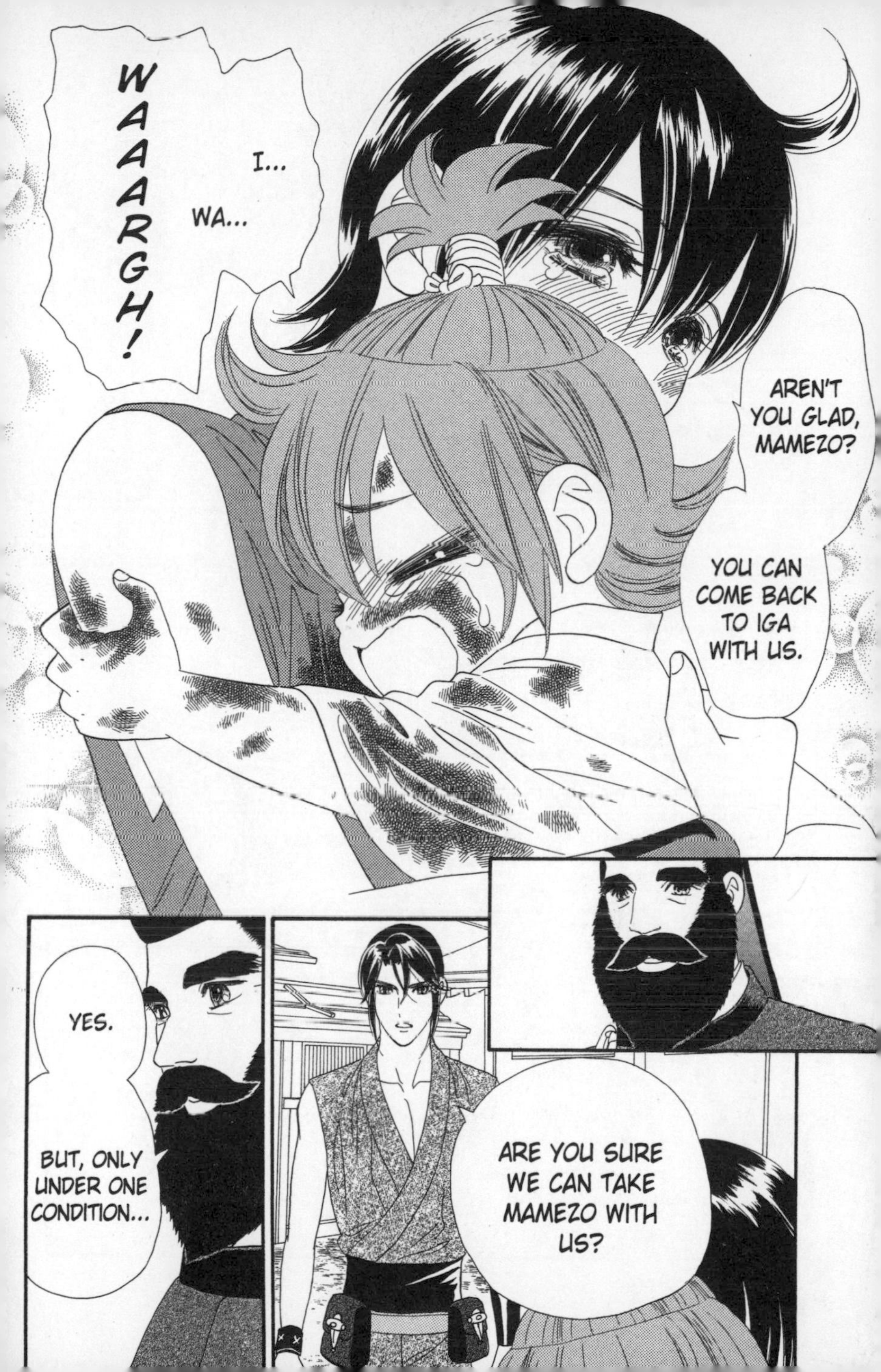
AREN'T YOU GLAD, MAMEZO?
YOU CAN COME BACK TO IGA WITH US.
I... WA...
WAAAARGH!
ARE YOU SURE WE CAN TAKE MAMEZO WITH US?
YES.
BUT, ONLY UNDER ONE CONDITION...

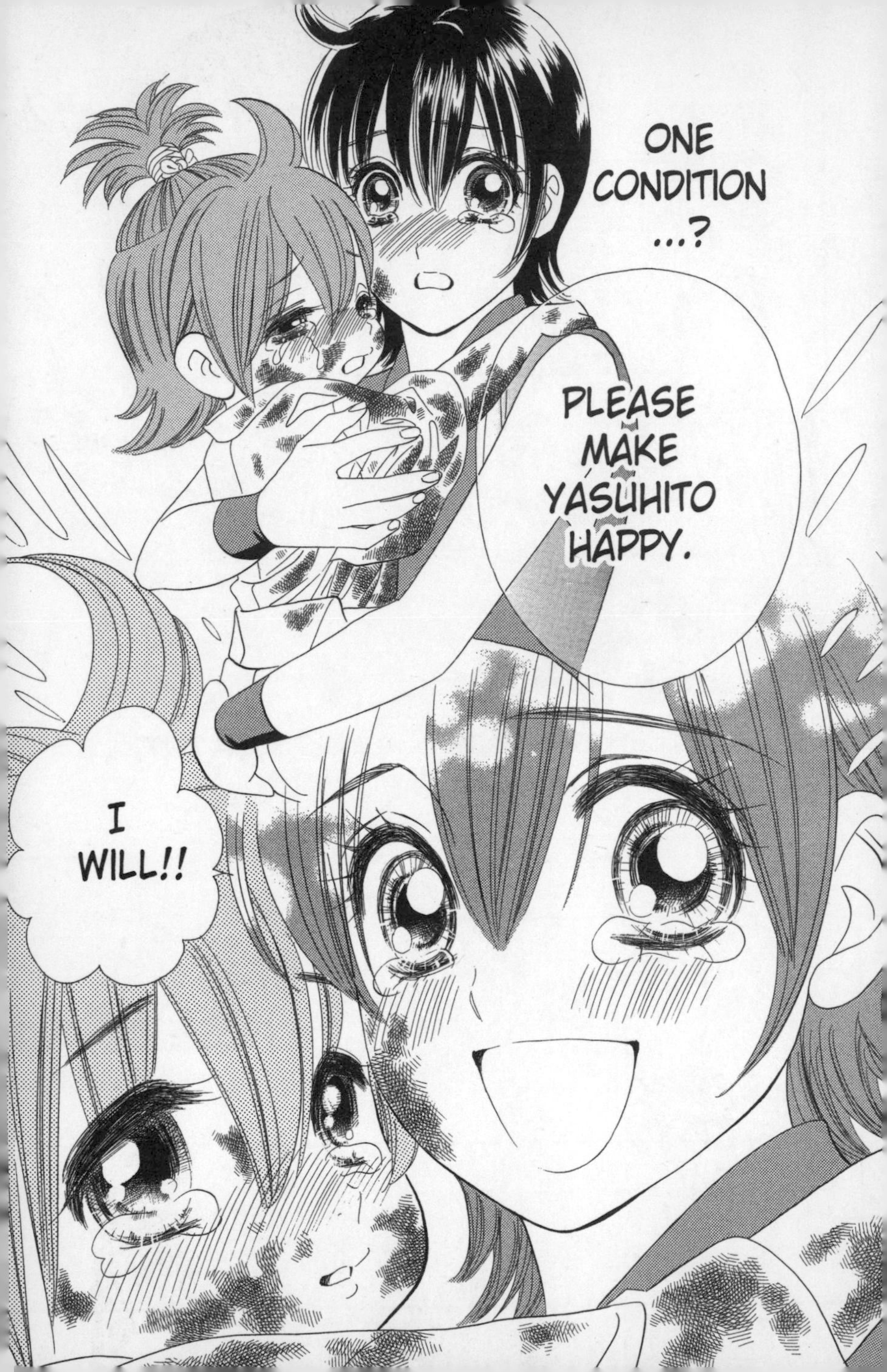
ONE CONDITION ...?
PLEASE MAKE YASUHITO HAPPY.
I WILL!!

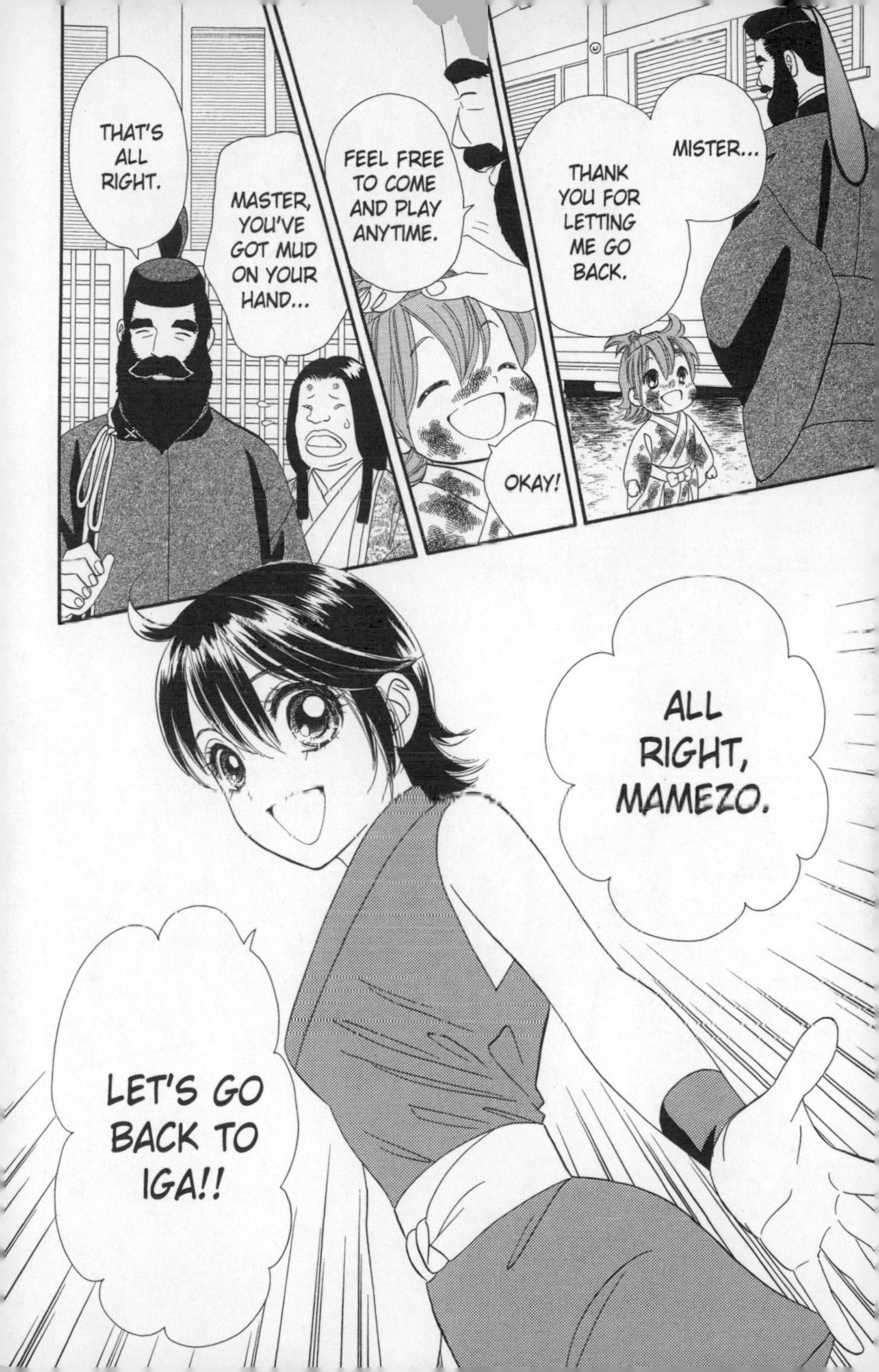
MISTER...
THANK YOU FOR LETTING ME GO BACK.
FEEL FREE TO COME AND PLAY ANYTIME.
OKAY!
MASTER, YOU'VE GOT MUD ON YOUR HAND...
THAT'S ALL RIGHT.
ALL RIGHT, MAMEZO.
LET'S GO BACK TO IGA!!

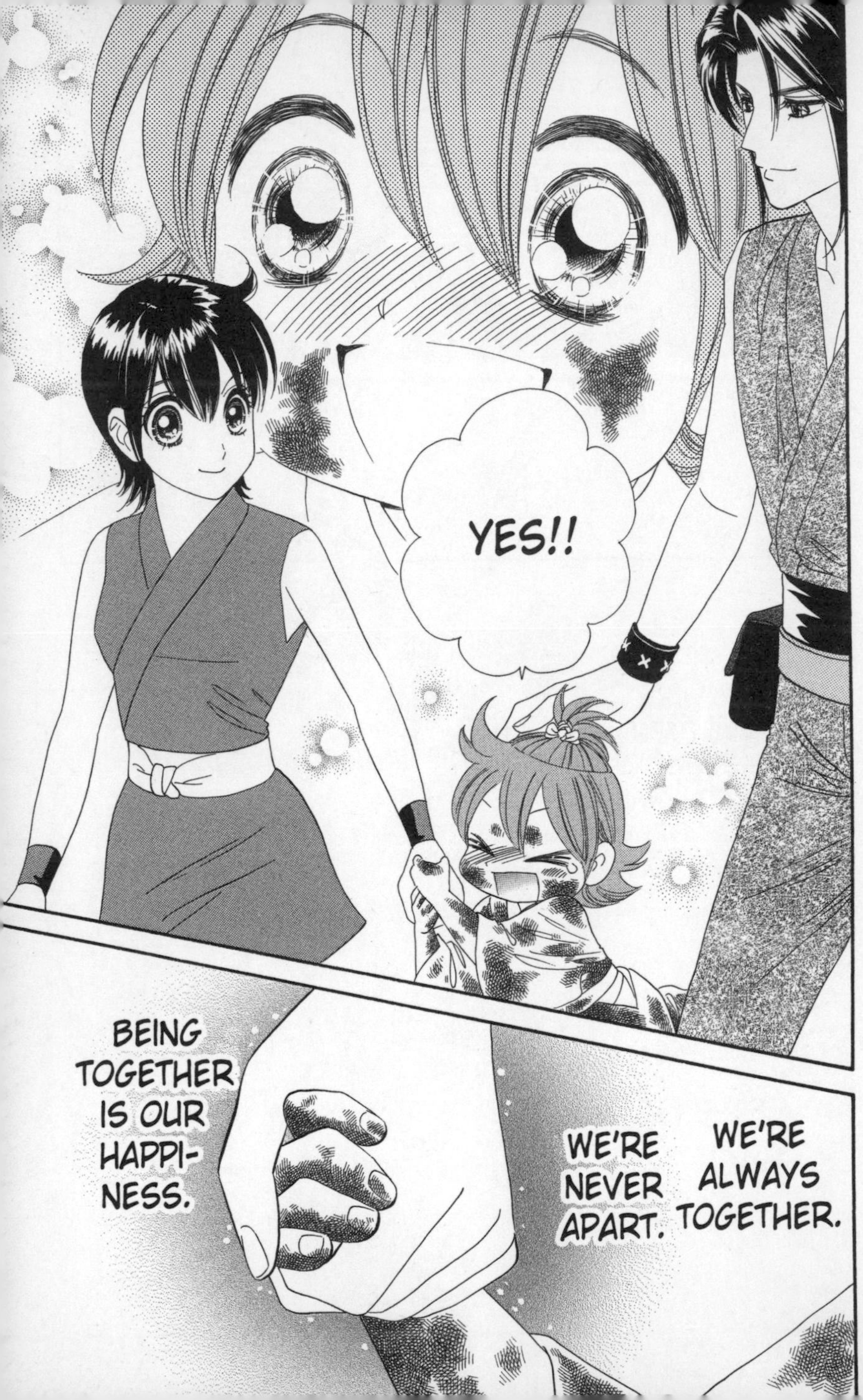
YES!!
WE'RE ALWAYS TOGETHER.
WE'RE NEVER APART.
BEING TOGETHER IS OUR HAPPI-NESS.

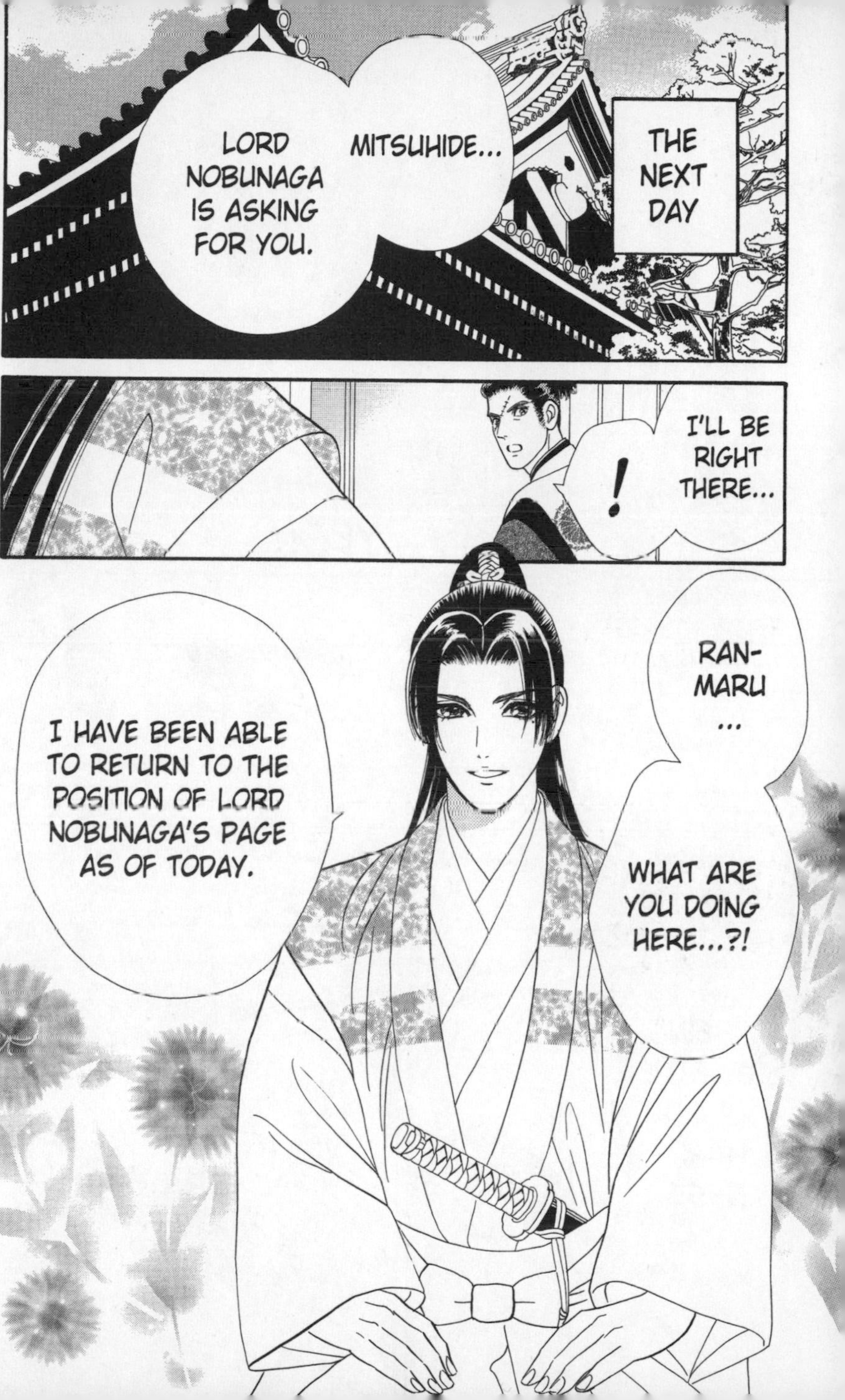
THE NEXT DAY
MITSUHIDE... LORD NOBUNAGA IS ASKING FOR YOU.
!
I'LL BE RIGHT THERE...
RAN-MARU ...
WHAT ARE YOU DOING HERE...?!
I HAVE BEEN ABLE TO RETURN TO THE POSITION OF LORD NOBUNAGA'S PAGE AS OF TODAY.

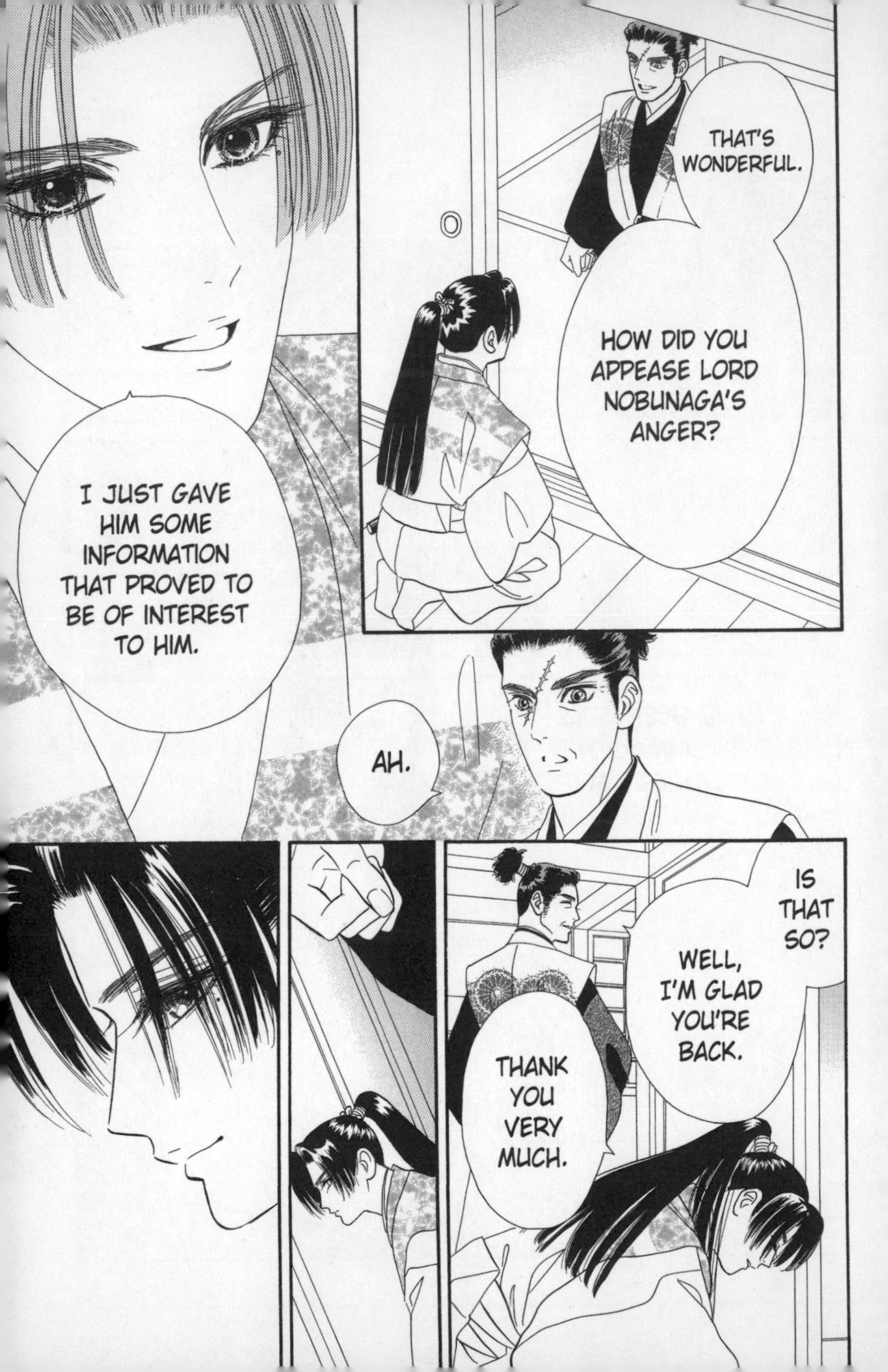
THAT'S WONDERFUL.
HOW DID YOU APPEASE LORD NOBUNAGA'S ANGER?
I JUST GAVE HIM SOME INFORMATION THAT PROVED TO BE OF INTEREST TO HIM.
AH.
IS THAT SO?
WELL, I'M GLAD YOU'RE BACK.
THANK YOU VERY MUCH.

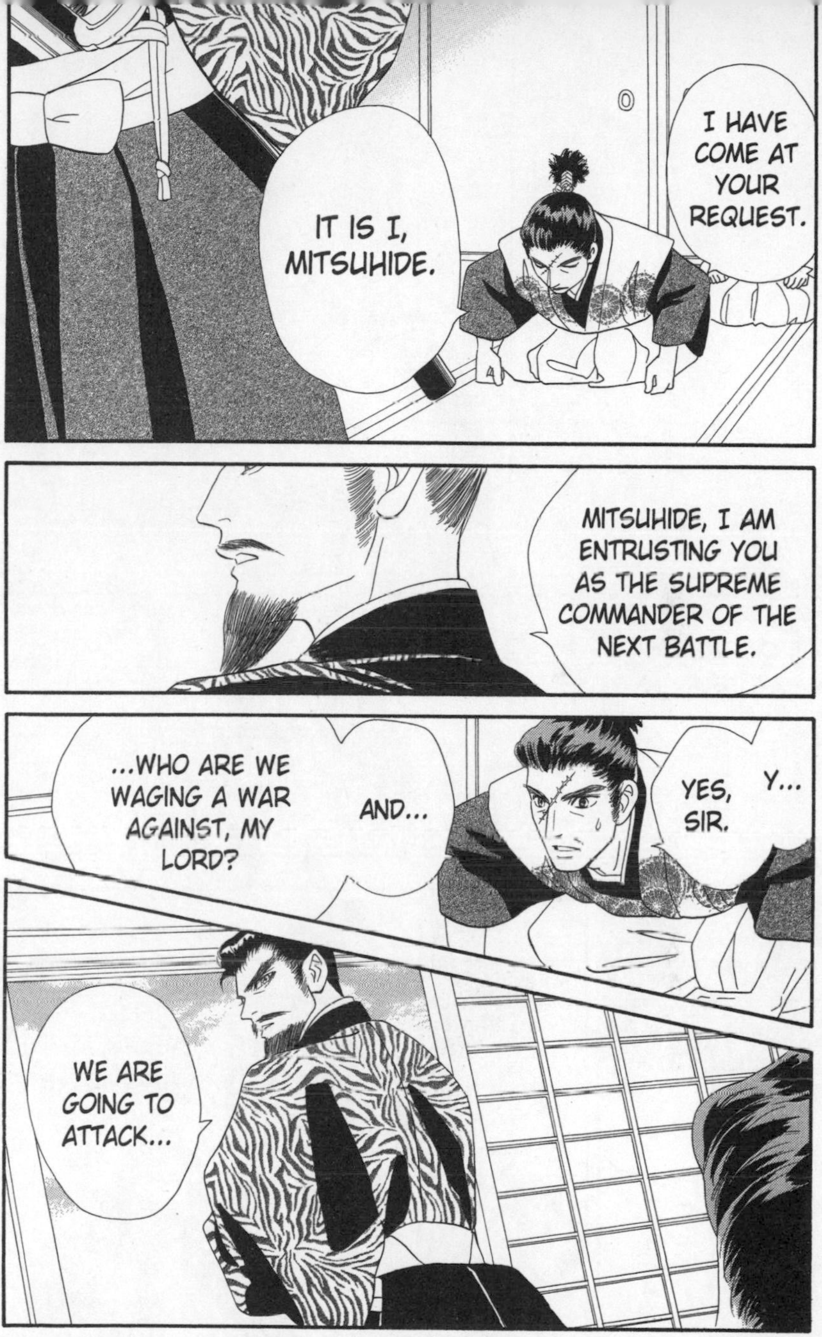
I HAVE COME AT YOUR REQUEST.
IT IS I, MITSUHIDE.
MITSUHIDE, I AM ENTRUSTING YOU AS THE SUPREME COMMANDER OF THE NEXT BATTLE.
Y...
YES, SIR.
AND...
...WHO ARE WE WAGING A WAR AGAINST, MY LORD?
WE ARE GOING TO ATTACK...

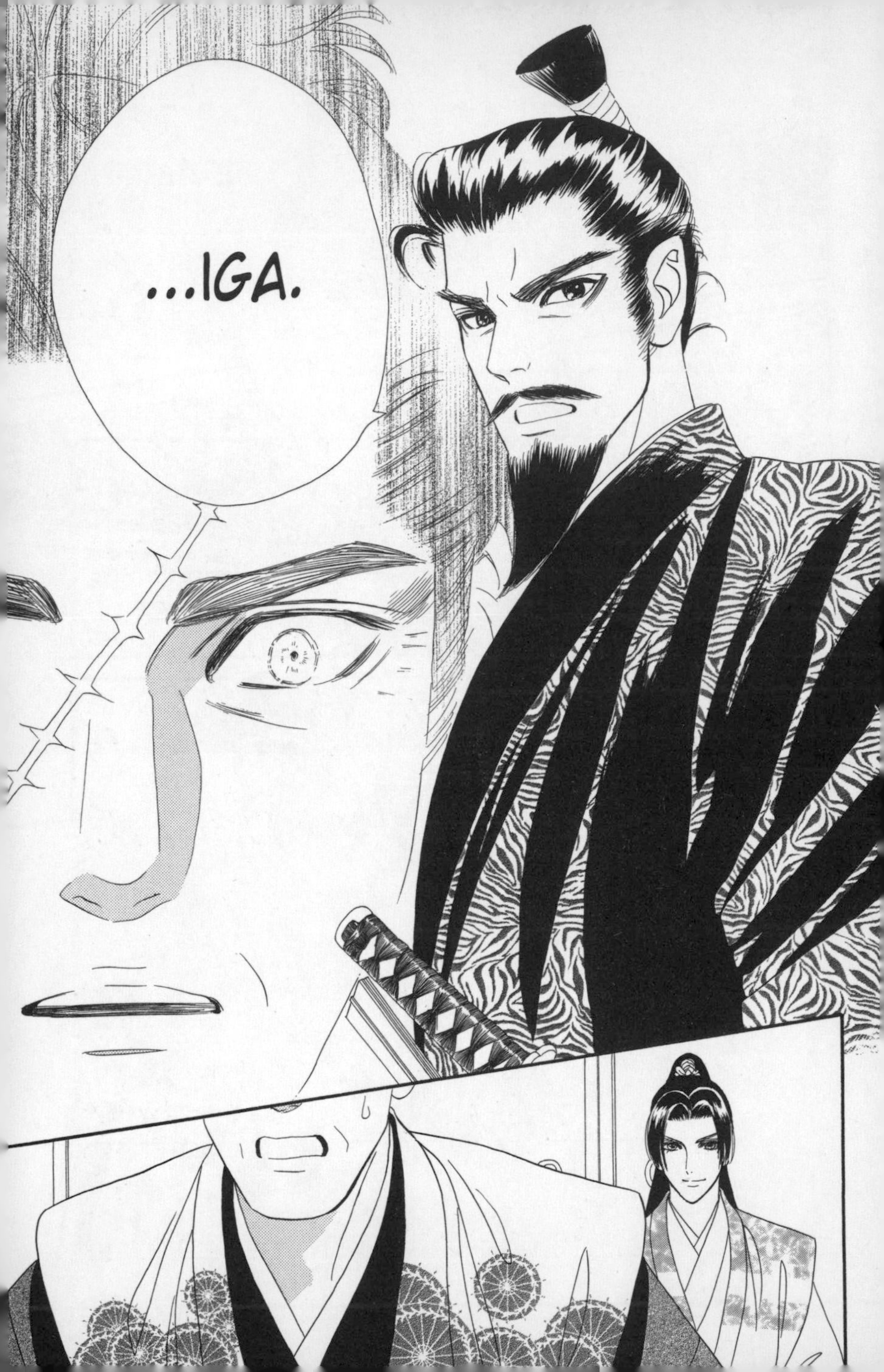
...IGA.

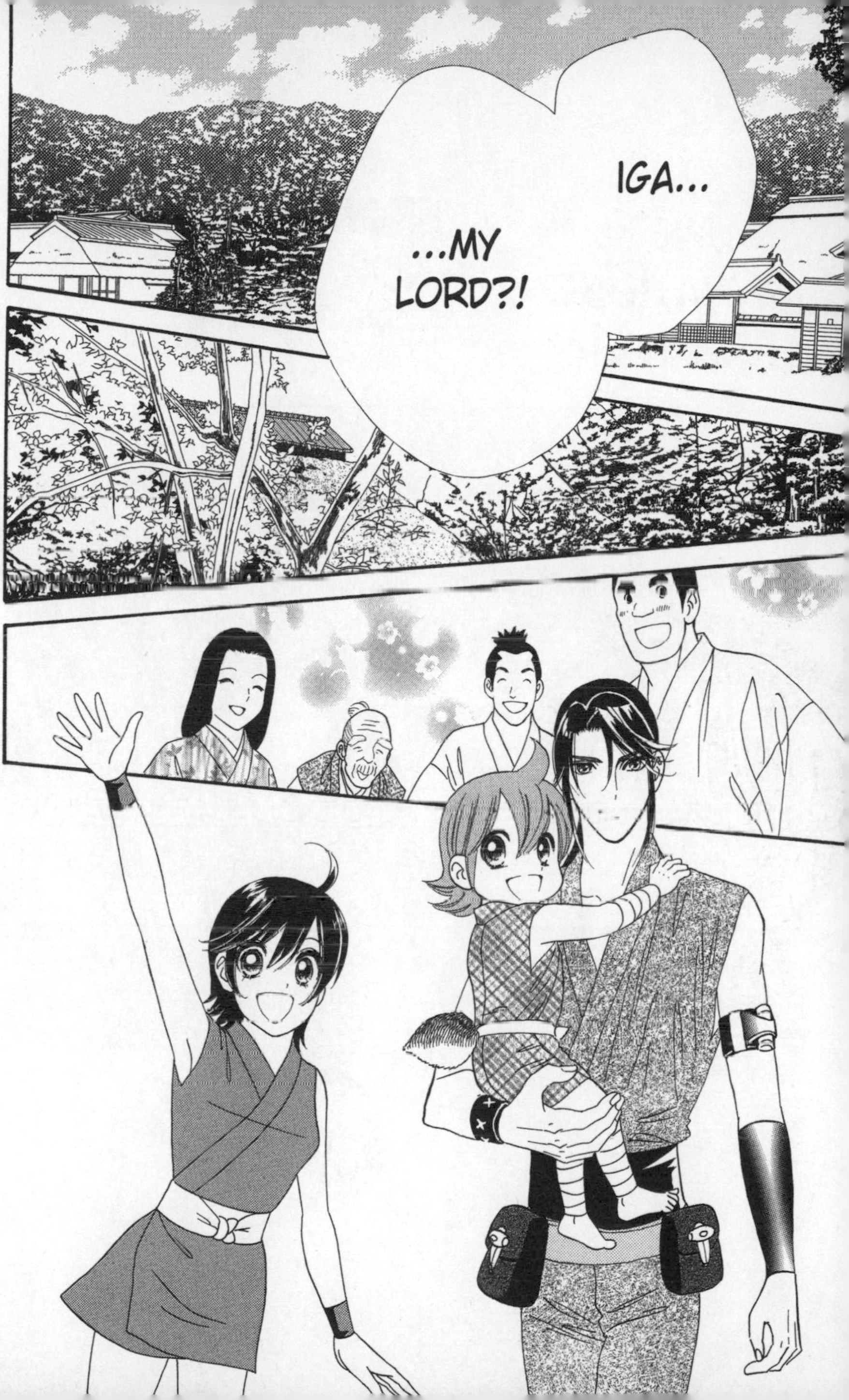
IGA...
...MY LORD?!

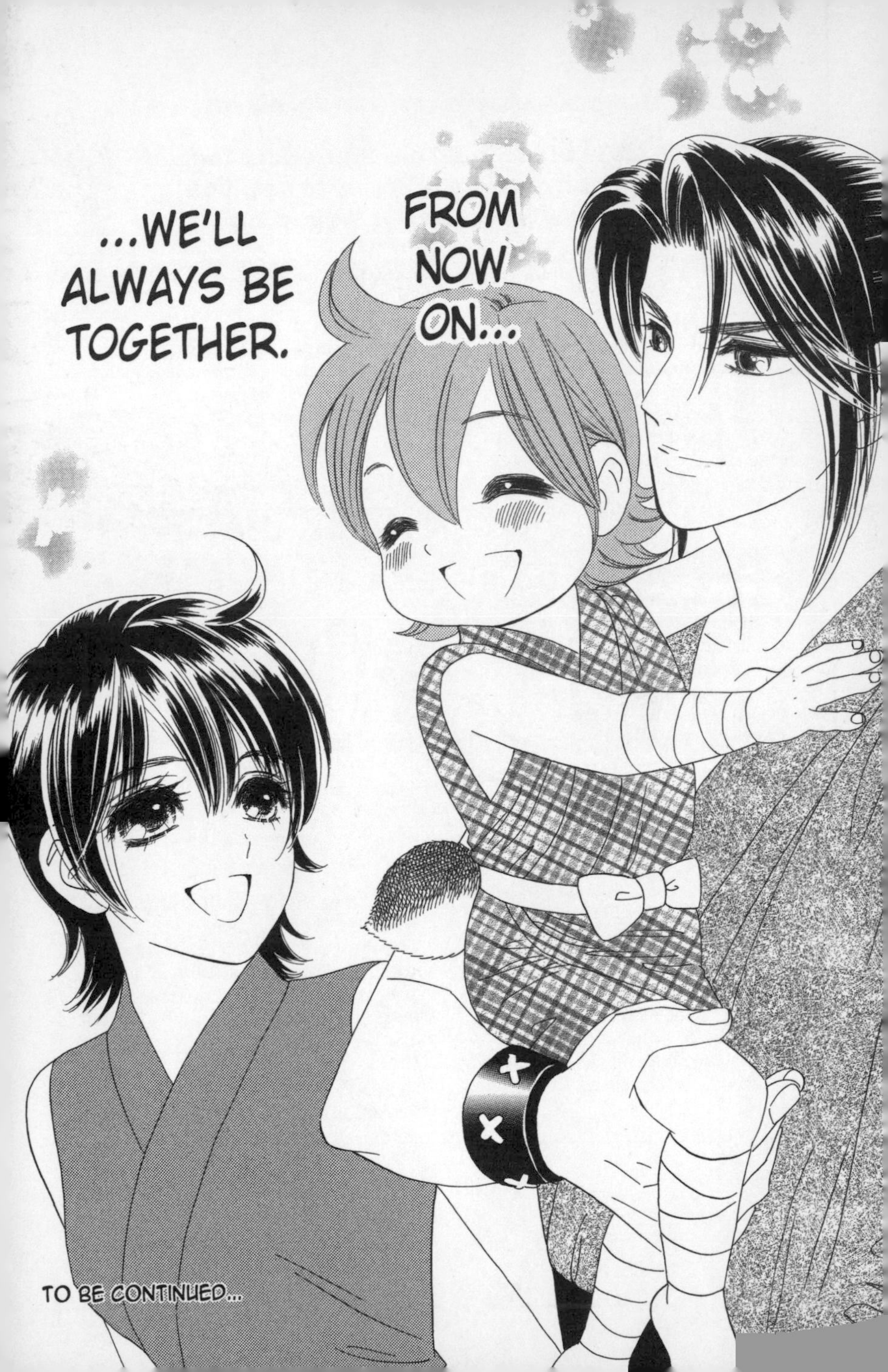
FROM NOW ON...
...WE'LL ALWAYS BE TOGETHER.
TO BE CONTINUED...

> *The ways of the ninja are mysterious indeed, so here is a glossary of terms to help you navigate the intricacies of their world.*

Page 24, panel 4: Aconitum
Also known as aconite, monkshood, or wolfsbane, Aconitum is a genus of flowering plants belonging to the buttercup family. There are over 250 species of Aconitum, and several species have been used in poisoned arrows.

Page 28: Mochi
Rice cake made of glutinous rice that is pounded into paste and molded into shape. When making *mochi*, one person pounds the rice with a large mallet while another person quickly folds the rice so that the mallet will keep pounding a different area of the rice. That way, the rice will be evenly pounded.

Page 32: Gelende
In Japanese, the word *gelende* means "ski slope" whereas in German, *gelände* means "terrain" or "land."

Page 39, panel 2: Oda Nobunaga
Oda Nobunaga lived from 1534 to 1582, and came close to unifying Japan. He is probably one of the most famous Japanese warlords. He was the first warlord to successfully incorporate the gun in battle and is notorious for his ruthlessness.

Page 2: Shimo no Hanzo
Shimo no means "the Lower," and in this case refers to Hanzo's geographic location rather than social status.

Page 2: Ranmaru Mori
Ranmaru Mori is one of Nobunaga's most famous vassals. He became Oda Nobunaga's attendant at a young age and was recognized for his talent and loyalty.

Page 2: Iga
Iga is a region on the island of Honshu and also the name of the famous ninja clan that originated there. Another area famous for its ninja is Kouga, in the Shiga prefecture on Honshu. Many books claim that these two ninja clans were mortal enemies, but in reality inter-ninja relations were not as bad as stories might suggest.

Page 22, panel 1: Mitsuhide Akechi
Mitsuhide Akechi became one of Oda Nobunaga's retainers after Nobunaga's conquest of Mino province (now Gifu prefecture) in 1566. He is known to have been more of an intellectual and a pacifier than a warrior.

Page 23, panel 1: Kunoichi
A term often used for female ninja. The word is spelled くノ一, and when combined, the letters form the kanji for woman, 女。

Page 136, panel 3: Tsuntsun and Dere
Tsuntsun can mean "prickly" in Japanese, and Hanzo assumed *dere* to be an abbreviation of "delivery" here.

Page 136, panel 4: Kabaddi
A game that is like a combination of dodgeball and tag that's played in South Asia. It is a rule of the game that the attacking member is not allowed to breathe while attacking, so "kabbadi" is constantly chanted to prove that the player is not taking a breath.

Page 137: Ryoma Sakamoto
Ryoma Sakamoto (1836-1867) is considered to be one of the greatest contributors to the modernization of Japan. He was a leader who envisioned Japan without a shoganate and worked towards creating a modern naval force.

Page 58: Choju-giga
Choju-giga are a set of four picture scrolls that date back to the mid-12th to 13th centuries. They depict illustrations of frogs, rabbits, and monkeys acting human-like. Though they have no writing on them, these scrolls are considered to be the oldest form of *manga* in Japan.

Page 59: Yakitori
Yakitori literally means "grilled poultry" (usually chicken), and it is served on a skewer. However, *yakitori* in Higashi-Matsuyama City of Saitama Prefecture are actually made with pork instead.

Page 84: Razor Ramon HG
Razor Ramon HG is a character that Japanese comedian Masaki Sumitani portrays on TV. He wears a leather fetish outfit and goes around performing acts of charity to unsuspecting bystanders.

Page 85: Chikuwa
Chikuwa is a round, tube-like food product made of ingredients like fish paste and starch. The name *chikuwa* means "bamboo ring," referring to the shape that it looks like when it is sliced. *Kamaboko* is also made from fish paste, but it is usually shaped like a half-circle.

Page 100, panel 2: Honnoji
Honnoji is a temple in Kyoto. Oda Nobunaga often stayed here when he traveled to the capital.

Page 136, panel 1: Tsundere
Tsundere is a term that combines two Japanese words–Tsuntsun (which means "unfriendly") and deredere (which means "lovestruck"). It is used to describe people who are rather unfriendly at first sight but gradually become more lovely as you get to know them.

Of all the processes in creating manga, the thing I tend to be weakest at is dividing the page into various panels. If it's too simplistic, it gets dull. But if I make it too complex, then it will be too hard to read! So I usually aim for them to be "reasonably easy-to-read yet dramatic and daring in the big scenes," and I keep groaning every time I draw my manga.

–Rinko Ueda

Rinko Ueda is from Nara prefecture. She enjoys listening to the radio, drama CDs, and Rakugo comedy performances. Her works include *Ryo*, a series based on the legend of Gojo Bridge, *Home*, a story about love crossing national boundaries, and *Tail of the Moon (Tsuki no Shippo)*, a romantic ninja comedy.

TAIL OF THE MOON
Vol. 11
The Shojo Beat Manga Edition

STORY & ART BY
RINKO UEDA

Translation & Adaptation/Tetsuichiro Miyaki
Touch-up Art & Lettering/Mark McMurray
Design/Izumi Hirayama
Editor/Amy Yu

Editor in Chief, Books/Alvin Lu
Editor in Chief, Magazines/Marc Weidenbaum
VP of Publishing Licensing/Rika Inouye
VP of Sales/Gonzalo Ferreyra
Sr. VP of Marketing/Liza Coppola
Publisher/Hyoe Narita

Printed in Canada

Published by VIZ Media, LLC
P.O. Box 77064
San Francisco, CA 94107

Shojo Beat Manga Edition
10 9 8 7 6 5 4 3 2 1
First printing, June 2008

www.viz.com   store.viz.com

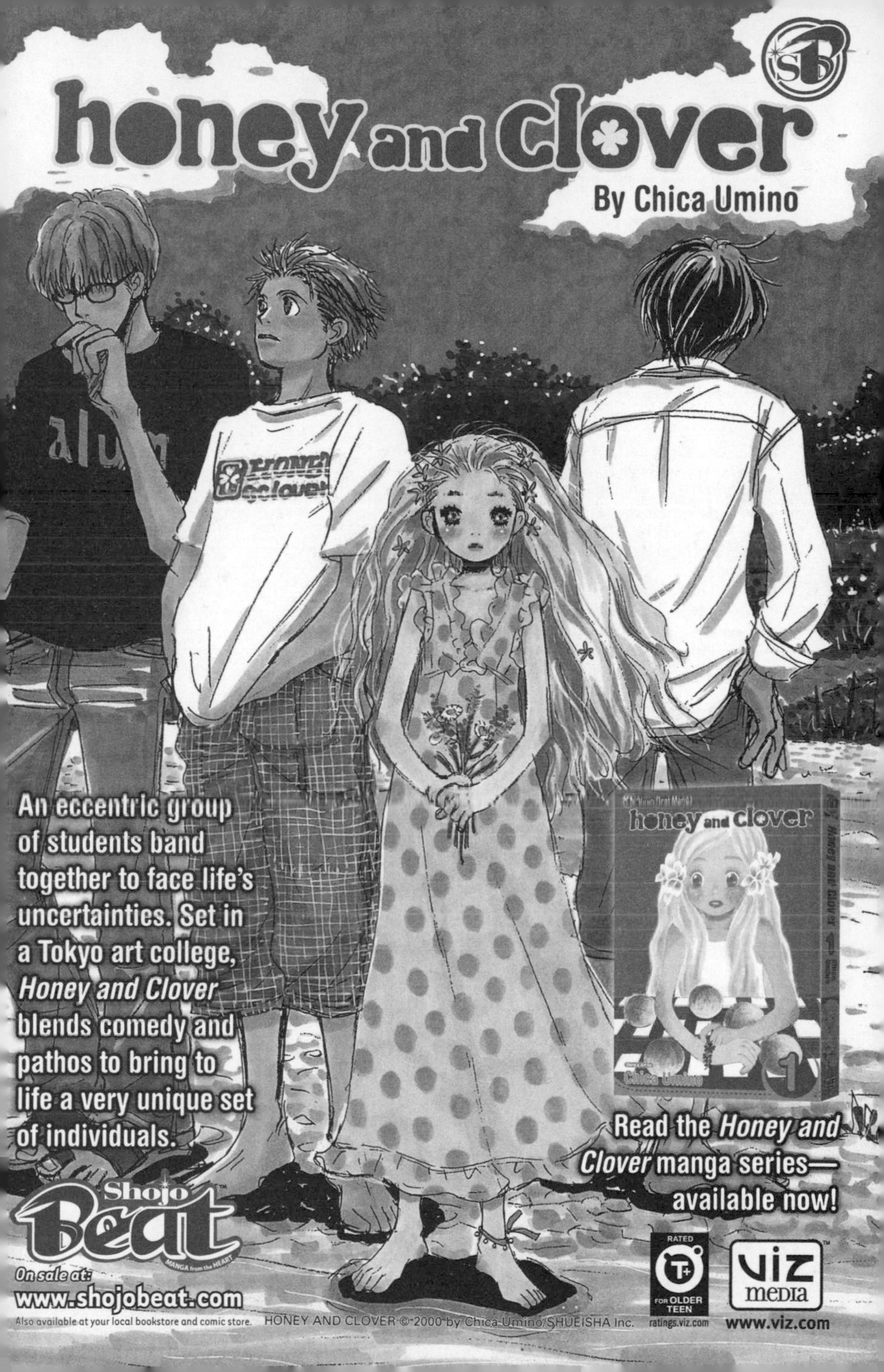

honey and clover
By Chica Umino
An eccentric group of students band together to face life's uncertainties. Set in a Tokyo art college, *Honey and Clover* blends comedy and pathos to bring to life a very unique set of individuals.
Read the *Honey and Clover* manga series—available now!
Shojo Beat
On sale at:
www.shojobeat.com
Also available at your local bookstore and comic store.
HONEY AND CLOVER © 2000 by Chica Umino/SHUEISHA Inc.
RATED T+ FOR OLDER TEEN
ratings.viz.com
VIZ MEDIA
www.viz.com

I·O·N

BY ARINA TANEMURA,
CREATOR OF *FULL MOON*
AND *THE GENTLEMEN'S
ALLIANCE †*

Ion Tsuburagi is a normal junior high girl with normal junior high problems. But when a mysterious substance grants her telekinetic powers, she finds herself struggling to keep everything together! Are her new abilities a blessing...or a curse?

Find out in *I·O·N*—manga on sale now!

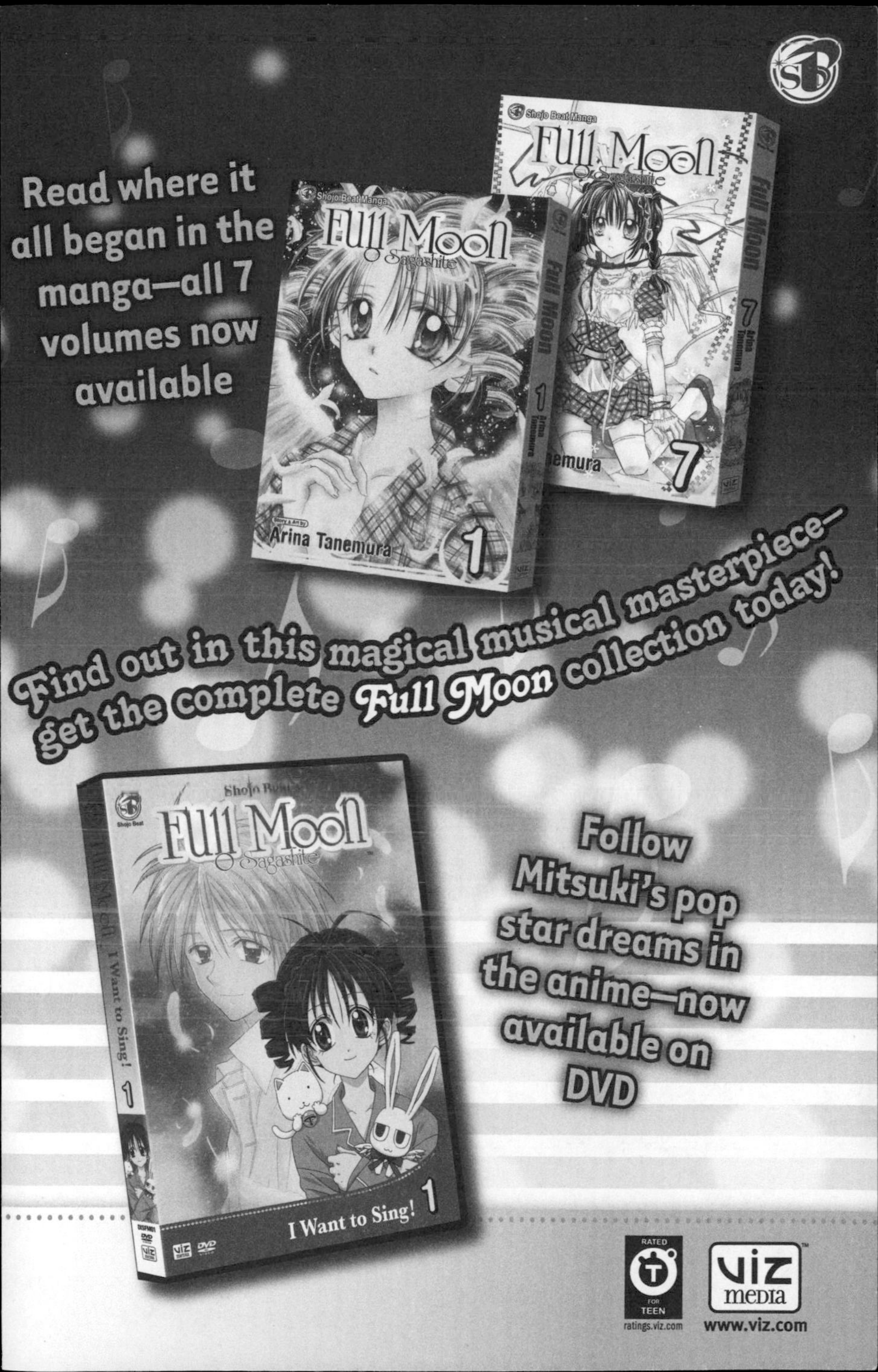
Read where it all began in the manga—all 7 volumes now available
Shojo Beat Manga
Full Moon O Sagashite
Story & Art by
Arina Tanemura
1
7
Find out in this magical musical masterpiece—get the complete Full Moon collection today!
Shojo Beat
Full Moon O Sagashite
I Want to Sing! 1
Follow Mitsuki's pop star dreams in the anime—now available on DVD
RATED T FOR TEEN
ratings.viz.com
VIZ media
www.viz.com

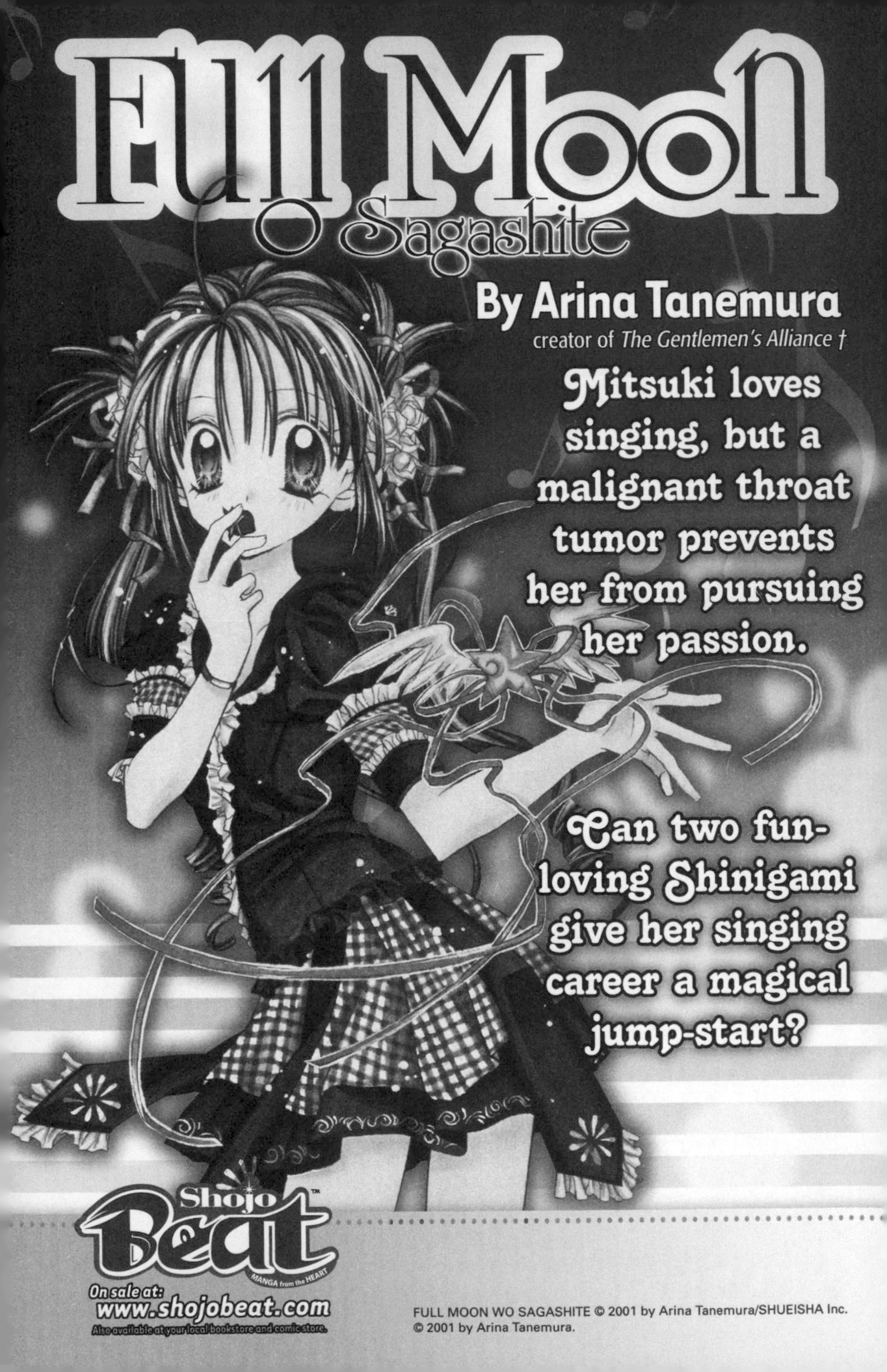
Full Moon
O Sagashite
By Arina Tanemura
creator of The Gentlemen's Alliance †
Mitsuki loves singing, but a malignant throat tumor prevents her from pursuing her passion.
Can two fun-loving Shinigami give her singing career a magical jump-start?
Shojo Beat
MANGA from the HEART
On sale at:
www.shojobeat.com
Also available at your local bookstore and comic store.
FULL MOON WO SAGASHITE © 2001 by Arina Tanemura/SHUEISHA Inc.
© 2001 by Arina Tanemura.

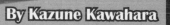
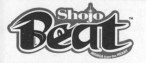

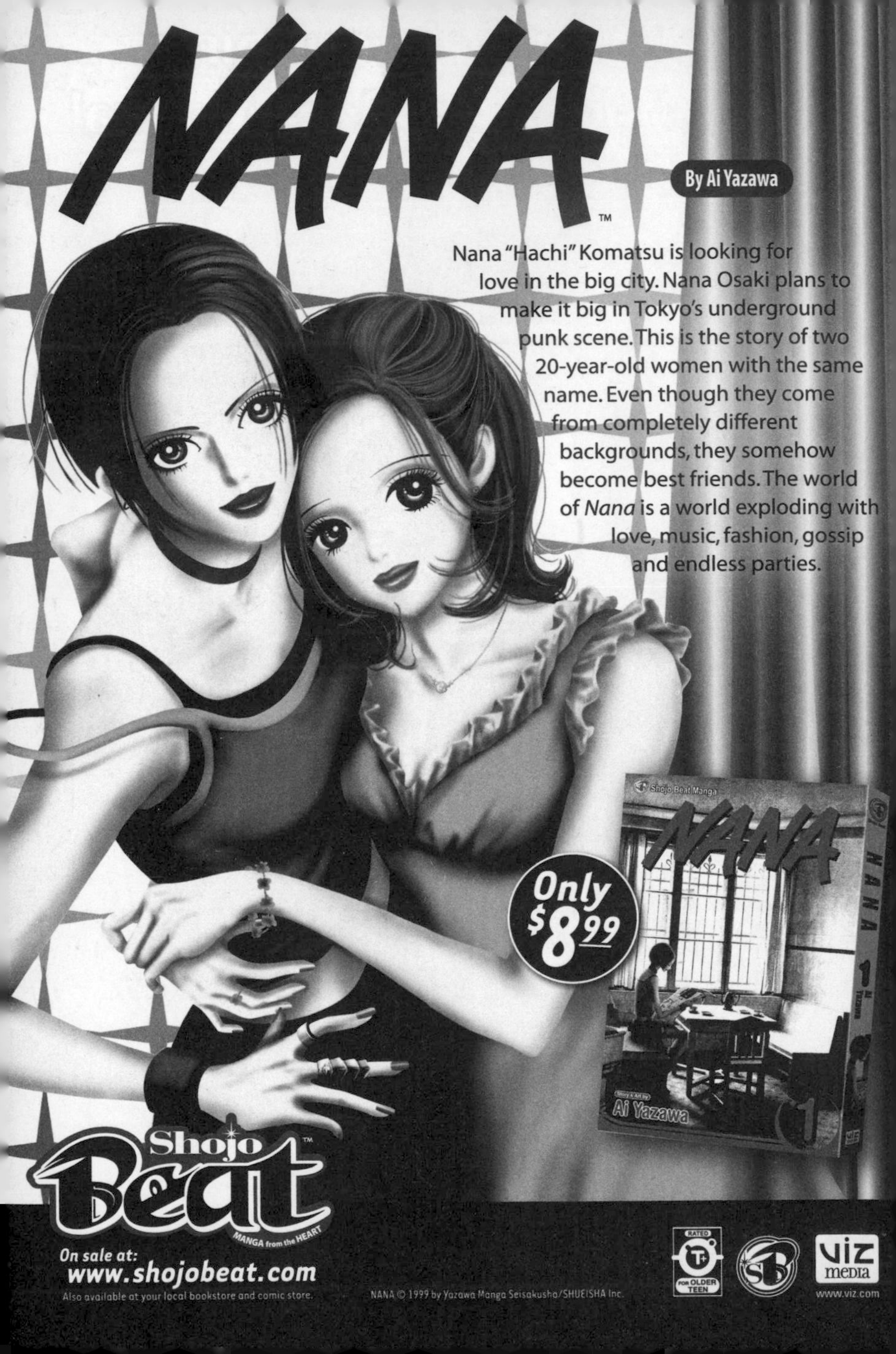
NANA™
By Ai Yazawa
Nana "Hachi" Komatsu is looking for love in the big city. Nana Osaki plans to make it big in Tokyo's underground punk scene. This is the story of two 20-year-old women with the same name. Even though they come from completely different backgrounds, they somehow become best friends. The world of *Nana* is a world exploding with love, music, fashion, gossip and endless parties.
Only $8.99
Shojo Beat Manga
NANA
Ai Yazawa
Shojo Beat™
MANGA from the HEART
On sale at:
www.shojobeat.com
Also available at your local bookstore and comic store.
NANA © 1999 by Yazawa Manga Seisakusho/SHUEISHA Inc.
RATED T+ FOR OLDER TEEN
viz media
www.viz.com

Tell us what you think
about Shojo Beat Manga!

Our survey is now available online. Go to:

shojobeat.com/mangasurvey

W9-AYS-521

Help us make our product offerings better!

VIZ media

Shojo Beat

MANGA from the HEART

THE REAL DRAMA BEGINS IN...